CW00402565

BYRON CUMMINGS

Byron Cummings

Dean of Southwest Archaeology

TODD W. BOSTWICK

The University of Arizona Press *Tucson*

The University of Arizona Press

∞ This book is printed on acid-free, archival-quality paper.
Manufactured in the United States of America

11 10 09 08 07 06 6 5 4 3 2 1

Library of Congress Cataloging-in-Publication Data

Bostwick, Todd W.
Byron Cummings : dean of Southwest archaeology /
Todd W. Bostwick.
p. cm.
Includes bibliographical references and index.
ISBN-13: 978-0-8165-2477-8 (hardcover : alk. paper)
ISBN-10: 0-8165-2477-7 (hardcover : alk. paper)
1. Cummings, Byron, 1860–1954. 2. Archaeologists—Southwest, New—Biography. 3. Indians of North America—Southwest, New—Antiquities. 4. Southwest, New—Antiquities. I. Title.
CC115.C77B67 2006
979'.0072'02–dc22

2005017318

Publication of this book is made possible in part by the proceeds of a permanent endowment created with the assistance of a Challenge Grant from the National Endowment for the Humanities, a federal agency.

The ages of the Gods make no account of definite time. Man grows as he is able to comprehend God's great plan, and appreciate the joy he may have in playing well his little part in that plan.

—BYRON CUMMINGS, Kinishba book inscription, 1943

Contents

Illustrations

FIGURES

TABLES

Acknowledgments

The author wishes to express his appreciation for all the assistance he received during this study. Numerous individuals from several research institutions and repositories provided access to their documents. These include Celia Skeels at the Amerind Library in Dragoon, Arizona; Deborah Shelton of the Arizona Historical Society in Tucson; the Arizona Historical Foundation, Hayden Library, Tempe; Robert Spindler of the Department of Archives and Manuscripts at Arizona State University, Tempe; the Arizona State Libraries and Archives, Phoenix; Alan Ferg, Mike Jacobs, Susan Luebbermann, and Jeannette Garcia of the Arizona State Museum, University of Arizona, Tucson; Bee Valvo of the Cline Library at Northern Arizona University, Flagstaff; Chris Turnbow and Diane Bird of the Laboratory of Anthropology, Santa Fe, New Mexico; Tomas Jaehn of the Fray Angélico Chavéz Library, Museum of New Mexico, Santa Fe; David Wilcox of the Museum of Northern Arizona, Flagstaff; Roger Lidman and Holly Young of the Pueblo Grande Museum, Phoenix; Joanne Cline of the Smoki Museum, Prescott, Arizona; Lorri Carlson of the Sharlot Hall Museum, Prescott, Arizona; University of Arizona Special Collections, Tucson; Paul Mogren of the J. Willard Marriot Library, University of Utah, Salt Lake City; Jean Hengesbaugh and Kathy Kankainen of the Utah Museum of Natural History, Salt Lake City; Gene Morris of the National Archives and Records Administration, National Civil Records, Washington, D.C.; John Welch of the Fort Apache National Historic Landmark, Arizona; and David C. Manning of Scottsdale, Arizona. In addition, Andrew Christenson, Christian Downum, Harvey Leake, James Snead, and David Wilcox graciously shared unpublished materials in their possession. Noel Stowe, Robert Trennert, Peter Iverson, Andrew Christenson, Wesley Holden, and Allen Dart provided many useful comments on an earlier draft. I also wish to thank those individuals who allowed me to interview them for this study: Loren Haury, Mike Jacobs, Donald Sayner, and John Tanner. The editorial guidance provided by Allyson Carter, Anne Keyl, and Nancy Arora of the University of Arizona Press and freelance editor Sally Bennett also is greatly appreciated. Six of the maps used in this book were expertly drafted by Stephanie Sherwood of Compass Rose, with financial support from the Michael Steiner family. Finally, my wife, Heidi Bostwick, deserves praise for her patience and editorial comments. Thank you so much to all for your help.

BYRON CUMMINGS

1

"One of the Leading Figures in Southwestern Archaeology"

The Life of Byron Cummings

Byron Cummings, a small but sturdy man with blue eyes and the nickname "The Dean," had a profound influence on the archaeology of Arizona and Utah during its early development from the turn of the century to World War II (fig. 1.1). Cummings was an explorer, archaeologist, anthropologist, teacher, museum director, university administrator, active supporter of student athletics, state parks commissioner, and member of the board of directors for a variety of organizations.[1] During the first half of the twentieth century, he was involved in many important archaeological discoveries throughout the American Southwest and was a pioneer in the education of several generations of archaeologists and anthropologists.

A Man of Many Accomplishments

Senator Barry Goldwater gave high praise to Cummings on the cover jacket of his 1953 book, *First Inhabitants of Arizona and the Southwest*: "Prosperity will ever owe him a debt of gratitude for his industry, perseverance, his wise interpretations. Those who have had the privilege of knowing him, as friend or student[,] are even more indebted to him for this wise counsel, his generosity in giving of himself and his knowledge to all who sought it." Archaeologist Richard Woodbury (1993:29) has called Cummings "one of the leading figures in Southwestern archaeology."

Energetic, friendly, and seemingly ageless, this man Byron Cummings had a big heart and great vision. Born and educated in the New York-

1.1 Byron Cummings, circa 1930 (courtesy of Arizona Historical Society/Tucson, #BN92.677)

New Jersey area, he deeply admired the Greeks and Romans, and as a young man he wished to engage in a life of adventure exploring the ancient past. He chose the teaching of ancient languages for his professional career. In 1893 he moved to the West to pursue teaching and administrative opportunities at the expanding University of Utah. Ancient ruins in Utah soon attracted his attention, and after many years of teaching Latin and Greek, he developed a lifelong passion for the archaeology of Utah and Arizona.

From the beginning of his career, Cummings demonstrated excellent teaching and administrative skills. From 1893 to 1915, he taught ancient languages and literature at the University of Utah and served as dean of the School of Arts and Sciences for ten of those years. In 1915 he resigned from the University of Utah in a dispute over academic freedom and was then invited by the University of Arizona to teach and to develop the Arizona State Museum, which he directed until 1938. In 1915 he also established the university's Department of Archaeology, which was later recast as the Department of Anthropology by his former student, Emil W. Haury. Cummings also was dean of the College of Letters, Arts, and Sciences and the dean of men at the University of Arizona for five years. In addition, twice he served in the 1920s as acting president of the University of Arizona, the second time after a political crisis forced the resignation of the university president, Cloyd Marvin.

A compassionate man with a charming personality, Cummings was also a modest and generous person and could converse comfortably with the man on the street as well as with high-ranking government officials. His circle of friends included Navajos who lived in hogans without electricity or running water, as well as powerful lawyers, senators, and governors. He was a good negotiator and had excellent diplomatic skills, which he successfully used in his sometimes difficult relationships with Native Americans, university faculty and administrators, politicians, and government officials. However, he also could be quite stubborn, usually because he felt strongly that he was in the right.

Blessed with a strong will and lots of nervous energy, Cummings' early explorations of Navajo canyon country were highly successful and widely reported in local newspapers. Neil Judd (1952:xi), Cummings' nephew and a student assistant on several of his early adventures, recalled how Cummings explored the rugged areas of northeastern Arizona at a time when "white men were not wanted." Judd (1952:xi) witnessed the strength in Cummings' character when facing obstacles in his path: "the Dean was on the trail of ancient history and he had no fear. Repeatedly challenged and often threatened, he called more than one Indian's bluff. Eventually he won the respect even of the villainously inclined by his ready smile, his consideration for others, and his steadfastness of purpose." The Dean became well known for his physical stamina on the trail and for his tasty Dutch oven biscuits.

Cummings' first fame as an explorer occurred in 1909, when he was one of the leaders of the party that discovered the magnificent stone arch called Rainbow Bridge in southern Utah. The national attention created from this discovery led to its designation as a national monument the next year. He would thereafter be intimately linked to Rainbow Bridge, returning to visit in 1920 and again in the mid 1930s, when he was in his seventies (fig. 1.2).

Cummings was also the discoverer, along with John Wetherill, of the

1.2 Cummings at Rainbow Bridge in 1935 (photograph by Tad Nichols; courtesy of Northern Arizona University, Special Collections and Archives, #NAU.PH.99.3.1.1.9)

famous Pueblo cliff dwelling called Betatakin Ruin, another national monument that resulted from Cummings' explorations. Completely enthralled with the beauty and mystery of this part of the Southwest, Cummings continued his explorations of ancient sites in northeastern Arizona and southeastern Utah for another twenty years from his university office in Tucson (fig. 1.3). Throughout these years he maintained a close friendship with the John and Louisa Wetherill family, using their trading post in Kayenta as his field headquarters and mentoring and employing their two children.

Cummings was active in archaeology at a time when the discovery and interpretations of ancient ruins in the Southwest were used by local Anglo-Americans for constructing their own cultural identity that rationalized their place in the nation (Snead 2001). The rugged wilderness that was initially strange and frightening became a place of beauty and reverence. By combining science, education, and regional pride, the Native American past was used in the growing American West to build up

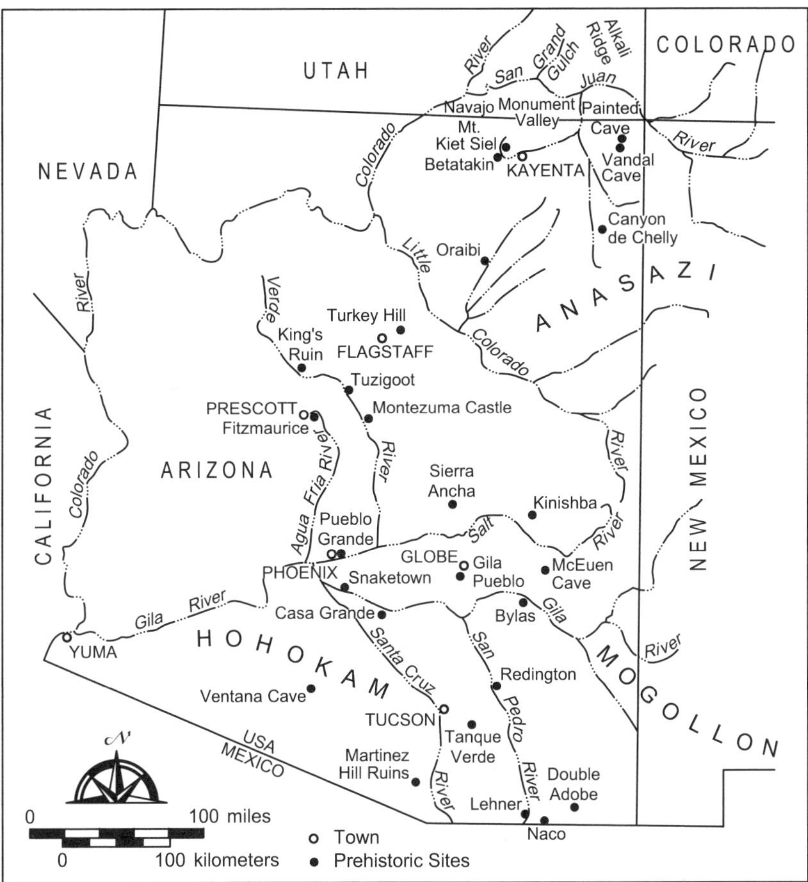

1.3 Important archaeological sites investigated by Byron Cummings and his students in Arizona

popular constituencies that adopted the notion of archaeology as heritage. Well-preserved ruins situated in stark landscapes came to be seen as unique regional resources, something of cultural value that the eastern United States did not have.

One of the first ruins in the Southwest to receive national attention, through the writings of Ralph J. Hinton (1878) and Adolph F. Bandelier (1884), was Casa Grande Ruin in southern Arizona. This multistory adobe structure was given federal protection by Congress in 1889. However, few professional archaeologists lived in the West, so for many years museum men from New York, Boston, and Washington, D.C., competed with western relic hunters for the Southwest's ancient treasures (Fowler 1999; Hinsley 1981). Between 1893 and 1930, a "Western Coalition" of archaeology organizations and museums was established in Arizona, Colorado, New Mexico, and Utah (Snead 2001:76). Archaeology became a source of local pride and identity in the Southwest.

Just as Cummings was transforming himself from Latin teacher into archaeologist, three distinct "communities of interest" were competing for control of archaeology in the Southwest: scholars in eastern institutions who sought the scientific value of the ruins and their informative artifacts; the states and territories, which wished to control their own ancient resources, free of federal influence; and entrepreneurs, who wanted to convert ruins into profit (Snead 2001:25). Cummings sided with the second group. All three played important roles in the development of tourism in the Southwest by providing colorful descriptions of human survival in a harsh but beautiful desert landscape.[2] Cummings personally contributed to the growth of Arizona tourism with his well-publicized archaeology adventures and his involvement in the establishment of national monuments.

In the early stage of his archaeology career, while at the University of Utah, Cummings worked closely with Edgar Lee Hewett of the School of American Archaeology (later changed to Research), in New Mexico, and the Archaeological Institute of America, headquartered in Boston. Hewett was a key player in the passage of the federal Antiquities Act of 1906, helped found the Archaeological Society of New Mexico and the Museum of New Mexico, helped establish the journal *El Palacio*, was director of the San Diego Museum of Man, and was professor of anthropology at San Diego State Teachers College, the University of New Mexico, and the University of Southern California (Chavenet 1983; Fowler 1999). Cummings appreciated that Hewett involved students and members of the public in his archaeological investigations in New Mexico; Cummings did the same in Utah and Arizona. And similar to Hewett, Cummings summarized his archaeological findings in short, popular articles rather than detailed site reports, much to the chagrin of later archaeologists. This absence of reports has obscured current views of Cummings' archaeology abilities.

During his forty-plus years as a dirt archaeologist, Cummings and his students dug well over a hundred archaeological sites, the exact count unknown.[3] The more famous of these include Kiet Siel and Betatakin in Navajo National Monument, Tanque Verde and Martinez Hill ruins near Tucson, King's Ruin north of Prescott, Turkey Hill Pueblo northeast of Flagstaff, Tuzigoot Pueblo in central Arizona, and Kinishba Pueblo in east-central Arizona. The later two were given national monument and national historic landmark status, respectively, because of Cummings' excavations and restorations. He also spent two seasons, in the mid 1920s, excavating the pyramid at Cuicuilco, Mexico, for which he received international acclaim. He was involved in the 1926 discovery of Ice Age artifacts in southeastern Arizona, a significant find that went mostly unnoticed outside the state. Upon his forced retirement from the Arizona State Museum at age seventy-seven, Cummings continued for several more years with his excavation and restoration of the Kinishba ruin near Fort Apache.

Archaeological sites excavated by Cummings were located in all three major environmental regions in Arizona: Colorado Plateau, central mountains, and desert basin and range. These sites also represented the entire suite of prehistory in Arizona—from Paleo-Indian big-game hunters to Archaic hunters and gatherers to Formative period agricultural societies (Reid and Whittlesey 1997). The latter include the Anasazi of the Colorado Plateau, the Mogollon of the central mountains, and the Hohokam of the southern desert. Unfortunately, Cummings did not write scientific reports on many of the sites he dug, and therefore he did not publish data that could be incorporated into other archaeologists' analyses. During the 1930s, however, his graduate students began to publish data obtained from Cummings' excavations, and several students published reports on work directed by them for other organizations.

Cummings dug year after year because he felt he was in a race not only against the ravages of time, but also against others—local relic hunters and archaeologists from eastern institutions who took the artifacts they found out of the state, never to return. Cummings had seen Hewett deal with the same challenges in New Mexico, because Southwestern archaeology in general had been dominated for many years by the well-financed Smithsonian Institution in Washington, D.C.; the American Museum of Natural History in New York; and the Peabody Museum at Harvard in Cambridge, Massachusetts (Hinsley 1981; Fowler 2000). This competition for Utah's and Arizona's relics with eastern-based archaeologists

—Alfred V. Kidder, Jesse W. Fewkes, and Earl Morris in particular—soured Cummings toward out-of-state archaeologists and they toward him. Although Cummings has been described as "a gentle kindly man who lacked the drive of Hewett" (Lister and Lister 1968:12), he managed to assume considerable control over Arizona archaeology with passage of the Arizona Antiquities Act in 1927.

In Cummings' mind, Arizona's ancient resources should stay in Arizona and preferably be investigated by local organizations working with the Arizona State Museum. Consequently, he was pleased with Harold Colton's development of a museum in Flagstaff, Arizona, in the late 1920s and had good relationships with Colton and his staff, many of whom were Cummings' former students. After a rough start, he came to appreciate the work of Harold Gladwin at the Gila Pueblo Archaeological Foundation in Globe, Arizona, especially after Gladwin hired Cummings' former student Emil Haury as the assistant director in 1930. Cummings even got along well initially with Odd Halseth at Pueblo Grande Museum in Phoenix, until Halseth tried to get a law passed that would make him the state archaeological inspector. In response, Cummings made several unsuccessful attempts during the 1930s to strengthen his control of archaeology through legislation.

Cummings' four decades of explorations gave him many opportunities to develop close personal relationships with Native Americans. He hired them as guides, wranglers, suppliers, and entertainers. His students benefited from these relationships, for he often took them to visit his Indian friends whenever they went on field trips. He wrote field notes on the Navajo, Hopi, and Apache ceremonies he and his students witnessed, and he occasionally published short ethnographic articles from the notes (Cummings 1936a, 1936b, 1939a, 1939b). He also published a book solely about his Native American friends (Cummings 1952). The Navajo called him Natani Yazzie, loosely translated as "Little Captain."

Understanding Byron Cummings

Several short biographies have been written on Cummings by his former students Clara Lee (Fraps) Tanner (1954a,b), Neil Judd (1954a,b, 1968), Walter Kerr (1955), and Gordon Willey (1988). These writings focus on Cummings' most notable achievements and give a few personal anecdotes. Cummings (1958) started to write an autobiography, but it was only partly completed at the time of his death in 1954. His son, Malcolm, and daughter-in-law, Jeanne, edited his incomplete autobiography into an informative manuscript, but it is not very comprehensive and was never published (Cummings and Cummings n.d.). A full-length examination of his life has yet to be written, the absence of which has contributed to the lack of understanding concerning Cummings' pioneering roles in Southwestern archaeology and anthropology.

This book describes Cummings' intellectual and cultural contributions to Southwestern archaeology, as well as his conflicts with other professionals and government officials. Consequently, his own words are used whenever possible to give a sense of his concise yet articulate communiqués with professionals and the public through his publications, newspaper articles, popular literature, unpublished papers, correspondence, and lectures. In addition, Cummings' original spellings for place-names are used here, as are his original measurements in the English system.

Cummings' life can be examined in relationship to three important concepts: his patronage, such as institutional and private support for his work; his professionalism, or his scientific approach and methods of interpretation; and his rationale for conducting archaeology (Snead 2001). In addition, two major factors greatly influenced Cummings' professional career and life. The first, a strong moral character, was developed largely during early childhood and was grounded in his political and religious beliefs. The second was his early archaeological mentoring with Edgar L. Hewett and the Archaeological Institute of America.

George B. Merriman (1891), professor of math and astronomy at Rutgers, praised Cummings in a letter of recommendation written early in his career. Merriman said Cummings had "a character exceptionally pure and amiable with manners courteous and pleasing . . . and a heart loyal to God and to His service." George A. Bacon (1891), principal of Syracuse High School and editor of a journal on secondary education, offered similar comments about Cummings that year: "His scholarship is excellent, his loyalty and earnestness worthy of the highest praise. He has tact and teaching ability in unusual measure. His whole record with me was such that I can recommend him with the utmost confidence to any committee that is looking for a genuine teacher. He is modest in hearing, but entirely competent for any position which he is willing to assume." Nearly fifty years later, friend Opal Le Baron Whitmore (1938) added parallel words about Cummings' character: "You are always so modest and unassuming yet we all know that in intellect and ability and achievement and in character, yes, most of all in character, you are so far ahead as to be a giant among pygmies." For five decades as a professional educator and archaeologist, Cummings was known as a person with tact, teaching ability, modesty, and competence at whatever he did.

Cummings' view of others and life in general were clearly influenced by his political and religious views. A Progressive Republican, Cummings greatly admired Theodore Roosevelt and Woodrow Wilson for their views on the importance of education and social science. (Roosevelt's picture hung in his office.) Throughout his life, Cummings practiced the Progressives' values of organization, application of scientific expertise, efficiency, rationality, conservation of natural resources, and social justice (Hofstadler 1955; O'Neill 1975).

A deeply religious man, Cummings was always honest and consistent in his beliefs. John C. McGregor (1987), another former student and a distinguished archaeologist, wrote in his memoirs that Cummings had his own homespun Christian philosophy about life that he infused into everything he did. While on a field expedition with Cummings, they visited a small church in a rural community one Sunday. When the preacher found out that the famous archaeologist Byron Cummings was in attendance, he asked Cummings to give the sermon. Without any preparation, Cummings walked up to the pulpit and delivered a speech about life and proper living based on his own personal views and experiences, which left a lasting impression on McGregor.

Cummings was a devout Presbyterian, and his personal attributes strongly reflected the Presbyterian belief that humans have a responsibility for service and stewardship and should celebrate simplicity and shun ostentation. The Presbyterian notion of predestination also is reflected in Cummings' belief that humans have been naturally progressing in abilities and enlightenment over time. He considered it his duty to educate people so that civilized man would continue to improve the conditions of all humankind.

The outdoors was seen by Cummings as a laboratory for learning, and he utilized it as one of his teaching tools whenever possible. A Victorian moralist, Cummings accepted the notion that scientific inquiry brought about not only the truth, but also spiritual "uplift" (Hollinger 1984:148). Nearly every summer of his adult life, and on many weekends and holidays, Cummings took a select group of his students to investigate ancient ruins in Arizona, Utah, or Mexico. These excursions were typically filled with incredible scenery, lively lectures, and visits with Native Americans, usually Navajo or Apache. They were often memorable, as well as educational. Many of the early expeditions traveled over very rough country—at least in part by horse, burro, or mule—and camped in tents or under the stars.

The spiritual qualities of the northern Arizona landscape, where many of Cummings' summer expeditions took place, are dramatically expressed in one of his unpublished papers.[4] Cummings (1936d) describes the incredible outdoor settings of these expeditions as "a beautiful plateau country, swept by the purest breezes the Gods waft to any quarter of the earth and warmed and cheered by the perpetual sunshine. . . . Here he sees Nature in all the magnificent beauty of form and color which she assumes in the great southwest—the country of God's great out-of-doors. Under the inspiration of the wonderful coloring of cliff and gorge and sky the soul expands and life never seems small and petty again." This spiritually charged experience is ultimately educational: "This is the influence of Arizona's canyons, desert, and cliffs. They give a wider vision, a keener understanding of Nature's forces, and a better appreciation of man's part in the drama of life." For Cummings, educational experiences were best served by democratic ideals and a progressive social and political outlook. Consistent with his ideals, Cummings was a hands-on person, not just planning all the details of his expeditions into the great outdoors, but also sharing in the mundane tasks during those expeditions. His personal concern for others was well known to his students and friends.

Cummings was a better field archaeologist than is generally recognized, although he was not a meticulous excavator, even considering the standards of his time. However, he understood and applied the concept of stratigraphy by at least the 1920s, especially in his excavations of the pyramid at Cuicuilco, Mexico, and later at the Kinishba Pueblo in eastern Arizona. Indeed, it was his personal observation of the stratigraphy at the Silverbell Road site near Tucson that convinced him that the lead artifacts must be authentic despite various translations of the inscriptions on the artifacts that indicated otherwise. He preferred to excavate with a shovel but allowed his students to use trowels if they wanted. He would never have considered excavating a site with a plow and scraper, such as Don Maguire (1894) had done in Utah and both Jesse W. Fewkes and Harold Gladwin had done at Casa Grande Ruins in Arizona (Elliot 1995; Hackbarth 2001a).

Cummings took numerous black-and-white photographs of most of the sites he excavated, although many of the pictures are currently unidentified. He understood the importance of note taking and accurate record keeping, but he apparently was inconsistent in his application of that knowledge. There are field notes in his archives for nearly every survey and dig in which he was involved from 1908 to 1938. Unfortunately, for many of his later expeditions, those field notes are nothing more than very brief summaries containing a few architectural measurements and some short remarks on burials. In some cases, the notes appear to have been written not in the field but later in the office. Some of his original field notes may have burned in a 1949 fire in his garage (Judd 1968).

The thousands of excavated artifacts brought back to the Arizona State Museum by Cummings were all catalogued at the museum, and those catalog cards still exist today. However, they have yet to be computerized, making their analysis difficult. All his photographs, existing field notes, and museum catalog cards remain to be organized and correlated before the full story of his field expeditions can be told.

For most of his life, Cummings was a dedicated professor, and he is known to have consistently promoted professionalism to his students. He kept relatively up-to-date on the archaeology literature he assigned his students to read and generally incorporated advances in excavation strategies and techniques into his classroom lectures and field school training. He supported amateur archaeologists, as long as they cooperated with his request to donate all or a portion of the artifacts to the State Museum collections. Cummings wrote concisely and was cautious in his archaeological interpretations, even though they often were romantic and more impressionistic than scientific in tone. The numerous master's theses that he oversaw and approved reflect careful thought and clear writing. He instilled his professional approach to archaeology in his students, creating a strong foundation for those who went on to prestigious graduate schools such as Richard Aldrich, Gordon Baldwin,

Stanley Boggs, Paul Gebhard, Norman Gabel, Harry Getty, Emil Haury, Florence Hawley Ellis, Edward Spicer, Gordon Willey, and others.

In his efforts to make a wide range of anthropology topics available to his students, Cummings continually expanded the faculty and curriculum of the Archaeology Department, even during the financially difficult times of the 1930s Great Depression. The department grew from four archaeology courses and about two dozen students during the 1916–1917 academic year to sixteen courses and more than 250 students in 1936–1937. When Cummings retired from teaching in 1937, the Archaeology Department was nationally known and recognized for its high standards.

Cummings had no formal training in museum work, yet he founded or played a major role in the development of several Arizona museums, including the Arizona State Museum in Tucson, the Smoki Museum in Prescott, Tuzigoot National Monument in Clarkdale, Montezuma Castle National Monument along Beaver Creek, and the Kinishba Museum near Fort Apache. Fort Lowell in Tucson was set aside as a state historical park at his urging (Cummings 1935c). He also substantially built up the collections of the Arizona State Museum, acquiring more than 26,000 relics and specimens, as he called them.

However, Cummings' view of museum exhibits was rather static, a reflection of the Victorian "cabinet of curiosity" approach in which artifacts were seen as the same as natural history specimens (Conn 1998). Numerous objects of diverse origins were crammed into cases, with prehistoric artifacts and historic craft items placed alongside stuffed animals. Interpretive text was limited or nonexistent. Cummings believed that the educational value of museums was best achieved by a friendly staff that patiently answered all questions from interested visitors, a role his sister Emma served for many years at the State Museum. When Cummings' former student and successor, Emil Haury, took over as director in 1938, he had to reorganize the State Museum, updating the exhibits and repository practices.

The educational and consequently moral value of archaeology was the main rationale used by Cummings for being an archaeologist. He carefully laid out his goals in an unpublished paper on archaeology nomenclature that he delivered in 1930 to the American Association for the Advancement of Science. For Cummings (1930b), archaeology provided an opportunity to learn "truths all must know," by revealing "the facts of men's lives and their relationship to the universe in which they move." In Cummings' opinion, men needed to be become more intellectually interested in other people's welfare, which could be achieved through proper education. Archaeologists' nomenclature, he strongly argued, must be simple to ensure that terms and expressions don't "mystify the reader or confuse him with a large number of words whose application need special explanation." Rather, facts should be correlated with those already known and assigned "a place in the cabinet of truth that will lead to the easiest and clearest understanding of their significance." Cummings did not mention, but we can assume, that he considered his museum display cases to be those cabinets of truth.

Cummings believed that an archaeologist's goal should be "to secure an intelligent appreciation of their work on the part of thinking men and women everywhere." Writing that was to be understood by the public, one of Cummings' favorite audiences, required "clearness, brevity and simplicity." Therefore, classification should be developed "for the benefit of the beginner and the intelligent population, and not merely for the hair-splitting investigator."

Most of Cummings' writings on Southwestern archaeology were designed for the thinking general public. Some archaeologists—those hair-splitting investigators—didn't understand this aspect of his work. They wrote mostly for other professional archaeologists and seemed "to think that an extensive and unusual vocabulary is an index of the profundity of their investigations." For Cummings, newly acquired knowledge about ancient Native Americans was to be disseminated chiefly through the schools and colleges, the places where "truth takes the place of conjecture, and dispels ignorance and superstition." This attitude partly explains why he wrote few technical reports on his explorations yet made sure that they were well covered in the local newspapers and in his numerous public lectures. In addition, many of his students also included the results of his excavations in their master's theses. Cummings probably was able to rationalize his excavations every year, without producing technical reports, because he had shared his expedition results with the public and his students—the thinking men and women everywhere.

Consequently, Cummings did not develop hypotheses and test them through an analysis of data systematically collected and examined, nor did he construct arguments through the marshalling of all relevant information. Rather, he offered some philosophical comments about the challenges of life in the past and described his adventures, which included brief comments on the more interesting natural features, ruins, and artifacts.

Because he excavated at a time before radiocarbon dating, Cummings was not overly concerned about chronology. He was interested in the general progress of humankind and believed that Native American culture represented the earlier stages of humans before civilization developed. When his close friend and colleague Andrew E. Douglass invented tree-ring dating in the early 1920s, Cummings dutifully had his students collect wood specimens for dating. Yet he did not use the dates for refining chronologies for the culture areas in which he worked. However, several of Cummings' advanced students made substantial contributions to the early development of tree-ring dating, working closely with Douglass (Nash 1999, 2000).

It is not surprising that Cummings readily adopted Henry L. Morgan's (1877) three-stage model of human social development, which proposed that humans had progressed from savagery through barbarism to civilization. He also adopted some of Morgan's (1881) ideas about the importance of house form. Cummings, like many progressives of his time, accepted Charles Darwin's ideas about human evolution but placed them within a cultural, not biological, context. By modifying the theory of natural selection to be God's means to create and sustain His creatures, progressives who were also devout Christians could accept the notion of biological and cultural change through time (Moore 1979).

Although Cummings (1935c) did not use Morgan's terms, he developed his own simplistic, three-stage model of human development in the American Southwest based on house form: cave to pit house to pueblo. This three-stage model was generally ignored by other archaeologists, and even his own students divided the Southwest into more specific cultural or geographic areas in their master's theses. Still, Cummings had little interest in defining regional culture areas—such as the Hohokam, Anasazi, and Mogollon—and stubbornly stuck with his generalized view of the past.

Interpreting the ruins that he investigated was not difficult for Cummings. He simply relied on behavioral analogies based on his many years of observations of Native Americans—Navajo, Paiute, Hopi, and Apache—on the reservations in the Southwest. For four decades, he observed and participated in numerous ceremonial and social dances. These experiences gave him a sensitivity to the importance of religion in Native American lifestyles.

Through his popular writings, the founding of museums in Utah and Arizona, and the education of hundreds of students, Cummings contributed to the creation of the Southwest's unique identity, a place where "one drinks in divinity with every breath" (Cummings 1920:31). His steady stream of newspaper articles reporting his annual expeditions, for more than thirty years, were part of what Curtis Hinsley (1996:188) has called the "discursive pattern of the Southwest discovery narrative." Cummings continuously expressed the repertoire of emotions that were called forth in that narrative—wonder, excitement, curiosity, and pensiveness. He saw the Southwest as an American wilderness, where the story of cultural development revealed by the archaeologist and anthropologist was as ancient and important as it was in Europe. His life story reflects his great reverence for the Southwest, a place where he could work for the betterment of humankind through the building of moral character in his students and the enlightenment of the general public about human progress in the American past.

2

"If We Live, at All, Let Us Be Alive"

Early Life in New York and New Jersey

Franklin County in upstate New York is a beautiful but cold region of spruce forests and numerous lakes. Moses C. Cummings, Byron's father, was of Scots-Welsh ancestry and owned a farm in Westville, New York, only a few miles south of the Canadian border. The Cummings' small farm was valued at $280 in 1850.[1] Moses' wife, Roxana ("Roxie") Hoadley Cummings, was a strong-willed member of an old New England family. They were married on March 5, 1843, in Westville by Justice of the Peace Buel H. Man. Together they had eight children: Maurice, Emily (Emma), John, Lydia, Moses, Phoebe, Thoreon, and Byron. Roxana gave birth to her last child, Byron, on September 22, 1860.[2] He had been a "blue baby" when born, and only his mother thought he would live to feel the breezes of the nearby Adirondack Mountains. Perhaps this auspicious beginning was a portent of his strong will to live.

The Civil War had a profound effect on the Cummings family. Just after Byron turned a year old, in October of 1861, Moses voluntarily enlisted in the Union Army and became a private in Company D of the Ninety-eighth Regiment of the New York Infantry. Byron later remembered sitting on the fence waiting for his father to come home. His older brother John ran away and tried to enlist, unsuccessfully, at age fourteen. During the last major campaign in the war, Byron's father experienced severe sunstroke. He died in the army hospital in Petersburg, Virginia, on August 18, 1864, and was buried in the Coal Hill Cemetery in Westville.

With no father to earn wages or run the farm, the Cummings family learned to be thrifty, since Roxana's income was a widow's stipend of only $8 per month plus $2 for each of her three children under sixteen years of age. Byron was later known as a frugal man, a quality he may well have acquired during his early family days in upstate New York.

A strongly religious person, Roxana had a creed that she instilled in all her children. It included the following seven commands: set a goal, have perseverance, study the scriptures, be courteous, be self-contained, be kind, and adhere to the truth (Cummings and Cummings n.d.:7). She taught that following these guidelines would lead a person to gain in stature and merit the respect of those around him. Young Byron must have listened carefully to his mother because he practiced her seven commands throughout his life.

The blue-eyed, sandy-haired Byron was slender and underweight as a child but athletically determined. Studying the ancient Greeks inspired Byron to pattern his life after them. He wished to become a marathon runner. At the age of eleven, however, Byron had a serious illness that the family doctor thought might be fatal. Byron recovered, but he gave up the thought of becoming a marathon runner. Nonetheless, he kept his intense interest in ancient Greek and Latin literature, deciding to become a teacher of ancient languages. He also was hopeful of some day visiting the Holy Land, Greece, and Rome in search of Classical ruins. From an early age, Byron had a deep-seated interest in archaeology and ancient history.

The Cummings' family farm was sold soon after the Civil War ended and they moved to a larger farm in Bangor, New York, where the schools provided more opportunities for Roxana's children. When Byron was ten years old, in April 1871, his mother married Stephen Wells, a neighbor and successful farmer. A few years later, Byron left home because he did not get along with his stepfather. He had asked that his father's pension money of $2 a month be given to him, but his father-in-law refused, and a court investigator agreed with his father-in-law. Byron then went to live with his brother-in-law and newly chosen guardian, George Donaldson, south of Bangor.

Byron initially worked in Donaldson's creamery but soon took on a job with a merchant in town, while attending a private school. However, at age fifteen Byron had a nervous breakdown from working too hard. Because his mother had become unhappy with her second husband, she left him and moved to her sister's house in Vermont. Byron soon joined them and attended a nearby school. One day when his teacher was ill, Byron was asked to teach her class until she returned. Although only sixteen years of age, he managed to keep the class together and had them complete some assignments. He knew then that he was destined to become a teacher (Cummings 1958:6).

When his mother moved to Brushton, New York, Byron came along. He worked with his brothers in their tombstone cutting business in Norwood. He then got a job with a local merchant, and one day, without any previous experience, he was told to drive a group of young oxen to the country by himself. His success at this difficult task impressed him so much that he later commented, "I found out that you never know what you can accomplish until you try" (Cummings 1958:6). This spirit of determination would remain with him his entire life.

In 1879, Cummings enrolled at Potsdam Normal Teacher Training School, and he also obtained a temporary job teaching thirty-two students in a country school when the school lost one of its teachers. Because it took a while to find another regular teacher, he taught there for two years. Then, because he was not happy at Potsdam School, he transferred to Oswego Normal School, located on the shore of Lake Ontario. He convinced his sister Emma, who was fifteen years older than him, to attend Oswego for a two-year elementary teacher degree. Still enthralled with outdoor athletics, Byron practiced with the football team, but after he broke his ankle, his family made him give up sports. Byron tutored and taught classes while at Oswego. He taught one school term in Governour, New York, during a severe winter, when temperatures dropped to twenty degrees below zero for two weeks. The following spring, he taught school in South New Berlin, New York.

Byron graduated in January 1885, with his sister Emma graduating the following summer. In September 1885, Cummings entered Rutgers Preparatory School at Rutgers College in New Brunswick, New Jersey. Dr. Edgar S. Shumway, a former Oswego Latin teacher and published scholar, supported Cummings' application to Rutgers, got him a scholarship, and paid for part of his board during the first semester. Cummings was fortunate to find a Presbyterian family that offered him board at the inexpensive rate of $3.50 per week. Perhaps because of this experience, he remained a member of the Presbyterian church for the rest of his life.

While at Rutgers, his scholarly aptitude and good penmanship got Cummings a job cataloging in the library for twenty-five cents an hour. He also helped a young attorney in the Wykoff family search his family history by inspecting public records and the graveyards of old churches in New Jersey. During his freshman year, Cummings learned what it meant to fight, literally, for his principles. When one of his classes rebelled against the strenuous assignments of their teacher, Cummings refused to participate. In retaliation, two of the leaders of the class mutiny tried to throw Cummings headfirst down a stairway. Though he was not very big, he was very strong for his size and was able to resist his attackers. His physical strength and strong will would serve him well throughout his life.

From 1887 to 1888, Cummings taught classes at Syracuse High School while on an excused leave of absence from Rutgers. He made up his class work during the summer and with tutors, and in 1889 he received his A.B. and was initiated into Phi Beta Kappa. Three years later, he obtained his master's degree and all the while taught Greek, Latin, and mathematics (algebra and geometry) at Rutgers Preparatory School from 1889 to 1893. It was during this time that he learned to become a disciplinarian, perfecting his "crushing look" to keep students under control in class (Cummings 1958:22).

By his early thirties, Cummings had obtained a solid education and teaching experience in the field of his choice—ancient languages. His study of ancient cultures, especially Greek, helped him develop his own philosophy about people and living, one that guided him throughout his own life and which he passed on to his students. Notes from one of his later (undated) lectures in Greek art and literature concisely expressed Cummings' position: "If we live, at all, let us be alive: let us have our share in solving the questions—social, political, and moral, that are crowding upon us today; but let us at the same time remember that the most nearly perfect-picture of the present that can be found is the past."[3] The past was to become even more significant in Cummings' life when he decided to move west, abandoning his eastern roots for a new life among Mormon pioneers, Native Americans, and ancient ruins.

3

"The Climate Is Delightful, the Scenery Unsurpassed"

Cummings at the University of Utah

In 1893, Cummings carefully examined his future and made a decision that became a turning point in his life. Seeking new opportunities in a drier climate, Cummings wrote the National Teachers Association and asked if there were any teaching positions available in the West. As a result of that inquiry, he received a telegram from the president of the University of Utah offering him a job teaching English and Latin. Although his headmaster at Rutgers told him that Salt Lake City was the last place on earth that he would consider moving to, Cummings accepted the offer without hesitation (Cummings 1958:23).

In early September, Cummings relocated to Salt Lake City, country that he had never before seen. On his way west, he met his mother and Emma in Chicago, where they spent a week at the World's Columbian Exposition. This opulent display of America's new industrial power included well-financed anthropology exhibits coordinated by Frederick Putnam of the Peabody Museum at Harvard University. Several exhibits on the Southwest were prepared by Frank Hamilton Cushing (1890), who had conducted the first systematic excavations in the Salt River valley five years earlier. At the Chicago exposition, Cummings would have seen the Wetherill family's extensive collection of artifacts from southwestern Colorado, Gustaf Nordenskiöld's photographs of cliff dwellings at Mesa Verde, and Cushing's artifacts from the Salt River valley excavations; Cummings also would have enjoyed craft and cooking demonstrations by Navajo, Hopi, and Zuni Indians (Fagin 1984; Fogelson 1991). His weeklong visit to these exhibits exposed him to some of the ancient and living cultures of the Southwest that would come to fascinate him for the rest of his life.

In his unpublished autobiography, Cummings (1958:22) explained why he chose to leave his eastern roots to live in the "Promised Land" of the Mormons in sparsely populated Utah Territory. He described an incident in which he tried to get a lazy student expelled from his algebra class, which created an uproar with the student's well-established Dutch family. Ultimately, the student withdrew from his class, but Cummings vowed to move to a place out west, where he could teach students who were willing to work hard in school to improve their life, rather than depend on their family's wealth and standing. To Cummings, hard work was one of life's greatest virtues.

There may have been other reasons as well. A former student and friend of Cummings', John McGregor (1987), wrote in his unpublished memoirs that Cummings had contracted tuberculosis and moved west to alleviate his deteriorating health, not expecting to live long. Ironically, McGregor noted, Cummings not only survived but lived into his nineties. Although Cummings was not able to achieve his childhood dream of being a marathon runner, his long and incredibly active life was like a marathon.

Cummings adapted well to his new home. Salt Lake City was nestled against the beautiful Wasatch Mountains, with peaks more than 11,000 feet in elevation, and had a view of the shimmering Great Salt Lake. He told friends that "the climate is delightful, the scenery unsurpassed" (Cummings and Cummings n.d.:14). The town was laid out in a well-planned grid with wide streets, and the impressive temple and tabernacle buildings of the Church of Jesus Christ of Latter-day Saints (whose members are popularly known as Mormons) were situated in the center of the grid. Although originally settled by Mormons in 1847, Salt Lake City in the 1890s contained many Gentiles, or non-Mormons (Talmadge 1901). Cummings joined a number of non-Mormon faculty already on the staff of the University of Utah, which during that academic year had 384 students enrolled (Chamberlin 1960:194). Cummings got along well with the Mormons because he appreciated that they were hard working, industrious, and progressive. He felt so comfortable in Salt Lake City that in November, his mother moved there and shared his apartment with him.

A photograph of Cummings, taken in 1893, was published in Ralph Chamberlin's (1960) history of the University of Utah. This photograph shows that at that time Cummings had a round head that was going bald, a bushy but trimmed mustache, and a broad and slightly hooked nose. He wore small, round-lensed glasses. Later photographs show that he changed very little in appearance over the next thirty years.

By 1894, Cummings was an assistant professor of Latin and Greek at the University of Utah and treasurer of the Athletic Association, an organization that he helped create (Chamberlin 1960; Kerr 1955). He soon became one of the most popular professors on campus, providing interesting lectures and participating in many student activities. In the spring of that year, his older sister Emma moved to Salt Lake City to live with him and his mother. From then on, Emma lived with her beloved brother for the rest of her life. In August, some of Cummings' new friends took him and Emma to see Yellowstone National Park in Wyoming, which he found very inspiring. After living and traveling in the region for a year, he knew that he had made the right decision to reestablish his roots in the West.

In the fall of 1894, one of Cummings' other sisters, Phoebe, and her five children came to live with him for a while. Her husband, Judge Lucius P. Judd, had been elected to the United States House of Representatives and moved to Washington, D.C. Cummings had to get up early to fix breakfast for everyone, a skill he would later put to good use during his field expeditions. He enrolled Phoebe's two young sons, Dell and Neil, in a local school so they would not fall behind in their schooling. This was Neil Judd's first experience in the Southwest but would not be his last. A few years later his family relocated permanently to Utah, and with Cummings as his mentor, he became a public school teacher for two years and then a professional archaeologist for the rest of his life.

With just two years of teaching experience at the University of Utah, Cummings achieved the status of full professor and head of the Department of Ancient Languages and Literature. His salary afforded him a two-story brick house with a lawn in front and a pasture for his horse and cow in the rear.[1] However, the pet cow, "Red," kept escaping from the backyard. Conveniently, a streetcar line ran near his house, and he frequently rode it.

Cummings proposed marriage that year to Mary Isabelle McLaury, a high school teacher from New Brunswick, New Jersey. She was slender and attractive, with dark eyes and a quick smile. She also was very intelligent and was a graduate of the New York School of Speech. Her friends knew her as Isabelle, and Cummings called her Belle. The McLaury family owned the Cold Springs Berry Farm in New Jersey, and Isabelle's father, Daniel McLaury, had been trained as a teacher as well. Cummings had courted her with hand-stitched, pressed flowers in his letters. One of the poems he sent her, written during his trip to Yellowstone, reveals the romantic and spiritual side of his personality (Cummings 1895):

This the sculptor who the artist
  That in some dim distant past
Wrought with patient hand unerring,
  Nature's temples grand and vast?
Sure the gods must look with favor
  On that being who in might
Has these lofty towers enacted
  Painted heavenward towards the light.
Note their massive sturdy structure
  See their graceful columns bright.
Don't they seem like souls immortal
  Towering toward the infinite?
Did you ever view such coloring
  Such firm blending here with hue,
All the shades and tints conceived of
  Yet not one that mars the view.
Sure no mortals raised these turrets
  Lifting high their time worn wall,
Human architects could never
  Give such form and grace to all.

In one of his letters to Isabelle, Cummings informed her that he had not attended church that day because he was too busy with university business, and he stated, "I guess you'll think I need a guardian, and I do. I need just your own dear self to keep me straight." She was soon given that opportunity (fig. 3.1).

Looking to enhance his professional credentials, Cummings decided to obtain a Ph.D. Because there were few graduate programs in the West at that time, he had to look to the Midwest or East. In the summer of

3.1 Isabelle and Byron Cummings, 1917 (courtesy of Arizona Historical Society/ Tucson, #PC29F.21A)

1896, he enrolled at the University of Chicago (perhaps because he had relatives residing there) and attended three classes.[2] His mother traveled with him back east, where she stayed with her daughter in Bangor, New York. Cummings apparently planned to study under Professor Frank Tarbell, who specialized in Classical archaeology and was a published expert on Greek and Roman art. One of the classes taken by Cummings, Old World archaeology, was taught by Professor Tarbell. Cummings' notes for this class include discussions on Mycenaean, Greek, Egyptian, and Syrian ruins. Another class was on Latin languages and literature and was taught by Professor Abbott. The third class was on Roman politics and was taught by a Mr. Walker. For unknown reasons, after the summer Cummings did not attend any more classes at the University of Chicago, nor was he involved with that university in any other way.

During one of his few trips back to the New York–New Jersey area, on August 12, 1896, Cummings married his fiancée in a New Brunswick wedding. They honeymooned in Montreal before returning to Salt Lake City and their brick house. They regularly attended the Third Presbyterian Church of Salt Lake City together. Their son, Malcolm—their only child—was born September 23, 1897. The joy of having a healthy child was tempered, however, when Cummings' mother died two months later in Bangor, New York.

When Malcolm was eighteen months old, Isabelle became sick, and her doctor recommended that she spend some time at a higher elevation. Cummings acquired an isolated camp at Lake Blanche in the Wasatch Range, east of Salt Lake City, as a family retreat. To get to his camp, located at about 8,000 feet in elevation, required three miles of horseback riding or hiking. The fresh air and quiet helped Isabelle recover from her malady.

Cummings also prospected a silver mine near his camp, which he and his students occasionally worked, digging a tunnel seventy-five feet in length. He also purchased five hundred shares of stocks in an unsuccessful mining company. He continued to buy small amounts of stocks in other mining companies over the next twenty years, although none turned out to be profitable.

Isabelle was blessed with good social skills and learned to entertain, on a limited budget, her husband's frequent guests. He often invited students home for dinner unannounced, and she was expected to feed everyone on a moment's notice. Isabelle also was very active in the women's clubs of Salt Lake City, serving as the president of the Ladies Literary Club and twice as the president of the Utah Federation of Women's Clubs.

In 1900, the University of Utah moved to old Camp Douglass on the east bench of the Wasatch Range, where it is currently located. Cummings was given a small office in the library building, and students would often gather there. Cummings worked with Utah's first paid coach, Harvey R. Holmes, to construct a football field and track, and he personally awarded the first silver-and-crimson sweaters to the football team. He and his Latin students also built a fence around the football field so they could charge admission to pay for equipment. This was the second football field and track that Cummings constructed, because he had also built one at the university's previous location. Because of this dedication, Cummings Field was named after him, and the *Utah Chronicle* called him the "Father of Athletics" (Kerr 1955:147). Cummings also served for eight years on the Board of Education of the Salt Lake City Schools and seven years on the Utah State Park Commission. In 1931, Cummings was awarded an honorary life membership for the "U" Men's Club in Salt Lake City.

While at the University of Utah, Cummings developed a reputation as a popular teacher. This was partly because he showed a personal interest in his students, often loaning them money when they needed it. He also sponsored the Boy's Club in Sugar House, Salt Lake City. Cummings kept busy actively recruiting students to the University of Utah, taking family buggy trips on Saturdays to schools, post offices, and churches throughout Utah. He enjoyed the scenery and occasionally observed ancient ruins during these journeys. On one trip to Cedar City, the stage driver brought along some wine made from Utah grapes that he hoped to sell in town. Not all of the wine was sold, however, and the stage driver decided to drink what was left over. He got so drunk that he almost fell off his seat a few times before Cummings took the reins, driving the stage himself all night and trusting the horses to find their way home.

Cummings continued to receive promotions while the University of Utah continued to grow. In 1906, when the university had more than 1,100 students, he was appointed dean of the newly created School of Arts and Sciences, a position he held for the next ten years (Chamberlin 1960:586). Four years later, Cummings insisted that the developing Department of Medicine be treated as a subdivision of the School of Arts and Sciences, partly because he was unhappy about the appropriation of the whole second floor of the Biology Museum for the expansion of the Medical School several years earlier (Ralph Chamberlin 1960:261). Since university president Joseph Kingsbury supported Cummings, for a short while Cummings served as both the dean of the School of Arts and Sciences and the dean of the Medical School.

Sometime in the early 1900s, at least by 1905, Cummings dedicated himself to the study of Utah archaeology, perhaps stimulated by his recruitment excursions. This new interest forever changed his life, as his exploration of ruins in 1906 began his decades-long, annual search for undiscovered ruins in Utah and Arizona. He used a spare room in his house as a museum, as well as part of his office in the University of Utah Library, where classes also were held. Cummings' field interests were soon incorporated into his teaching, and he eventually began developing a variety of archaeology classes in addition to his Latin and Greek classes. Archaeology was soon to become one of his main passions.

4

"Archaeology of Our Own Region"

The Utah Society of the Archaeological Institute of America, 1906–1909

Few archaeologists have discovered and excavated more archaeological sites in the Southwest than Byron Cummings and his students. The thrill of discovering hidden places in undeveloped country and digging for treasures more than five hundred years old motivated Cummings to explore thousands of miles of wilderness in Utah and Arizona for more than thirty-five years. When he was in his seventies, Cummings listed his sole hobby as "exploring."[1]

An energetic and tireless man with a strong sense of curiosity and a love of the outdoors, he was ideally suited for extended explorations of rugged country on horseback or with mules. For Cummings, discovery was the desire both to find ancient treasures heretofore unseen or unrecorded and to communicate with the divine through rigorous interaction with nature's wonders. His search for the best relics was contested by eastern institutions, but the outdoor adventures that were experienced became legendary among those who participated in his expeditions.

Cummings' favorite place to explore was the colorful and deeply incised canyon lands in southeastern Utah and northeastern Arizona. This part of the American Southwest is known as the Colorado Plateau physiographic province. It is a region of folded and faulted layers of different sedimentary rocks, colored by past geologic events and more recently eroded by wind and rain into innumerable canyons. Portions of this high desert landscape have an unusual grandeur and beauty. Geologist Herbert Gregory (1917:11) described the region as "a bewildering array of scattered mesas, buttes, isolated ridges, and towering spires, among which dwindling streams follow their tortuous paths." Rising above the tops of these eroded sedimentary deposits are various volcanic formations, including massive mountains, such as Navajo Mountain, where permanent springs and dense forests can be found. Many of the incised canyons drain into the San Juan River, which in turn flows west into the mighty Colorado River. Sandstone deposits stained dark red to orange have eroded into numerous pockets, recesses, and alcoves. Scattered among these fantastic formations are numerous archaeological sites, exhibiting a variety of architectural styles and dating to different time periods stretching back into the distant past. Many of the cave sites within the canyons contain rare, perishable objects. It was in this wilderness wonderland that Cummings developed a lifelong fascination with exploration and archaeology.

Cummings' search for ruins started in southeastern Utah but soon focused on the canyons located to the south and east of the majestic Navajo Mountain, which straddles the Utah-Arizona line and looms like a big blue-gray shadow above the canyons. His favorite location was the Tsegi (Sagie) canyon system southwest of Kayenta, but he also explored the sides and top of Navajo Mountain, which rises more than 10,000 feet above sea level. He also visited an important water source on the south side of Navajo Mountain, called War God Spring by the Navajos.

Ruins, Cummings believed, were physical evidence for the progress of mankind in the Southwest. Archaeology provided information about ancient people whose cultures represented earlier stages of human development compared to modern civilization. Cummings wished to know about the lifestyles and accomplishments of these people, but the primary goal of his adventures was to obtain artifacts (which he called "relics") for his university museum before they were taken by pothunters and out-of-state archaeologists. He also wanted to give his students an outdoor education they would never forget.

Cummings considered his expeditions into the wilderness as inspirational. He once commented about the emotional response from exploring such a magical landscape: "You feel that the Creator has surrounded you with mighty forces and great beauty that are helpful and not destructive, and that all seek to encourage and cheer you rather than to discourage you or retard your progress" (Cummings 1936d:2). Spending time camping under the stars, Cummings believed, also revealed the great plan for the human race:

> As the Ruler of the Universe turns on, one after another, the friendly illuminators of the canopy above you, you seem to catch a wider vision of the great plan and be able to reach out and touch the fingertips of the infinite. The world no longer seems sordid and mean. You forget the petty selfishness of men and see these as an essential part of the great plan that is moving on to the conquest of truth and the salvation of the world. Your eyes close, and you dream of the part you may play in that procession. (Cummings 1936d:3)

The notion of a predetermined plan greatly influenced his ideas about the past, which he saw as a series of progressive stages in the development of culture.

Although a highly religious man, Cummings thought of himself as a scientist as well, seeing no conflict in the two. He understood the importance of documentation in the discovery process, writing field notes and taking photographs, in most cases, during all of his University of Utah explorations. He embraced his responsibility to share the results of his expeditions but preferred to do that with the public more than with other professionals. He often provided more information about the expedition to the newspapers than he did in his brief archaeology reports (those few that he wrote). Consequently, the locations of some of the sites he found and their characteristics are unclear (table 4.1).

The origins of Cummings' archaeology career remain sketchy, and his involvement with Edgar Hewett and the Archaeological Institute of America has not been fully documented. Nevertheless, some of his early archaeological experiences and expeditions undertaken on behalf of the Archaeological Institute of America are known.

Utah Archaeology in the 1890s

When Cummings arrived in Utah in 1893 to begin his new position as assistant professor of Classical languages at the University of Utah, he was naturally inclined to develop an interest in American archaeology because he was already knowledgeable about ancient ruins in the Old World. Many of the local ranchers and farmers in Utah had known about the numerous ruins in the state since the 1850s. During Lt. George Wheeler's explorations in Utah in the early 1870s, Mark Severance and H. C. Yarrow excavated into ancient mounds in Beaver and Provo (Janetski

TABLE 4.1. Some of the Archaeological Sites Explored by Byron Cummings, 1908–1909

1908	1909
Alkali Ridge	Batwoman House
Long House	Betatakin
Snake Ruin	Cave No. 2
	Dogoszhi Biko
	Gulch
	Inscription House
	John's Springs
	Kiet Siel
	Ladder House
	Little Snake House
	Near Snake House
	Redhouse Ruin
	Redhouse Caves
	Skeleton Cave
	Snake House
	Swallows Nest

Source: Turner 1962.

1997). Museums in the eastern United States soon became interested in obtaining artifacts from the Southwest, and the Smithsonian Institution sponsored Edward Palmer's excavations in southern Utah to retrieve artifacts for exhibits at the 1876 United States Centennial celebration in Philadelphia. Palmer also collected for the Peabody Museum in the late 1870s (Fowler and Matley 1978).

Beginning in 1880, Don Maguire (1894) of Ogden began excavating ruins in central and southern Utah, sometimes using a team of horses and a plow and scraper to expose walls and obtain artifacts. Because he was one of only a few individuals digging in the state at that time, he was hired by the Utah Territorial World's Fair Commission to prepare an exhibit on Utah's ancient ruins for the 1893 World's Columbian Exposition in Chicago. Cummings may have seen this collection when he visited the exposition. Maguire's work was later called "promiscuous relic hunting" by Cummings' student Neil Judd (1926:5).

When Cummings began teaching at the University of Utah, he soon must have met Henry Montgomery, professor of geology and mineralogy and curator of the Museum of Natural History at the university. Montgomery had traveled throughout the state in the early 1890s to promote a school of mines and develop a museum. He visited Nine Mile Canyon and dug into some of the same sites as Maguire. Unlike Maguire, Montgomery (1894) was proud to note that he used a shovel, trowel, and brush during his excavations. The 1891 catalog of the University of Deseret (changed to Utah in 1892) mentions an archaeological collection, under the care of Henry Montgomery, at the university (Smith 1950:23).

Montgomery (1894) published an informed paper entitled "Prehistoric Man in Utah," in which he perceptively argued that the ruins of southern Utah were left by the same people as other Pueblo ruins in the Southwest. Furthermore, Montgomery believed that the Southwestern Pueblo people were related—but peripheral—to the greater civilizations of Mexico, as did many other early explorers and settlers of the Southwest in the 1890s (Fowler 1992).

When Cummings first became involved in archaeology is unclear, but he later stated that he had read Montgomery's paper (Cummings and Cummings n.d.). Cummings also may have been aware of excavations during the 1890s in southeastern Utah by Charles McLoyd and Charles Graham, as well as by a group that included Richard and John Wetherill and Talbot and Fred Hyde (Janetski 1997). Elmer R. Smith (1950:24), assistant professor of anthropology at the University of Utah, wrote that Cummings befriended Professor Montgomery and assisted him with his surveys and excavations throughout Utah from 1895 to 1914 to increase the University of Utah's museum collections. However, Montgomery left Utah in 1894, and in Cummings' discussions of his early archaeology experiences, he does not mention working with Montgomery.

Cummings and the Archaeological Institute of America

In Cummings' own words (1939c), his first archaeological exploration was in 1906, when he spent his summer vacation on horseback exploring Nine Mile Canyon in central Utah. His goal was to trace the northern boundary of the region occupied by the so-called Cliff Dwellers. The small villages, pictographs, granaries, and pottery sherds he found confirmed their presence in the area.

Cummings' 1906 exploration was done on behalf of the Archaeological Institute of America (AIA) of Boston, after he met Mitchell Carroll and Edgar L. Hewett at one of their lectures in Salt Lake City. The AIA had been established in 1879 by Charles Eliot Norton to promote American participation in archaeology of the Classical world. To increase membership, the AIA promoted the creation of local societies in western states, and local societies were soon established in Kansas City, San Francisco, Los Angeles, Denver, and Salt Lake City. Soon thereafter, Charles Lummis, a colorful and talented journalist who helped develop the Los Angeles society, argued that western affiliates should focus their resources on investigating and preserving the archaeology of their own region, rather than Classical archaeology. The results of those excavations could then be used to build local pride and create local museums—what Lummis (1910) later called the "Western Idea" (Snead 2001:65).

The Western Idea suited Edgar Lee Hewett, a former teacher and university administrator–turned-archaeologist, who had been excavating in northern New Mexico for several years before he was appointed AIA delegate, in 1905, for the Colorado Society of the AIA (Fowler 1999; Hinsley 1986). By December of that year, Hewett had been given an AIA fellowship in American archaeology. He conducted surveys, gave public lectures, and took on the position of spokesman for the western societies. He also lobbied Congress on behalf of American antiquities and helped write the first federal Antiquities Act (Lacey Act), which was signed by President Theodore Roosevelt in June 1906 (Lee 2000; Thompson 2000).

After talking with Hewett in Salt Lake City, Cummings was eager to help the newly created Utah society. A Progressive Republican, like President Roosevelt, Cummings believed that American antiquities were important and merited preservation. The AIA was happy to have his assistance because of his impressive credentials as dean of the newly formed School of Arts and Sciences at the University of Utah. Cummings became a member of the AIA in May 1906 and was closely affiliated with them while at the University of Utah. His exploration during the summer of 1906 was one of several planned by Cummings and Hewett for the Utah Society of the AIA (Cummings 1906a).

In July, Cummings (1906b) wrote President Thomas D. Seymour of the AIA in Boston, informing him that the Utah society had fifty-nine members, including President Joseph T. Kingsbury of the University of Utah and Colonel Williard Loring, president of the Church of Jesus Christ of Latter-day Saints. The next month Colonel Enos A. Wall and Cummings, acting as president and secretary of the Utah society, distributed an announcement throughout Utah that invited educational institutions, students, and citizens of Utah to furnish information about archaeological sites by filling out blank cards that identified the kinds of remains and their locations (Snead 2001:79). The information was to be sent to Cummings, who would use it for a publication on the state's resources and for future expeditions by the Utah society for the purpose of exploring, mapping, and excavating ruins. Establishing a states' rights position that he would maintain for the rest of his life, Cummings made sure everyone knew that the material collected would be kept within the state of Utah for scientific and educational purposes. The Utah society also created a series of parlor talks, which were designed to gain support for a state museum and the protection of Utah's ruins. One of the talks, scheduled for April, was by Cummings, on his Nine Mile Canyon survey.

In the fall of that year, Cummings planned a six-week field school for the following summer, to begin in mid June. In March of 1907, he proposed to Hewett that their next expedition go through Monticello, then to the Elk Mountains and on to Bluff, before returning to Salt Lake City (Cummings 1907a). Hewett approved Cummings' plans and sent him a list of recommended equipment: an army knapsack, a miners' tent, a camp bed, a saddle and bridle, a rubber coat, heavy shoes, an extra old suit, and a good camera to take plenty of quality black-and-white photographs (Hewett 1907b).

When summer came, Cummings took with him four of his University of Utah students, a journalist (Burl Armstrong), a minister (F. F. Eddy), and a guide to explore his targeted area—Montezuma Creek Canyon, Grand Gulch, Armstrong Canyon, and White Canyon in southeastern Utah (table 4.1). The isolated country they visited southeast of the town of Bluff was described in the *Grand Valley Times* (1907) of Moab as 160 miles from a railroad, 50 miles from a post office, and 40 miles from the nearest habitation. One of the students on the trip was Cummings' nephew and Latin student, Neil Judd, who also was a member of the Utah society. Munroe Redd, a local cattleman, served as guide for $7 a day,

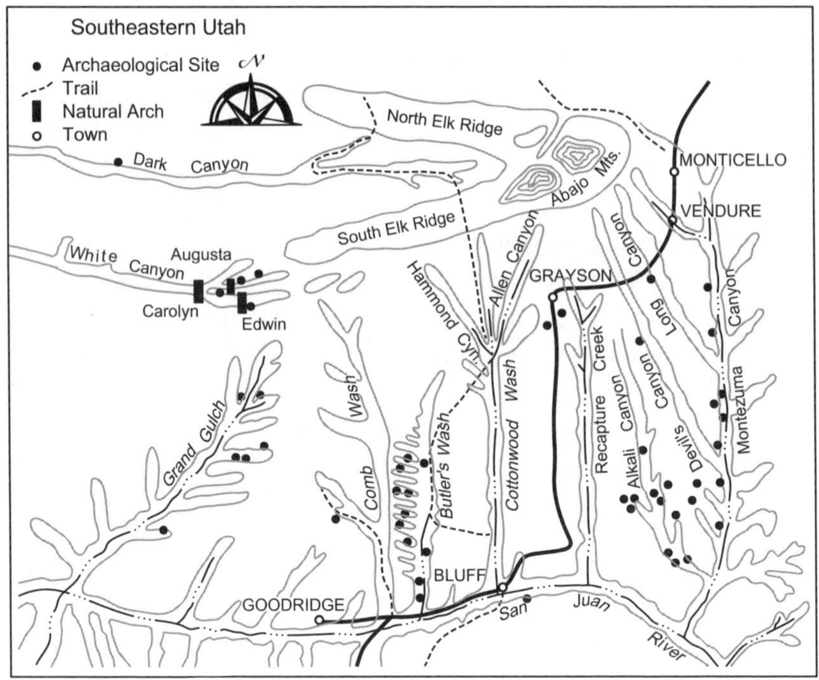

4.1 Redrawn portion of Cummings' (1910a) map of southeastern Utah, showing locations of archaeological sites

which included driving the group around in a wagon drawn by a four-horse team. Edgar Hewett visited with the group for a while and then returned to Santa Fe.

Cummings stated that the purpose of the expedition was to map the area where rumors said there were large natural bridges and prehistoric ruins, and to identify bridges worthy of protection. He and his students visited three large bridges called the Edwin, the Carolyn, and the Augusta Bridge. They also inspected many ancient pueblos located in the cliffs, along the canyon bottoms, and on the upper mesas (fig. 4.1).

On the basis of Cummings' and Hewett's recommendations and Fred Scranton's topographic map, President Theodore Roosevelt declared the area to be Natural Bridges National Monument on April 16, 1908 (Rothman 1989). Cummings was forever grateful to Roosevelt for his support. Soon thereafter, William B. Douglass of the General Land Office resurveyed the Natural Bridges National Monument, and it was subsequently enlarged by President William Taft on September 25, 1909. Douglass, a former Indiana lawyer turned federal surveyor, changed the names of the bridges to Kachina, Sipapu, and Owachoma. In a *National Geographic* magazine article he wrote about his explorations, Cummings (1910b) included a photograph of eleven horses and riders on top of Edwin (Owachoma) Bridge, which stands more than 100 feet in height.

Cummings and his crew observed many ruins but undertook little or no excavation (Judd 1968). They found circular rooms of poles and mud along with rectangular masonry rooms with beautifully intact roofs. One of the ceremonial kiva (round, semisubterranean) chambers had a two-pole ladder protruding through the hatchway. Well-preserved storage chambers were made of bent willow poles bound with horizontal withes and plastered with mud. Petroglyphs were abundant at habitation sites and along travel routes.

Judd (1968) vividly remembered the primitive food they lived on—coffee made from beans ground by smashing them between a folded blanket, biscuits made in a Dutch oven, and bacon. He had a not-so-amusing educational experience one evening in Hatch Wash, when he learned not to place a bedroll in a roadway. This lesson came from a sudden rainstorm that passed over; before he could get out of the way, a muddy stream of water ran down the road and through his bed tarp and blankets. Another lasting impression for Judd was an encounter with a mountain lion in their camp under Carolyn (Kachina) Bridge. This large cat apparently was not aware of Judd when it went to get a drink of water, and when it did see Judd, it made a spine-chilling scream that caused him to jump in the air in fear of his life.

After the summer field school, Cummings continued his efforts on behalf of the Utah society, requesting that Hewett visit Salt Lake City and lecture on American archaeology. Cummings (1907b) happily informed Hewett of his progress: "We have the people throughout the state quite awakened to the fact that we are attempting to do something in the line of the archaeology of our own region and I believe we are gaining their cooperation." The idea of an archaeology of his own region stayed with Cummings throughout his life.

But Cummings was not entirely content with the archaeology of Utah, and he starting coveting northern Arizona, where the ruins were thought to be less disturbed by relic hunters. However, a location in Utah was chosen for the summer dig, because financial assistance for the expedition came from Colonel Wall, a wealthy copper miner from Salt Lake City who wished to support Utah archaeology. The AIA was a cosponsor under the permit issued to Edgar Hewett. While Hewett was in Europe completing his Ph.D., Alice Fletcher (1908), chair of the Committee on American Archaeology, wrote Cummings in April, authorizing him to spend AIA funds. Cummings was listed as a member of the School of American Archaeology's staff in Hewett's (1909a) annual report for the following year, and the work of the Utah Society of the AIA was mentioned in Hewett's (1910a, 1911a, 1912, 1913) annual reports through 1912. Cummings held the title of field assistant for the AIA.

Hewett's and Cummings' plans for the summer of 1908 were for Cummings and his crew to conduct a survey of Montezuma Canyon, through which ran a northern tributary of the San Juan River, which was reported to contain many Pueblo ruins (Prudden 1903). After their survey, a large pueblo on Alkali Ridge in Utah, near present-day Blanding, was then chosen for excavation, and arrangements were made with Hewett to provide students to assist Cummings in the digging of the pueblo and its burial grounds.

One of the students Hewett recruited from Harvard University was Alfred V. Kidder, who had briefly met Cummings the year before while conducting a survey for Hewett. Kidder had been put in charge of the Alkali Ridge excavations by Hewett without Cummings' knowledge (Judd 1968). The twenty-two-year-old Kidder offered to be the codirector with Cummings, who was more than twice his age. Kidder had just received his B.A. from Harvard University and would enroll, the following year, in the Ph.D. program there, obtaining it in 1914. Within a few years, Kidder would become one of the most prominent and influential archaeologists to work in the Southwest.

Another crew member on the Alkali dig was Sylvanus G. "Vay" Morley, a civil engineer–turned-archaeologist, whom Kidder (1950) characterized as a small, nearsighted dynamic bundle of energy. Morley was with Kidder on Hewett's survey the year before and obtained his master's degree from Harvard in 1908. Morley later directed the Carnegie Institution's excavations at Chichén Itzá, where he also served as a spy during World War I for the U.S. government in Central America (Harris and Sadler 2003). He later served on the National Geographic Society's advisory committee for Cummings' excavations at Cuicuilco, near Mexico City, in the mid 1920s.

Another crew member at Alkali was the tall and slender Jesse Nusbaum, a skilled photographer and mason from Colorado, who would later direct the stabilization of the Palace of the Governors in New Mexico and Mesa Verde ruins in Colorado (Nusbaum 1980). During the 1930s, Nusbaum was the consulting archaeologist with the National Park Service for Cummings' excavation permits at Kinishba Pueblo. Two University of Utah students, including Neil Judd, also participated in this expedition.

The Kidder/Cummings crew camped at Cave Springs for five weeks and barely sampled the Alkali Ridge ruin. They dug seventeen rooms, three kivas, and two burial mounds containing dozens of human remains. Kidder was satisfied by their results, since they procured about four hundred museum specimens, including thirty whole pots. Cummings drew a sketch map in his field notes of a grid system that was set up over the burial mound. The materials collected from the dig were sent to the University of Utah Museum under Cummings' care. Some of the skeletal remains were sent in September to the Smithsonian Institution by Cummings, and in exchange he received 178 flint artifacts collected by the Smithsonian from sites in the Midwest. Judd (1950:21) reported that two of the local crew members at the Alkali Ridge dig were indicted for murder shortly after leaving camp because of their involvement in the death of a Mexican laborer during an argument in an Espanola tavern.

Because Cummings was eager to explore the red rock country of northern Arizona, he arranged to meet John Wetherill at his trading post, in Oljato (Place of Moonlight Water), on August 1, 1908. Wetherill and his wife, Louisa, had established the trading post in 1906. Neil Judd and Cummings' other student went along. Cummings also kept detailed field notes on this trip. When Cummings arrived in Oljato, he found that John and Louisa Wetherill had to participate in military negotiations as trusted allies of the Navajos. Consequently, Cummings and his two students set out by themselves for the beautiful and rugged Sagie-ot-Sosi (with varied spellings including Sega-at-Sosa and Tsegi Hatsosie) Canyon and Sagie—or Tsegi ("Inside the Rock")—Canyon, southwest of Kayenta.

Cummings (1908a) was very impressed with Wetherill, calling him "a very capable and honest man," whose experience, Cummings correctly predicted to Hewett, "will be of great value to us." One of five sons of the famous Wetherill family from southwestern Colorado, John had explored canyons and dug Pueblo ruins since he was a young man. He had a craggy face and a drooping mustache and was slight in stature but had remarkable physical strength (Comfort 1980). Raised in a Quaker family, he was compassionate and modest and had good peace-making skills, which served him well as a guide in Navajo country. Cummings developed a lifelong friendship with John and Louisa and their children, Ben and Georgia Ida. Louisa was a strong but charming woman who loved to sing and dance, and she was also a trusted friend of the Navajos because she spoke their language fluently. Ben was a skilled horseman at an early age but lost an eye at age eight, when he was kicked in the face by a horse at Chaco Canyon, New Mexico. Nonetheless, Ben helped his father and later became a guide himself. Cummings' sister Emma lived with the Wetherill family one year, in 1912, to serve as tutor to Ben and his sister, whom everyone called Ida. Ben and Ida also lived for a while with Cummings' family in Tucson.

The San Juan River was dangerously swollen when Cummings' party attempted to cross in the summer of 1908, so he looked for ruins on the north side of the river, where he traveled to Butler's Wash and excavated in Cold Spring Cave. After safely crossing the San Juan River, Cummings' party was guided by Wetherill for four days in search of ruins. Judd (1968) later recalled how they left a human skull conspicuously placed upon their equipment to keep Navajos, because of a fear of the dead, from taking the equipment while they were away from camp. However, this technique did not work with the Navajo dogs that were always rummaging through their campsite. The group examined a burial cave and two cliff dwellings. Cummings collected artifacts for his University of Utah museum, including a well-preserved wooden ladder from Dogozshi Bokho. Thrilled with his first exploration in Arizona, Cummings (1908a) informed Hewett that "it is so much more satisfactory to study a region before others have partially destroyed it."

Two months later, Cummings (1908b) expressed interest in returning to the Kayenta region the following summer, telling Hewett that he did not object to the Los Angeles–based Southwest society digging in the same area. He probably did not object at that time because they were a western chapter of the AIA and Cummings worked in Utah. A decade later, when Cummings was at the University of Arizona, he was not pleased about the Los Angeles group taking artifacts to California from Arizona.

Hewett (1909b) wrote Cummings in January with the news that Cummings and Colonel Wall had been made members of the governing board of the AIA. Hewett was happy that Cummings wanted to dig in the Kayenta region, instructing him to do "enough to preempt the field," presumably from archaeologists associated with eastern institutions. He also warned Cummings that their work would be carefully scrutinized: "We must take every precaution to have every word we publish up to scientific standards for the work in American archaeology is on trial for its life and will be subjected to the most rigid criticism both within and without our ranks." Cummings' delays in submitting his field reports to Hewett may have stimulated Hewett to make this pointed statement.

Cummings (1909a) let Hewett know that the Utah Legislature was probably going to approve his request for $2,000 for two years of University of Utah archaeological expeditions. He also reported to Hewett that he had exchanged letters with William B. Douglass, surveyor for the General Land Office, and was irritated with Douglass' opposition to the AIA digging in the Kayenta region. Convinced that the Smithsonian Institution was behind Douglass, Cummings (1909a) complained that "I don't see why its men should not be more than willing to help build up local museums in this country." This incident increased Cummings' resentment of eastern institutions.

In March, Cummings (1909b) told Hewett that he hoped to attend Columbia or Harvard University that year, before leaving for Europe, as part of his graduate studies. Also that month, William Douglass helped convince President Taft to establish Navajo National Monument to protect ruins in the Tsegi Canyon area, about forty miles south of the Utah-Arizona state line. Although he had not yet seen the area, Douglass (1909a) informed Walter Hough that he was motivated to move quickly to reserve the region's archaeological treasures for professionals at the Smithsonian Institution, rather than have them removed by Cummings and taken to the University of Utah.

Undeterred by Douglass' attempts to stop him, Cummings returned to the Kayenta area that summer, sponsored by Colonel Wall again and working under a permit issued to Hewett for the AIA. In addition to excavating ruins in Tsegi Canyon, Cummings was interested in finding a legendary sandstone arch called Rainbow Bridge and located west of Navajo Mountain, in an extremely rugged area. John Wetherill had informed Cummings of this stone arch after hearing about it from a Navajo friend, One-eyed Man of the Salt Clan (Gillmor and Wetherill 1934:161).

When Cummings arrived at Oljato, he found that Wetherill was preoccupied with other problems. So without Wetherill's guidance, Cummings explored canyons in the area around Oljato with his son, Malcolm, and four students from the University of Utah, including Neil Judd again. Stuart Young, a grandson of the legendary Mormon leader Brigham Young, took some fine photographs during the trip, and artist Donald Beauregard (1909) kept a diary of their adventures that was published by the *Deseret Evening News*.

Cummings' group set up camp at a well-preserved cliff dwelling that has the Navajo name Kiet Siel (also spelled Keet Seel), commonly translated as "broken pottery" but more correctly as "Shattered House" (Linford 2000:101–102). Containing more than 150 rooms and six kivas in a cliff opening high above the canyon bottom, this picturesque site had been discovered in the winter of 1894–1895 by two of John Wetherill's brothers, Richard and Al, and their friend, Charlie Mason. After a week of excavations, Cummings (1909c) wrote to inform Hewett that he had decided to delay his plans to go on a sabbatical to Germany that fall to study for a doctorate degree. Rather, he would continue his excavations through the end of the year and then travel to Germany.

In July, John Wetherill and his family took Cummings, his son, and Stuart Young to some ruins near Nitsie (also called Nitsin) Canyon, west of Kiet Siel. Here, a Navajo named Pinietin offered the group hospitality, and the Wetherill children and Malcolm explored nearby ruins. Scratched into a wall of one of the cliff dwellings was a difficult-to-read inscription that appeared to be "Anno Domini 1661" (Cummings 1953:48), and thus the seventy-four-room cliff dwelling was named Inscription House. The date indicated that the inscription had been made by a Spanish explorer. Other scholars have since argued that the inscription is actually 1861 and was probably made by Mormons (Miller 1968; Ward 1975). Cummings returned in the summers of 1914, 1915, 1916, and 1930 to conduct additional excavations at Inscription House.

While Cummings was exploring Tsegi Canyon, he encountered a local

Navajo named Needacloy ("Whiskers"), who was unhappy that Cummings' party was digging into Pueblo burial sites and disturbing their spirits. He ordered Cummings to leave immediately. Cummings refused and offered to pay for the pasture his horses would eat and for any other assistance that Needacloy would provide. Cummings then moved his camp farther from Needacloy's hogan but continued to dig. He and Needacloy later became good friends, visiting with each other whenever Cummings was in the area.

In early August, John Wetherill had to travel to Bluff, Utah, on business. There he ran into Douglass, who was not pleased that Cummings was excavating in the region under a permit issued to Edgar Hewett, without Hewett being present. Douglass had asked the General Land Office to cancel Hewett's permit and to force Cummings to stop his excavations. Douglass (1909b) also contacted Walter Hough of the Smithsonian Institution to complain that Cummings would take the objects he excavated, a "very remarkable collection," to the museum at the University of Utah. Douglass believed the artifacts belonged to the federal government, not to some western university. Cummings, obviously, had the opposite view.

When Wetherill returned from Bluff to Tsegi Canyon, he gave Cummings the bad news. He suggested that Cummings meet with Douglass and offer to conduct a joint expedition to Rainbow Bridge. Hoping to lessen the growing conflict between him and Douglass, Cummings agreed.

Many different accounts have been written about the adventures of this joint exploration party. Numerous discrepancies are present in the accounts, and there is not a consensus on who first heard about the existence of Rainbow Bridge, which route was taken by the joint expedition, what time it was discovered, who saw the arch first, and which of the Native American guides was most responsible for the success of the expedition (Cummings 1926d; Hassell 1999; Jett 1992; Judd 1927; Rothman 1993; Wetherill 1955).

To meet Douglass for the joint expedition to Rainbow Bridge, Cummings' group left Tsegi Canyon for Oljato, passing the hogan of Needacloy (also Nedi Cloey or Nide-Kloi) on the way. One version of the story states that Needacloy's wife informed Cummings' group that her children had seen a large ruin up the canyon. Because their horses were tired,

John Wetherill rested the horses and hired Clatsozen Benully, Needacloy's son-in-law, to take a group of six to this ruin on August 9 (Gillmor and Wetherill 1934:169). Upon finding this ruin nestled into a sandstone alcove in a deep canyon, they named it Betatakin, Navajo for "House on a Rock Ledge" (Linford 2000:115). Since they had little time, no excavation was undertaken, but Cummings planned on returning to further investigate it later.

Cummings' group, including his eleven-year-old son, Malcolm, returned forty miles from Piute Canyon to Oljato to wait for Douglass to arrive and join their party. After a day or two, they decided to go forward without him. To keep their travel gear light, they took two blankets each but no tents or extra clothing, and minimal food. Cummings had made arrangements to meet Nasja Begay[2] ("Son of the Owl"), a Paiute guide, at his hogan in Piute Canyon, northeast of Navajo Mountain. From there, Nasja Begay was to lead his group the rest of the way to Rainbow Bridge, on the northwest side of Navajo Mountain.

Douglass and his surveyors' group of five other men—including his Paiute guide, Mike's Boy (also called Jim Mike)—eventually caught up with Cummings on the trail. Douglass was accustomed to being in charge and stated that the combined group was under his control, annoying Cummings and Judd. Communication with Douglass was challenging because he was hard of hearing and everyone had to speak into his long ear trumpet. The Navajos called him "Man Who Hears Through a Rope" (Jett 1992:17). Altogether, the group now numbered eleven determined men and one boy on his way to becoming a man.

Because of their late start that day and slow progress through shifting sands, the exploration party was forced to camp only a few miles north of Oljato that night. They had a dinner of Dutch oven biscuits and boiled rice, stained red from the sediments in the water.

The next day, they followed an old mining road down Copper Canyon to the south bench of the San Juan River, between No Man's Mesa and Monitor Butte. Some of their horses were already showing wear from the rocky terrain. They pushed on to the west, to the mouth of Nokai Canyon, where they set up camp a short distance up the canyon.

On the third day, one of the horses lost a shoe, and Wetherill had to use nails from an old tomato carton to reshoe the horse. When the group arrived at their place of rendezvous in Piute Canyon that day, Nasja Begay was not there, having left to attend to his goats and sheep after waiting for the delayed party. After a lunch of watermelon and fry bread with Nasja Begay's father, Nasja, the exploration party marched on, concerned that they did not have a guide who knew where Rainbow Bridge was located. The group climbed out of the canyon over a precipitous trail and across the Rainbow Plateau on the north side of Navajo Mountain, camping that night along Beaver Creek in Cha Canyon. Mike's Boy and Dogey Begay, Cummings' Navajo wrangler and cook, became discouraged. There was talk about turning back until Wetherill challenged their pride, threatening to spread the word among their neighbors that they had not shown the same endurance as the white man.

The next day, the exploration team crossed over slippery domes of bare red rock along the edges of steep cliffs, frightening some of the horses. They finally descended from the mesa top down a narrow pass that contained an ancient trail, later called Hoskininni's Steps, where two of the horses fell. Fortunately, the animals were not seriously hurt. The group camped in Surprise Valley, and some of the men began to doubt that they could find the one canyon out of hundreds in the area that contained the seemingly mythical arch.

Just when things were beginning to appear hopeless that night, the fourth on the trail, Nasja Begay appeared out of the darkness and into their camp. His ability to travel the steep trails in the dark amazed everyone. He agreed to lead the group to their destination and back for $3 per day, a price quickly accepted. The following day, Nasja Begay and the exploring party traveled the last eight miles up the talus of Hellgate, past Owl Bridge and Oak Creek, to Rainbow Bridge—standing majestically 290 feet above Bridge Creek. Stuart Young took a picture of the exhausted but happy group in the midday of August 14, 1909 (fig. 4.2). John Wetherill inscribed his name and the date on a cliff above the bridge.

Douglass (1955) wanted to be, and convinced himself that he was, the first Anglo to see the bridge. After all, it was he who surveyed the 640-acre monument and named it Rainbow Bridge ("Barahoine" in Paiute, "Nonnezoshe" in Navajo). But both Wetherill (1955) and Judd (1927) stated that Cummings was the first of the group to see the bridge, with Wetherill outracing Douglass to become the first Anglo to stand under the bridge. Malcolm was the last of the group to see the bridge, being completely exhausted when he arrived. Moreover, other Anglos, includ-

4.2 Rainbow Bridge crew, 1909 (*left to right, top row*: Ned English, Dan Perkins, Jack Keenan, Vern Rogerson, Neil Judd, Don Beauregard; *bottom row*: Jim Mike, John Wetherill, Byron Cummings, William Douglass, Malcolm Cummings) (photograph by Stuart Young; courtesy of Northern Arizona University, #NAU.PH.643.1.130)

ing Wetherill, probably already had seen this tremendous sandstone arch before the Cummings and Douglass party rediscovered it (Hassell 1999).

As a diplomatic gesture to Douglass, Cummings instructed Judd to guide Douglass and his surveyors to Kiet Siel and Betatakin ruins, while he and Wetherill explored some canyons in a tributary of Piute Canyon. On the way to Kiet Siel, Judd's party accidentally came upon a forbidden Navajo war ceremony attended by six hundred Navajos and punctuated by intense drumming and blazing fires that lit the night sky (Judd 1927). Douglass' crew then surveyed the ruins and prepared a map for the proposed boundaries, which were later changed. Douglass' crew only had half-rations of food, but they were able to purchase corn and watermelons from local Paiute and Navajo farmers. Cummings' group could not find any melons and had to rely on parched green corn and inedible goat meat bought from Nasja, and they returned to Oljato hungry and wet from summer thunderstorms.

Local newspapers including the *Grand Valley Times* of Moab (1909a), the *Montezuma Journal* of Cortez (1909), and the Salt Lake City *Deseret News* (1909) ran stories on the discovery of Rainbow Bridge. Gaining some notoriety from his expeditions, Cummings was eager to continue exploring that year as long as the weather permitted. With his AIA excavation permit still valid, Cummings took sabbatical leave from the University of Utah and returned, in September 1909, to the San Juan River region for further exploration. Several local citizens served as guides.

Cummings returned to Salt Lake City in late September to get Malcolm back to school, then headed to Kayenta to dig more ruins. On his way to Arizona, Cummings read in a local newspaper that Douglass had tried to take credit for the discovery of Rainbow Bridge. To set the record straight, Cummings gave an interview in early October to the *Grand Valley Times* (1909b) of Moab, stating how "disgusted" he was with the "petty little spirit" shown by Douglass. He proposed that Douglass was jealous of the accomplishments of the University of Utah.

In November, Cummings and his crew rode horses and explored Indian Creek, Cottonwood Canyon, Beef Basin, and Fable Valley in southeastern Utah. Cummings' wife, Isabelle, accompanied the group. One morning that month, while packing the horses, they experienced a blinding snowstorm. But that didn't slow Cummings down, and he continued to dig in a cave ruin and a pueblo. Later, at a pueblo in Ruin Park, they sank five-foot-deep prospect holes in search of human burials and their grave materials (Cummings 1909f).

One of the ruins Cummings excavated that winter was the beautiful Betatakin, a semicircular pueblo with 135 rooms tucked under an overhanging cliff five hundred feet in height. Located at the head of a forested canyon containing a reliable spring, this cliff dwelling was better built and had received far less excavation than Kiet Siel (fig. 4.3). No special chambers, called kivas, were found, but one rectangular room in the center of Betatakin was thought to be ceremonial because of its kivalike interior features: a stone shelf, a fire box with a stone screen, and a pecked depression in the floor that could have been the sacred entrance into the underground, called a *sipapu* (Cummings 1915a:277). He also photographed a large, circular pictograph at the site. Cummings was happy to be the first one to "clean out," as he called it, the well-preserved rooms.

Hewett (1909c) provided specific instructions to Cummings for work

4.3 Betatakin, 1909 (photograph by Byron Cummings; courtesy of Arizona Historical Society/Tucson, #PC29F.15A)

at Betatakin that fall: avoid destruction or weakening of the ruin during excavation; don't put dump from excavations on areas to be dug later; don't restore ruins beyond necessary repair, and do that well; consider all objects to have value and save them; "take great pains" to make complete maps and photographs showing the condition of the ruin before, during, and after excavation; prepare detailed field notes; and prepare a special report on the excavations "in the shortest time consistent with thorough scientific study of your notes and materials." These well-thought-out instructions would hold up to scrutiny today. For the most part, Cummings followed Hewett's advice. He created a specimen list for the excavated artifacts and drew detailed sketch maps of the site. Excavations retrieved a number of important items, many of which were later analyzed by Keith Anderson (1971) for his detailed study of Betatakin and Kiet Siel.

Cummings managed to send Hewett, in late October, a preliminary report on his work from June 21 to September 30. He expressed his concern that officials in Washington, D.C., were uncooperative at a time when "the Far West is struggling to develop its resources, build up its educational centers, and live a larger and more cultured life" (Cummings 1909d). Surely, he reasoned, no government agency would "stand in the way of this progress."

In late November, while Cummings was in Tsegi Canyon, Douglass (1909b) wrote Hough to complain again. He could not understand why Cummings would not stop excavating ruins in the Navajo National Monument. Douglass was disappointed that Cummings, "with all the fruits of the Garden of Eden before him, in the matter of excavations, must eat of the forbidden tree." Furthermore, Douglass felt that Cummings had acted unfairly toward him, because Cummings had "denied making excavations of any ruin I surveyed, and yet I find the statement untrue." Douglass also accused Cummings of seeking only museum specimens and getting few details of the ruin itself. Although Cummings did seek museum specimens, his field notes indicate that he also recorded important details about the ruins (Christenson 2002).

Cummings and his party left Betatakin at the end of December, during a severe winter storm. There was two feet of snow on the ground and it was still snowing when Needacloy arrived with horses, according to Cummings' prearranged plans, to take them out of Tsegi Canyon. On December 27, Cummings (1909e) wrote Hewett from Bluff, Utah, noting that it had been minus twenty degrees the morning before and all of their food had frozen, leaving them with little to eat for breakfast. He also reported that they had excavated nearly all of the rooms at Betatakin but hadn't finished all that had been planned.

Cummings (1909f) prepared a list of all of the materials he collected from November through December 1909 under his AIA permit. Most of these materials were collected from Tsegi Canyon, but a few others came from Beef Basin, Cottonwood Canyon, and Allen Canyon. This list shows an amazing collection of artifacts, including beautiful ceramic vessels, finely woven cotton cloth, buckskin leather, feather cordage, sandals, wood and bone implements, hafted stone tools, and carved stone and shell jewelry. Most of these objects are still stored at the University of Utah, where Cummings deposited them, although he never did prepare a report on his excavations.[3] Kathy Kankainen (1995) of the Utah Natural History Museum has published color photographs and descriptions of more than eighty woven yucca sandals collected by Cummings in 1909 from six different locations: Sega-at-Sosa (Sagie-ot-Sosi) Canyon,

Betatakin, Batwoman, Double Cave Ruin, Hostein Canyon, and Navajo John Canyon. Many of the sandals from Hostein and Sagie-ot-Sosie canyons were made during Basketmaker times (AD 1–700). These sandals have decorative, raised geometric patterns on their soles. With such a fine collection of material tucked away and secure at his university museum, Cummings was ready to travel to Europe.

5

“A Picture of the Past and Present Mingled”

Adventures in Europe

In 1910, Cummings decided to travel to Europe and fulfill his lifelong ambition to see Classical ruins. He also hoped to get a Ph.D. from a foreign university, much as Edgar Hewett had done in 1908 after studying in Geneva, Switzerland, for a few months (Chavenet 1983). Cummings chose to attend the University of Freiburg in Germany, perhaps because one of Hewett’s close friends, Charley Wallace, had recently attended the university there, and because many Americans were studying at German universities at that time.

The governor of Utah, William Spry, wrote a letter of introduction for Cummings to take with him to Germany. This letter called Cummings “a scientist of ability, and a gentleman of the very highest personal traits” (Spry 1910). With this letter in hand, Cummings, Isabelle, Emma, and Malcolm began their journey overseas. They were delayed, however, when Malcolm caught scarlet fever on the way to the East Coast. He was quarantined for thirty days in a room in Isabelle’s aunt’s house in Chicago.

While waiting for his son to recover, Cummings spent time at the Field Museum and the Art Institute in Chicago. With the red rock country of northeastern Arizona ever present in his mind, Cummings (1910c) wrote Hewett a letter from Chicago. He expressed to Hewett his displeasure with William Douglass, characterizing him as “one of the type of men that still thinks the West exists merely to be exploited by the East and that there can be no educational centers in this particular part of the world.” Douglass’ actions only made Cummings more determined to establish one of those educational centers in the West at the University of Utah.

After Malcolm had recovered from his illness, the Cummings family took a train to New York City. From there, they traveled on the German steamship *Wilhelm Kaiser* to Europe through a terrific Atlantic storm, landing in Naples, Italy. They visited Herculaneum and Pompeii, where Cummings was disturbed by the "apparent licentiousness of the times" (Cummings and Cummings n.d.:55). They also toured the Vatican and Saint Peter's Cathedral in Rome, which Cummings believed were built for the "uplift of all mankind" (Cummings and Cummings n.d.:55). At the Capitoline Museum in Rome, they just missed seeing Theodore Roosevelt, who was visiting the city at the same time. This would not be the last time Cummings narrowly missed meeting Roosevelt. In Florence, Cummings was struck by the magnificent art but found it ironical that the wealth that allowed such fine art to be made also created leisure, which in his mind was the reason for the fall of the Greek and Roman civilizations. After two months in Italy, the Cummings family made a short trip to Greece and visited the Temple of Apollo at Corinth.

Cummings and his family then traveled to Freiburg, an ancient German town "where one finds a picture of the past mingled with the present" (Cummings and Cummings n.d.:58). In April, Cummings (1910d) wrote Hewett, calling Freiburg a delightful town but expressing disappointment in the university. One of the individuals he hoped to study under, Professor Sellar, was in Mexico. Professor Tiersch urged Cummings to try the university in Berlin. Cummings (1910d) confided in Hewett, "If I can earn a degree I want it, if not, I don't." The Cummings family then relocated to Berlin for his place of study, since the royal museums there were known to have archaeological collections from the Americas, as well as from Greece and Rome.

Cummings and his family stayed at a widow's house in Potsdam, outside of Berlin. They then moved to an apartment on Sachsenwald Strasse in Steglitz, closer to the Berlin museums, where his son, Malcolm, could be admitted into a German gymnasium. Cummings began learning German again because it had been two decades since he had studied German at Rutgers College. He enrolled in the University of Berlin and studied the extensive collections in the Natural History Museum in Berlin, where he was given a desk. There Cummings (1910b) wrote his article on the natural bridges of Utah for *National Geographic* magazine. In Berlin, the capital of Germany, Cummings noticed the rising military presence and the growth of the Socialist Party. One day he watched for two hours as twenty thousand high-stepping young men marched through the streets. Cummings also visited the Black Forest and attended a performance of the passion play at Oberammergau near the border of Austria. And in the winter of 1910–1911, he traveled alone to England to visit a former University of Utah student and family friend, Frank E. Holman, who was attending Oxford University on a Rhodes scholarship. Holman would later become a prominent attorney in Utah and president of the American Bar Association.

While Cummings was in Europe, William H. Holmes of the Bureau of American Ethnology sent Jesse W. Fewkes to Navajo National Monument to make a comprehensive record of the ruins. Called "Codfish" because of his straitlaced New England manners, Fewkes had originally trained at Harvard University as a marine biologist. He had a keen intelligence along with good artistic skills and was a prolific writer of short articles. He also was not a meticulous excavator or note taker and was an ambitious and jealous man (Hinsley 1983:63–64). In lectures given that winter, he had attempted to take credit for discovering Betatakin. But Fewkes had first visited the site on October 16, 1909, after working at Mesa Verde, and John Wetherill had inscribed in stone at the site Cummings' name and date of discovery: August 8, 1909. Concerned about his friend's reputation, Wetherill (1910) wrote to Cummings in Germany to remind him of this fact.

Once Cummings learned of Fewkes' work in Betatakin, he wrote Hewett in the summer of 1910, complaining that it was "mighty shabby treatment" that Fewkes was free to do as he pleased in the Navajo Monument region (Cummings 1910e). Hewett (1910b) in turn wrote Frederick W. Hodge at the Smithsonian, asking him to issue a statement about what Fewkes was doing in the region, since his activities appeared to be in "absolute disregard of and disrespect for the work of Professor Cummings." Hewett did not elaborate on why the investigation of ruins on federal land by an archaeologist employed by the federal government should be disrespectful to Cummings.

Senator Reed Smoot of Utah, an old friend of Cummings', responded to Cummings' request to find out what was happening. Senator Smoot (1910) wrote Cummings a long letter informing him that Smoot had been told by the Department of the Interior that Fewkes had had an interest in the ancestral sites of the Hopi in the Navajo Monument region for many years but only recently had been given the opportunity to investigate them. Senator Smoot also noted that the region was rich in archaeology and the field so vast that "there is work enough for many institutions for many years to come." Cummings (1910f), however, did not agree with that position, telling Hewett in August that he did not understand why they were not willing to tell the truth in Washington. His frustration with the East's control of archaeology in the Southwest was reflected in his comment that "they can vent their spleen on me—a Western upstart that in his ignorance assumes to criticize the great powers that be."

During Cummings' European trip, the Utah Society of the AIA struggled. Neil Judd kept Hewett updated on their activities, and Hewett offered Judd a job in the summer of 1910 assisting with excavations at Puye Ruin in New Mexico. In September, after the summer dig, Judd (1910a) informed Hewett that he was working with the Utah State Fair people on an exhibit for their museum at the fair. In December, Judd expressed his concern that the previous Utah society meeting had been poorly attended. Judd (1910b) explained the challenges that he and Cummings faced:

> The situation is often discouraging from the mere fact that we cannot make people believe that we are serious in our work. If we had a place to display our material it would be much easier to build up a strong society but until we secure suitable quarters we cannot secure the support of any great number of Salt Lake people. Then too there is the constant chore of trying to show the good saints that the Cliff-dwellers were not their distant ancestors.

After receiving his bachelor's degree from the University of Utah in 1911, Judd left the state to work at the U.S. National Museum at the Smithsonian Institution in Washington, D.C., where he was employed for more than thirty-five years (Wedel 1978). George Washington University awarded him a master's degree in 1913. Judd returned to Utah from 1916 to 1920 to conduct extensive fieldwork in the state as a staff member of the U.S. National Museum (Judd 1926).

At the end of the year, Cummings (1910g) expressed his concerns about a suggestion by Hewett that Alfred Kidder lead another expedition in Utah. Cummings told Hewett that it would be a mistake because Kidder "did not give our Utah boys the right encouragement when we were at work on Alkali Ridge." Rather, Cummings argued that "it will be much better for the Institute to encourage and guide the State University in carrying forward these investigations." He requested that he be allowed to return to Betatakin that summer to finish his excavations. Hewett (1911b) responded to Cummings with a "hearty approval" for his Utah plans.

In April 1911, Cummings took a trip, by himself, from Germany to Greece on a freight boat. His purpose was to gather information about artifacts he was studying in Berlin. On the way he stopped to see the opera building in Vienna, Austria. While the boat was docked overnight in Brindisi, Italy, Cummings took a photograph of an old Roman wall. Because he was wearing German clothes, he was arrested as a suspicious character. He was released, but as he was leaving town he saw an Italian man-o'-war ship that had been decorated with underwear, a humorous image that Cummings found so irresistible that he took a photograph. He was arrested again, released again, and barely made it to his boat as it was leaving the dock.

During his trip to Greece, Cummings visited the coast of Corfu, Tiryns, the ruins of Argos, the temples of Olympia, the harbor of Patrai, the shrine of Delphi, and the Acropolis in Athens. While in Corfu, he had a rare drink of alcohol, toasting Ulysses with a glass of fine wine (Cummings and Cummings n.d.:67).

The return trip to Berlin was by train from northern Greece through Austria. Realizing that a German Ph.D. was not going to happen, Cummings and his family left Berlin. They took a train to Paris and a ship to London, where Cummings spent long hours at the British Museum. He was especially intrigued with a Mexican mosaic mask, which sparked an interest in Mexican archaeology that he would later pursue. The Cummings family then returned to the United States by boat, this time on a calm sea.

Cummings made good use of the pictures he had taken during his stay in Europe, showing them to students in his Greek and Roman classes at the university. Curiously, his European trip instilled in him an even greater interest in the ruins of the Southwest. He had come to realize that while the Greek and Roman empires had assured the world of a "true picture" of their life and times through their literature, the absence of a written record for the ancient Southwest had obscured its people's place in history. Excavating in the ruins of the cliff dwellers and mesa pueblos, however, provided a means to answer the "where, when, and why of ancient man in the Southwest" (Cummings and Cummings n.d.:75). This was something he could do in his own state.

6

"The Path Man Has Traveled in His Progress"

Return to the Red Rock Country, 1911–1914

With only two years of explorations in the Navajo Reservation in northeastern Arizona, Cummings was hooked on the land and its people. The mesas and canyons that drained into the San Juan and Colorado rivers became his home away from home, his place of physical exertion, intellectual inspiration, and meditation.

Ancient Inhabitants of the San Juan Valley

While Cummings was in Europe, a summary report on his 1908 and 1909 explorations in the San Juan Valley region was published in the *Bulletin of the University of Utah* (Cummings 1910a). This forty-five-page report was one of the longest archaeology reports that he wrote during his entire career. A detailed map of the region he had explored and nearly fifty photographs of ruins and artifacts were included. His map showed the locations of more than forty-five cliff ruins and prehistoric villages south of the San Juan River in the Kayenta region and nearly fifty sites in southwestern Utah, north of the San Juan River.

In this report, Cummings spelled out one of the reasons for his continued explorations of the red rock country of southeastern Utah and northeastern Arizona. By revealing the lives of the prehistoric peoples of the Southwest through archaeological excavations, Cummings (1910a: 45) was confident that Americans would become "acquainted with the struggles through which the human race has passed here on our own continent." Cummings was thus in favor of an archaeology of not only his own region, but also his own continent. He argued that knowledge about the Indians' industry, esthetics, and persistence in surmounting difficulties would "awaken the sympathy and interest of every student of mankind." Indeed, he felt that "surely no more noble theme can challenge man's best thought than the path man has traveled in his progress from mere animal living and thinking today." And why could not that development have occurred in the Americas rather than just in Europe?

Some of the artifacts recovered during Cummings' digs showed a level of skill previously unknown for the prehistoric inhabitants of the Southwest. For example, one of the items found in Sagie-ot-Sosi Canyon was a medicine bag woven of colored yucca fibers with four square-toed sandals, each a different size, which Cummings suggested represented the four stages of life. Another medicine bag was made of woven human hair. Feather and fur robes were found wrapped around the bodies of the dead, indicating respect for the deceased. Pottery was found in abundance, and the report contained twelve photographs of several pottery groups or types. One of the more unusual vessels was a jar in the shape of a prairie dog with a painted design on the animal's body.

Cummings also described the architecture of the ruins he recorded. In some places it was so well preserved that there were still the impressions of fingers and knuckles left in the clay used to cover the masonry walls. He noted the presence of springs in the back of many of the caves that contained prehistoric structures. Recognizing that individual structures were sometimes parts of larger community groups, he identified an architectural pattern in which a large building that served as a fort or place of assembly, perhaps both, was surrounded by many smaller structures grouped around it. He also briefly described tower ruins in southeastern Utah.

Cummings addressed the question of why the cliff-dwellers had abandoned their homes, suggesting that decreased rainfall had brought about long periods of drought, causing crops to fail and resulting in famine and disease. These forces would have weakened the people until they "became an easy prey to the piratical Ute and the warlike division of the Navajos" and were eventually forced southward, losing their tribal identity (Cummings 1910a:45).

By 1910 standards, Cummings' report is a respectable description of his explorations, even if his writing style was more impressionistic and philosophical than scientific. The report is full of useful information at a

TABLE 6.1. Some of the Archaeological Sites Excavated or Surveyed by Byron Cummings, 1911–1914

1911	*1912*	*1913*	*1914*
Turkey House	Batwoman House	Batwoman House	Ceremonial Cave
Twin Cave House	Juniper Cove	Twin Cave House	Eagles Nest Ruin
	Oraibi	Water Lily Canyon	Inscription House
	Twin Cave House		Little Kiet Siel
			Pine Tree House
			Red House Ruin
			Red House Caves
			Sand Cave House
			Terrace House
			Tsegi Caves
			Twin Cave Ruin
			Yellowhead Canyon

Source: Turner 1962.

time when little was known about the prehistory of northeastern Arizona and southeastern Utah. His approach was one that he continued throughout the rest of his career—a colorful and romantic but well-written general discussion of the archaeology of the region, with occasional details provided only for example or for something of special interest. A detailed survey report it was not.

Back in the Saddle

After returning from Europe in 1911, Cummings managed a brief summer field trip to Tsegi Canyon, excavating some well-preserved sites (table 6.1). On September 3, he wrote to Hewett, from Bluff, informing Hewett that Cummings had just completed his fieldwork and had done it without a permit, expecting that it would arrive later, as it did (Cummings 1911). Cummings was now so intrigued by the ruins in Tsegi Canyon that he returned to the area for the next five summers, from 1912 to 1916 (Christenson 2002).

The year of 1912 was an eventful one for both the state and the nation. After half a century of territorial status, Arizona and New Mexico became states. Woodrow Wilson, a Progressive Democrat and former president of Yale University, was elected president of the United States. Novelist Zane Grey (1912) published his now-famous *Riders of the Purple Sage*, which introduced readers of American fiction to the people and landscapes of southern Utah.

Grazing permits had become a controversial issue that year for the Navajo National Monument. Because the national monument was considered too large to manage and officials were concerned about the negative reaction to the denial of grazing permits, the General Land Office persuaded President Taft to decrease the size of the national monument. On March 12, 1912, the monument was reduced to a total of only 360 acres, broken into three separate parcels surrounding each of the three cliff dwellings (Rothman 1989).

During the summer of 1912, Cummings had a small crew, including his sister Emma as cook and John Wetherill as guide, but they still made many exciting discoveries in the Kayenta region (fig. 6.1). His party excavated in Batwoman House, a seventy-five-room cliff dwelling that has a prominent white pictograph interpreted by him as the Navajo deity Batwoman, grandmother of Slayer God. Cummings spent that summer and the next digging this well-preserved ruin and others. At Batwoman House, Cummings excavated a burial of a mummified corpse wrapped in seventeen layers of matting, some carefully woven. This burial contained planting sticks and wooden scythes. The crew also found a painted jar containing small flint corn and a variety of beans. Ten burro loads of boxes filled with artifacts were retrieved from this ruin (Cummings and Cummings n.d.:99).

Another important site excavated that summer by Cummings was called Juniper Cove. This site, located about five miles west of Kayenta, was not a cliff dwelling but a large village containing numerous circular structures that appeared to be earlier than the cliff dwellings. He would return eleven years later to dig more of this site. Cummings' group also traveled to the Hopi mesas, watched Hopi dances, and explored ruins east of Oraibi.

By 1913, the rugged and beautiful landscape of the Kayenta region was becoming a destination point for intrepid travelers, artists, and writers. Visitors were especially interested in visiting Rainbow Bridge by following a treacherous trail around Navajo Mountain. Novelist Zane Grey visited Monument Valley, Rainbow Bridge, and Kiet Siel ruin with John

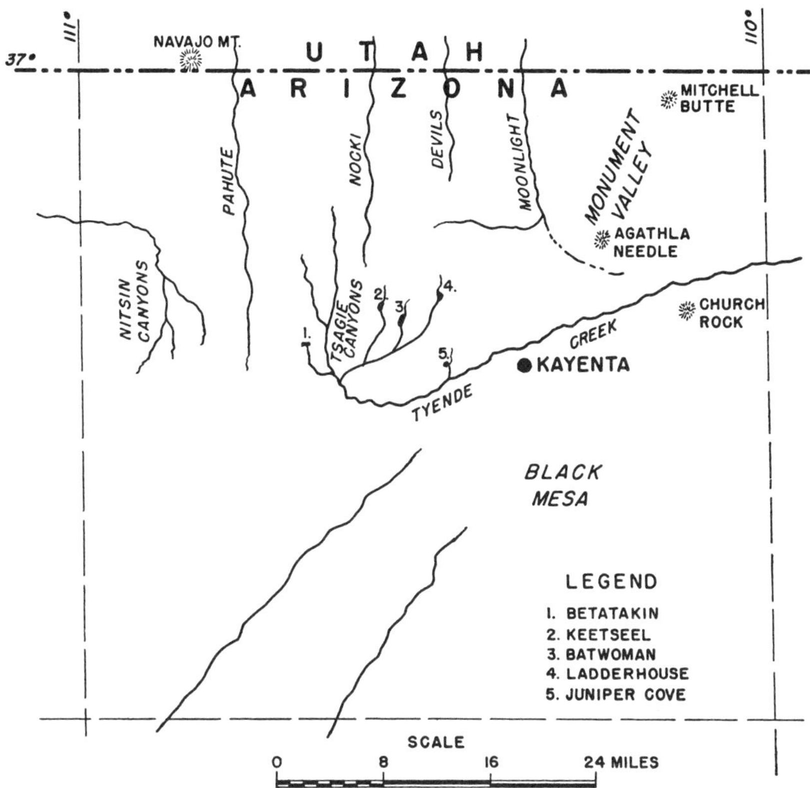

6.1 Cummings' (1953:149) map of major sites he investigated in the Kayenta region of northeastern Arizona

Wetherill and Nasja Begay that year (Grey 1972). Grey later incorporated John and Louisa Wetherill as characters in his novels set in the Kayenta region, calling them the "Withers" (Grey 1915; May 1997).

Cummings wrote in his autobiography that Theodore Roosevelt made arrangements in early 1913 to meet him during Roosevelt's trip to Rainbow Bridge later that year (Cummings and Cummings n.d.:81). Honored to receive such an invitation, Cummings offered to meet Roosevelt in Kayenta on August 15, after doing some exploring he had already planned. Even a visit from the president would not detour Cummings from his annual summer dig.

Early in the summer of 1913, Cummings took a quick trip to western Utah and eastern Nevada, visiting Lehman Cave. His summer expedition that year to the Kayenta region was the largest yet undertaken by the University of Utah, but it got started late, on August 1. A description of the trip was reported in the *Deseret Evening News* (1913) in mid September. The party of twelve rode horses and led a pack of eight burros into the rugged canyon lands. Members of the group included Cummings' wife and son, two other women, a reporter, an attorney, a naturalist, and a student named Andrew Kerr. They were guided by two Navajo men: eighty-year-old Huddlechessy (also known as Hosteen Luca, "The Joker") and Sie Soci (Navajo John), who was in his twenties. One of the women, Isabelle Brooks, startled everyone by wearing a pair of men's riding breeches. Hosteen Luca gave her the nickname "Boy-No."

Cummings' group covered up to twenty miles a day, but they were slowed one day when it took their Navajo guides all afternoon and evening to find a place to ford the surging San Juan River. The party visited Oljato—John Wetherill's trading post, which he had recently abandoned—and then moved south to Kayenta to visit Wetherill and his partner Clyde Colville at their new trading post. They arrived late for their scheduled meeting with Roosevelt at Wetherill's trading post, missing him by only three hours. Roosevelt had waited for Cummings for two days but became anxious and left to go see the famous Snake Dance at the Hopi mesas. Later that fall, Roosevelt ([1913] 1990:39) would publish a colorful account of his adventures in the Kayenta region, describing the fantastic rock formations near Navajo Mountain: "The cliffs were channeled into myriad forms—battlements, spires, pillars, buttressed towers, flying arches: they looked like the ruined castles and temples of the monstrous devil-deities of some vanished race. All were ruins—ruins vaster than those of any structures ever reared by the hands of men—as if some magic city, built by warlocks and sorcerers, had been wrecked by the wrath of the elder gods." This adventure article attracted even more attention to the area.

While in the Tsegi Canyon area that summer, Cummings excavated the Twin Cave ruins, an eighty-two-room cliff dwelling that contained a large amount of material, including numerous baskets. He explained to the *Deseret Evening News* (1913) that his method of investigation that summer was to "excavate every room carefully so as to preserve the walls intact and to preserve the interior arrangement and also find everything that may lead to a better understanding of this people." During their excavation of Twin Cave House, the group found a huge ceramic jar measuring nearly five feet in diameter and some turkey bones and feathers. They also excavated a room they interpreted as an artist's room, where they found a brush of fine straw and several pointed sticks. Cummings returned the next summer to dig more of the Twin Cave ruins. This time he excavated a circular structure that was twenty feet in diameter and had the characteristic interior features of some kivas: a bench paved with flat stones, a ventilator shaft, and a fire pit with a screen made of upright posts that had been plastered (Cummings 1915a:276).

During the summer of 1914, Cummings took thirteen men with him to undertake excavations at Inscription House and a few other ruins and to conduct additional explorations of the Piute (Pahute) Canyon region. He paid an Indian guide $4 for his assistance. Cummings dug into Pine Tree House, a cave pueblo with thirty-six rooms that was located on the Nitzenoeboko branch of Tsegi Canyon. Two small kivas at this site, both containing ventilator shafts and fire pits, dated to different time periods. The earlier, circular one was only about 8.5 feet in diameter. The later, rectangular kiva was 10 feet in diameter (Cummings 1915a:179).

A ceremonial cave in Monument Park was very difficult to enter, but Cummings used ropes to swing his crew over the cliff seventy-five feet to a small ledge and then another hundred feet to a landing from which they could climb hand over hand into the interior of the cave. Inside, they found a circular room with walls made of upright stones and wooden branches. Inside that room was a black jar covered with a flat stone that contained four carved wooden birds, a bundle of prayer sticks, thirty-six wooden pendants, bone awls, and other objects (Cummings 1915a:280, plate XX). Each of the carved birds was a different size, and Cummings surmised that they were part of a shrine to the rain gods, representing the four cardinal directions.

One of Cummings' more notable discoveries that summer was a female burial in Tsegi Canyon that contained nineteen ceramic pots. Field notes from those investigations fill three notebooks, which are currently located in the Arizona State Museum archives (Cummings 1914). Descriptions of architecture and plan maps are present for Batwoman House, Ladder House, Swallow Nest, Priestess Cave, and several other ruins.

One of the participants in Cummings' 1914 expedition, Clayburn Elder (1957), later recalled that Cummings was endowed with so much energy that he had trouble getting to sleep at night. One way for him to calm down was to tell stories around the campfire, and Cummings had many stories.

The Kayenta region increasingly attracted the attention of archaeologists from eastern institutions, and in 1914 Harvard University sent out two young but capable individuals, Alfred Kidder and Samuel Guernsey, to get their share of the fabulous artifacts that were being found in the cliff dwellings of northeastern Arizona. Kidder, who had worked with Cummings in southern Utah in 1908, had just completed his Ph.D. from Harvard University. Guernsey was a curator of art at the Harvard Peabody Museum. John Wetherill's trading post at Kayenta served as their headquarters, and they hired Clayton Wetherill, John's brother, as their guide. Kidder and Guernsey started their investigations in Monument Valley but had to abandon that area when their water sources dried up. At the suggestion of Cummings, who happened to be visiting John Wetherill at the time, Kidder and Guernsey moved to the Marsh Pass area, southwest of Kayenta. Their following Cummings' advice was to have a profound effect on Basketmaker archaeology (Blackburn and Williamson 1997).

In the Marsh Pass area, not far from where Cummings had dug previously, Kidder and Guernsey excavated three "caves" (rockshelters) that were full of well-preserved, perishable items and dozens of circular slab cists. Some of the cists held human burials. In 1915, Guernsey returned without Kidder to excavate more in that area. Kidder and Guernsey's (1919) report on their 1914–1915 investigations was 228 pages in length and profusely illustrated with 102 figures and 97 plates. The preservation of some materials was unbelievable and included food remains such as acorn nuts, piñon nuts, cactus fruits, corn, and squash; mountain sheep and deer skins; sandals and hairbrushes; woven baskets and bags; and several atlatls, or throwing sticks, and their associated darts. This report set new standards in the reporting of excavation results for northern Arizona. Kidder and Guernsey (1919) noted that they had found evidence of a people who had undeformed crania, unlike the shaped crania of the Pueblo Culture, as well as different burial practices. Because their findings were similar to those in Grand Gulch, Utah, that the Wetherill brothers had called Basketmakers, Kidder and Guernsey also assigned their materials to the Basketmaker tradition.

Guernsey also returned in 1916–1917 and again in 1920–1923 to excavate additional sites. This work was also well reported (Guernsey 1931; Guernsey and Kidder 1921). Interesting discoveries included two dogs, one accompanying a male burial and another buried with a female person.

In their first report, Kidder and Guernsey (1919:13) acknowledged that "the opening up of the immensely fertile archaeological field of northeastern Arizona is due to the initiation of Byron Cummings." Cummings, however, was not pleased that so much well-preserved Basketmaker material was removed from the state. In addition, he may have been jealous of the high quality of the reports that his former coworker was able to publish. Certainly the reports far exceeded anything he had written, or would write in the future, about his excavations in the same region.

7

"Not in Harmony with the Forces"

A Controversy at the University of Utah

When Cummings was hired at the University of Utah in 1893, he joined a university founded by Mormon pioneers but seeking its own identity in an increasingly modern world. The United States was becoming heavily industrialized, and urban settlements were rapidly expanding across the nation. Declared a state in 1896, Utah wanted to be incorporated into the national economy, but on its own unique terms. Because its mining and agricultural industries were relatively young and the Mormons wished to appear as political moderates, the corrupt political and business alliances found in many urban environments at this time had not developed in Utah (May 1987). The state constitution, drafted in 1895, has many Progressive elements, including workers' health and safety regulations and women's suffrage.

Living in Utah's capital, Salt Lake City, Cummings witnessed the rapid growth of one of the West's important urban settlements. This electrified city had 50,000 inhabitants in 1900 and 93,000 in 1910. The Progressive movement, a diverse group of social reforms that swept the country at the turn of the century, also gained a foothold in the Salt Lake region. In 1902, Mormon apostle and Republican Reed Smoot of Provo was elected U.S. senator, and for the next thirty years he assisted in the passage, or death, of all Progressive reform legislation in the state. In 1911, a coalition of Mormons, Protestants, and Socialists established a city commission form of government for Salt Lake City to insulate it from political pressures. Some Progressive reforms were acceptable in Utah, as long as they were done by local choice.

The administration of the University of Utah wanted the school to become a modern university, Progressive in outlook but still politically conservative. A liberal curriculum that emphasized desert agriculture and science, in an urban institution located adjacent to a wilderness setting, attracted eastern professors with Progressive ambitions, such as Cummings. For a while, this mixture of liberal and conservative political views worked within the university.

After conservative Republican William Taft defeated Theodore Roosevelt, a Progressive, for U.S. president in 1912, the University of Utah administration began to clamp down on its professors' participation in Progressive Party activities. A strong supporter of Progressive ideals, Cummings found himself in the midst of a raging controversy between the professors and the administration over faculty rights and the influence of the Mormon church. This fight reached such intensity that seventeen professors resigned from the university, a sudden loss of teachers so dramatic that it received the attention of the *New York Times* (1915).

Some accounts of this war between the faculty and administration focus on a student's controversial speech at the university in 1914. The *New York Times* (1915), however, reported that the problems began earlier, when the congressional Vreeland Commission visited Salt Lake City to take public testimony concerning national banking reform and mineral smelting and railroads in Utah. One of the persons who testified, George Q. Coray, professor of economics at the University of Utah, was a member of the Progressive Party. His testimony was not well received by local banking interests or by Governor John C. Cutler. Members of the university's board of regents were not happy, and Regent William W. Riter demanded that Professor Coray be fired. In addition, when Professor W. P. Merrill, head of the School of Mines, was nominated for the state senate on the Progressive ticket, the board of regents forced him to withdraw.

According to Ralph Chamberlin (1960), the faculty's dissent with the administration had been brewing since at least 1913. In September of that year, the faculty had submitted a petition to the board of regents, signed by more than forty members of the faculty. This petition expressed concerns about faculty dismissals by President Kingsbury without adequate explanations and a perceived policy of repression by Kingsbury, who had been president of the university since 1897.

The dissatisfaction among the faculty and the heavy-handed approach of President Kingsbury came to a clash with the June 1914 commencement speech by Milton H. Sevy, a sheepherder from southern Utah and class valedictorian. Sevy's speech criticized the university for its general conservatism and for several recent administrative decisions, including the denial of a women's dormitory in 1913 in favor of housing cattle at the state fair. Sevy also argued that "some vestige of the old time church antagonism" remained at the university and that the university should assume a "vigorous progressive policy" (Chamberlin 1960:327). Sevy's speech set off a firestorm of complaints. Governor William Spry wrote letters to the board of regents and the university president requesting that they find out who was behind Sevy's speech. The governor, a friend of Cummings', was embarrassed and demanded that those responsible be held accountable, including terminating their appointments with the University of Utah. He would soon learn that Cummings was to be implicated in the scandal.

An investigation ensued, and it was revealed that Sevy had written his own speech but three professors had read it before it had been delivered at the commencement. Cummings was one of the three; the other two were W. G. Roylance, a former newspaper editor and professor of history, and Instructor Charles W. Snow of the English Department—who was Sevy's debate coach.

To assert control over the situation, on February 26, 1915, President Joseph Kingsbury recommended, for the good of the university, that four members of the faculty, all non-Mormons, should not be reappointed. These included Snow; another member of the English Department, Instructor Phil C. Bing; Associate Professor Ansel A. Knowlton of the Physics Department; and Associate Professor George C. Wise of the Department of Modern Languages. All four professors were popular, but Progressive-minded, teachers (Chamberlin 1960:328). In addition, Professor George M. Marshall, chair of the English Department and a member of the faculty for twenty-three years, was demoted. A Mormon bishop and high school teacher was nominated to fill his chair position. A fifth professor, F. W. Reynolds, had left town before his employment could be terminated (Jeppson 1973:165).

The faculty was immediately up in arms over these actions and demanded an explanation. President Kingsbury met with the faculty in early March and stated that he would not back down on what he had done, nor would he explain the reasons for terminating the professors.

The alumni association, students, faculty, the Literary Club of Utah, the Federation of Women's Clubs (of which Isabelle Cummings was a member), two state senators, and three of the five local newspapers called for an investigation of Kingsbury's actions. The board of regents, with William Riter as chairman, refused to discuss the matter. On March 5, an alumni meeting was held, and a resolution in the state senate for an investigation was proposed but failed after Kingsbury lobbied against it.

Cummings, who had just received a fellowship in the American Association for the Advancement of Science, was understandably angry that Kingsbury had terminated professors without Cummings' advice as dean. On March 6, he wrote a letter of resignation to the president. Cummings' (1915c) letter clearly indicated that he was unhappy with President Kingsbury:

> Inasmuch as you deem it necessary to make sweeping changes in the work and teaching force of the school of Arts and Sciences and seem to consider it unnecessary to advise me in any way regarding these changes, and inasmuch as your reticent attitude toward me in our recent interview both indicate that you no longer have confidence in my ability and judgment and inasmuch as I am not in harmony with the forces and the policy now guiding the University, I would respectfully tender my resignation as Dean of the School of Arts and Sciences and Professor of Ancient Languages and Literature to take effect with the termination of my contract at the close of the present school year.

In mid March, the board of regents issued a statement supporting President Kingsbury and stating that Snow and Wise were not needed in the future reorganization of the English Department. It was also reported that Knowlton and Wise had made derogatory comments in their classes about the administration. Since the board of regents saw an irreparable breach in the relationships of the four dismissed individuals and President Kingsbury, the board believed it best to support the president in his actions.

The response from the faculty was explosive. The next day, March 17, fourteen professors submitted their resignations. One of them was the dean of the School of Law, Frank E. Holman, who later stated that he "was not in harmony with a policy of repression, suspicion and opportunism in University administration" (Chamberlin 1960:341). Three other professors submitted their resignations a short time later. As many as eight different departments were represented. The president and the board of regents quickly accepted all of the resignations, including Cummings', and began seeking replacements.

The Salt Lake City newspapers were divided in their opinions on the university controversy. The *Deseret News* and the *Herald-Republican* supported the board of regents, while the *Tribune* and *Telegram* did not. The *Herald-Republican* (1915), on March 25, called Cummings and Roylance weak men because they had read Sevy's speech and had done nothing to change it. Six days later, Cummings told the *Utah Chronicle* (1915) that he no longer wanted to work at the University of Utah with "a large portion of the public in the State violently antagonistic to the University." He also informed the paper that he was looking around for another position, in Arizona in particular.

Concerned about the large number of resignations, the newly formed American Association of University Professors (AAUP) set up an investigative team to conduct an inquiry. Professor Arthur O. Lovejoy of Johns Hopkins University headed the team. The AAUP investigative report determined that the professors had indeed been dismissed without basis and that the atmosphere on campus could have an effect on free speech and academic freedom. The board of regents ignored the report, although at the beginning of the next year Kingsbury was removed as president and made president emeritus.

In March 1915, Cummings had written the University of Arizona seeking a position in archaeology or in museum work. A few months later, he had a new job there as a professor of archaeology and director of the Arizona State Museum. He put his Utah experience behind him and relocated his family to Tucson in September. Tucson was a much smaller town than Salt Lake City, but the University of Arizona was growing and progressive enough to satisfy his educational philosophy. Just as important, he could continue his annual summer expeditions to explore ancient ruins in northern Arizona.

8

"The Confidence and Esteem of His Pupils"

Teaching Archaeology, 1912–1925

Byron Cummings is generally thought of as an archaeologist, yet first and foremost he was what he was trained to be—an educator. He spent his whole life in the field of education, from a high school teacher to an instructor, a professor, a museum director, a department head, a dean, and a university president. Even when performing a variety of administrative duties, he actively taught classes in ancient languages and archaeology, presenting class lectures and grading papers almost continuously for more than fifty years. And he was very good at it. Cummings' archives at the Arizona Historical Society are full of letters of appreciation about how he made a huge difference in students' lives. But he not only educated students, he also made concerted efforts to educate the public through civic and professional organizations, such as the Arizona Archaeological and Historical Society. His field schools were legendary in their own time and would be difficult to re-create today because of modern safety and liability requirements.

Cummings the Classroom Teacher

Early in his career, Cummings was recognized as a talented teacher. E. H. Cook (1891), secretary of the National Education Association in New Brunswick, called Professor Cummings a Christian gentleman and an excellent disciplinarian who "wins the confidence and esteem of his pupils." Nearly fifty years later, Gordon Baldwin (1938b), former student assistant to Cummings, stated that Cummings was "always accessible to everyone; always ready with wise counsel and advice; always helping students from his private means."

An example of the strong impression Cummings made on former students is found in a letter from Howard M. Jones of Salt Lake City. Jones (1944) informed Cummings that four members of the class of 1909 had met for lunch to talk about their past experiences at the University of Utah and that Cummings was remembered as a kind and understanding dean. Jones didn't expect Cummings to remember his four former students but wanted to tell him that "even after 35 years the memory and appreciation of your services to the University of Utah are still fresh and clear."

Cummings' education at Rutgers College in the late 1880s had taught him that the purpose of college was to instill a mental and moral discipline in young students to make them better Christians and citizens. This combination of discipline and piety was typical for nineteenth-century American universities, which borrowed it from European universities (Veysey 1965). Learning ancient languages was important in these institutions because wrestling with Latin and Greek grammar built character, a primary objective of education. This educational and theological orthodoxy became forever ingrained into Cummings' core beliefs about life.

Most of Cummings' original class records for the period from 1893 to 1921 are on file at the Arizona Historical Society in Tucson. These records show that when Cummings took the job at the University of Utah in 1893, he started the fall semester with a full load of four classes: English grammar, rhetoric, Latin (Caesar), and Greek. In addition, he soon expanded his course selection—in 1895 he taught Roman history, and in 1896 he taught a class in mythology. Moreover, as early as 1897 he taught summer school classes; that summer's offering was Roman history.

Cummings' class records indicate that his first class in archaeology was given in 1912 at the University of Utah (table 8.1). Walter Kerr (1955), who accompanied Cummings on his 1912 summer expedition, stated that Cummings taught archaeology classes beginning in 1906, but no listing of archaeology classes appears in his class records before 1912. Ralph Chamberlin (1960:586), in his comprehensive history of the University of Utah, reported that Cummings taught his first American archaeology class in 1912–1913 and was in charge of a separate Archaeology Department in 1914–1915.

TABLE 8.1. Classes in American Archaeology Taught by Byron Cummings at the University of Utah, 1912–1915

Academic Period	*No. of Students*	*No. of Withdrawals*
Summer 1912 (June 10–July 19)	36	3
1912–1913 Extension (Ogden)	31	0
1912–1913 Extension (Morgan)	9	0
1912–1913	22	3
Summer 1913	20	0
1913–1914	44	1
1914–1915	49	2
1914–1915 Extension	14	0

Source: AHS, Byron Cummings Papers (MS 200, box 8).

Teaching archaeology was not only enjoyable to Cummings but also served another purpose in his career. During the first twenty years of the twentieth century, the American university system promoted utility and research in higher education, with less focus on discipline and piety (Veysey 1965). Having students recite a dead language took on less importance at many universities, especially ones that endorsed Progressive educational ideals, which emphasized problem solving through science. Committing himself to the emerging fields of anthropology and archaeology provided a means for Cummings to adhere to the notions of discipline and piety but to also continue to be useful to the modern university. Teaching archaeology allowed him to satisfy his and his students' intellectual curiosity, yet to still build character through the study of the American past, both in the classroom and in the great outdoors.

When Cummings received his job offer from University of Arizona president Rufus von KleinSmid (1915), the job was twofold: to develop the existing Arizona State Museum and to teach one or two courses in archaeology in a new Archaeology Department. Cummings' starting salary was $1,400 for a ten-month period ($25,340 when converted to 2003 dollar value). With additional administration duties, his salary would rise to $3,800 in 1919 ($40,300 in 2003 value) and to $4,500 in 1920 ($41,200 in 2003 value). In 1925, Cummings was paid $4,800 in annual salary (the equivalent of $50,300 in 2003 dollars).

Because Cummings had been hired in the summer, the University of Arizona's (1915) catalog for the fall and spring semesters had already been printed. Therefore, no classes are listed for Cummings for that academic year. His class notes indicate that he taught a class in European archaeology in the fall of 1915 at the university, but because the class started late, in October, only seven students attended. Clearly pleased with his new institutional patron, Cummings (1916) informed the Rutgers alumni newsletter, *The Targum*, that the University of Arizona had an excellent president and faculty and was "a young, progressive institution."

In the spring, Cummings taught his American archaeology class, with twenty students attending. The University of Arizona (1916) catalog listed four archaeology classes for the next academic year: general archaeology, American archaeology, Greek archaeology, and Roman archaeology. Not only did he teach archaeology classes, but for his first five years at the University of Arizona, he also taught Latin and Greek. He soon found that his archaeology classes were far more popular than his Latin and Greek classes (table 8.2). The number of students attending his archaeology and anthropology classes steadily increased over time, partly a result of the university's nearly tripling of enrollment in five years: from 450 students in 1915 to 1,635 students in 1920 (Martin 1960:278–279). Cummings' exciting archaeology classes coincided nicely with a major expansion of the university.

Arizona Archaeological and Historical Society

Cummings understood well the importance of public support for archaeology. He had actively participated in the development of a Utah branch of the Archaeological Institute of America and had watched the masterful promotion, by Edgar Hewett and Charles Lummis, of the educational and civic values of archaeology in the Southwest.

Soon after arriving in Tucson, Cummings began organizing a local archaeology group to support his field expeditions and to provide a means to educate the local citizens about archaeology in Arizona. On April 14, 1916, he and a group of sixty friends and associates formed the Arizona Archaeological Society (Johnston 1966). This group soon thereafter merged with a defunct Phoenix group called the Arizona Archaeological and Historical Society (AAHS) and took its name.

Curiously, Cummings did not request that the AAHS become affiliated with the Archaeological Institute of America (AIA). This became notice-

TABLE 8.2. Classes Taught by Byron Cummings, 1915–1921

Academic Period	*Class*	*No. of Students*	*No. of Withdrawals*	*"A" Grade*
1915–1916	European Archaeology	7	0	20%
Spring 1916	American Archaeology	20	2	35%
Fall 1916	General Archaeology 1	24	1	17%
	Greek Archaeology 5	2	0	0
	Greek 1	3	0	0
	Latin 3	8	3	60%
Spring 1917	Roman Archaeology 6	9	0	56%
	Latin 4	6	0	33%
	Greek 2	2	0	?
	General Archaeology 2	40	3	35%
Fall 1917	General Archaeology 1	19	2	41%
	American Archaeology 3	4	0	50%
	Greek Archaeology 5	4	0	50%
	Latin 1	6	0	0
	Latin 5	6	0	17%
Spring 1918	Anthropology/Archaeology 2	35	3	38%
	American Archaeology 4	8	1	29%
	Roman Archaeology 6	6	2	50%
	Latin 2	40	2	0
	Latin 6	3	0	33%
Fall 1919	university closed—no classes			
Spring 1919	Anthropology/Archaeology 2	40	2	34%
	American Archaeology 4	17	3	57%
	Roman Archaeology 6	8	1	29%
	Latin 7	1	0	0
	Latin 8	4	0	?
Fall 1919	Anthropology/Archaeology 2	49	2	13%
	American Archaeology 3	18	2	19%
	Greek Archaeology	7	0	29%
	unidentified class	6	1	0
Spring 1920	Anthropology	81	13	30%
	Ethnology/Archaeology 8	35	5	33%
	Roman Archaeology 6	11	1	17%
Summer 1920	Field Course	9	0	0
Fall 1920	Anthropology 1	58	5	18%
	American Archaeology 3	24	3	48%
Spring 1921	Anthropology 2	66	10	11%
	American Archaeology 4	27	1	20%
Summer 1921	Mexican Archaeology Field Course	3	0	33%

Source: AHS, Byron Cummings Papers (MS 200, box 8).

able to Hewett (1916), who wrote Cummings that fall and asked "if with the extinction of the Utah Society you let your membership in the Institute lapse, and if so whether you would not let us carry you in either the Santa Fe or the San Diego branches." Cummings joined the Santa Fe society but did not ask for the AAHS to become an Arizona society of the AIA, perhaps because by then Hewett had created a number of powerful detractors and because the AAHS's support, without AIA influence, gave Cummings a better chance of wresting control of Arizona archaeology from eastern institutions.

A monthly program meeting and occasional field trips were the main functions of the AAHS, where archaeologists and other scholars shared their experiences with members of the society. Cummings' 1916 summer expedition, for example, was financed by a $500 grant from the AAHS and $500 from his University of Arizona budget (Johnston 1966).

Between 1916 and 1936, Byron Cummings made approximately thirty-four presentations at AAHS meetings, and his students gave dozens more. AAHS programs in the fall of each year typically consisted of Cummings and several of his advanced students presenting lectures on the results of their annual summer expeditions. Cummings also shared his experiences from travels to Mexico and Egypt. Only his student and successor, Emil Haury, gave more programs to the AAHS than did Cummings (Hartmann and Urban 1991).

A sporadic newsletter was an important part of the early AAHS, but not until 1935—when Harry Getty, Thomas Hale, and Father Victor Stoner started the quarterly journal called *The Kiva*—did the society have a regular publication (Fontana 1985). All three were students of Cummings'. The fact that Cummings did not feel a need to establish a professional journal as part of his support group in 1916 reflects his general approach to archaeology: he was less motivated to share his archaeology results with other professionals through written reports than to give lectures and talks to his local supporters.

The early membership of the AAHS comprised a few professional archaeologists but mostly Arizonans who had an active interest in the state's history and prehistory (Hartmann and Urban 1991; Wilcox 2002). Cummings was the first president. The four vice-presidents were Charles F. Solomon, president of Arizona National Bank; Reverend Julius W. Atwood, bishop of Trinity Episcopal Cathedral; Mrs. Anna Belle Morgan, wife of the president of Wilcox Bank and Trust; and Professor Frank W. Hart, principal of Prescott High School. The secretary was Thomas K. Marshall, president of Pima Publishing Company, and the treasurer was John S. Bayless of Carlink Ranch. Dr. Joel Ives Butler, a local surgeon, served on the executive committee. Most of the members of the AAHS lived in southern Arizona, but Cummings also had supporters from the Flagstaff area. Many of them would become an integral part of his statewide archaeology activities.

Cummings' Early Field Schools

Cummings was a great believer in the value of a hands-on outdoor education. Nothing built moral and physical character better than hardships in the wilderness, sweetened with a sense of discovery about the past and a feeling of accomplishment. A longtime supporter of the Young Men's Christian Association (YMCA), Cummings most likely had read YMCA leader Luther Gulick's (1913) book, *The Efficient Life*, on the Greek ideal of strenuous activities serving as an aid to human efficiency. The Victorian culture in which Cummings was raised believed that body strength built character and righteousness and, consequently, personal usefulness for God's and the nation's work (Haley 1978; Whorton 1982). A wilderness journey with Cummings was meant to be both educational and enlightening, with both aims achieved through physical and mental exertion.

From his first explorations into Arizona in 1907, Cummings took students and friends along with him. Not until 1919, however, were students able to get college credit for their adventures with Cummings. University president Rufus von KleinSmid had inaugurated a summer school program the year before, and Cummings immediately asked to participate (University of Arizona 1918). He was familiar with Hewett's field projects in the Frijoles Canyon area in northwestern New Mexico, where archaeological field surveys and excavations were combined with anthropological, geological, and botanical observations in the region (Springer 1910). Consequently, Cummings designed his field schools to include a variety of different experiences, including interacting closely with the Native Americans who lived in the area where he and his students excavated.

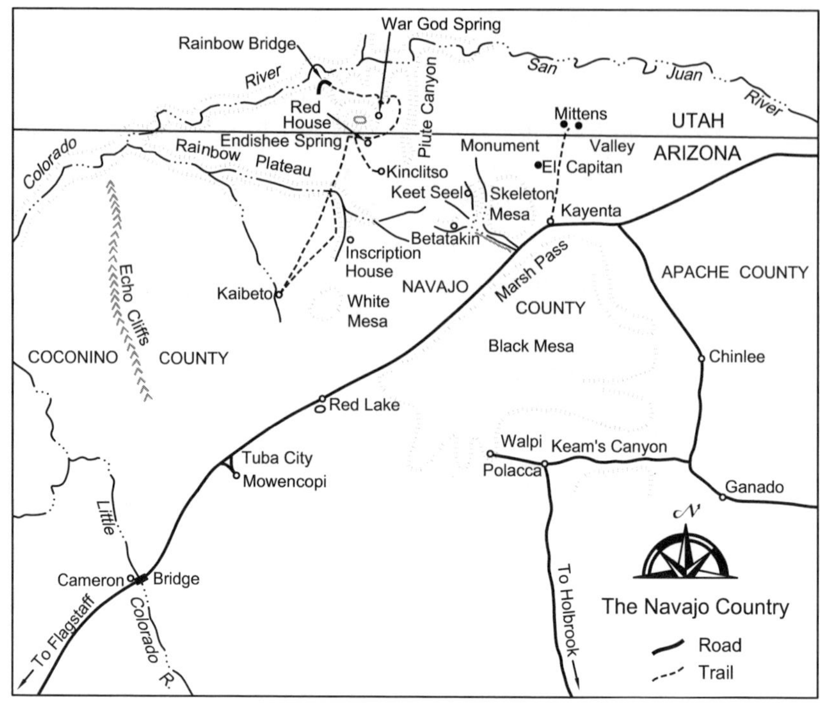

8.1 Franklin Walker's redrawn map of Cummings' 1919 field school expedition to the Navajo Country, northeastern Arizona

Cummings' 1919 field school was a memorable experience for the eight men and seven women who paid $153 and a university fee of $2 to $8 per person to attend the "Summer Course Among the Cliff Dwellers." Travel from Tucson to Flagstaff was an additional $14 expense. According to the University of Arizona (1919) catalog, the participants had to be able to ride horseback and camp out. One of the students, Franklin Walker (1919), described their trip in his class paper: "There were many experiences, many sights more wonderful than those many see in a lifetime. There were a few hardships which only added zest to the trip. When that same group returned they had all changed. Health was stamped in every action; happiness and satisfaction were everywhere in evidence; and a deep realization of the benefits in knowledge and experience gained was rooted in the heart of each individual." Walker noted that the participants traveled over a thousand miles by auto, by horse or mule, and by foot (fig. 8.1).

Another student, Violet Rubens, recorded in her paper that breakfast consisted of bacon, Dutch oven bread, and lots of coffee with canned milk; dinner was usually beans, bread, and stewed fruit, and occasionally mutton. John Wetherill provided supplies and served as guide, charging $10 per day for his services and $1.50 per day for each of the twenty pack animals (Brace 1986; University of Arizona 1919). Rubens (1919) vividly remembered that one night there was a "most terrific electrical storm" that was made even worse by red ants, rattlesnakes, and bright moonlight.

Cummings' 1919 field school contained elements that became common to the Southwestern field school tradition: scenic splendors, natural hardships, anthropological experiences, side trips to other places, interdisciplinary activities, and practical jokes (Gifford and Morris 1985). It was not until 1928 that his mentor, Edgar Hewett, was able to give college credit for Hewett's field schools in New Mexico.

Anthropology in the Classroom

Whenever possible, Cummings exposed his students to indigenous people and the knowledge they were willing to share. One of his Navajo friends, Hosteen Luca, spent several weeks in Tucson in 1919, along with the John and Louisa Wetherill family. Cummings convinced Luca to speak to the morning assembly at the university. Wearing his traditional Navajo black velvet shirt and red headband, Luca talked about the futility of war (Cummings 1952). The moral message of Hosteen Luca's talk was most likely appreciated by Cummings.

Honorary Degrees and Some Help

For five years, from 1915 to 1920, Cummings was the sole professor in the Archaeology Department and head of the Classics Department. By 1919, he offered six different classes in archaeology (University of Arizona 1919). Frank Fowler, newly hired professor of ancient languages, was also listed under the Archaeology Department course schedule for the 1920–1921 and 1921–1922 academic years (University of Arizona 1921a, 1922a). Proud of the notoriety that Cummings brought the University of Arizona, the administration rewarded him, in 1921, with an honorary doctorate of law degree (L.L.D.). It was not accompanied by a raise in his salary, but from now on he would be referred to as Dr. Cummings.

From 1922 to 1925, Cummings was assisted by Karl Ruppert, a shy but multitalented individual from Phoenix in his mid twenties (University of Arizona 1922b, 1923, 1924a). Hired as an instructor in the Department of Archaeology after assisting Cummings with his summer excavations as early as 1916, Ruppert taught archaeology classes and worked in the Arizona State Museum.

In the summer of 1924, the Rutgers Class of 1889 held a class reunion. The *Los Angeles Times* (1924) announced that Cummings was attending and would receive an honorary doctor of science (S.D.) from his alma mater. The paper also reported that Cummings would visit the American Museum of Natural History and the American Indian Museum in New York before leaving for Mexico to excavate the Cuicuilco Pyramid in Mexico, for the second time, on behalf of the National Geographic Society. Cummings was at the height of his career.

Karl Ruppert took care of the State Museum while Cummings was excavating at Cuicuilco in 1924 and 1925. With Cummings out of the country, Ruppert was the first professional archaeologist to participate in the controversial lead cross discovery on Silverbell Road in Tucson. Fortunately for him, in 1925 he left for a job in central Mexico, avoiding the nastiness that resulted over arguments about the authenticity of the lead crosses. Ruppert was equally skilled as an archaeologist and as an architect (Lambert 1961). For more than thirty years he was employed by the Carnegie Institution of Washington, D.C., working with Sylvanus Morley and others on several famous Mayan ruins, including Bonampak (Ruppert et al. 1955) and Chichén Itzá (Ruppert 1935; Ruppert et al. 1952).

9

"The Organizing and Building Up of Our University Museum"

Development of the Arizona State Museum, 1915–1926

Today, the Arizona State Museum is an internationally known anthropology institution housed on the west side of the campus of the University of Arizona. It has come a long way since 1915, when Byron Cummings was hired to organize and develop the State Museum. During his twenty-three years as the museum's director, Cummings substantially expanded its collections from a few hundred to more than twenty-six thousand catalogued items. His desire to obtain materials became an obsession, because he feared if he didn't collect Arizona's relics they would end up on someone's fireplace mantelpiece or in storage at the American Museum of Natural History in New York or the Smithsonian Institution in Washington. He also knew that the 1893 originating act of the museum (then called the Territorial Museum) had stated that it would exhibit archaeological objects, minerals, and animal and bird specimens from the territory.[1]

The first director of the Territorial Museum, who remained in that post for more than fifteen years, was Herbert H. Brown, owner of the *Tucson Daily Citizen* and warden at the Yuma Penitentiary. A typical Victorian amateur scientist and collector, he also was a founding member of the Arizona Antiquarian Association in the late 1890s. In addition, he published a short article on a Pima-Maricopa cemetery in the *American Anthropologist* (1906). The Territorial Museum was first housed in a single room in University Hall in the Old Main Building, where most of the university departments were located. In 1904, the museum was moved into parts of the first and second floors of the new library and museum building, which later became the law building. Brown died in 1913, and the collections were placed in storage until the new Agriculture Building was completed. Professor John J. Thornber and his wife, Harriet, looked after the collection until Cummings arrived.

The museum's hope for future development took a significant turn for the better when a new University of Arizona president, Rufus B. von KleinSmid, was hired in August 1914. Von KleinSmid's educational background was in psychology and philosophy, and he clearly understood the important educational role a museum serves at a growing university. Von KleinSmid was eloquent and dynamic and constantly promoted the university throughout the state with his theme of "Greater Arizona" (Martin 1960:13). To have a museum that highlighted the unique and significant qualities of Arizona's past fit well with this theme.

When President von KleinSmid (1915) informed Cummings that the board of regents was offering him a three-fifths position of professor of archaeology, von KleinSmid specifically stated that the job would involve "the organizing and building up of our University Museum." Cummings immediately accepted the position and then undertook his annual summer archaeological expedition to northeastern Arizona and southern Utah under the auspices of the University of Arizona. After his summer field expedition, he stayed in Salt Lake City a short while to finish cataloging artifacts he had collected while at the University of Utah, before packing his bags for Arizona.

When Cummings arrived in Tucson in September 1915, von KleinSmid took him to the second floor of the not-yet-completed Agriculture Building and showed him a pile of stone implements, ethnological material, and cases of bird skins on the floor in the hall. Von KleinSmid is reported to have said, "Here is your museum, go to it" (Wilder 1942:27–28). After a few days, Cummings began installing displays in two rooms, with a small office between them. Cummings was not inexperienced in museum work, since he had established a small archaeology museum at the University of Utah, and he quickly began sorting the material according to three primary categories: natural history, archaeology, and ethnology. He also back-cataloged Brown's collection, filling out 5 × 7 inch catalog cards, a procedure he followed for all of his later acquisitions (fig. 9.1).

To ensure a constant flow of ancient and historical objects into the State Museum's collections, Cummings continually acquired material

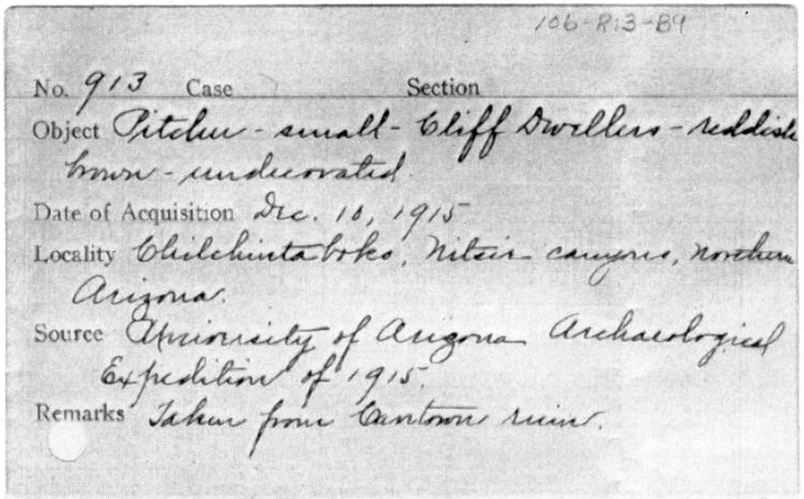

106-R13-89

No. 913 Case Section

Object Pitcher - small - Cliff Dwellers - reddish brown - undecorated.

Date of Acquisition Dec. 10, 1915

Locality Chilchintabito, Nitsie canyon, northern Arizona.

Source University of Arizona Archaeological Expedition of 1915.

Remarks Taken from Cantown ruin.

9.1 Example of Cummings' handwritten museum catalog card (courtesy of the Arizona State Museum, University of Arizona)

through donations, purchases, loans, and his annual summer excavations. Museums, in Cummings' view, were places where people learned about the past through visual examination of their relics. The more material on display, the better. Exhibits in the State Museum also were used as part of Cummings' archaeology classes, which covered topics ranging from the Americas to Old World ruins. To accommodate his broad interests in anthropology and history, and the expansion of his class topics, Cummings accepted a very eclectic collection of objects for the State Museum. But the building up of the quantity and variety of the collections created a constant need for more display cases and room to put those cases. Since the museum's budget was very limited, he formed a support group called the Arizona Archaeological and Historical Society (AAHS). The AAHS provided volunteer labor and financial assistance to the museum, such as cosponsoring Cummings' 1916 field expedition to obtain archaeological materials from ruins in northeastern Arizona.

The first major acquisition of objects with the assistance of the AAHS was the purchase of the Dr. Joshua Miller Collection. Miller was the superintendent of the State Institution for the Insane, in Phoenix, and one of the founders of the Arizona Antiquarian Association in 1895. He spent a decade in the late nineteenth century investigating ruins and gathering archaeological and ethnological materials from the Salt River valley, Prescott, Flagstaff, and the Hopi and Zuni reservations (Wilcox 1987). It was under his leadership that the Arizona Antiquarian Association excavated a tunnel in the platform mound at Pueblo Grande. Miller's large collection was offered to the University of Arizona in 1897, but President Howard Billman declined the offer. The Arizona Antiquarian Association then offered Miller's collection to Tempe Normal School (which later became Arizona State University), and President James MacNaughton was interested, but the school's effort to purchase the material failed to get enough support in the legislature (Wilcox 1988).

One of the reasons Tempe Normal School did not obtain Miller's collection was that Herbert Brown, curator at the Territorial Museum at the University of Arizona, wanted it to go to his museum. However, no purchase money was available, and Miller's collection remained in Phoenix. It was not until 1917, when Cummings and the AAHS came up with the $500 purchase price, that the State Museum "secured the collection" (University of Arizona 1918). Thirteen individuals, mostly from Tucson, donated $430, and the AAHS covered the remaining $70 with its organizational funds. Dr. M. P. Freeman of Tucson was the most generous benefactor, with a donation of $100.

In his first few years, Cummings was able to substantially increase his collections. His summer field expedition of 1916 was a huge success, recovering 1,500 specimens for the museum. Although the museum's focus was on the Southwest, Cummings accepted donations of archaeological and ethnological materials from elsewhere in the United States as well as from other parts of the world. Several individuals donated items in 1916, including Governor George Hunt, who gave the museum eighty Apache baskets, five Pima baskets, and three baskets from Alaska. President von KleinSmid also donated ethnological objects he had obtained during his travels in Madagascar, Jerusalem, and India. Historical artifacts included the first organ brought to Arizona and a collection of Mexican money. With limited staff, the museum was kept open only in the afternoon, from 2:00 to 6:00 p.m.

From early in his tenure at the University of Arizona, Cummings had a vision of the State Museum being located in its own building. In the university's 1917 catalog, Cummings noted that the Agriculture Building served as a useful place for the State Museum "until such time as the institution can secure a museum building" (University of Arizona 1917:29).

In April of 1917, U.S. president Woodrow Wilson declared war on Germany, and the university began preparing for participation in World War I by planting a war garden to grow produce to be used by the dining hall. The university also starting losing many of its male students, who eagerly enlisted in the military, and a variety of military training exercises began to dominate the campus.

Because of the war, Cummings was limited in his field expedition activities, but he still managed to obtain objects for the museum through small excavation projects, by donations, and through AAHS purchases. By now, the AAHS had 182 members. In April, Cummings obtained his first Hohokam ceramic vessels for the museum through excavations at Saint Mary's Hospital (University of Arizona 1919:31). In addition, the AAHS purchased from Elizabeth C. Stanley a collection of ethnological materials from the Hopi, Chippewa, and Ute Indians. Other materials accepted as donations came from near and far, including stone implements from mounds near Florence, Arizona, and from Seneca River, New York. Cummings also accepted Mrs. J. W. Wheeler's 175 mounted bird specimens from Arizona.

A worldwide influenza epidemic, called the Spanish flu, rapidly spread throughout the United States in the fall and winter of 1918. This epidemic, which killed more than half a million Americans, reached Arizona, causing the University of Arizona to shut down in October and become under quarantine. All classes were suspended until January of 1919. True to his humanitarian religious convictions, Cummings and his wife stayed on campus and spent many hours nursing sick students. Andrew Douglass (1950:2) later wrote that Cummings worked in the campus hospital day and night, with his selfless actions probably saving the lives of many students.

In October 1919, Louisa Wetherill became a staff member at the State Museum while pursuing her studies on the Navajo tribe. She worked closely with Sam Chief, also known as Yellow Singer, to research the history of Navajo clan symbols and the use of medicinal plants (University of Arizona 1920a:31). At Cummings' request, Sam Chief reluctantly made six sandpaintings from Beauty Way and Plume Way for the museum's collections. Cummings' sister Emma later wrote an article on these sandpaintings (E. Cummings 1936). During a lecture in November for one of Cummings' classes, Sam Chief stated that he made the sandpaintings, rarely seen by the public at that time, because Cummings had shaken his hand when they met and had treated him as Cummings would a white man (Comfort 1980).

Cummings' summer field school excavations, initiated in 1919, resulted in the acquisition of 125 prehistoric pots, specimens of feather and fur blankets, sandals, and other objects from northern Arizona. Donations accepted during that academic year included a wide range of objects, such as cliff-dweller pottery from the Babbitt brothers of Flagstaff, numerous pieces of old pewter and other historical items from Mrs. Alice S. Cameron, and several mounted specimens of Arizona animals. Mrs. Agnes Hunt Parke donated an old spinning wheel.

Cummings allocated money every year from his museum budget for the purchase of museum objects, which he identified as "relics and specimens." This allocation, included under the category of capital expenses, varied annually depending on the museum's overall budget and other museum needs. For example, in 1919–1920, Cummings budgeted only $112.50, but the next academic year he increased the sum to $651.01 (University of Arizona 1920b). For 1922–1923, he could only manage $142.20, but in 1924–1925 money for relics and specimens was $433.50 (University of Arizona 1924b).

In 1920 and 1921, Cummings served as acting president while von KleinSmid was in Latin America promoting pan-American academic exchange. Subsequently, Cummings spent the summer and fall of 1921 in Mexico. One of his students, Karl Ruppert, served as the assistant in the museum, although from April to September of 1921, Ruppert worked with Neil Judd at his famous excavations in Chaco Canyon, New Mexico. Emma also helped Ruppert run the museum in Cummings' absence.

Cummings continued to collect an odd assortment of artifacts for the museum through donations, exchanges with other museums, and purchases. These included, in 1922–1923, a variety of prehistoric Arizona artifacts donated by A. Ogilvie from Star Valley, Lionel F. Brady from Mesa, Walter German from Higley, and Captain L. W. Mix from Nogales. Cummings also used some of his relics and specimens budget to purchase twenty-five pots from C. A. Reedy of Christmas, Arizona (University of Arizona 1922a:31). Cummings and the museum staff had been allowed to excavate in the ruin on Mr. Reedy's ranch for a few days in the spring of 1921. The AAHS also purchased sixty-two Hopi flat-basket plaques from E. C. Stanley, three pots from Guadalupe, and two pots from Teotihuacán in Mexico. In addition, Cummings accepted a donation of a hundred-year-old quilt from Mrs. R. D. Kennedy of Globe and a case of bird eggs from Mr. and Mrs. Walter Bennett of Phoenix.

Probably at the request of the university administration, Cummings (1924a, 1924b) wrote short reports on the activities of the State Museum. He noted that the museum's archaeological and ethnological collection numbered more than fifteen thousand items, a huge increase from when Cummings first started. He estimated the value of this collection at $1.5 million and boasted that it comprised the most complete representation of the prehistoric population in the Southwest in existence. But he also complained that the collection was crowded into two rooms—which were inadequate to arrange the material so that it would tell the story of the life history of the different branches of the human family. Although the museum had thirty-five display cases and three storage cases, there was a need for additional space for a laboratory and storerooms. Always thinking about the ways in which the museum served as a teaching tool of the university, Cummings argued that increasing the size of the museum's facilities would attract more graduate students.

Personnel for the 1923–1924 academic year included Karl Ruppert, assistant director and part-time cataloguer; part-time assistant Emma Cummings; and three student helpers—John Braezeale, Fred McNeil, and H. M. Sayre. Cummings defended the employment of his sister and requested a $250 raise in her salary.[2] He noted that she looked after the museum, dusting and keeping the display cases in order and explaining the artifacts to visitors. In defense of her age (mid seventies), he commented that she "is not young, I know, but far more valuable in the place she holds than a young, uninformed person would be" (Cummings 1924b:3).

A report on the activities of the State Museum was published in the spring catalog of 1925. Emma Cummings was listed as assistant. Museum hours had been expanded to a schedule of 9:00 a.m. to 5:00 p.m. every day during the academic season and 9:00 a.m. to 12:00 noon except Sundays during the summer school season. A museum mission statement, of sorts, also was presented in the 1924–1925 catalog (University of Arizona 1925:30):

> [The museum] is maintained as an educational factor in the institution and the State. Its chief aim is to present the life history of Arizona and the great Southwest. Its archaeological collections emphasize the conditions and the achievements of the ancient Cave, Cliff, and Pueblo people of the region, and its ethnological collections present the manufactured products of the various modern Indian tribes. Its natural history collections show the bird life of the State and present many other forms of animal existence.

The statement also explains that the reason the State Museum contained such a diverse collection was that these materials provided "a reasonable basis of comparison with other lands." This collecting of materials for world comparative purposes represented a very broad mission statement that led to a hodgepodge of objects without any real unifying theme, a criticism leveled by Cummings' successor, Emil Haury (1985, 2004c).

Artifacts acquired in 1924 were, once again, far ranging in origin. Frank and E. John Hands donated several stone tools from their ranch in Pinery Canyon near the Chiricahua Mountains (University of Arizona 1925:196). John Hands had made a small fortune in Arizona mining, which gave him the financial freedom to spend time exploring ruins and to help Cummings with several excavations during the 1920s (Hayes 1999).[3] Other examples of donations included fifty-one prayer sticks from Phoenix, historic artifacts from the Gila Valley, a Civil War rebel overcoat, World War I gas masks, a hand grenade, a silver spoon, a Freemason's sash, a Sioux Indian warbonnet, an infant mummy whose location was not identified, an unidentified skeleton, a table spread from India, and a collection of seventy-three sacred figures, sixty-nine lamps, and sixteen ornaments from Egypt. Consequently, a class on Egyptian archaeology was added to the Archaeology Department's curriculum the next year (University of Arizona 1925).

In 1925, Cummings acquired another diverse number of objects for the museum. These included more than 230 artifacts he had excavated from the pyramid of Cuicuilco and 190 items purchased while in Mexico. Donated items came from San Salvador, Babylon, China, Honduras, New York, California, and Arizona (University of Arizona 1926a:197–198). In addition, Governor George Hunt donated thirteen figurines and pots from Greece. That fall, Emil Haury was assigned to work as a student assistant at the museum. Among his many duties was the task of feeding two caged Gila monsters that Cummings kept to interest visitors (Haury 2004c).

The world of Arizona archaeology, in Cummings' opinion, was to be coordinated as much as possible by the Arizona State Museum in Tucson. When learning of a proposal to move the State Museum to the state fairgrounds in Phoenix, Cummings scoffed at the idea. Speaking to the *Tucson Citizen* (1925b), he insisted that the state fairgrounds as a location for the State Museum was totally inappropriate because of "the incongruity of Arizona's antiquities being displayed in common with a cattle-exhibit and in close proximity to the lively strains of carnival revelry." The State Museum, according to Cummings, was located at the University of Arizona because that was where future citizens of the state were trained, and therefore, the museum served a "very necessary adjunct to the work of men and women in providing them with a proper view of life." For him, the State Museum was "an educational force and should at no time cater to the mere curiosity seeker." The proposal failed, and the State Museum stayed in Tucson.

Only a year later, in 1926, Cummings was upset by the State Parent-Teachers Association's (PTA) endorsement of the Arizona Museum Society's plans to build an archaeology museum in Phoenix. He was especially angry about the plan to finance the building of the new Arizona Museum with the help of schoolchildren. In April, he told the *Tucson Citizen* (1926f) that the movement was a clever scheme on the part of the people of Phoenix to "put it over" on the rest of the state. Because Cummings found no mention of the State Museum in any of the literature promoting the new Arizona Museum, he accused the Phoenix group of "misrepresentation and falsehood" and not worthy of support. To counter the endorsement of the PTA, he sent out letters to all of the superintendents of schools in Arizona. In these letters, he stated that there was only one State Museum in Arizona, at the University of Arizona, and that this museum contained twenty thousand specimens that formed the "best illustration of the arts of the ancient and living Indian tribes of the southwest in existence." Cummings concluded by asking, "Should the public school children of the state be called upon to help build a home for a local museum in one of the towns of the state, when the extensive collections of the Arizona State Museum have to be crowded into one corner of one of the University buildings, and we have no state museum?"

The Arizona Museum Society moved forward with their plans and in 1927 opened the Arizona Museum (later called the Phoenix Museum of History), not far from the state capitol building in Phoenix. The first director of this museum was Odd Halseth, a strong-willed Norwegian, who, like Cummings, had trained under Edgar Hewett and agreed with Hewett's emphasis on public interpretation in archaeology (Wilcox 1993). Halseth and Cummings would later clash over control of archaeology in the state, especially over the makeup of the Arizona Antiquities Act.

10

"The Great Onward Movement of the Human Race"

Expeditions to Northern Arizona, 1915–1926

By 1915, Cummings had established himself as a professional archaeologist: he had a decade of field experience, had held an official staff position with the prestigious Archaeological Institute of America (AIA), had organized a small museum, and had published articles on Southwestern ruins. His future in the field of Southwestern archaeology looked promising. Even his resignation from the University of Utah, in March 1915, was a step forward for Cummings. Hired within a few months as head of his own archaeology department at the University of Arizona, he could now count on the department's annual budget to fund his archaeological expeditions into northeastern Arizona.

Back to Kayenta for More Explorations, 1915–1923

Cummings accepted his new position in early summer and then took off for an expedition under the auspices of his new employer. He returned to a place he called Nitsin (or Nitsie) Canyon, south of Navajo Mountain. The Kayenta region, and its wealth of Basketmaker and cliff-dwelling materials, occupied most of Cummings' summers for the next fifteen years.

Cummings' fascination with the Kayenta region continued while he was employed by the University of Arizona. He returned to excavate ruins in that region from 1915 to 1920 (table 10.1) and again in 1923, 1926, and 1930. The exciting adventures of Cummings' 1915 expedition were reported in the *Salt Lake Tribune* (1915) in early September. The headline of this article was a bit melodramatic but did reflect the difficulties of the

TABLE 10.1. Archaeological Sites Excavated by Cummings in Northeastern Arizona, 1915–1917

1915	*1916*	*1917*
Sun Priest Cave	Gourd Cave	Slab House Ruin
Sun Symbol Cave	Terrace House	Fort Cave
Cave Town Ruin	Lime Terrace Ruin	Noschaw Cave
Little Kiet Siel	Prospect Cave (Snake House)	West Canyon
Mirror Ruin	Inscription House	Pahute Cave
High Terrace Ruin	Crows Nest Ruin	Navajo Cave
Two Mummy Cave	Sheep Corral Cave	Kinclachie (Red House) Cave
Kishmiklaboko	Kay Kodie Basin	unidentified sites
Inscription House Cave	Needacloy Cave	
Turkey House Ruin	Alcove House	
Terrace House Ruin	Princess Cave	
High Balcony House	Scaffold House Ruin	
Baby Mummy Cave	Double Wall Ruin	
Fort Cave	Little Kiet Siel	
unidentified sites	Nitsin Ruin	
	Lime Terrace Ruin	
	unidentified sites	

Sources: Turner 1962; Webster 1991; Wilcox 2001.

trip: "Archaeological Expedition Suffers Greatly on the Desert, Thrilling Tale Told of Trip across Monument Valley." Accompanying Cummings were Wallace Grace, a University of Utah student, and C. E. Purviance, a Granite High School teacher. Cummings' party left Salt Lake City in mid July, traveling the same route he had taken many times: the train from Salt Lake City southeast to Thompson's Station, then a stagecoach south to Moab and a wagon ride to Bluff, located on the north side of the San Juan River.

At Bluff, Cummings rented six horses (three to ride and three to pack). Thinking they could save some time, the group took a shortcut across the arid Monument Valley rather than following the wagon road to a known spring. Crossing miles of sand in scorching heat took its toll, evaporating their twenty-one-gallon water bags and exhausting their horses. Two of the packhorses eventually gave out. Loads were transferred to two other horses, and two riders had to walk alongside the horses. The student, who had a gun, became depressed and threatened to shoot himself. Cummings chastised him for thinking such selfish thoughts since his tired and thirsty companions would then have to pack his body out of the desert. The young man's spirits improved considerably after he shot a rabbit and they cooked it for dinner.

The group survived their Monument Valley ordeal and camped in the Chilchiniaboko Canyon, a branch of Nitsie Canyon, in search of "higher" Pueblo culture. Soon after arriving, Cummings was confronted by a local Navajo, Hosteen Jones, also known as Pinietin ("No Sense"). Jones wanted Cummings to give him the medicine bag that they had just found and to leave the area immediately. This deerskin bag contained hematite cylinders, shell beads, dried roots, obsidian disk mirrors, and other unusual items. Cummings refused to give Jones the bag even after Jones' son, Taddytin, threatened the group. After more discussion and meals together, Jones accepted Cummings' intrusion into his domain and thereafter, on occasion, assisted with Cummings' expeditions. Later, in 1930, Cummings redeemed Jones' turquoise jewelry from pawn at the Inscription House Trading Post as a gift to him.

Cummings paid two Indian guides, Atalie Nez and Sharkey, $1.50 a day to assist his group's explorations. Eight ruins were located that summer in the Nitsie Canyon area, each containing from two to a hundred or more rooms. Cummings observed a variety of wall construction material and techniques, including crude bricks with straw and walls made of wattle-style sticks and clay. Two of the ruins closely examined that summer were Sun Symbol Ruin and Two Mummy Cave. Sun Symbol Ruin contained only five rooms, but a set of concentric circle pictographs, interpreted as sun symbols, interested Cummings enough that he excavated the rooms and prepared a plan view of the site. Two Mummy Cave contained eighteen rooms and yielded woven sandals, a yucca basket, a wood comb, a corrugated jar, and other artifacts.

Cummings considered the 1915 summer expedition one of his most successful for obtaining quality artifacts for his museum—which had just become the State Museum at the University of Arizona. His crew excavated more than fifteen sites that summer (Webster 1991). Expenses for the trip totaled $402.84 (table 10.2). It is not clear who paid for this expedition since Cummings was not yet on the University of Arizona's payroll.

That year Cummings published two short but informative articles on

TABLE 10.2. Byron Cummings' Archaeological Expedition Expenses for the Summer Expedition of 1915

Activity or Purchase	*Amount*
Transportation—Salt Lake City to Thompson's	$10.10
Stage—Thompson's to Bluff	$13.50
Meals—Thompson's to Bluff, 4 days	$4.30
Excess baggage—saddles, etc.	$2.40
Cinches, straps, etc., to fit packsaddles	$1.35
Saddle pads at Bluff	$4.05
Care of horses and board of Indian at Bluff	$5.00
Trips of Indian to Bluff with horses	$17.00
1 bridle	$2.35
⅓ expenses of trip from Bluff to Kayenta, and provisions	$17.15
⅓ bill of provisions for Nitsie	$7.70
2 shovels	$2.00
2 sheep pelts for pack pads	$0.75
Bill of provisions from Red Lakes	$3.40
Indian labor in Nitsie:	
Paul Goodman—10 Days	$15.00
Allen Nezlea—14⅔ Days	$21.90
John Klein—15 Days	$22.50
Allen's brother by day and piece	$9.00
Dick by day and piece	$17.75
Leslie by day and piece	$14.50
Hostein Jones and family by pieces	$17.00
Indian guide	$2.75
Mutton, milk, and corn	$13.60
Bill of dried potatoes	$6.02
Bill of provisions and Indian labor in Sagie, etc.	$118.52
Assistance of Ernest Smith in Sagie—6½ days	$9.75
Freight—on specimens to Tuba	$10.85
Meals at Tuba, provisions for Indian, corn for Horses	$2.50
Stage—Tuba to Flagstaff	$10.00
Hotel and meals at Flagstaff	$2.20
Railroad fare—Flagstaff to Tucson	$14.95
Hotel and meals in Phoenix	$1.80
Corn for horses, etc., in Red Lakes	$1.20
Total	$402.84

Source: ASM (A-468, 00051).

his archaeological investigations. One was written for the *American Anthropologist* (1915a) while he was still at the University of Utah. This article discussed the variety of ceremonial chambers, called kivas, he had excavated in the San Juan River region. His discussion focused on a description of construction techniques and provided information about kivas at Twin Cave House in Water Lily Canyon, Pine Tree House (now called Trickling Springs House) in the Nitzenoeboko branch of Tsegi Canyon, and other sites in Montezuma Creek Canyon and in Monument Park. A photograph of a black-on-white jar from Twin Cave House was published by Cummings (1953:147) many years later.

Cummings' (1915a) article on San Juan kivas also included a romantic description of his view of ancient Pueblo religion. He had come to learn that the land and sky of the Southwest has a profound effect upon those who live in its wide-open spaces. He argued that anyone who had traveled over the beautiful but harsh landscape of the Hopi and Navajo reservations without finding a spring or decent waterhole (as he had) understood why Mother Earth and the rain gods were important in the theology of the Indians. Under these circumstances, the worship of rain clouds as benign beings coming from the four quarters of the earth to bless mankind was not surprising to Cummings. The reason the kivas were mostly sunk beneath the floor level of the living rooms was because they represented an expression of the Pueblo belief in the sustaining power of Mother Earth. Although many Anglos thought Native American religions were full of superstition and primitive imagination, for Cummings (1915a:272) "they grasped germs of great truths."

The other publication by Cummings that year was a summary of prehistoric textiles he had found in various Pueblo ruins; it originally was a paper given at the annual meeting of the National Association of Cotton Manufacturers. Cummings (1915b) discussed the simple tools used in the production of prehistoric cotton and yucca textiles and described examples of cords, rope, sandals, and belts. He also mentioned girdles and headbands made of mountain sheep wool, and bags and belts made of human hair. However, he provided little information on the provenience of these textiles.

In this paper, Cummings also provided a preliminary outline of his views on the progress of culture during prehistoric times in the Southwest. This early version of his three-stage model consisted of (1) cliff-dwellers with crude pithouses, (2) cave-dwellers with substantial stone and clay homes, and (3) villages in canyons and on mesa tops. Although he later modified and expanded this model, Cummings adhered to a three-stage succession of house types for his entire career.

Concerned about the future impact of World War I on the U.S. economy, in 1916 Cummings homesteaded a 160-acre parcel of land in southeastern Utah, near Monticello, and planted wheat (Cummings and Cummings n.d.:128). During the summer and fall, Malcolm lived in the small house they built on the property and farmed the homestead with a new tractor. His efforts yielded a good harvest, but the homestead was too far from the railroad and consequently he could not get the wheat to a market to sell it. Their wheat farm experiment was terminated.

Despite his worries about World War I, Cummings was not going to give up his summer expedition. That summer he returned to Tsegi and Nitsie canyons, taking with him four University of Arizona students. Professor Charles T. Vorhies, with whom Cummings had worked at the University of Utah and who had also resigned in 1915, joined the group later in the summer. The expedition was sponsored by the Arizona State Museum and the newly formed Arizona Archaeological and Historical Society (AAHS). An old Model T Ford and several other vehicles were used to transport the crew and their baggage from Tucson to Kayenta over washed-out and flooded roads. It took them more than fourteen hours to get from Tucson to Phoenix (Cummings and Cummings n.d.:128).

Excavations that summer, from June 15 to September 15, retrieved for the State Museum about a thousand specimens. Several hundred ethnographic items also were purchased from the Hopi villages. Cummings named one of the ruins he investigated "Needacloy Ruin," after the Navajo man who lived in the area and had confronted him during his 1909 expedition. The total cost of this expedition was $888.53, which included $177.80 in purchases for the State Museum (Cummings 1916). The students participating in the expedition gave presentations to the AAHS at its October meeting. Karl Ruppert gave a paper on his first archaeological experience in the southwestern desert.

While at one of the Hopi dances in Oraibi that summer, Cummings first met Harold Colton and his wife, Mary-Russell (Colton 1961). Harold was a professor of zoology at the University of Pennsylvania vacationing with his family in Flagstaff. He and Mary-Russell soon developed a love of the archaeology of northern Arizona and every summer conducted surveys of prehistoric sites and systematically identified their pottery types. In 1926, Colton retired and moved permanently to Flagstaff. Two years later he established, mostly with his own inherited wealth, the Museum of Northern Arizona (Miller 1991). Several of Cummings' students, including John McGregor and Lyndon Hargrave, would later hold prominent positions at Colton's museum.

Even with World War I ongoing, Cummings made another expedition, with Malcolm, to northeastern Arizona and southeastern Utah from June 6 to August 20, 1917. He may have been inspired by the fact that Judd had been hired in March to conduct a $3,000 stabilization program at Navajo National Monument, with an emphasis on Betatakin. Cummings had thought he would be hired for the job, especially since he had worked with Senator Reed Smoot of Utah to get the appropriations passed on May 18, 1916, and had been recommended for the job by Special Agent W. J. Lewis of the General Land Office. But at the last minute it was determined that only a federal employee could be hired for the work, and since Judd was a federal employee at the U.S. National Museum and had worked with Cummings at Betatakin in 1909, he was hired (Judd 1931).

Cummings' 1917 summer exploration of the canyons south and west of Navajo Mountain was undertaken with his two Navajo friends Atalie Nez and Sharkey. During this expedition, he found human mummies in Duggagei Canyon that were in excellent condition. He prepared a sketch map of an interesting site he called Slabhouse Cave and took a set of photographs. In Duggagei, Cummings excavated his first pithouse, a form of subterranean architecture completely different from the masonry pueblos. Total expenses for the summer of 1917 were $280.47, which included paying John Wetherill $6 a day as guide and $4.50 a day for a horse and two mules during an eleven-day trip to the top of Navajo Mountain (Cummings 1917). At the Wetherill and Colville Trading Post, Cummings purchased two shovels for $1 each.

Although travel was by horseback over rugged terrain, Cummings' group ate well. Their food supplies for the trip were relatively diverse, consisting of coffee, tea, cans of milk, cans of tomatoes and peaches, crackers, cracked wheat, rice, oatmeal, baking powder, raisins, oranges, sugar, pepper, salt, bacon, and lard. These supplies were obtained from

Cummings' friend John Wetherill at the Wetherill and Colville Trading Post in Kayenta. In November of that year, Cummings gave an illustrated lecture on his summer excavations to members of the AAHS.

In 1918, because of World War I, no official University of Arizona–sponsored fieldwork occurred. In addition, Cummings' expedition partner Malcolm was in the infantry at Camp McArthur in Texas. Still, Cummings could not refrain from his summer exploration that year. In July he made a short field trip to southeastern Utah, west of Monticello. Two friends, Clarence G. White and Wilford Frost, and Cummings took six horses into Beef Basin. White financed the trip, and Parker Titus served as guide. Their goal was to find previously undiscovered ruins and obtain some tree-ring samples for Andrew E. Douglass (University of Arizona 1919).

Douglass was an astronomer at the University of Arizona interested in determining whether tree-ring growth patterns could be used to date Pueblo sites in the Southwest, which proved to be highly successful (Douglass 1921, 1929). Cummings had met Douglass soon after being hired at the University of Arizona in 1915, the same year that Douglass became dean of the College of Letters, Arts, and Sciences. Both also served as executive officers of the AAHS and were family friends. Douglass later became director of the Steward Observatory at the university.

Cummings' 1919 expedition is now famous, for it was his first official university field school (Brace 1986; Gifford and Morris 1985). It was mostly sightseeing but also included four weeks of excavations. Cummings must have expected to be climbing some rough terrain because he purchased a pair of overalls and two ropes from D. C. Lowery at the Ka'-pe-toe Trading Post. His group explored, with the help of John Wetherill, a rugged mesa that overlooks the Colorado River at the border of southern Utah and northern Arizona. This mesa was unnamed at the time of Cummings' ascent but would be named Cummings Mesa by the time Charles Bernheimer of the American Museum of Natural History climbed it five years later (Ambler et al. 1964:6). Two of the ruins Cummings' crew excavated that summer were located near Navajo Mountain and were given Navajo names: Kinklitso, "Yellow House," and Kinclachie, "Red House." Cummings would return to these sites to dig into them again. In the fall of 1919, Cummings and eight students gave brief talks to the AAHS about their explorations.

Another field school expedition to the Navajo Mountain area was undertaken in 1920, with the intent to further excavate Red House and Yellow House ruins. Cummings wanted to prove that this group of pueblos on the south of Navajo Mountain was the final stopping place of the ancestors of the Hopi before that people moved to their present location. Red House was a multiroom structure built from a local red sandstone that had been well dressed and then laid in double walls with clay mortar. Some of the blocks of the outer courses were four feet in length; those in the interior were smaller. Rooms surrounded a large interior courtyard, with a wide entrance to the south (Dean 2002:fig. 6.15). Within the courtyard was a circular, semisubterranean kiva that Cummings (1945:32) and his students excavated. Another kiva also may be present. Both food storage and corn grinding activities took place inside the courtyard. Later work at Red House by Alexander Lindsay dated it to the Tsegi phase, AD 1250–1300, a time when Pueblo architecture was becoming increasingly concentrated into room clusters organized around courtyards, representing a multihousehold group (Dean 2002).

Nine individuals participated in the six-week course that summer, including Karl Ruppert and Ben and Ida Wetherill. Before and after the 1920 field school, Cummings and Ruppert spent several weeks excavating sites in the Kayenta region (University of Arizona 1921a). At the October meeting of the AAHS, Cummings and three students gave presentations about their excavations that summer. One of the presentations, entitled "The Trials of an Archaeological Guide," was by Ben Wetherill. Trained by one of the best—his father, John—Ben would later play an important role in the last major archaeological expedition to the Kayenta region in the mid 1930s (Beals et al. 1945; Christenson 1987a).

That summer, Cummings (1920) published an article on the national monuments of Arizona in *Art and Archaeology*. This article again revealed Cummings' romantic and Progressive notions about the past. He wrote that nature's monuments had inspired man to "fulfill his part in the great plan of the universe and rear monuments that tell their story of the constant upward struggle of the human race toward such a knowledge of the truth that it brings peace and happiness" (Cummings 1920:27). Nations and tribes, according to Cummings, either advanced or retarded the great onward movement of the human race. He felt that if people in the past made the most of the knowledge, materials, and opportunities at their disposal, then the monuments they left behind were worthy of preservation. In his opinion, there were many examples in the Southwest.

Only limited work was done in Arizona during most of 1921 and 1922, during which time Cummings traveled and worked in Mexico. At the urging of Hewett, Cummings and Louisa Wade Wetherill (1922) published the article "A Navajo Folk Tale of Pueblo Bonito" in an issue of *Art and Archaeology*. In addition, an expedition was organized to go into Mexico in search of the builders of Casa Grande, the national monument south of Phoenix. This group included Karl Ruppert, John and Louisa Wetherill, Ben Wetherill, a Mexican guide, and two Navajo medicine men—Hosteen Luca and Navajo George.

Cummings was eager to return to northeastern Arizona in the summer of 1923 because Charles Bernheimer, a wealthy benefactor to the American Museum of Natural History in New York and to the Smithsonian Institution, had written an article in the February issue of *National Geographic* magazine about his successful effort to encircle Navajo Mountain the year before (Bernheimer 1923). Earl Morris, archaeologist for the American Museum of Natural History, accompanied Bernheimer on the 1922 expedition, as well as his trip to the same area in 1921. Morris, raised in Colorado and trained by Hewett, was an "indefatigable digger" (Woodbury 1993:46). He had been excavating at Aztec Ruin in Colorado for several years and would soon be digging in Canyon de Chelly in northeastern Arizona, much to Cummings' chagrin (Lister and Lister 1968). While with Bernheimer on his 1922 Navajo Mountain expedition, Morris dug in Charcoal Cave in Cliff Canyon, finding well-preserved Basketmaker material that included a child wrapped in a fur-string blanket (Bernheimer 1924).

Concerned about Morris's excavations in an area that he thought was his turf, Cummings planned a major expedition in the Kayenta area for the summer of 1923. From June to September, Cummings led more than two dozen people, including his wife, into the canyons southwest of Navajo Mountain and excavated two sites near Marsh Pass. John and Ben Wetherill participated in the expedition. One of the students on this adventure was Winslow Walker, who began his archaeological career that year. The son of archaeologist Edwin F. Walker of the Southwest Museum in Los Angeles, Winslow Walker attended the University of Arizona under Cummings from 1923 to 1925 and also conducted fieldwork with

Cummings at Turkey Hill Pueblo in 1928 and at Kinishba in 1940. In the 1930s, Walker gained recognition for his tree-ring dating research in the southeastern United States (Nash 1999).

Walker (1923) wrote a diary for this field expedition, providing a rare insider's record of the group's daily activities. His mother, father, and brother also participated. The expedition arrived in Kayenta on June 13. The group began excavating a ruin on top of Gnat Mesa, seven miles from Kayenta, where several burials were uncovered. Three days later, at Wetherill's trading post, members of the group cast dice to determine the order of taking a bath. The Wetherills' home, a one-story stone house covered with vines and framed by healthy box elder trees and a fresh-looking grass lawn, provided quite a contrast with the surrounding red-and-yellow rock canyons that the group would soon be exploring.

On the way into Tsegi Canyon, their main destination, Walker was fascinated by the sight of a Navajo boy and his tethered pet owl at the side of the road. After visiting Betatakin, the group took a wrong trail and had to ride their mounts over a narrow rock trail where only a few feet separated them from a drop of five or six hundred feet—more adventures for Cummings' students and friends.

In late June, the group began exploring the very rugged country east and north of Navajo Mountain. For two days, they mapped the Red House ruin, which had been dug by Cummings and his students a few years earlier. Cummings' crew dug several other ruins in the area, interrupted occasionally by afternoon thunderstorms. Walker recorded their regimented schedule: breakfast at 7:00 a.m., field or laboratory work from 7:45 a.m. to 11:45 a.m., lunch at noon, an afternoon siesta, back to work at 3:00 p.m. until 6:00 p.m., and supper at 6:30 p.m. Cummings also gave lectures during some of the evenings.

In mid July, Cummings took part of the group to the top of Navajo Mountain, a five-hour trip by horse and mule from their camp. The group then returned to Gnat Mesa, where they continued to dig out burials. A hole that Cummings was digging caved in, and he narrowly escaped being buried twice, with one of the cave-ins breaking his shovel into two pieces. While at Gnat Mesa, Cummings' group was visited one day in July by Alfred Kidder. A person can only wonder what Kidder, the grand master of Southwestern archaeology and a meticulous excavator, thought of Cummings' excavation techniques. That month, one of Cummings' as-

10.1 Excavation of Juniper Cove pithouse by Winslow Walker, 1923 (photograph by Byron Cummings; courtesy of Arizona Historical Society/ Tucson, #PC29F.131A)

sistants, John Huffman, injured his foot with a pick while digging and later had to leave for Flagstaff to receive medical treatment.

In early August, Cummings and Walker went to Juniper Cove, two miles from Kayenta, where they uncovered two or three rooms made of slabs of stone set on edge and erected in a circle (fig. 10.1). Cummings had dug at this large village ruin in 1912. This Basketmaker village is now known to date to the seventh and eighth centuries (Nichols 2002:71). It contains at least a hundred pit structures and a large circular structure, thirty-six feet in diameter and with a raised bench, that is possibly a kiva (Cummings 1953:18, 23, 62). Juniper Cove represents the beginning of village nucleation resulting from the intensification of agriculture, although the placement of storage facilities and work areas in open areas within the village suggests a relatively egalitarian society.

On August 18, the group celebrated the twenty-third wedding anniversary of Walker's parents with a gift of a Navajo rug. A few days later, Cummings took the crew over rough roads to the famous Hopi Snake Dance at the village of Walpi.

On the last day of August, Cummings and his crew began digging at another site near Kayenta called Tachini Point, which he characterized as a pithouse pueblo. Although they did not find any burials after a week of excavations, they did find a square room made of slabs that Cummings believed represented a transition from round to square pithouses. They also found pottery that he thought was a transitional type between earlier ceramics and later Pueblo pottery. Altogether, 350 prehistoric artifacts were collected during the 1923 expedition.

Cummings' Three-Stage Model of Cultural Development, 1924 Version

Cummings' reputation as a leading Southwestern scholar was recognized with his selection in 1923 as president of the Southwestern Division of the American Association for the Advancement of Science (AAAS). On May 5, 1924, Cummings presented the president's address at an AAAS meeting in El Paso. His paper was entitled "Development of Prehistoric Pueblo Culture," and it presented his three-stage, progressive model of human cultural development in the Southwest. Cummings had briefly outlined the model as early as 1915, but this was a more fully developed version. The three stages were (1) the First Pueblos, who lived in "huts" at the base of cliffs; (2) the Pithouse People; and (3) the Cliff and Mesa Pueblos. Cummings argued that the Southwestern culture had originated in Mexico. The paper was never published, although a revised summary of Cummings' progressive model was published more than a decade later (Cummings 1935c).

Summer of 1926

Once again Cummings went north to the Navajo country for the summer. He returned in late July to the large Juniper Cove site for more digging and explored the Kayenta region until mid September. He was assisted by student Henry Lockett, John Hands, and four Indian laborers named Atalie Nez, Shorty, Yellow Head, and Sharkey. At Calamity Ruin, thirty miles northeast of Kayenta, they found four prehistoric individuals who had been killed by slabs of rock that fell from the ceiling of the rockshelter. A well-preserved ladder was retrieved, which Hands carried on his shoulders for thirty-five miles while mounted on a mule, so that it could be taken to the State Museum (*Tucson Citizen* 1926g). Cummings told the *Arizona Daily Star* (1926e) that he had learned that the Cliff Pueblo people of northern Arizona had not knocked "their squatty little predecessors over the head with their stone hammers" and then built a new civilization but instead had "completed and rounded out the civilization begun by their ancestors—the Cave People."

Cummings' 1926 Science *Article*

By 1925, Cummings had spent many years excavating ruins in Utah and Arizona. That fall, the AAAS appointed Cummings to the prestigious Committee of One Hundred on Scientific Research. One of their tasks was to look into the working conditions of professional archaeologists and anthropologists. Cummings' (1926c) opinions about those conditions were published the next year in the March issue of *Science*. In this article, entitled "Problems of a Scientific Investigator," Cummings complained that some archaeologists sensationalize their discoveries, giving in to popular demand. This creates "a great temptation to shake one's plumage and cluck instead of sitting on the nest till the eggs are hatched" (Cummings 1926c:321). He expressed concern for the loss of professional ethics and personal justice. He also discussed the fear among many American archaeologists of finding cultural remains with Pleistocene deposits and having to defend their work to aggressive critics. Little did he know that later that year, he would become involved in such a discovery in Arizona.

Cummings concluded his *Science* article with eight suggestions for achieving greater efficiency and a larger degree of successful results. These were, and still are, reasonable and appropriate suggestions: (1) complete devotion to the problem in hand, (2) an ethical attitude toward the work of other investigators, (3) constructive criticisms of results, (4) adequate funds for equipment, (5) sufficient time to reach stable conclusions, (6) living salaries for workers, (7) a central organization to aid investigations and correlate results, and (8) a definite and comprehensive policy. Cummings' seventh suggestion—advocating a central archaeology organization—was made nearly a decade before the Society for American Archaeology was created (Guthe 1967).

11

"A Mexican Pompeii"

Uncovering the Cuicuilco Pyramid, 1922–1925

In the mid 1920s during two different field seasons, Byron Cummings directed the excavations of a massive pyramid at the site of Cuicuilco, near Mexico City. His investigations of this early Mesoamerican temple were highly successful and well publicized. At a time when archaeological dating techniques were poorly developed, Cummings argued that he had found the earliest ceremonial structure in the Americas. This finding reinforced his belief that humans had developed an impressive, but primitive, culture in the Western Hemisphere independent of those of Europe and Asia. Although his estimate for the age of Cuicuilco is now known to be incorrect, the site is still considered one of the earliest pyramids in Mexico, and much of what we know about this unusual circular pyramid is a result of Cummings' work.

Cummings' excavations were sponsored by the University of Arizona, the Mexican government, and the National Geographic Society. The results of this important project were reported by Cummings in numerous published articles, newspaper accounts, and public lectures. Indeed, this project is one of Cummings' better-reported archaeological excavations, in contrast to his earlier expeditions in Arizona. The following summary of Cummings' Cuicuilco project is derived from both his published writings and previously unpublished materials, including his field notes, correspondence, and excerpts from a 1925 diary kept by Cummings' student assistant, Emil Haury (2004a).

The origins of the Cuicuilco excavations can be traced back to the winter of 1915–1916, when the board of regents sent President Rufus B. von KleinSmid to the Pan-American Scientific Congress in Washington, D.C., to deliver an address to twenty-one nations (Martin 1960). Von KleinSmid was then invited to visit the University of Mexico, but World War I intervened, and he was unable to follow up on that invitation until 1919. In Mexico City, President Venustiano Carranza gave him an honorary degree. The next year, José N. Macías, rector of the University of Mexico, came to Tucson, and the University of Arizona bestowed upon him an honorary degree.

Within this atmosphere of cooperation between the two countries, and with a year of paid leave from the University of Arizona, Cummings devised an ingenious plan to learn more about Mexican archaeology. He and Professor Charles A. Turrell, of the Department of Spanish, designed an exciting, eight-week summer field course in Spanish and Mexican archaeology that included the Education Congress in Mexico City. This class of twenty-seven teachers and students traveled throughout western and northern Mexico visiting colonial towns, archaeological ruins, and museums and then settled down in Mexico City to attend the Education Congress and take classes in Spanish and Mexican archaeology at the University of Mexico.

After the Education Congress had ended in September, Cummings extended his stay until late October, spending time in the National Museum studying its collections. While in Mexico City, Cummings had met Manuel Gamio, director of anthropology and archaeology of Mexico and a Ph.D. graduate of Columbia University under Franz Boas. Gamio had participated in Boas' International School of Anthropology, Archaeology, and Ethnology in Mexico City from 1911 to 1915 and is credited with being the first archaeologist in Mexico to use the stratigraphic method of excavation to determine ancient cultural sequences (Boas 1912; Gamio 1913). From his excavations at Atzcapotzalco, Gamio (1924) identified an "Archaic Culture" located below the well-known Teotihuacán and the Aztec cultures, establishing a three-stage cultural chronology for the central highlands of Mexico.

Cummings was aware of the excavations by Gamio and other Mexican archaeologists that tunneled underneath an extensive lava flow, called El Pedregal. This basaltic lava flow had been created by a long-dormant volcano called Xitli, which was located at the southern edge of the Valley of Mexico. These tunnels under the Pedregal revealed skeletons and ancient pottery, and it was assumed that the villages of these Archaic people would eventually be found as well. South of Mexico City was a hill located in San Cuicuilco, at the edge of the Pedregal flow, which intrigued Gamio, and he showed it to Cummings. Gamio invited Cummings to investigate the hill if he was interested. Cummings accepted, and the Mexican government agreed to pay for laborers and equipment. This agreement resulted in two field seasons of excavation for Cummings at Cuicuilco, in 1922 and again in 1924–1925.[1]

The first season of excavations began in early April of 1922, when Cummings and Gamio began preparing the site for the arrival of the Mexican laborers. Four laborers started working by the end of April, and the workforce was gradually increased to twenty-five individuals. Work continued until September of that year. Cummings' (1922b) field notes stated that laborers were paid $1.50 per day by the Mexican government, with the foreman, Ignacio Sanchez, paid $2.25 per day. Byron and Isabelle stayed in an old hacienda at Tlálpam. Malcolm joined them in June, after he had graduated with his B.A. from the University of Arizona.[2]

The first digging done by Cummings' crew was on top of the so-called hill, which was covered with a thick layer of ash, earth, and piles of rock, but not lava. These excavations soon revealed that the hill was artificial, and additional digging determined that it was a truncated conical pyramid about 350 to 400 feet in diameter at its base and about 90 feet in total height. Located on top and in the center of the pyramid were superimposed altars, with the upper one made of river-worn boulders built on a circular foundation of boulders, packed clay, and sand. The altar was horseshoe-shaped, with the opening pointing southwest, and measured 22 feet in length and 9 feet wide. Cummings noted that river-worn boulders were not easily obtainable in the area, although the Cuicuilco River

11.1 Excavation of the side of Cuicuilco (photograph by Byron Cummings; courtesy of Arizona Historical Society/Tucson, #PC29F.31B)

and the Pena Probre stream are located nearby, under the Pedregal lava (Cordova et al. 1994).

After digging on top of the pyramid, Cummings placed two long trenches from east to west into the side of the pyramid and over its top to determine the architecture of the pyramid, the depth of the cultural deposits, and the stratigraphic relationships of the deposits to the lava flow. Manuel Gamio may have suggested this modern method of exploration, but the trenches were hand-dug by the laborers under Cummings' direction, and Cummings wrote all the field notes. The trench on the east side was dug to a depth of more than eighteen feet to examine earlier cultural deposits (fig. 11.1), and Cummings prepared a sketch of the trench profile. Northern and southern trenches were dug more than eighty feet in length to trace the nature and extent of the lava flow at the edge of the pyramid. Information obtained from these trenches allowed Cummings to describe the deposits around the base of the pyramid and to determine its actual height. Cummings also dug a tunnel under the pyramid to examine its internal structure. The tunnel was shored up with sixteen-foot-tall timbers, but cave-ins were a serious problem, and the Mexican government eventually asked Cummings to stop tunneling.

Excavations into the sides of the pyramid discovered massive stone walls sloping at a forty-five-degree angle, with the walls broken by three different terraces. The sloping wall to the first terrace was forty-six feet in height; that to the second terrace, twenty-four feet in height; to the third terrace, four feet; and the top platform rose five feet above the third terrace. On the eastern side of the pyramid, a "platform" extended down on an incline from the first terrace and presumably had served as an entrance ramp. Another ramp was later found on the opposite side of the pyramid. On the south side of the pyramid, Cummings found some unusual rooms that had walls that included columns or "pedestals" of lava rock laid upright in clay mortar. The stones were hewn, with their corners sharply squared; some had shapes that gave them the appearance of stone heads. The rooms were covered with lime plaster up to half an inch thick, inside and out.

A few burials were also found during the first field season, but information on them is limited. Cummings' (1922b) field notes suggest that as many as eleven burials were recorded. Plain black pottery was found with most of the skeletons.

The outer wall of the pyramid was constructed of unmodified chunks and shells of lava compactly piled on top of a central core of filled earth. Cummings noted that some of the holes in the lava wall were filled with smaller stones, but no other filling material was used and there was no effort to make a completely smooth wall. He called this type of architecture "cyclopean." All of the lava rock used in the construction of the pyramid predated the Pedregal lava flow, which suggested a great age for this massive structure. Cummings (1923b:212) determined that the Pedregal lava flowed against but only partly covered the pyramid: "On every side are encountered the black, forbidding faces of the Pedregal, which pressed their numerous noses against the covering of old Cuicuilco until they were flattened and rounded and buried deep in its yielding soil. In some places, where the more gentle slope of the covering permitted, the many-headed lava monster climbed up the slope, burying the base far beneath and holding the great temple in its iron-like embrace."

Cummings' excavations showed that fifteen to seventeen feet of sand, clay, and rock had accumulated on the pyramid before the Pedregal flow occurred, indicating that it had already been abandoned when the lava came to its edge. George E. Hyde, a geologist from New Zealand, studied the Pedregal during the winter of 1921–1922 for the Mexican government. Without any methods of direct dating available at that time, Hyde guessed that the Pedregal was at least 7,000 years old (Cummings 1923a). Given that three major periods of construction had occurred before the Pedregal lava flowed, Cummings thought Cuicuilco could be the earliest pyramid in the New World.

In about five months' time, Cummings had recovered a considerable amount of information about the Cuicuilco Pyramid. Newspaper accounts that appeared at the time of his excavations, and afterwards, proclaimed the importance of Cummings' findings. *El Universal* (1922), a newspaper in Mexico, printed a story in July with the title of "Un Sensational Describrimiento de Arqueológia" ("A Sensational Archaeological Discovery"). The *Excelsior* (1922) followed shortly thereafter with a story entitled "Un Describrimiento de Gran Merito Arqueológico" ("An Archaeological Discovery of Great Merit"). The *Science News Bulletin* called Cuicuilco a "Mexican Pompeii" that extended history back centuries. Cummings (1923a:57–58) compared Cuicuilco with other Mexican pyramids: "Cuicuilco is an illustration of one of the first pyramids created by the ancestors of those tribes who adorned Mexico not only with mighty pyramids, but also with richly decorated temples and palaces before the first century of our era. This crude pyramid, unembellished and unadorned, yet massive and solid, stands as a mute evidence that the native Americans developed this masterful architecture here on American soil." In August, the *New York Post* (1922) and the *Literary Digest* (Cummings 1922a) published similar articles about Cummings and the Cuicuilco Pyramid.

The *Tucson Citizen* (1922) wrote a story in early September, stating that the University of Arizona had just extended Cummings' leave of absence for another six months so he could pursue further investigations at Cuicuilco. In that article, Cummings surmised that the top of the pyramid may have been used as a stage where "the best singers of the age praised and thanked their gods for deliverance from storm and enemy."

In early 1923, Cummings gave fifteen slide programs on Cuicuilco in cities on the Pacific coast under the sponsorship of the Archaeological Institute of America. Articles about his program appeared in the *Walla Walla Bulletin* (1923), the *Seattle Times* (1923), the *San Francisco Chronicle* (Boyden 1923), and the *Los Angeles Times* (1923). At his talk at the University of Washington, Cummings argued that the great age of the pyramid, which he estimated to be 8,000 years old, raised the question of whether the Western Hemisphere, rather than the Eastern, was the birthplace of human progress. As a *San Francisco Chronicle* reporter noted, this meant that Cuicuilco was older than the tomb of King Tut, another sensational archaeological discovery of the 1920s (Boyden 1923).

Two romantically written but well-illustrated articles were published by Cummings soon after his excavations were completed. A summer issue of *Art and Archaeology* (edited by Cummings' old colleague Edgar Hewett) contained an eight-page article with eight photographs. In this article, Cummings (1923a:52) proposed that Cuicuilco was built to "propitiate the anger of fire, wind and water and win the continuous favor of the sun and the earth."

A nineteen-page article with sixteen photographs of Cuicuilco appeared that same year in the *National Geographic* magazine. Here, Cummings (1923b:213) conjectured that "some ancient Indian chief of the Valley of Mexico was forcing his subjects and slaves to rear a mighty structure on which to honor the gods of this land." Cuicuilco is not spectacular, he conceded, but it represents "the results of stolid, vigorous Youth, Youth just beginning to feel his strength and daring occasionally to straighten up and ask the spirits to teach him."

The 1924–1925 National Geographic Society Excavations

Cummings had garnered international attention for his work at Cuicuilco. Eager to return, he applied for a National Geographic Society research grant to support another season of excavation. Cummings' proposal was approved by the three members of the research committee: Frederick V. Coleville, John C. Merriam, and Sylvanus G. Morley. In mid January, the *Tucson Citizen* (1924) reported that Cummings had received a grant for $2,500 from the National Geographic Society, but this amount appears not to have been adequate for his plans. In April, he submitted a revised application that was found acceptable, with the National Geographic requesting the option to publish the results first. He was then awarded a grant for $6,000, based on his estimate of $5,378. In addition, N. H. Darton, geologist with the United States Geological Survey, was hired by the National Geographic Society to assist Cummings with a geological study of the lava.

Cummings' National Geographic Society–sponsored Cuicuilco investigations began in late June. Four "student" workers assisted him: H. Melville Sayre; William Carrigan; Cummings' son, Malcolm; and John Hands, a retired miner who served as tool sharpener and was in charge of blasting. Hands, who had worked with Cummings previously on excavations in northern Arizona, volunteered his time and probably set up the railroad track used to move push cars full of dirt and lava stone. Isabelle accompanied her husband to Mexico City for the second time. By July 7, a crew that varied from ten to thirty-six Mexican laborers began working under Cummings' direction. Some of these men could trace their ancestry back to the Aztecs. They were paid the equivalent of seventy-five cents per day. The front of Cummings' 1924 field notebook contains the names of all the men who worked for him each week; he also tracked all the interest-free loans he gave the workers, most of which were paid back.

Cummings' field notes show that he excavated a test pit for stratigraphic purposes east of the pyramid; it went down thirteen levels, each level 1.5 feet in depth. All but the lowest level contained cultural materials. Cummings also had his laborers dig a huge trench 200 feet in length, 6 feet wide, and 22 feet deep to obtain additional stratigraphic information. Dynamite was used to blast through some areas of the lava that were up to 21 feet thick, because it was a very effective technique and there was no apparent damage to the stone facing of the pyramid.

In mid August, Isabelle and Malcolm returned to their home in Tucson to attend to family affairs. Once back in Tucson, Malcolm was interviewed about his father's work at Cuicuilco, and he had to defend his father's use of dynamite in his excavations, a method of digging totally unfamiliar to Southwestern archaeologists. Cummings returned to Tucson in late September but had already received permission to extend his leave from the university until the spring semester of the next year. On November 1, he wrote Gilbert Grosvenor, president of the National Geographic Society, and informed Grosvenor of his plans to continue the excavations (Cummings 1924c). Cummings' three goals were to find the homes of the people who built the pyramid, determine whether the interior of the pyramid was a tomb, and better understand the function of the boulders surrounding the base of the pyramid.

In early November, Cummings returned to Mexico with Sayre, Carrigan, and Hands. The *Arizona Wildcat* (1924) informed University of Arizona students that Cummings was in Mexico for the winter, using mining cars and track to excavate Cuicuilco. In this article, William Carrigan stated that they had built a half-mile road over the very rough lava to allow tourists to visit the pyramid. In mid January of the next year, Cummings received the good news from Grosvenor (1925) that the National Geographic Society had awarded him another $4,000 for the excavations.

During the months of June through early September, a twenty-one-year-old University of Arizona student, Emil Haury, assisted Cummings with the excavations. Cummings had met Haury in Kansas when he gave a lecture at Bethel College, where Haury's father was a professor (Thompson 1995). The young Haury asked Cummings if he could join Cummings on the next summer field trip to northeastern Arizona, but Cummings informed Haury that he probably would be working in Mexico. When Haury wrote Cummings in March 1925, Cummings responded with an invitation to Haury to assist him at Cuicuilco, even paying Haury's train fare to Mexico City. Cummings also offered to hire Haury as a student assistant in the Arizona State Museum after the Cuicuilco dig was over. Haury happily accepted both offers, and thus began the career of one of the most influential American archaeologists of the twentieth century.

Haury's handwritten diary, written during his time in Mexico, was apparently misplaced and was only recently published by his son, Loren. The diary begins on June 11, 1925, in the train station in Newton, Kansas, Haury's hometown, and ends in Tucson, Arizona, on September 12 (Haury 2004a). Some of the entries in this diary are incorporated into the following discussion.

Haury's first day in Mexico was eventful. Cummings and he took a mule train to Tlálpam, where their living quarters were located. He sketched the floor plan of the three-bedroom house in which they were staying and noted that one of the residents, Kathryn McKay, a registered nurse, kept several pets, including a tame deer that liked to be petted. Manuel Gamio visited Cummings at the house, and Haury noted that Gamio had just been asked to resign from his position of government secretary in charge of archaeological investigations of the region because he had publicized some problems he had uncovered in his department. Cummings, who had become good friends with Gamio, was not pleased.

Haury was excited about being put in charge of some of the Mexican laborers, commenting on how it was a new experience to be "boss." He also complained about the large number of dogs that roamed the area, because they created havoc at the site, even breaking pottery that had been excavated. Because Haury's Spanish was very poor, Cummings gave lessons to him on those nights that Cummings wasn't teaching English to the Mexican laborers. In the meantime, Haury gave instructions to his laborers through hand signals.

In mid June, the jokester side of Haury's personality was revealed when he tried to trick Cummings with an artifact. He showed Cummings a piece of green glass and told him it was green obsidian. Cummings was not fooled. On the way back to the house after work that day, Haury was fascinated to see a man use a long hollow gourd to draw up the sap from a maguey plant. He learned that this sap, or pulque, after fermenting for a few days, would knock over the strongest man. Cummings had prohibited the drinking of pulque by his laborers, but a few of them disobeyed him, and he had to terminate their employment (Weadock 1925).

Excavations were shut down on Saturday afternoons and Sundays, so Cummings and Haury would visit the markets, explore the region, and attend church on those days. On June 21, they visited Professor Hoffman in San Angél to talk about his archaeological collection of some twenty thousand objects. Cummings wanted to purchase some of the collection for the Arizona State Museum, and Professor Hoffman was willing to sell it for $10,000. Cummings later thought he had a commitment from University of Arizona president Cloyd Marvin to purchase this collection, but Marvin did not honor his commitment, which angered Cummings.

Many visitors came to watch the Cuicuilco dig. In late June, about a thousand schoolgirls came out to the ruin around noon for lunch. Cummings, however, asked them to leave because the crew was getting ready to use dynamite to blast away some of that lava. A few days later, a rainstorm forced the crew to quit work a little earlier, and when Cummings and Haury got back to their house, Karl Ruppert, a former assistant to Cummings, was waiting for them. He had recently worked in the Yucatán for the Carnegie Institution and had some interesting stories to tell.

The next day, a large group of visitors from Germany showed up at the site, and Haury was able to use his knowledge of the German language to provide them with a tour.

On the first day of July, Ruppert visited the site at noon to take Cummings with him to Casa de Alvarado for dinner with a number of other scholars including Sylvanus Morley, director of the Carnegie expedition in Yucatán; Mr. Brown, an ornithologist; and an unnamed botanist. As Haury was closing up the dig that afternoon, a group from Arkansas City, Kansas, arrived at the site. Haury was thrilled to give some people from his home state a tour.

The following Sunday, Haury complained that he was awakened at 5:00 a.m. by fireworks and a band playing for a nearby festival. Cummings and Haury learned that morning that Kyotano, a friend of Miss McKay, had stabbed and killed another man the night before. Haury noted in his diary that Kyotano had visited their house that Friday and was seemingly a nice person.

In early July, a portion of the lava under which they were excavating collapsed, bringing down tons of material. Haury had written in his diary that he had anticipated that this might happen, and fortunately no one was injured. That day, Morley came to the site again for a short tour. In mid July, C. C. James and some guests visited and gave Haury nine heads of Teotihuacan-style figurines for his collection. Around that time, an engineer started to survey the ruin to make a topographic map.

The morning of July 20 brought a surprise, as the volcano Popocatepetl became active. Popo, as it was called, was shooting steam and smoke that could be seen very well from Cummings' house. Haury wrote that the column of smoke must have risen several thousand feet. The next day, Popo issued another huge column of smoke.

In late July, Haury was involved in a cave-in while digging a deep shaft on top of the pyramid. Some dirt fell on his head from the shaft, and it almost knocked him unconscious. At forty-two feet below the surface, his crew found bone, obsidian, and carbon, which indicated artificial fill inside the pyramid. After hearing of Haury's accident, Cummings instructed them to stop digging in the shaft—at a depth of forty-four feet. However, for an additional eighteen feet they dug with a two-inch-diameter probe and continued to find cultural fill.

The first day of August, a Saturday, was another eventful day. In the morning, Haury went to the Chapultepec Country Club to go swimming with several other fellows. Upon his return to their house, he found that Cummings had put together a fiesta for the laborers because the crew was to be reduced the next week to only eight men. Haury was irritated to learn that Cummings had been instructed to cease digging the tunnel under the pyramid. Mr. and Mrs. Pallendini came to the house that evening and brought Cummings some pre-Columbian objects for the Arizona State Museum. These included a skull that was artificially flattened in back, pottery, figurines, and an obsidian tool.

On August 14, Mexican officials visited the site for an inspection but could not provide Cummings with any information about the future of the investigations. The next day was the last day of work for the Mexican laborers. Cummings planned to stay at the site until September, when classes began at the university.

Haury finished his plan map of the Cuicuilco Pyramid on August 18 (fig. 11.2). His map shows four terraces and a top platform, for a total of five levels. The base is 387 feet in diameter, and the top platform, 218 feet in diameter. Haury also sketched some of the idols while Cummings reconstructed one of the crushed skulls. For the next three weeks, Cummings and Haury organized the materials they collected, finished photographing the site, and completed the cataloging of artifacts. Haury (2004a:86) also wrote in his diary that Cummings and he sorted through the human burial remains and picked out what they wanted to save; the rest was given "a decent burial."

On the second day of September, after the artifacts had been boxed, Cummings was informed by Mexican officials that photographs would have to be taken of all the artifacts leaving the country, including the broken pottery. Cummings and Haury then unpacked three boxes of artifacts ready for shipment to take the photographs. Several days later, nine boxes of artifacts, two bundles, and a trunk were taken to the train depot in Mexico City. Cummings, Haury, and the artifacts left the next morning on the train for Tucson, ending their Cuicuilco adventure.

On September 10, 1925, the Cuicuilco excavations were officially closed down. Cummings' (1925a) expense report to the National Geographic Society for the period June 15, 1924, to September 10, 1925, showed that the National Geographic Society had given Cummings

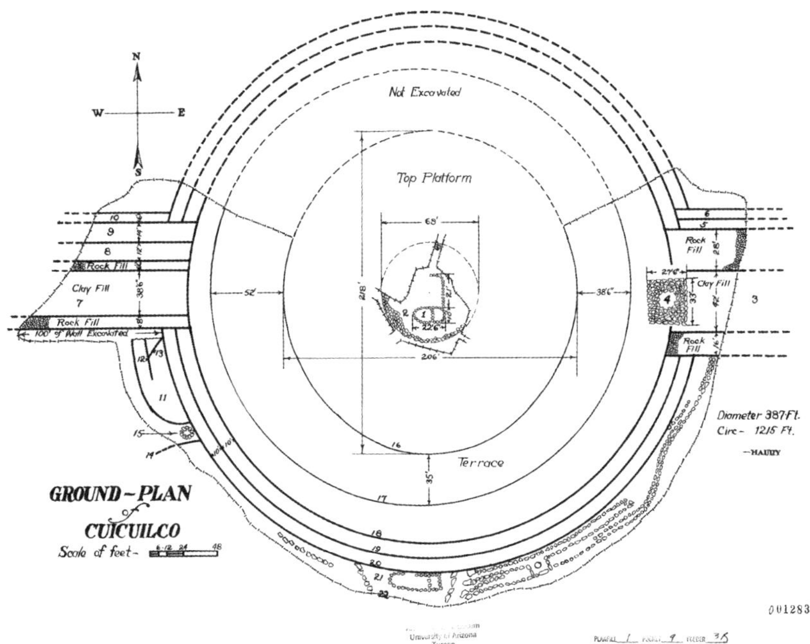

11.2 Emil Haury's plan map of Cuicuilco excavations, 1925 (courtesy of Arizona State Museum, University of Arizona)

$8,400. He was also able to sell one of the mules for $67.50 and the typewriter for $47.50. The other mule was in such bad shape that Cummings had to give it away. Two push cars and the railroad track were left behind for use by future excavators. Cummings' total receipts for the 1924–1925 investigations were $9,481.00, and his total expenditures were $9,768.64. A small shortage—$284.54—was personally paid by Cummings.

Cummings was in great demand as a speaker, and he gave several talks on Cuicuilco that fall. In early October 1925, Cummings gave lectures on his Cuicuilco work to the Men's Brotherhood of the Tucson United Methodist Church and to the American Association of Engineers (*Arizona Daily Star* 1925a). In late October, he was honored by the Southwestern Division of the American Association for the Advancement of Science with his selection to the prestigious Committee of One Hundred on Scientific Research, partly due to his well-publicized investigations at

Cuicuilco (*Arizona Daily Star* 1925b). At the November 17 meeting of the Arizona Archaeological and Historical Society, Cummings showed lantern slides of burial urns and figurines from his Cuicuilco excavations.

Publishing the Excavation Results, 1926–1933

In an April 17, 1926, letter to Gilbert Grosvenor, Cummings apologized for his delay in submitting a final report. He noted that his notebook—"in which I had my report worked out"—was stolen at the train station in El Paso by someone attracted to its leather cover (Cummings 1926e). This required him to work out the outlines of another report for the National Geographic Society. Haury (1975:199) mistakenly thought that Cummings' field notes were stolen, but they are currently located in the Arizona State Museum archives.

Cummings published an article and a professional paper on his work at Cuicuilco after his second season. That article, which appeared in an October issue of *Scientific Monthly*, included twenty photographs, two of which were upside down. As a result of the latest excavations, Cummings (1926b:293) was able to better describe the eighty-six-foot-wide inclined ramp, or "causeway," on the east side of the structure, where he believed "it requires very little imagination for one to see a gaily decorated procession of ancient tribal priests slowly mounting that long incline and stepping from boulder to boulder up that last ascent to the great dancing place on top." Another inclined ramp was also described for the west side of the pyramid.

Eight years after he completed his excavations, Cummings (1933b) published his longest report on Cuicuilco in the University of Arizona's Social Science Bulletin no. 4. This fifty-two-page paper contained thirty photographs and eleven illustrations. He started the paper by commenting that it was only a preliminary report, since only two-thirds of the pyramid had been excavated and additional comparative studies still needed to be done. However, he would not write any other reports or articles on Cuicuilco.

Cummings presented some additional information in his 1933 paper that was not discussed in previous articles. During the second season of excavation, the pyramid walls had been better delineated, and he had determined that the pyramid's walls were ten feet thick at the bottom and six feet thick at the top. Each of the three enlargements of the pyramid consisted of new walls built over the older ones and a new altar on top of the older altar. Water-washed sediments inside different wall construction episodes indicated that the structure had experienced several floods as well as lava flows.

Further excavation on the top of the pyramid in 1924–1925 had helped to better characterize the sequence of altars. Cummings found six platforms and their surrounding pavements superimposed to a depth of eighteen feet from the top of the pyramid. Each platform had an altar, except the last, uppermost platform, which contained a fifteen-foot-tall cone of rock and earth to the southwest of the center on the top of the pyramid. This platform may have had a wooden structure on top of it. All of these construction episodes predated the Pedregal lava flow.

Cummings' stratigraphic trenches and test pits provided more information about the lava flow. His excavations revealed that a lava sheet five feet to twenty feet thick had flowed around the structure in three successive flows. However, the pyramid was covered with earth and rock, and he found no places where the lava came into direct contact with the outer wall.

Additional architectural details were discovered during the 1924–1925 investigations. Huge boulders were encountered in the debris that had fallen from the walls to the base of the pyramid. These boulders were so large that it took four to five of Cummings' laborers to move them, and many had to be broken up with big hammers or dynamite. Cummings wondered how those boulders had been put into the wall forty to sixty feet above the ground's surface.

He also examined more closely the unusual circular rooms on a stone terrace adjacent to the southwest side of the pyramid (fig. 11.3). Some of the dark blue, upright stone slabs in the walls of these rooms had drawings of geometric lines on them. A few of the slabs were so large that several men would have been needed to lift and carry them. All three rooms were built after the pyramid had been abandoned, as indicated by the use of stones from the outer wall of the pyramid to build the terrace upon which the rooms were located. Perhaps this is why the name "Cuicuilco" is interpreted to mean "the place of the paintings or hieroglyphs" (Broda 1991:92).

Another unusual architectural feature at Cuicuilco was the presence of

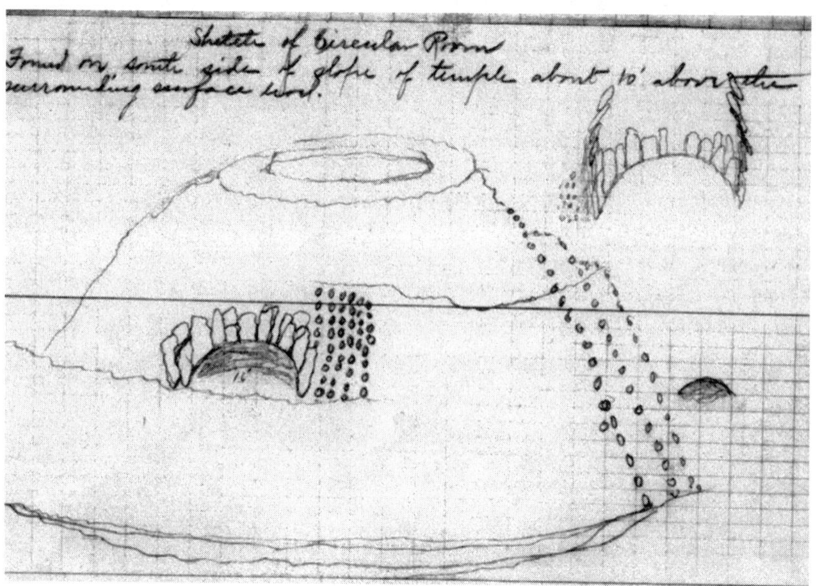

11.3 Cummings' sketch of room feature on side of Cuicuilco Pyramid (courtesy of Arizona State Museum, University of Arizona)

three parallel rows of upright stones 1.5 to 4 feet in length set into a clay bed and encircling the southern side of the base of the pyramid. In the middle of these rows was a rectangular room that contained, in its center, an upright stone column that had been smoothed. Cummings speculated that it was a shrine to a water-spirit. One of the photographs included in Cummings' 1933 paper on Cuicuilco shows Emil Haury standing among the rows.

Surprisingly, in all of his articles, Cummings only briefly mentioned the numerous burials he encountered.[3] In the 1933 paper, he included two photographs of burials and a brief statement saying that most of the human bones were fragments of skeletons crushed by the lava or falling stones. His field notes, however, provide valuable information on fifty human burials, including their position of interment and associated grave goods. Most of the burials were badly crushed or disintegrated, but those that could be identified included both adults and children and both males and females. Although the locations of the burials were not plotted on a map, Cummings' (1924–1925) field notes indicate that they were located on top of, within, and adjacent to the pyramid. Grave objects included ceramic vessels (black, red, or yellow), obsidian tools, polishing stones, beads, minerals, and animal bones.

Cummings focused his nonarchitectural analysis on the human figurines that were found in relatively large numbers. Some of them were illustrated by Emil Haury and included in Cummings' 1933 paper. The upper levels at Cuicuilco contained Toltec and Aztec pottery left behind after the pyramid was abandoned.

Altogether, Cummings traced out four levels of cultural deposits at Cuicuilco. The lowest level contained a natural reddish brown, polished pottery. Also present were small, standing figurines with a receding forehead and a high, crested head with hair arranged in elaborate braids. The second level contained plain pottery with grooved necks on some of the ollas. Seated figurines, absent in the lower level, occurred in the second level. The third level was located two feet below the lava and contained many artifacts and human remains. Pottery in this stratum was thick, unpolished black and reddish brown types. Figurines were flat and squatty with a turbanlike headdress; their eyes and mouths were small strips of bent clay, often called "coffee bean" types. Cummings thought that the people who left their remains in this level were a different people than those of the lower two levels, primarily because the artifacts were more "crude" in the third level compared to the lower levels. Cummings speculated that the third-level people may have been invaders from outside the region.

Cummings' investigations at Cuicuilco included a study of the volcanic lava that partly covered the pyramid. Three geologists worked with Cummings: Tempest Anderson of England, Karl Vittich of Germany, and N. M. Dalton of the U.S. Geological Survey. At a time when absolute dating techniques were not yet developed, in 1924 Dalton estimated that the Pedregal lava flow had occurred at least 2,000 years ago, which was 5,000 years younger than Hyde had estimated in 1922. Cummings still believed that the pyramid was at least 8,000 years old, based on his estimate of the amount of building and rebuilding of the pyramid that had taken place before the Pedregal flow occurred.

Cummings believed that Cuicuilco, with its elevated platform and wide causeways and terraces, had been built as a ceremonial temple for sacred dances and other rituals. Locals told him that on the fifth of May, a special light danced across the top of Cuicuilco and then passed across the Pedregal to the crest of Zacatepec, another hill lying to the west. More recently, Johanna Broda (1991:111) has noted that one of the main orientations of Cuicuilco faces one of the Aztec's sacred mountains, Popocatepetl, and that the sun can be seen rising over this still-active volcano on the winter solstice, marking this very important day in the Mesoamerican calendar.

Cuicuilco after Cummings

Cummings' excavations of the pyramid at Cuicuilco were one of the highlights of his long career. He used a variety of excavation techniques—long trenches, deep trenches, test pits, a tunnel, and auger holes—and studied their profiles and the contents of different excavation levels to understand the stratigraphic relationship of the Pedregal lava flow to this ancient monumental building. He exposed about two-thirds of the pyramid and revealed its size, shape, and methods of construction.

Cummings' excavations at Cuicuilco remain, as of today, the only major work on the pyramid, and the quality of his excavations has been praised by later archaeologists who have worked at the site (e.g., Schavelzon 1983). Cuicuilco is considered by other archaeologists as one of the early important urban centers in the Valley of Mexico, perhaps competing with the great urban city of Teotihuacán (Adams 1991:108; Evans and Webster 2001:199; Muller 1990; Weaver 1993:78).

In the mid 1950s, additional excavations were carried on at Cuicuilco by Robert Heiser and J. Bennyhoff (1958). On the basis of radiocarbon dates obtained from charcoal, Heiser and Bennyhoff dated the Pedregal flow to AD 400. Combining the absolute dates with the types of ceramics recovered by Cummings from under the lava, they estimated that the pyramid of Cuicuilco was first constructed between 800 and 600 BC and continued in use until about 1 BC. These data support Cummings' argument that Cuicuilco was abandoned before the volcano erupted. However, more recent investigations have provided additional dates, and there is currently no consensus on when the eruption took place (Cordova et al. 1994; Gonzalez et al. 2000; Martin del Pozzo et al. 1997; Perez-Camp et al. 1995). Consequently, the debate continues on whether or not the pyramid was in use when the volcano erupted. Cummings' work remains an important contribution to this debate.

12

"A Good Detective Story"

The Silverbell Road Artifact Controversy, 1924–1930

In February 1927, Harold H. Bender of Princeton University wrote Byron Cummings a brief letter that began with the following words:

> I have never been able to get out of my mind the excavated swords and crosses which you were kind enough to show me here in Princeton a year or two ago. It has been as if a good detective story had been taken from me just as I was going to read the last chapter. Won't you be good enough to write me at your convenience, and entirely for my private information, whether any new light has been thrown on their origin, and what your present opinion is as to their authenticity. I should be grateful indeed. (Bender 1927)

Professor Bender's letter refers to a real detective story that to this day has not been satisfactorily solved. This case involves what the *New York Times* (1925a) called the "puzzling relics," a group of thirty-one lead artifacts and an inscribed stone found deeply buried at an old limekiln near Tucson. What made these crosses, crescents, batons, swords, and spears so intriguing was their inscriptions and drawings. In addition to Latin phrases and Hebrew words, eighth- and ninth-century dates were also inscribed. Drawings consisted of poorly drawn heads, altars, angels, axes, doves, temples, crowns, snakes, menorahs, and other unidentified symbols. Individuals who examined these drawings recognized Christian, Muslim, Hebraic, and Freemasonry symbols (fig. 12.1). Did they show that Europeans had come to America hundreds of years before Columbus?

The interpretations of these inscriptions and symbols, their date of manufacture, and the artifacts' context of discovery became embroiled

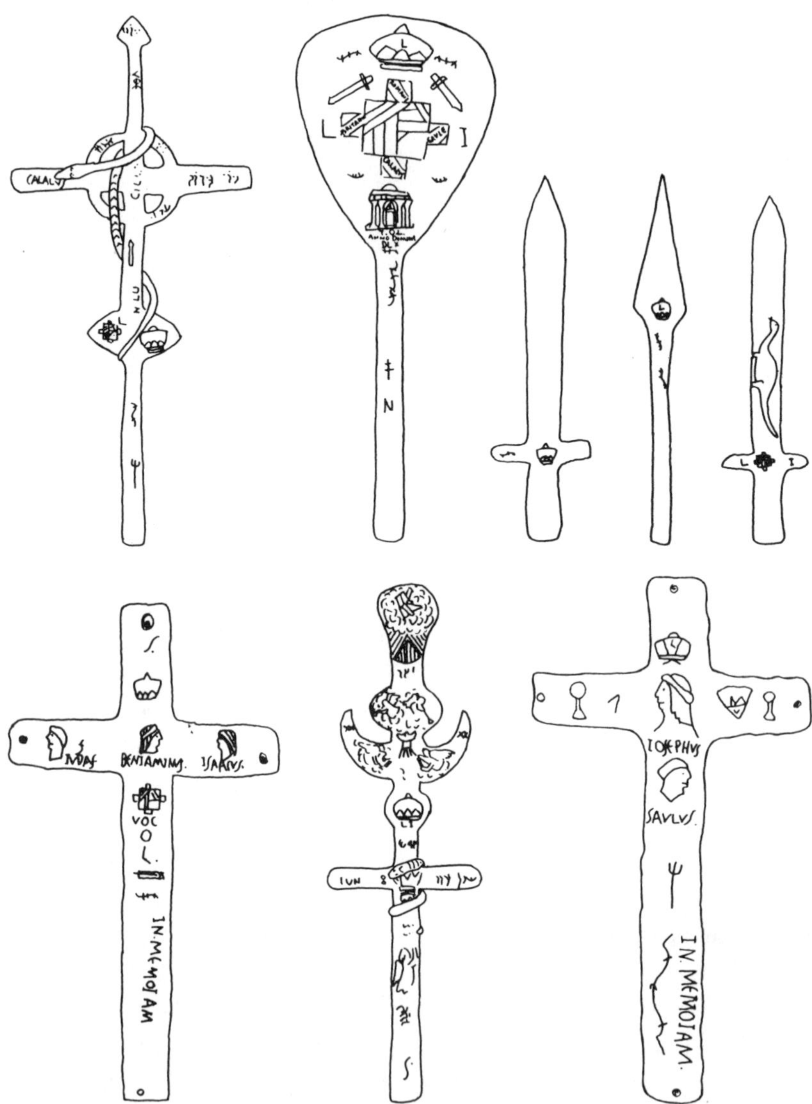

12.1 Illustrations of some of the inscribed lead artifacts from the Silverbell Road site (from Sayles 1968:109)

in controversy soon after they were found. For a little more than a year, from September 1924 to early November 1925, the kiln site's hard caliche (calcium carbonate) deposits were hacked at with picks, shovels, screwdrivers, and pocketknives, first by two Tucson citizens and several Mexican laborers, and later by a variety of geologists, archaeologists, and students.[1] Exciting finds occurred on at least nineteen different days over the fourteen-month period of excavation. Reporters, professors, and other curious visitors would arrive soon after a new discovery. The ensuing public disagreements over their authenticity, printed in local and national newspapers, developed into one of the most difficult challenges Cummings had to face in his entire career.

Charles E. Manier's Discovery

The plot of this story involves an interesting cast of characters, ranging from the amateur discoverers to the numerous experts brought in to analyze the materials. The two individuals who started it all—Charles E. Manier from Ohio and Thomas Bent Sr. from New York—were both World War I veterans. Manier, a retired police officer and prison warden who suffered from respiratory illnesses, discovered the artifacts on September 13, 1924, while on an outing in the desert with his family. Manier was examining an old Spanish limekiln site located on Silverbell Road, several miles northwest of Tucson, when he noticed an object sticking out of the side of an eroded trench in a high bank of hard, calcified desert soil (*Arizona Daily Star* 1925c). Manier is reported to have tapped the object with his cane and realized it was metal. Getting a pick and shovel out of his car, Manier hacked away the caliche matrix and removed the metal object. The metal object turned out to be a lead cross weighing more than sixty pounds. Examination of the cross by Manier's neighbor, D. M. Bruce, determined it to be two crosses pegged face to face with lead dowels and then coated with wax. Manier was amazed at what he found under the coating—crudely inscribed words, dates, and a variety of symbols. Another neighbor, the wife of Professor A. F. Kinnison of the University of Arizona, recognized some of the inscriptions as Latin.

Manier immediately took the cross to the University of Arizona to get advice. Because Cummings was in Mexico at the time, Manier showed it to Cummings' assistant Karl Ruppert at the State Museum. The next day Ruppert visited the old kiln site with Manier, and they found a flat piece of stone made of caliche and with inscriptions carved into it. This object came from an exposed cut into the earth at a depth of more than five feet below the surface. Ruppert was intrigued by the finds and suggested that Manier excavate the site systematically to lend credibility to the objects that were found.

Newspapers, Naysayers, and Defenders

Manier's discovery had the potential to be a sensational story if the artifacts could be proved authentic. He partnered with Thomas W. Bent, an attorney who had homesteaded the property, to conduct additional excavations. Bent erected a tent and a metal storage shed (Sayles 1968) and then began a detailed log of all future discoveries.

A week after the discovery of the artifacts, the local news was on the story. The *Arizona Daily Star* (1924) ran the headline, "Tablets Found Here Bear Inscription of '800 A.D.'" The tablets were actually the two lead crosses discovered by Manier the week before. He had shown them to Frank Fowler, professor in the Classical Languages Department at the University of Arizona. Professor Fowler was quoted that he had not yet translated the inscriptions because the words were disjointed and the Latin very poor. Nonetheless, he did find what appeared to be the ninth-century date, which he noted was highly improbable, since no one in America knew the Latin language at that time.

Andrew E. Douglass, astronomer at the University of Arizona and vice president of the Arizona Archaeological and Historical Society, had been shown the artifacts and, in Cummings' absence, began writing letters to solicit opinions from experts. In late October, Archer M. Huntington (1924), president of the Hispanic Society of America in New York, suggested to Douglass that he contact the British Museum. Douglass followed up on Huntington's advice. Six weeks later, O. M. Dalton (1924), keeper of the British Museum, informed Douglass that Dalton's staff found it difficult to believe that the artifacts were "anything but the work of a person living long ago and desirous of mystifying other persons." But Douglass and others at the University of Arizona were not so quick to discount the artifacts.[2]

Convinced that the artifacts were authentic, Bent prepared a formal agreement with Manier on November 25, 1924, that gave each partner one-half of the profits obtained from any objects that were found. Only a few days later, additional crosses were recovered by Mexican laborers working for Manier and Bent (table 12.1). Bent also contacted officials of the Church of Jesus Christ of Latter-day Saints (LDS) to determine if the Mormons would like to help with their investigations. Initially, the LDS church officials were not interested.

In early December, another cross weighing twenty-five pounds was found by some of the Mexican laborers working for Manier and Bent. All four crosses had been found within a radius of six feet. All were made of two halves put together face to face and covered with wax; the inscriptions were on the inside faces (fig. 12.2).

On January 19, 1925, Douglass inspected the Silverbell Road site deposits. Having received less than enthusiastic responses to his inquiries by letter, he was very skeptical, initially taking the position that the crosses had been emplaced in recent years, perhaps to support certain religious claims. But five days later, Ruppert was at the site when two more crosses were found, and Douglass began to wonder if his first impression was correct.

The *Tucson Citizen* (1925a) published an article in early February that stated that more than one person must have assisted in the writing of the inscriptions because of a marked difference in the grammatical construction. All of the crosses appeared to have been molded in the ground. A detailed translation of some of the inscriptions was provided. They told a choppy tale of a journey by sea to an unknown land called Calalus, where the Toltezus lived. A man named Theodorus captured more than seven thousand warriors in a war and ruled for fourteen years. He was followed by Iacobus, for six years. The names of Israel, Seine, Rome, Gaul, and Theban are mentioned. In AD 880, Israel III was banished for liberating the Toltezus. Another inscription, signed with the initials "O L," was translated as the following: "An unknown land A.D. 895. May I be able to accomplish my endeavor to serve the King. It is uncertain how long life will continue. There are many things which may be said. While the war was raging three thousand men were slain, the leaders with their chiefs were taken, nothing but peace was sought, God ordains all things." The *Tucson Citizen* (1925a) asked, "Did Columbus really discover America, as history tells us, or was the discovery made hundreds of years earlier by

TABLE 12.1. Silverbell Road Artifacts Discovered by Charles Manier and Thomas Bent, 1924–1925

Date of Discovery	*Artifact Type*	*Artifact Number*	*Depth*	*Professional Involved*	*Comments*
Sept. 13, 1924	cross	1	65″		62 lbs.
Sept. 14, 1924	caliche slab	2	67″	Karl Ruppert	below cross
Nov. 28, 1924	cross	3	65″		10 lbs.
Nov. 30, 1924	cross	4	58″		incomplete
Dec. 5, 1924	cross	5	58″		11.5″ long
Jan. 24, 1925	2 crosses	6, 7	66″	Karl Ruppert	30 lbs. and 25 lbs.
Feb. 13, 1925	sword	8	64″		18″ long
March 4, 1925	javelin	9	54″	A. E. Douglass, Thomas Lovering, C. J. Sarle	18″ long
March 27, 1925	spear	10	59″	A. E. Douglass, C. J. Sarle	18″ long
March 28, 1925	sword	11	60″	A. E. Douglass, C. J. Sarle	18″ long
April 5, 1925	sword and baton	12, 13	62″	C. J. Sarle, Frank Fowler, Charles Vorhies	a map and dragons on sword hilt
May 26, 1925	sword blade and head	14, 15	58″, 42″	A. E. Douglass, Neil Judd, C. J. Sarle	
July 10, 1925	sword handle	16	?		in dirt pile
Aug. 27, 1925	sword tip	17	72″		
Aug. 29, 1925	cross with snake	18	72″	C. J. Sarle	Hebrew inscription
Aug. 30, 1925	spear	19	72″	C. J. Sarle	22″ long
Sept. 1, 1925	cross/crescent	20	72″	C. J. Sarle	21″ long, under rock
Sept. 2, 1925	spear shaft	21	72″	C. J. Sarle	in dirt pile
Sept. 18, 1925	spearhead and sword blade	22, 23	62″	A. E. Douglass, Byron Cummings, C. J. Sarle	
Nov. 6, 1925	sword and spear tip	24, 25	78″		3 pieces
Nov. 7, 1925	sword	26	72″		18″ long
Nov. 13, 1925	spear tip	27	72″		

Source: Bent 1964, AHS, Thomas Bent Papers (MS 1122).

12.2 Interior of one of the Silverbell Road lead crosses (courtesy of Arizona Historical Society/Tucson, #PC29F.16B)

an unknown people from overseas?" Manier and Bent must have thought they had made one of the most important archaeological discoveries in American history.

By early March, Douglass had visited the site; he helped to expose a lead spear and took photographs. He kept notes and observed in his written report (Douglass 1925a) that "there was no appearance whatever of recent disturbance of the earth" in the vertical face from which the artifact was protruding. Douglass then went back to the university, and he took T. S. Lovering, assistant professor of geology at the university, to the site to gain Lovering's opinion. Geologist Clifton J. Sarle, a consultant to Manier and Bent, also appeared at the site. All three men observed the removal of the artifact by Bent. Douglass (1925a) wrote in his report that they all agreed that there was no evidence of recent disturbance and that "it certainly looked as if the caliche had formed in place all about the lead pipe." Douglass also noted two recent scratches on the lead spear but concluded that it was "extraordinarily difficult for me to see any modern origin for these lead articles." A sketch map of the site was prepared.

Both Douglass and Lovering wrote letters on March 14 to Cummings in Mexico, informing him about the Silverbell Road artifacts and rendering their opinions about the context of discovery. Douglass (1925b) told Cummings that at first he had disregarded the artifacts as a joke but that after his visit with Lovering and Sarle "there is no doubt in my mind that it was cemented material and that the lime cement was of the ordinary caliche type."

Charles T. Vorhies, a friend of Cummings' and an entomologist in the Department of Agriculture at the University of Arizona, inspected the excavations on April 5 at Sarle's invitation. Vorhies was also of the opinion that the deposits did not appear to have been disturbed. The university's top scholars were beginning to wonder about these unusual discoveries.

Excavations continued in April and May, and additional artifacts were found. Neil Judd of the Smithsonian Institution in Washington, D.C., was visiting relatives in Tucson and assisted with the excavations for a short time in late May. He observed the removal of two artifacts. In June, Professor Charles H. Beeson of the University of Chicago gave a public lecture in Chicago of the lead artifacts, verifying Professor Fowler's Latin transcriptions.

In mid September 1925, Cummings returned from Mexico. He visited the Silverbell Road site on September 18 and witnessed the removal of a lead object from the side wall of a vertical exposure in the caliche deposits. A photograph was taken of him pointing to the object (fig. 12.3).

But local skeptics voiced their doubts. Omar A. Turney (1925), an engineer and amateur archaeologist who had just mapped the ancient Hohokam canals in Phoenix, wrote a letter in late September stating that the artifacts had to postdate 1540 since that was when Europeans had first entered southern Arizona. Turney suggested that the Silverbell Road crosses were connected to the San Xavier Mission southwest of Tucson.

To solicit the opinions of experts, in early October Cummings sent rubbings of the inscriptions to several scholars of ancient languages at eastern institutions. One of those individuals was Harold H. Bender of Princeton University in New Jersey. Bender believed that the artifacts could not possibly date before the arrival of the Spanish in Arizona in the sixteenth century.

Cummings also sent rubbings to Professor Emil Kraeling of Union Theological Seminary in New York. Kraeling (1925) confirmed that some of the inscriptions were Hebrew and commented that "the matter is rather curious, to say the least." He found, however, that some of the He-

12.3 Cummings pointing to artifact in situ at the Silverbell Road site (courtesy of Arizona Historical Society/Tucson, #AHS62107)

brew showed incorrect usage, which would not have been perpetrated by a Hebrew speaker. Furthermore, Kraeling observed, Hebrew was almost unknown to Christians during the period AD 750–950. Ira Price (1925) of the University of Chicago's Department of Oriental Languages and Literatures confirmed to Cummings that some of the characters were Hebrew.

Professor Bender leaked news of the discovery to the *New York Times*, and they telegraphed Cummings to get his opinion. Cummings referred the *Times* to Manier and Bent, and they were interviewed. After confirming with Cummings that Manier and Bent were reliable, the *New York Times* (1925a) ran a six-column, front-page story on the Silverbell artifact discovery. Photographs of six different crosses accompanied their mid-December story. One was pointed, spearlike on its upper end, intertwined with a serpent on its vertical and horizontal parts, and contained Hebrew script. The upper portion of another cross included a crescent, an intertwining snake wrapping around the vertical and horizontal crossmembers, and Masonic symbols and Hebrew script.

Cummings was quoted in the *New York Times* (1925a) article as being convinced of the antiquity of the finds based on the dates on the inscriptions and the geological and archaeological contexts within which the artifacts lay. Three University of Arizona professors supported Cummings' position: Frank Fowler, Andrew Douglass, and Charles Vorhies. In contrast, Bashford Dean, curator of arms and armor of the Metropolitan Museum of Art, identified inconsistencies that he felt were very childlike, indicating that the objects were forgeries. Frederick Hodge of the Museum of the American Indian in New York also thought they were fakes. Even Neil Judd, who had found two items embedded in caliche, believed that they were not planted but that they could not date before AD 1540.

The same day as the *New York Times* article, the *Arizona Daily Star* (Cosulich 1925a) ran its own story with the headline, "Roman Relics Found Here Baffle Science." Geologist C. J. Sarle provided a detailed description of the geological characteristics of the deposits in which the lead artifacts were found. He observed three distinct geological deposits in the exposed profiles at the site. The upper section was a dark stratum of soil about fifteen inches in thickness. Underneath that stratum was "a thick zone solidly cemented by [the] deposition of lime," called caliche. Under that second zone of caliche was the third level, a gravel stratum, where the artifacts were found. In Sarle's opinion, the geological characteristics of the deposits represented "a seal which nature has placed on these artifacts, not to be counterfeited." Unknown to the paper's readers, however, was that he had a vested interest in the authenticity of the find because as project geologist he had signed a contract on December 8 with Manier and Bent and was to receive 5 percent of profits from the artifacts and 50 percent of any money received from publications (Bent 1964).

Andrew Douglass was interviewed for the *Arizona Daily Star* article, and he described how he had seen six of the lead relics extracted from the rocklike caliche at depths from thirty to sixty inches and had photographed each of these in place as they were being uncovered. Douglass thought that the premise that the artifacts had been put in the ground recently was impossible, because "their position in the firm caliche indicates great age." He argued for continuing with the excavations. Because of the interest in the story, the *Arizona Daily Star* (1925c) published Bent's log of the discoveries.

The next day, the *New York Times* (1925b) published another front-page story on the discovery and was even stronger in its skepticism of the authenticity of the lead artifacts. The experts cited in this article generally regarded the finds "as a fantastic and absurd dream, with little scientific or logical support." Cloyd H. Marvin, president of the University of Arizona, was quoted as saying that those involved were keeping an open mind and that the university was "going to work on the problem to prove or disprove it." A university-sponsored investigation was suggested for implementation in January.

The second *New York Times* (1925b) article identified one of the key issues in the discovery—the geological context and position of the artifacts. The article noted that thus far, only one geologist had been involved, Clifton J. Sarle, and he supported the idea of a Roman-Jewish expedition. Although giving Sarle his due as an excellent field geologist, the *Times* stated that he had taught for eight years at the University of Arizona but had been released upon determination that he was not well equipped for teaching. In addition, the *Times* pointed out that Sarle's collaborator and Latin translator, Laura C. Ostrander, was only a teacher in the Tucson public schools.

Cummings, the *Times* noted, had been careful not to commit himself to the Roman-Jewish expedition theory but had expressed puzzlement as to how they could be fakes. He had personally witnessed one of the artifacts being excavated, and Douglass and Fowler, whom he highly respected, had seen other items come out of the ground. Cummings was convinced that the artifacts had not been planted there. However, he also acknowledged that Native Americans of the Southwest do not have any oral traditions about white men visiting them with lead crosses and swords.

The twenty-six artifacts thus far discovered were put on display in Tucson in the Tucson Bank Building. Admission was twenty-five cents for adults and ten cents for children. Mrs. Ostrander gave a talk about the artifacts' significance, and Thomas Bent collected money at the door. Half of the proceeds were to go to the Community Chest fund and the other half to pay for further excavations.

A few days later, a third article by the *New York Times* (1925c) provided additional evidence damaging to the authenticity of the lead artifacts. The *Times* reported that the abbreviation "A.D.," which stands for "Anno Domini," was not in general use until about AD 1000, a century after the latest date on the Silverbell Road artifacts.

Additional articles appeared in the *Tucson Citizen* in mid December, reporting that Thomas Bent had given a presentation about the lead artifacts to the joint meeting of the chamber of commerce and the merchants association. He defended himself and Manier from criticisms that they were "capitalizing" on their finds. He noted that they had tried to involve local archaeologists and other professionals in their excavations, had resisted efforts by some people to finance their dig with cash from private sources, and anticipated eventually donating the artifacts to the University of Arizona. Playing to the promotional interests of the local business crowd, Bent reminded them that "this is a Tucson achievement and we want it to remain as such" (*Tucson Citizen* 1925d).

The *Arizona Daily Star* (1925d) also ran another story at this time, adding further elements to the growing controversy. The local Mormon community claimed that the inscriptions related a story similar to the epic tale of the Book of Mormon, the story of the wandering Nephites and their extermination by the red-skinned Lamanites (Native Americans). Evidence for this connection could be found in the names of the kings mentioned in the inscriptions—Benjamin, Israel, and Jacob—who were also mentioned in the Book of Mormon. Some local individuals even intimated that the artifacts were a hoax perpetuated by Mormons, but it was pointed out that none of the individuals involved in their discovery or excavation were Mormons. The *Arizona Daily Star* (1925d) article also stated that Cummings and the University of Arizona would be taking over the excavations and that Cummings would be taking some of the artifacts back east in January to show them to "doubting scientists there."

On December 20, the *New York Times* (1925d) published its fourth article on the Silverbell Road artifacts. This one was a summation of the other three articles, with an emphasis on recounting other rare objects that had been proved to be fakes. On December 17, the *Arizona Daily Star* followed up with a summary of the criticism lodged in the *New York Times* articles. Despite this "flood of doubt," Cummings was still determined "to get to the facts."

As the debate over the artifact's authenticity became more heated, the *Arizona Daily Star* (Cosulich 1925b) printed a defiant editorial in which several influential Tucson citizens claimed that the artifacts were authentic. The headlines boldly stated, "If Cummings Says They're Genuine, They Are, Declare Tucsonans." Those Tucsonans were the mayor, John E.

White; the famous novelist Harold Bell Wright; Albert Steinfeld; Postmaster Annie Dickerman; and A. H. Condron, secretary of the chamber of commerce. The paper did note that Pima County Superior Court Judge Gerald Jones was highly skeptical.

Excellent detective work was demonstrated by the *Tucson Citizen* (1926a) when in January the newspaper broke the story that Leandro Ruiz, a pioneer cattleman in the Tucson area, remembered a young sculptor with an obsession for buried treasure who had lived with his family at the old kiln site on Silverbell Road in the 1880s. This young member of the Odohui family had been educated at a Mexican university and could have known Latin. A follow-up story was printed by the *Tucson Citizen* (1926b) three days later, and more information was forthcoming from Leandro Ruiz. He remembered that the young sculptor had once skillfully made a model of a horse in lead and a cross in stone. In addition, the Vincenti Odohui family was known to have had a collection of Greek and Hebrew classics, which the young sculptor could have read.

Cummings was skeptical of Ruiz's claims and even after interviewing Ruiz was not convinced by his story. However, the *Tucson Citizen* (1926d) later revealed that another informant, Eduardo Machado, confirmed that the well-educated Odohui family had once lived at the old limekiln on Silverbell Road and that their son Timotio had been an artist.

Later that month, the *Tucson Citizen* (1926c) reported that Cummings had returned to Tucson from his three-week trip back east. This trip first led him to Lawrence, Kansas, where Cummings attended the Cosmopolitan Clubs' annual conference, and then to Kansas City, where he gave a paper, with lantern slides, on the Silverbell Road artifacts at the meeting of the American Association for the Advancement of Science. He also traveled to Washington, D.C., with Douglass, where they gave a presentation to members of the Washington Academy of Science.

The *Arizona Daily Star* (1926a) continued to side with the stubborn Cummings. An article published in mid January described Cummings' trip back east and quoted him as saying, "I am firmer than ever in my belief that they are genuine." The article also reported that Professor Bender of Princeton University had identified some Mithraic symbols on some of the artifacts, adding more intrigue to the inscriptions. In addition, assays of the metal were reported to have revealed lead with antimony and traces of tin, gold, silver, and copper. Ore of this type could be found in the Tucson Mountains and in mountains to the south of Tucson, suggesting that the artifacts could have been made locally. However, two of the artifacts, a labrum and a serpent sword, seemed to contain more copper and the workmanship was better; these artifacts were thought to have been made elsewhere. No Spanish markings were present among the inscriptions and symbols. Additional excavation was recommended to uncover evidence of a camp or "the bones of these brave men." If there was a great battle, some wondered, where were the dead buried?

At the February meeting of the Southwest Division of the American Association for the Advancement of Science in Phoenix, Cummings, Sarle, Douglass, and Ostrander all gave papers on the lead artifacts (Bloom 1926). Ostrander surprised the audience with her view that the personage identified as Israel III in the artifacts' inscriptions may be Quetzalcoatl (*Arizona Daily Star* 1926b). Sarle argued that deposits above the artifacts were undisturbed and must have taken considerable time to harden.

On February 19, the *Arizona Republican* (1926) jumped into the controversy with an article that defended the awkward position that Cummings found himself in: "This discovery encountered incredulity in what are regarded as authoritative quarters. That was to be expected. Such an astonishing discovery demanding a sweeping reconstruction of theories, must at once awaken genuine suspicion. But mere suspicion may be removed with proof. There was something more obdurate than suspicion, the intolerance of scientists of developments which disturb preconceived opinions." To the *Arizona Republican*, it was not so much a matter of whether or not the Silverbell Road artifacts were genuine but how Arizona scientists were treated by their colleagues back east.

The Arizona Archaeological and Historical Society held its February meeting that year in the University of Arizona auditorium to a packed audience, with a number of the university faculty and boosters club present (*Tucson Citizen* 1926e). The topic was the Silverbell Road artifacts. Cummings and Douglass gave presentations. Andrew Douglass tried to systematically address the main issues concerning questions about their context. He identified four charges: (1) the artifacts were placed there during excavation, (2) the artifacts were inserted at some time in the recent past, five to fifty years ago, (3) the artifacts were inserted during the

Spanish occupation of Arizona, and (4) the artifacts were inserted during a pre-Spanish period.

Douglass had a rebuttal to the first three charges. He doubted that the artifacts could have been placed there during their excavation because University of Arizona professor Ruppert had encountered artifacts six feet from the vertical face and geologist Sarle had found artifacts ten feet from the vertical face, with no reported signs of holes. Douglass also discounted the idea that the artifacts had been inserted in the recent past because no vertical outlines of holes were seen. Douglass also did not believe that the artifacts came from the San Xavier Mission because he felt it was unlikely that the Spanish would have carried a group of artifacts weighing between two hundred and three hundred pounds a distance of fifteen or twenty miles before burying them.

F. L. Ransome, professor of geology at the university, was asked to speak about the geology. He shocked the audience and Cummings by proclaiming that the lead artifacts were simply "puerile toys," with the inscriptions the work of a "demented man." The so-called weapons, he argued, would be useless in a battle. In Ransome's opinion, the artifacts were buried under a dump of caliche "detrital" by human hands during the last hundred years. He believed that the caliche at the kiln site was not the same he had found elsewhere in the city. Cummings refused to back down, reiterating his belief that the artifacts and their context were genuine. Douglass summed up the controversy by stating that "caliche constitutes the crux of the problem."

Cummings soon thereafter announced in the *Arizona Daily Star* (1926c) that the University of Arizona was withdrawing its financial support of the Silverbell Road artifact excavations. Cummings wanted the artifacts to be shared equally, with Manier and Bent getting half and the university the other half. Manier and Bent, however, did not want to split up the artifacts. Cummings criticized them for their position, stating that their attitude "smacks too much of commercialism."

Without financial support from the university, Manier and Bent sought other funding, including private investors. They were unsuccessful. Bent, an experienced lawyer, responded to a critical editorial in the *Arizona Daily Star* with a detailed letter to the editor, stating his objections to the editorial (Bent 1926). He noted that the excavations had never been financed in the past by the university, so to say that it withdrew its financial support was not correct. The university's only involvement to that point had been an occasional visit by Professors Cummings, Douglass, Butler, Vorhies, and Fowler to verify the discoveries. In addition, Bent stated, "we have had to contend with ridicule and discouragement from several of the other members of the faculty." Bent argued that their requests for compensation were not commercialism because they had invested a lot of their own money thus far. He concluded by noting that they did not believe that "a glass case in the University Museum is a sufficiently safe place to display relics that are as valuable as our collection appears to be."

The editor and reporters for the *Arizona Daily Star* (1926d) retreated from their earlier support and took a position firmly against the authenticity of the lead artifacts. In early March, they published a sensational piece supporting this position. Professor Frank Fowler had found the original Latin texts from which the phrases and words of the artifacts' inscriptions had most likely been taken. All of the Latin was present word for word, and often in the same chronological order, in *Harkness' Latin Grammar*, the *Latin Grammar of Allen and Greenough*, and *Rouf's Standard Dictionary of Facts* (the earliest edition published in 1864). Nonetheless, Cummings would not budge from his position that the artifacts were not fakes. He asked but could not answer the question, "why should anybody go to so much trouble and painstaking work to make and hide them . . . ?"

The University of Arizona Takes Control

After a while, Bent and Manier reconsidered Cummings' offer and, with Manier's health failing, decided to renegotiate with Cummings to get the university involved in their excavations. On December 11, 1927, Cummings formally transmitted an agreement to the board of regents for their approval so that he could "undertake to solve the problem presented by these relics." One of the conditions of this contract was the payment of $16,000 to Bent and Manier for the artifacts if they were proved to be authentic by Cummings and deserving of a place in the Arizona State Museum collections.[3] While this was a large sum of money at the time, the artifacts would be extremely valuable if deemed genuine. The board of regents, happy to have the scandal of the previous university president over with and Cummings in charge, approved the agreement.

The University of Arizona excavations at Silverbell Road began on February 6, 1928, with John Hands and Charles P. Conrad in charge of the fieldwork (*Tucson Citizen* 1928). Hands and his assistants were instructed to contact Cummings in the event that a discovery was made so that Cummings or another member of the faculty could observe its removal. Dean Gurdon Butler was placed in charge of the geological study of the site, with Ransome no longer associated with the project after his negative comments. Cummings went into these excavations with some trepidation.

Within two weeks of digging, on February 15, Hands found two fragments of spear shafts that appeared to be parts of previous finds (*Arizona Daily Star* 1928). Butler examined these objects and declared that there was no evidence of disturbance or of recent burial. Other individuals who were present when the artifacts were removed included Thomas T. Waterman, newly hired professor in the University of Arizona Archaeology Department, and Cummings' students Emil Haury, Clara Lee Fraps, Lyndon Hargrave, Florence Hawley, and John C. McGregor; geologists Alexander A. Stoyanov, Raymond J. Leonard, and William H. Brown and their students Robert Heineman and Robert Reid; and members of the press. Manier and Bent were not present during these excavations, which lasted five weeks. Emil Haury, a talented artist, prepared a sketch map of the university excavations and the locations where the artifacts were recovered.

Altogether, four lead spearhead fragments and handles were found by the University of Arizona crews. None of these artifacts had inscriptions. Haury later claimed that because of the presence of fresh scratches, he thought the spearheads and handles were planted even while they were digging at the site (Mahoney 1956).

Rumors questioning the authenticity of the Silverbell Road artifacts reached the board of regents. In early March, Regent Robert Tally (1927a) wrote Cummings and informed him that Tally had heard "that there is some question, or at least criticism, of the age and condition of these artifacts leading many people to believe that they are not pre-

Columbian Age." He told Cummings not to make any recommendations to the board "unless convinced of the age and general value of these artifacts." In addition, Tally suggested that Cummings meet with the university's chief geologist, soil chemist, and other interested parties to have "a frank discussion of this entire subject to the end that the facts with both favorable and unfavorable opinions may be submitted to the Board at their next meeting." Cummings (1928g) responded that they would need much more time with their study than was available before the next meeting of the board of regents. Cummings expected the excavations could be completed by summer.

The excavations did not last that long, however, because they were not productive, and the dig was shut down in April. The university's investigation did not provide Cummings with the evidence he needed to allow him to state with conviction that the artifacts were genuine. He still believed the artifacts were authentic, but without additional supporting data, he was not willing to make a recommendation to the board of regents. So he did nothing.

Nearly a year later, in late February, Sarle (1929) wrote Bent a letter stating that Sarle had spoken with the secretary of President Shantz of the University of Arizona. The secretary had told Sarle that the university was no longer interested in the Silverbell Road artifacts. He questioned why Cummings had been silent on this matter and accused Cummings of plotting to discredit the artifacts and then purchasing them "for a song."

Bent (1929) then wrote Cummings from the veterans' care facility in Phoenix, asking him about the status of the university's position concerning the artifacts. Bent mentioned that he had heard the university was no longer interested. Cummings responded immediately to Bent's letter and assured him that no decision had been made.

The University Declines Purchasing the Artifacts

Despite Bent's plea to Cummings for action on the Silverbell Road artifacts, Cummings apparently paid little attention to the matter for the rest of that year. On January 2, 1930, Cummings finally wrote a summary report on the artifacts, which was published in the *Arizona Daily Star* (1930). This report provided a brief history of the excavations and outlined discrepancies in the artifacts' inscriptions and their context of discovery. Because of the series of problems relating to the artifacts, Cummings could not verify their authenticity, he wrote, and he therefore recommended that the university not purchase them.

Concerning the context of discovery, Cummings focused on the university excavations of 1928. He noted that the artifacts excavated by the university had not been encased in caliche and that all of them had been only a few inches from the face of the banks left by former excavations. In addition, fresh scratches that looked recent were visible on the underside of one of the artifacts, even though the excavator had taken great care to remove the artifacts without damaging them. The artifacts were scattered over an area more than seventy-five feet in diameter, so they were not a cache. Yet none of the excavations at the site found any fire pits, charcoal, or other artifacts of human workmanship such as articles of wearing apparel. Even if the artifacts were deposited by a flood at the same time that the rock, sand, and gravel under the caliche were brought down from the higher benches of the Tucson Mountains, this geological process would have occurred well before the earliest date on the artifacts, AD 560. Finally, during the removal of one of the objects, the university crew found a round hole extending about an inch beyond where the artifact was recovered. This hole was suspicious, and it "could have been made in the sand and gravel by driving some implement into the pocket and then withdrawing it and inserting the piece of lead and tamping in the sand and gravel around it." The presence of the hole implied that this artifact had been planted, although Cummings did not actually state that in his report.

Cummings also discussed problems with the artifacts themselves. He pointed out that lead is a poor material for weapons and that the hacks and nicks that were present on the swords did not look as if they had been made in battle. The lack of any skeletons also suggested that a battle had not taken place at the site. The weight of one of the crosses, more than sixty pounds, precluded it from having been carried very far.

The inscriptions and symbols used also were problematic. They were brief, disconnected, and illogical. In Cummings' words, "they get the reader nowhere." Cummings mentioned Fowler's discovery of the Latin grammar books from which the words and phrases were lifted. He argued that the combination of Latin and Hebrew words with a variety of symbols, such of which are similar to those used in Freemasonry, "form a strange and rather incongruous mixture." Moreover, the metal of the artifacts was determined to be a local ore, and one of the artifacts had a piece of copper embedded in it that was traced to the Bisbee region.

Curiously, Cummings did not specifically state that the artifacts were not authentic in his report, perhaps because he still felt they might be genuine. He merely concluded his report with the statement, "From the foregoing facts, I do not feel justified in advising the State Museum to purchase these lead articles from Thomas W. Bent and Charles E. Manier." As far as Cummings was concerned, that was the end of the university's involvement with the Silverbell Road artifacts.

Cummings was not able to completely wash his hands of the lead artifacts, as he received occasional requests for information about the objects for the remainder of his tenure at the Arizona State Museum. Bent, disappointed in the university's rejection of the artifacts, compiled a huge file on the project and in 1964 prepared an unpublished manuscript on their discovery and interpretations. Other people have examined that file and reached their own fanciful theories about the origins of the lead artifacts (Covey 1975). Bent's file and the artifacts are currently in storage at the Arizona Historical Society in Tucson.

Whether one believes that the Silverbell Road lead artifacts were made by Roman-Jewish people, Spanish explorers or missionaries, early Mormons, Quetzalcoatl, or a clever and imaginative sculptor of the late nineteenth century, they represent one of the more bizarre stories in American archaeology (Williams 1991).

13

"Life to Them Had Ceased to Be a Struggle for Existence"

Cummings and the Archaeology of the Sonoran Desert, 1925–1938

In the 1920s, Cummings began to investigate archaeological sites in the Sonoran Desert of southern Arizona. He usually escaped the extreme summer heat of the southern desert, where temperatures often exceed one hundred degrees, for milder locales in northern Arizona. But ancient ruins in the arid land of the stately saguaro cactus, where annual rainfall is less than fifteen inches, started to receive his attention during the cooler time of the year. Soon after he arrived in Tucson, he must have become aware of ruins in the area because local farmers and ranchers knew of many sites scattered throughout the Santa Cruz Valley, especially along the ridge tops that flanked the mountains. In addition, both Jesse W. Fewkes (1909) and Ellsworth Huntington (1912) had recorded sites in the region. But it was not until the 1920s that Cummings and his students systematically excavated some of those ruins.

With the assistance of modern dating techniques, archaeologists are now convinced that the prehistory of southern Arizona extends back at least 12,000 years. Cummings did not have the advantage of precise dating tools and had to rely on general estimates of age based on geological interpretations. Nonetheless, he understood the principles of geological deposition and archaeological superposition, and he could recognize changes in material culture through time. His archaeological explorations in southern Arizona brought him and his students face to face with the remains of the entire sweep of human history for the region, from the Ice Age big-game hunters we now call Paleo-Indians, to Archaic hunter-gatherers, to irrigation farmers given the name "Hohokam."

It is not known when Cummings' first excavation of ruins in the Sonoran Desert region took place. The 1919 university catalog states that in April 1918, Cummings—along with a student named Arthur Vaughn and R. F. Gilder of Nebraska—dug a few prehistoric features deeply buried at Saint Mary's Hospital in Tucson (University of Arizona 1919). He may have dug there again later, because Arizona State Museum catalog cards for the site are dated 1920 and 1930 (Jacobs 1979). A photograph of a plain red storage jar from St. Mary's Ruin is shown in Cummings' book on the first inhabitants of Arizona and the Southwest (1953:196, center left).

At that time, ruins located over the entire Southwest were considered Puebloan (Bandelier 1892). The term "Hohokam" was not yet in common use for ruins in southern Arizona and would not become so for another decade. In addition, most of the adobe architecture and artifacts of the Sonoran Desert were assumed to be contemporaneous. In his 1924 landmark book on Southwestern archaeology, Alfred Kidder encouraged archaeologists to more closely examine—through stratigraphic excavations—the archaeology of southern Arizona because the red painted pottery of this region looked very different from Pueblo pottery types. Since Cummings was headquartered in southern Arizona, he may have taken this as a challenge, especially from someone with whom he had previously had unpleasant experiences.

Tanque Verde Village

Cummings' systematic investigation of the archaeology of the Sonoran Desert began in 1925, when he and his students started a long-term excavation of a pithouse village called Tanque Verde Ruin, about twenty miles east of Tucson near the Rincon Mountains. This is probably the same ruin, called "Estanque Verde," that was described by Adolph Bandelier (1892:470–471) as a few houses "of the detached dwelling type" scattered beneath dense and thorny brush. Bandelier thought that the ruin belonged to the Pueblo Culture and noted that J. B. Girard had obtained from the site a red corrugated ceramic canteen in the shape of a duck.

The *Tucson Citizen* (1925b) ran a story on Cummings' Tanque Verde dig in mid November. Cummings knew he was working on a ruin older than the "Valley Pueblo" (aboveground adobe) sites that had been previously excavated in the Salt and Gila River valleys. Consequently, he estimated that his pithouse village was over a thousand years old. He called the Tanque Verde Ruin a "Pit House Pueblo" and claimed that it was the farthest south that ancient Pueblo dwellings had been found. Excavations continued for the next few years, with John Hands in charge in 1926 and 1927 (Zahniser 1966).

Several of Cummings' more talented students worked at Tanque Verde, including Clara Lee Fraps, Lyndon Hargrave, Emil Haury, Florence Hawley, Henry Lockett, John McGregor, and Edward Spicer (Thompson 1995:644; Smith 1983:75). Haury presented a paper on the excavations at the April 1928 meeting of the American Association for the Advancement of Science (AAAS) in Flagstaff, and both Clara Lee Fraps (1928) and Emil Haury (1928) incorporated data from the site in their master's theses under Cummings. Fraps (1935) also wrote a four-page summary article in *The Kiva*, but no other site reports were prepared by Cummings or his students.

More than a dozen houses were excavated, about half the village (fig. 13.1). Three types of houses were distinguished, based on differences in wall construction. One of the houses at the site was connected with a smaller one by stairs and a passageway. Two burial grounds also were dug, and the students found seventeen cremation burials in urns and another one uncontained. Haury (1928) noted that by maintaining a vertical face in the digging, field crews could observe stratigraphic relationships and record the superpositioning of structures. This process allowed confirmation that there was an apparent evolution at the site, with rectangular pithouse architecture changing, over time, into aboveground adobe-walled architecture.

Many years earlier, Fewkes (1912a) had reported a pithouse under a later adobe compound at Casa Grande, north of Tucson, and Cummings had observed similar changes in architecture in northeastern Arizona as early as 1916. Two years after Cummings had initiated the Tanque Verde dig, Harold Gladwin (1928), first with the Southwest Museum in Los Angeles and later with the Gila Pueblo Archaeological Foundation, also accepted Kidder's challenge; Gladwin excavated into several trash mounds at Casa Grande Ruins. From these excavations, Gladwin defined a "Red-on-Buff Culture" that predated the polychrome pottery

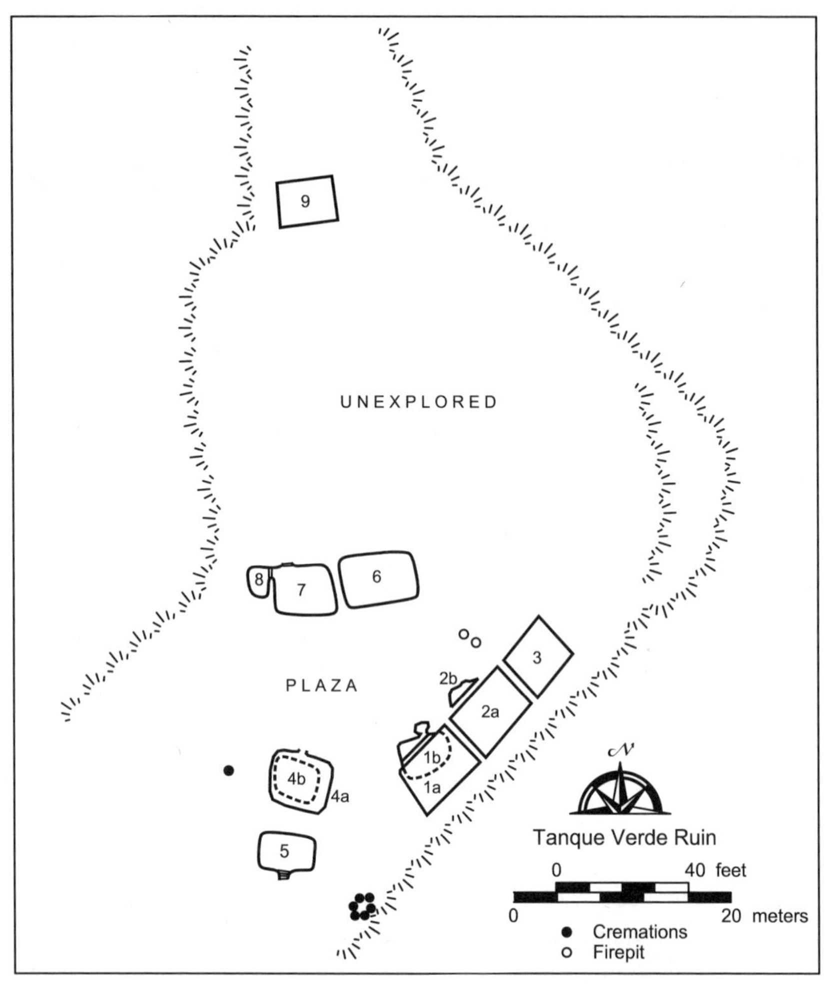

13.1 Plan map of the Tanque Verde excavations, based on Haury 1928 and Zahniser 1966 (fig. 4)

associated with the adobe compounds at Casa Grande. All these investigations reinforced Cummings' ideas, developed while working on the Colorado Plateau, about the uniform evolution of house types throughout the Southwest (cave-pithouse-pueblo).

A cave located a few hundred feet above the Tanque Verde village contained ceremonial objects, including textiles and miniature bow arrows, as well as plain and painted pottery similar to that found at the village. Norman Gabel's (1931) master's thesis defined this beautiful pottery type as Tanque Verde red-on-brown. It has since been found at many other prehistoric villages in the Santa Cruz Valley.

Casa Grande Canals

The year after Cummings started digging Tanque Verde, he took an interest in prehistoric canals in southern Arizona, most likely stimulated by the well-publicized canal investigations of Omar Turney (1922) in the Salt River valley. In March 1926, Cummings received a report from J. H. Duahey about a large prehistoric canal at Casa Grande. Concerned about the destruction of canals by farming activities along the Gila River, Cummings sent Emil Haury, who had demonstrated his mapping skills at the Mexican pyramid of Cuicuilco, and A. Larson to Casa Grande to map the canals. Cummings (1926a) authored a short article about the canals, accompanied by a detailed map, in an issue of *Progressive Arizona* magazine. Five main canals were recorded: two on the south side of the Gila River and three on the north side (fig. 13.2). One of the canals on the south side was traced for at least eighteen miles across the desert. The farmers that had used these canals, Cummings argued, proved themselves no less capable agriculturalists than the inhabitants of Mesopotamia and the Valley of the Nile in Egypt.

A few years later, one of Cummings' students, Carl Miller (1929), wrote his master's thesis on ancient irrigation systems in southern Arizona. Miller noted that Frederick W. Hodge (1893) had investigated prehistoric canals and a reservoir in the Phoenix region during Frank Hamilton Cushing's (1890) pioneering excavations and that H. R. Patrick (1903) had mapped many of the canals that Omar Turney (1924) was later credited with discovering. In 1930, Cummings gave a paper on the Casa Grande irrigation systems at the AAAS meeting held in Tucson.

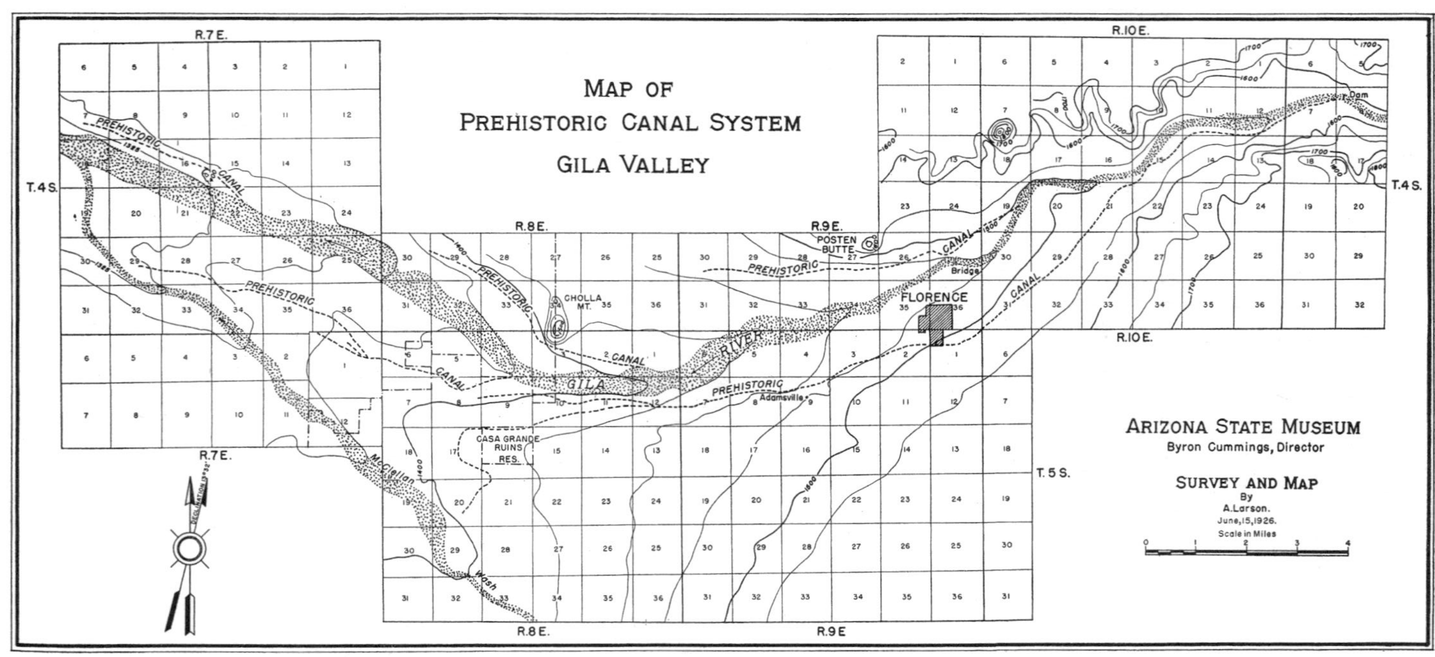

13.2 Cummings' (1926a) Gila River canal map

Gila River Ruins

During the winter of 1928–1929, the completion of Coolidge Dam threatened prehistoric villages and other sites located along the terraces of the Gila River upstream from the dam (*Coolidge News* 1929). Cummings and seven of his students—including Emil Haury, John McGregor, Lyndon Hargrave, and Waldo Wedel—undertook salvage archaeology on several of these sites. They dug a large rectangular "pithouse pueblo," called the Gila Bank Ruin, next to the Gila River, fifteen miles below Bylas (Cummings 1953:23, 25). This large adobe compound had more than a hundred "apartments" (Cummings 1953:21) and was as big as a modern-day football field, although a portion of it may have eroded into the river channel. According to Cummings' field notes (1929d), about twenty feet from the pueblo were one burial and five cremations in pottery jars. The jars had bowls turned over their tops, the bottoms of which had small holes punched into them. Pottery associated with the Hohokam culture—red-on-buff and Gila polychrome—were identified, but the punching of a hole into the funerary vessel is a trait common in the Mimbres Culture of western New Mexico. Another ruin excavated by Cummings during this expedition was called the Stone Frog Ruin and was located about one-quarter mile from the Gila Bank Ruin. This site was described as a pit-house ruin with walls of clay embedded with rocks (Cummings 1929d). Harry T. Getty (1932) later wrote his master's thesis on the archaeology of the upper Gila River region.

Martinez Hill

Ruins located at the southeastern base of Martinez Hill, located ten miles south of Tucson, attracted Cummings' attention as early as 1929, when he and his students excavated burials from a prehistoric village in that locality (Cummings 1931a, 1935i, 1953:22, 27). Norman Gabel (1931) wrote his master's thesis on the site. He described seven mounds about one-half mile east of the Santa Cruz River. From 1930 through 1932, Cummings' students dug "shafts" and trenches into the site and revealed two main cultural periods. During the earlier period, residents lived in small, partly sunken structures in oval and rectangular shapes—pit-houses—with thin clay and caliche walls twelve to nineteen inches in thickness. The floors of these pithouses were found at a depth of two or three feet below the modern ground surface. Associated pottery comprised only plainware. The architecture of the later culture was larger and more substantial and was associated with pottery that was painted red-on-buff and other red colors. Walls of the later structures—compounds—were made of courses of hand-puddled adobe twenty-four to thirty inches in thickness. Long, narrow rooms ("galleries") and open courts were present, with living rooms encompassed by a compound wall. One of the adobe walls of these structures was eight feet in height. The roofs were flat and made of timbers overlaid with poles, willows, and mud. Evidence of flooding (indicated by deposits of fine sand, clay, and gravel) was present in some of the structures (Cummings 1931a, 1935i). Extra stone had been set into the base of exterior walls, and some these walls were reinforced by outer walls built against them two or three different times, all in an apparent attempt to deal with the flooding.

Cummings suggested that, similar to Tanque Verde, the two culture periods at Martinez Hill represented a transitional stage between the rectangular pithouse villages common to this region and the compound structures found in the Casa Grande and Phoenix areas. Pottery from the site showed a development from rough plainware through the various stages of red-on-buff or red-on-brown (Cummings 1953:196), with a small amount of Gila polychrome. The hill above the site has numerous walls and circular structures that Cummings interpreted as defensive ramparts and windbreaks. In April 1930, Cummings gave a tour of the site to participants of the AAAS meeting, held in Tucson that spring. Later, the Tanque Verde phase was defined by archaeologists to represent the beginning of the Classic period, around AD 1150 for the Tucson region.

Blackstone Ruin

Another prehistoric village excavated by Cummings and his students is the Blackstone Ruin. This large site, located twenty-seven miles west of Tucson in the Avra Valley, was dug in the fall of 1930. It was located on a hilltop that rises about two hundred feet above the surrounding terrain. In total, 114 circular or oval rooms were mapped, most of them free-standing. About 40 of the rooms were excavated. The walls were made of basalt boulders, apparently without mortar. Rooms varied from two to forty feet in diameter. Walls were a maximum two feet in height, suggesting that they once had been surmounted by brush superstructures. Artifact deposits were sparse. Bedrock mortars and rock art were present on the hillslopes. The only report written on the site was a brief summary by Clara Lee Tanner (1936) for *The Kiva*.

What Shall We Call These People?

By the early 1930s, archaeologists were becoming convinced that the prehistoric cultures of southern Arizona were different from the Pueblo cultures to the north and east, but they could not reach a consensus on what to call these ancient people. Alfred Kroeber (1928) referred to the people who made red-on-buff pots as the Gila-Sonora Culture. Omar Turney (1929) had called them the Canal Builders, but Harold Gladwin preferred the Red-on-Buff Culture, named after their decorated pottery (Gladwin and Gladwin 1929, 1930a, 1930b). More than a decade earlier, after his work at Casa Grande, Fewkes (1912a:97) had recommended calling them the Hohokam, from a Pima (the modern Indians of the Salt-Gila basin) word interpreted by ethnographer Frank Russell (1908:24) as "That which has perished." A 1926 publication on Casa Grande by the Arizona Historical Society referred to the inhabitants of that site as Hohokam (Pinkley 1926). This term, however, was not adopted right away by other archaeologists.

In April 1931, a conference was held at the Gila Pueblo Archaeological Foundation in Globe to discuss problems with the 1927 Pecos Conference culture classification system when applied to the Sonoran Desert. Cummings was one of twenty-two people in attendance, and he was from one of nine western archaeology institutions represented. The participants agreed that the ancient peoples of the lower deserts should be called the Hohokam. Cummings adopted the Hohokam concept in his writings, but he still viewed them as a Pueblo-type culture.

In a *Tucson Magazine* article two years later, Cummings (1933) praised the skills and knowledge of the Hohokam people. He noted that they had accomplished great achievements in their architecture, art, and irrigation systems. Because he believed that they had had leisure time to enjoy themselves, he took the romantic position that "Life to them had ceased to be a struggle for existence."

Sierra Ancha Cliff Dwellings

Spectacular cliff dwellings in the rugged Sierra Ancha Mountains, northeast of Phoenix, attracted interest in the early 1930s after being neglected by archaeologists. Ruins along Cherry Creek, in particular, contained remarkably well-preserved structures with wooden beams that allowed them to be precisely dated using Andrew Douglass' (1929) recently developed tree-ring dating technique. In October 1930, Emil Haury explored the area on behalf of the Gila Pueblo Archaeological Foundation. During Christmas vacation that same year, Cummings made a quick trip into the area, guided by Glenn R. Ellison. In April 1932, Cummings and two of his students, Harry T. Getty and Mrs. Anna McGrath, returned on horseback to visit some of the ruins. One of them was a large pueblo the size of a modern-day football field. Later that summer, Haury organized a major expedition to collect wood specimens for dating, along with other perishable artifacts. Two years later, he reported the results of his expedition in his typical detailed manner (Haury 1934). Cummings visited the Sierra Ancha Mountains again in the same year as Haury's publication, but his trips were mostly "siteseeing," and he failed to write any reports on these trips.

University Indian Ruin

Cummings had envisioned acquiring a ruin near the University of Arizona campus that could be used as a field laboratory for his students. This vision came to fruition in 1930, when a prehistoric adobe compound north of Tucson, called University Indian Ruin, was donated to the University of Arizona by Mrs. Dorothy A. Knipe (Kelly 1935). She had worked with Cummings at Turkey Hill Pueblo the year before. Taking advantage of federal New Deal work programs, Cummings arranged to have a Civilian Conservation Corps (CCC) camp set up on the property to make improvements so it could be developed as an outdoor laboratory for university students. During the spring of 1931, Cummings and students excavated the ruin. Cummings believed that this site was similar in age to the Martinez Hill site.

Excavations were again undertaken at University Indian Ruin in 1933 and continued through 1936.[1] At least seventeen rooms were found in one of the four mounds on the property, along with twenty-three urn cremation burials. A "transitional" pithouse also was excavated (Cummings 1953:24). Aerial photography experiments of the site were unsuccessful in 1937. Later attempts proved more successful. In 1940 and 1941, Julian Hayden meticulously excavated a Hohokam Classic period (ca. 1150–1450) platform mound at the site for the National Park Service as a CCC employee. Unfortunately, Hayden's (1957) detailed report, written soon after his excavations, was not published until many years later. Nonetheless, it remains a classic report in Hohokam archaeology.

Redington Ballcourt

Cummings also had an opportunity to examine an oval depression that was called a Hohokam ballcourt. In the fall of 1935, he took several students to Redington, in southeastern Arizona, to examine a site near the schoolhouse that was reported to include a prehistoric ballcourt (Duffen 1936). Although this unique type of archaeological feature had been identified years earlier by Bandelier (1892), Fewkes (1912a) had argued that they were instead reservoirs. Turney (1929) called them sun temples. Their possible function as semisubterranean courts for playing a game similar to the Mayan ball game was given support by Haury's excavation of two of them in 1934–1935 at Snaketown along the Gila River south of Phoenix (Haury 1937).

The highly eroded feature at Redington had curved sides lined with stones; it was over a hundred feet in length and about sixty feet in width. Red-on-buff pottery was found nearby. Cummings and his students dug a trench and a test pit into the feature, but neither he nor his students were completely convinced that it was a ballcourt (but see Wilcox and Sternberg 1983:121).

Exploring Archaic Caves in the Safford Region

Cummings had an interest in the archaeology of the lower Gila River region in eastern Arizona, especially cave sites where he might find fragile artifacts, such as textiles and wooden artifacts rare in Hohokam sites. He also was interested in documenting cultures that preceded the Hohokam, currently identified as the Archaic Period. But few opportunities arose in which Cummings could justify visiting the Safford area. That situation changed in 1934. In the spring of that year, he participated with the Men's Mutual Improvement Association in the exploration of caves near Safford (*Arizona Daily Star* 1934a, 1934b). Led by Professor Monroe H. Clark of the Gila Junior College, about a hundred Mormon men and boys scoured the rugged canyons of the Gila River and found six caves. Some of the caves in Bonita Canyon had prehistoric walls, and Cummings vowed to return for further investigations.

Later that fall, Cummings found himself involved in the Safford region again, but this time it was a situation in which an important discovery turned for the worse. In late October, seventeen-year-old Glenn McEuen (1934) wrote Cummings and informed him of a cave, located near the Diamond Bar Ranch forty miles from Safford, that contained well-preserved archaeology deposits. Cummings (1934e) wrote back promptly and told McEuen that he would visit the area the second week of November. Cummings and Tom Sanders, his student, met with McEuen on November 10 and were shown the cave. They knew right away their trip had been worthwhile.

Buried in the 25-foot-deep and 230-foot-long lava rockshelter was a large quantity of perishable materials and several short rows of stones from the front to the back of the rockshelter. Within the deposits were shell beads from the coasts of California or Mexico, along with three burials. One of the burials was interpreted by Cummings as a medicine man, whose securely bound and flexed body was wrapped in a large yucca-fiber bag forty-one inches long. It had been beautifully woven with alternating bands of red and black (Moreno 2000:fig. 3; Tanner 1976:64). The individual was in a seated position and wore yucca sandals and a rabbit-fur blanket with bird feathers woven into it. Also accompanying the individual were a carved wooden pipe with a bone stem and an unusually well-preserved atlatl, an ancient dart thrower that predates the bow and arrow in America (cf. Ferg and Peachy 1998). The handle of the atlatl had buckskin finger loops that had been bound with yucca and twisted rolls of human hair to provide a firm grip. The body of the atlatl had been painted red, and at the end opposite the handle there was a heart-shaped groove with a hook where the end of the dart shaft would have been set for throwing (Moreno 2000:figs. 1 and 2).

Small corncobs, large gourds, and wild grass seeds also were found by Cummings in the cave, but no pottery. Because the woven yucca bag and the atlatl were similar to those found at Basketmaker sites in northern Arizona, Cummings estimated that the McEuen Cave burial was 2,000 years old. This was an exciting discovery—these materials represented a culture stage predating the Hohokam villages of the Tucson area. He vowed to return to conduct more explorations when he could schedule it. Only three days after his visit to the cave, the *Arizona Daily Star* (1934c) quoted Cummings about his discovery. He stated that they had found convincing evidence for a Cave People who were plant gatherers and lived scattered through the country, with infrequent contacts with one another. Archaeologists now assign these hunting-and-gathering people to the Archaic period.

Soon after the newspaper articles appeared, Marion P. McEuen (1934), Glen's father, wrote Cummings asking for his son to be compensated for first discovering the materials in the cave. Cummings (1934g) responded with a letter immediately, telling McEuen that Cummings had used his own car and gas to get to the site. He expressed disappointment in the young man's attitude: "We thought you [were] chiefly interested in knowing the facts and assisting the State Museum in spreading the knowledge of Arizona and instructing the youth of the State regarding the prehistoric tribes once occupying this region." That same day, Cummings (1934h) also wrote to Harvey L. Mott, a friend and reporter at the *Arizona Republic* in Phoenix, and asked Mott to check the land office on the ownership status of the land on which the cave was located. Cummings then returned to the cave in late November and early December to excavate some more materials.

In December, Oscar C. Chapman (1934), assistant secretary of the Department of the Interior, issued a permit to Cummings to officially excavate in McEuen Cave since it was on unsurveyed public land that had been leased to McEuen. Only three weeks later, Harold Colton (1935) of the Museum of Northern Arizona told Cummings that he had purchased some exceptional Basketmaker material from two individuals from Safford: J. H. Smith and Arthur McEuen. This news was disturbing to Cummings, but he was unable to schedule a return to McEuen Cave until later that year. However, material from McEuen Cave purchased by Harold Colton was traded to Cummings for other artifacts.

Cummings also prepared an exhibit of the McEuen Cave materials at the State Museum, including displaying the oldest baby cradle in Arizona—a long, oblong frame with wood slats and two woven cross-supports. Cummings' greatest fears were confirmed when he was finally able to revisit the cave. In October 1935, he sadly told Harold Ickes, secretary of the Interior, that McEuen Cave had been "gutted completely" (Cummings 1935n). Additional materials, including around 120 perishable artifacts, were later given to Casa Grande National Monument. These materials were then loaned to the Gila Pueblo Archaeological Foundation, and Dorothea Kelly (1937) analyzed them, although her report was not published. When the foundation was dissolved in 1951, the artifacts were transferred to the State Museum.

McEuen Cave continues to interest archaeologists. Radiocarbon dates later obtained on the twined bag, cradle, and some cordage support Cummings' age estimate, dating them to 2,200–2,500 years of age (Damon and Long 1962). More recent analysis of the atlatl has dated it to around 2,300 years old (Moreno 2000), and corncobs from the cave have been dated even older, from 2,800 to 3,700 years before the present (Huckell et al. 1999).

Cummings' Southwestern Culture Development Model

By 1935, Cummings had been excavating Southwestern ruins for three decades. He had seen with his own eyes variations in architecture and other material culture dating to different time periods on the Colorado Plateau and in the Sonoran Desert. Some of these differences were expressed in deposits on top of each other, exhibiting a recognizable stratigraphic sequence. These changes represented, to him, advances in the culture toward a more perfect state of being, or cultural progress. For many years, he adhered to a simple, three-stage culture stage model based primarily on a perceived improvement in architecture—cave to pithouse to pueblo. In the mid 1930s, Cummings (1935c) modified his model to include existing chronological data and the terms "Archaic" and "Pueblo," but this model still represented a cave-pithouse-pueblo evolution. The revised model had five periods: Archaic (prefarming), Early Pueblo, Late Pueblo, Historic, and Modern.

Cummings' Explorations in the Mid to Late 1930s

Involvement in Hohokam archaeology declined significantly for Cummings in the late 1930s, as he focused on Kinishba Pueblo and Harold Gladwin and Emil Haury of the Gila Pueblo Archaeological Foundation (GPAF) took the lead in the exploration of the Hohokam culture. Under Gladwin's sponsorship, Haury directed the systematic excavations of Snaketown, located on the north side of the Gila River, twenty miles south of Phoenix. From September to May in 1934 and again in 1935, several archaeologists and twenty-five Pimas excavated forty pit-houses, two ballcourts, several trash mounds, an irrigation canal, and more than five hundred cremation burials. Their detailed report, published only two years later (Gladwin et al. 1937), set the standards by which the Hohokam culture would be known for the next three decades (Reid and Whittlesey 1997:83). Nancy Margaret Pinkley, who had just received her B.A. in archaeology under Cummings, was field secretary for the Snaketown excavations.

In 1935 and 1936, Cummings took his students on trips into northern Mexico, where they examined *trincheras* (terraced) sites in Sonora and visited Casas Grandes and Olla Cave in the Chihuahua Desert. Cummings also investigated, in 1936, the Hodges site, located near Tucson between the Santa Cruz River and Rillito Creek. Carl Miller, who had obtained his master's degree under Cummings in 1929, directed the excavations at the Hodges site in 1936. He and his crew dug thirty-one Hohokam houses. Originally called the "Gravel Pit Ruin," this important Hohokam village contained a ballcourt and was under the care of Mr. and Mrs. Wetmore, who had purchased part of the site (Kelly 1978).

When Cummings retired from the Archaeology Department at the University of Arizona in 1937, he no longer had a group of student helpers to assist him in his excavations; therefore, his involvement in the archaeology of the Tucson region decreased significantly. Perhaps it is no coincidence that Harold Gladwin of the GPAF hired Frank Mitalsky (better known as Midvale) from 1937 to 1938 to conduct a ceramic survey of the Tucson region. In addition, during the winter of 1937 and spring of 1938, Isabel T. Kelly directed the excavation of the Hodges site under the sponsorship of GPAF. Kelly had obtained her doctorate at the University of California–Berkeley in 1932. She dug several dozen houses and identified five different types of Hohokam architecture at the Hodges site. She correctly argued that the village had gone through a decline in the fourteenth century. Unfortunately, Kelly's report was not completed when she left GPAF in late 1938, and the results of her important work remained obscure, much like the results of most of Cummings' Hohokam excavations. However, a revised version of Kelly's report was published forty years later with the help of James Officer and Emil Haury (Kelly 1978). This report continues to be an important contribution to Hohokam archaeology.

Cummings' last dig in the Sonoran Desert occurred in April 1938, when he and eleven residents of Ajo dug a three-foot-wide trench into Hinton Cave, twenty miles north of Ajo in southwestern Arizona. This rockshelter is thirty-one feet deep and ninety-five feet long. Inside, Cummings found obsidian artifacts and plain red, reddish brown, gray, and red-on-buff pottery with life-form designs. No report was written.

14

"Why Shouldn't Man Have Been Created on American Soil?"

Cummings' 1926 Excavations into the Arizona Ice Age

One of the fundamental questions in American archaeology concerns the origins of humans in the New World. This question generated considerable interest during the mid nineteenth century. Charles Darwin's (1859) *Origin of Species* provided an evolutionary framework for pushing human origins far back in time beyond the 6,000 years approximated in the Bible, but how far back remained a subject of heated debate. By the 1860s, the discovery of human-made tools—flaked "hand axes"—found with the bones of extinct mammals in European caves had convinced most archaeologists there of the great antiquity of humans. Furthermore, geologist Louis Agassiz had shown that an Ice Age had once existed in Europe and covered the continent with huge ice sheets. Some of the extinct mammals found with human tools had lived during this Ice Age, and scientists accepted the notion of a "Glacial Man" (Fagan 1987). The exact timing of this Ice Age was unclear, but it was assumed to have occurred tens of thousands if not hundreds of thousands of years ago, placing it during the Pleistocene Epoch (ca. 2,000,000 to 10,000 years ago).

The skeleton of an Ice Age mastodon had been excavated in New York as early as 1801 (Semonin 2000), and when Agassiz recorded geological evidence of the Ice Age in North America, the search was on for an American Glacial Man.[1] Certain individuals became advocates for his presence here when stone tools similar in form to the "Paleoliths" in Europe were found in several locations in America (Abbott 1892; Wright 1892). However, scientists from the Smithsonian Institution and the U.S.

Geological Survey discounted these finds and argued that the human settlement of America had taken place long after the Ice Age. Smithsonian geologist-turned-archaeologist William Holmes (1918, 1925) argued that the geological context of an artifact, not its form, was critical to determining the artifact's age. For more than two decades, he evaluated each new find, discounting all claims for a Glacial Man in America.

Smithsonian physical anthropologist Aleš Hrdlička (1907, 1918) also carefully examined all human skeletal finds and their stratigraphic context and decided that none dated from the Ice Age. He argued that Americans were immigrants from Asia, with their migration dating to no more than 4,000 years ago. Any archaeologist claiming to have found evidence of Ice Age humans in America faced the intense scrutiny of Holmes and Hrdlička, which "frightened away" many archaeologists who might otherwise have gone searching for the origins of man in America (Kidder 1936b:144–145).

In the mid 1920s, Cummings (1926c) had expressed his concerns about the difficulties that archaeologists would encounter if they discovered evidence of Early Man in America. Later that same year, he was thrust into this situation. In June, the *New York Herald* (1926) announced that Cummings had exhumed the fossilized shoulder blade of a prehistoric elephant, probably a mammoth, from a mine twenty-five miles southwest of Tucson. Washington archaeologist Captain D. W. Page and the mine's owner, Charles Udall, assisted Cummings.

In September of that year, the San Pedro River in southeastern Arizona had a record flood, after a three-day rain, that destroyed nearly a dozen bridge crossings and ripped up railroad tracks (*Tombstone Epitaph* 1926a). This flood also exposed several locations where ancient bones were buried within its banks (*Tombstone Epitaph* 1926b). After these sites were brought to his attention, Cummings and his students excavated the sites, taking field notes and photographs. Although Cummings failed to write a site report on his findings, several newspapers published articles about his investigations, allowing the reconstruction of his excavations (Hallman 1999). The discovery of stone tools and the bones of large mammals that lived during the last Ice Age in Arizona created considerable local excitement.

The first materials to be examined by Cummings were human burials found by a ranch foreman named Jones, in a bank of the Cienega Wash on the Empire Ranch, fifty miles southeast of Tucson. On October 9, Cummings and several students recorded two flexed human burials that were located in purportedly Pleistocene clay and sand deposits at a depth of twelve to fourteen feet below the surface. The bones were fragmentary and fossilized. Their condition and "crude" appearance suggested great age. Cummings sketched a profile of the deposits, recording alternating layers of clay and gravel. He also noted the presence of plain pottery in a deposit five feet above the skeletons and decorated pottery in the uppermost level and on the surface. These materials appeared to him to represent a long sequence of cultural developments. In her master's thesis, Anna McGrath (1932) included several photographs of Cummings and his crew, including Emil Haury, in front of the exposed deposits.

Soon thereafter, Mrs. Boss, a teacher at the Double Adobe school in Sulphur Springs Valley, located east of the San Pedro Valley, showed Cummings a piece of ivory from a mammoth tusk collected by a schoolboy. Cummings scheduled an investigation of the location of this discovery on the next available weekend, October 23 and 24. Taking along four students to help him—Emil Haury, Lyndon Hargrave, John C. McGregor, and Elliot Wilson—he excavated the Whitewater Draw area where the tusk fragment had been found and located a nearly complete skull of a mammoth. Cummings identified six stratigraphic levels containing varying layers of gravel, sand, and clay (fig. 14.1). The skull was in an upright position within a five-foot-thick stratum of clay. Cummings suggested this huge animal, which when living stood more than nine feet in height, had been mired in the mud of an ancient lake.

No other skeletal elements, however, were recovered with the skull. Ground stone tools also were found in the same stratum as the skull, although not in direct association with it. If indeed the artifacts and the skull were associated, Cummings' party had made a significant discovery. On October 26, Cummings officially announced their find to the *Douglas Daily Dispatch* (1926a), stating that the mammoth was at least 25,000 years old, since scientists thought the Ice Age had ended by then. He also mentioned his previous excavation of the human remains in Pleistocene deposits at the Empire Ranch, sixty miles to the northwest of the Double Adobe find.

Cummings believed that additional excavation was necessary at the Double Adobe site before anything definitive could be said. He returned

14.1 Cummings and student digging mammoth skull at Double Adobe site, 1926 (courtesy of Arizona State Museum, University of Arizona, #70)

on October 29 to continue with digging into the riverbanks in other nearby locations. Excavations about 450 feet away from the mammoth skull, and on the opposite side of the wash, revealed another significant find: the intact skeleton of an extinct bison, ground stone tools, and a hearth containing charcoal in a stratum several feet deeper than the skull (Cummings 1953:xii; Hallman 1999:fig. 4).[2] Cummings was convinced that he had discovered evidence of humans living in Arizona during the Ice Age. Possible depositional mixing of the bones and artifacts was not given any more serious thought. The deeper deposition of the bison bones suggested to Cummings that this skeleton was older than the mammoth skull. Artifacts uncovered at both locations were thought to have been used for processing animal hides and for extracting marrow from the animal's bones. In its Sunday edition, the *Douglas Daily Dispatch* (1926b) announced that Cummings believed that man lived in the area "nearly 40,000 years ago."

Cummings may have known about the discovery, the year before, of spear points associated with ancient bison bones overlain with Pleistocene sands and gravels at Lone Wolf Creek in Texas (Cook 1925). He may or may not have been aware of another important excavation undertaken in the summer of 1926, which found finely made projectile points associated with extinct bison bones in a buried deposit at the soon-to-be-famous Folsom site in New Mexico (Cook 1926).

Cummings was eager to share his findings informally with others, and he gave several talks to the frequent visitors during the excavations. He also gave a lecture in the town of Douglas to a group of prominent citizens. The *Benson News* (1926) reported him saying that his discovery would prove that the area was inhabited in the Pleistocene age and that "a divine hand, a divine planner, is in charge and responsible." This statement reflects Cummings' deeply held religious belief that all of human history was part of God's predetermined plan and that his job as an archaeologist was merely to reveal that plan through the excavation and display of the remains of the past.

Unfortunately, all the attention to his excavation at Double Adobe resulted in a portion of one of the mammoth tusks being stolen. Cummings was forced to hire a guard during the week of October 25 to 31 to protect the site until he could return and carefully remove the skull. S. F. Moore of Lowell was paid $4 a day to be the watchman. On October 31, the recovery of the skull was completed.

Despite the significance of these discoveries, Cummings did not write any reports on them, partly because he rarely wrote excavation reports, but also because of his concern about criticisms from other professionals such as Holmes and Hrdlička. However, he did give a presentation on his investigations at the November meeting of the Arizona Archaeological and Historical Society, a group much less critical than some of his colleagues.

Cummings was motivated to write something about his discoveries at Double Adobe when Omar Turney (1928) authored an article criticizing Cummings' findings in an issue of *Arizona Old and New*, the journal of the newly created Arizona Museum in Phoenix. Turney, a retired engineer and amateur archaeologist, accepted the idea of Ice Age man in America but expressed skepticism about the validity of the association of the skull and the stone tools at Double Adobe. Turney then proposed that man had been in America for a million years.

Cummings (1928b) responded to Turney with an article entitled "Cochise of Yesterday" in the following issue of the same journal. He supported the validity of the association of tools and mammoth bones at Double Adobe and discussed the Empire Ranch and Parmalee Ranch discoveries as additional evidence. Without the aid of precise dating techniques, which were not yet developed, Cummings estimated (incorrectly) the age of the geologic deposits at about 50,000 years old. In Cummings' (1928b:27) opinion, his excavations had revealed that humans had occupied southeastern Arizona "long before . . . Noah had drawn his first plans for the Ark."

In the spring of 1931, Cummings was informed of the accidental discovery of mammoth bones in a wash bank on Parmalee Ranch in southeastern Arizona (McGrath 1932:55–56). These fossilized bones had been found by Carson Morrow of the U.S. Border Patrol in a side wash of the San Pedro River, south of Hereford (Hallman 1999). The bones, including the skull of a mammoth, were found at a depth of six feet below the surface. Within 120 yards of the bones, on the same side of the wash, Cummings found a hearth with charcoal and burnt stone. Little else is known about this investigation.

Two years later, in May 1935, Cummings gave a presentation on his Ice Age investigations at the American Association for the Advancement of Science meeting in Santa Fe. Cummings' paper was part of a symposium called "Pleistocene Man in Arizona." His paper was never published, although the abstract of the paper was printed in *The Kiva* (1935d) and in the *Pan-American Geologist* (1935h).

Soon after this symposium, Emil Haury and Edward B. Sayles (and later, geologist Ernst Antevs) of the Gila Pueblo Archaeological Foundation began exploring the Double Adobe area and initiated their own excavations in the region. Haury (1983) later stated that they chose that area intentionally because the University of Arizona was not actively pursuing archaeological studies there. The excavations done by Sayles and Antevs (1941) in Cochise County resulted in their now-classic monograph that argued for a lengthy and continuous occupation of the area by a preagricultural Cochise Culture, extending back thousands of years into the Pleistocene. The term "Cochise Culture," interestingly similar to Cummings' "Cochise of Yesterday," was adopted into the archaeological literature of the Southwest. However, connections between the Ice Age cultural deposits and later artifacts belonging to "Archaic" people were eventually challenged because of a misunderstanding of the complex depositional history of the geological strata (Waters 1986).

Cummings' failure to adequately publish the results of his excavations can be attributed in part to his fear of scrutiny by scientists from the Smithsonian. He knew of the importance of the geological context of his bones and artifacts, but at the time there were no agreed-upon methods for recognizing stratigraphic units and sequences. Consequently, without a geologist present during his excavations, acceptance by others of the artifact and extinct mammal association would rely exclusively on Cummings' personal testimony and integrity (Meltzer 1991). The initial negative reactions to the Folsom discovery in 1926—because of the absence of other professional witnesses to inspect the geological context and verify artifact associations—indicates that Cummings' claim of Ice Age man in Arizona would have been rejected if he had published his findings. Why Cummings did not bring a university geologist to assist him with the excavations is unknown, but his less-than-favorable experience with several geologists during the Silverbell lead artifact excavations the previous year may have soured him on the idea of geologists interpreting his archaeological contexts for him.

Nonetheless, Cummings' investigations at Double Adobe had an important impact on Arizona archaeology. One of his student assistants in 1926, Emil Haury, later became a pioneer in the study of Ice Age humans in Arizona. In the early 1940s, Haury found Pleistocene mammal remains buried with stone tools in Ventana Cave in southwestern Arizona. Later he and others carefully excavated two important sites in southeastern Arizona, Naco (Haury 1952; Haury et al. 1953) and Lehner (Haury 1956; Haury et al. 1959), which contained mammoth skeletons unquestionably associated with Clovis-style projectile points. The Lehner site had thirteen mammoths that had been killed by hunters nearly 11,000 years ago.

Deeply patriotic, Cummings believed that American prehistory was as ancient and important as that of Europe or Asia. Indeed, instead of accepting the "Mongol Invader" theory, as he called it (that is, humans migrating to the Americas from Asia), he posed the question, "Why shouldn't man have been created on American soil . . . ?" (Mott 1937). He believed he had answered this question affirmatively with his discovery of Ice Age mammals and tools in Arizona dating to 50,000 years ago. Although Cummings was wrong about the extreme age of his finds, he was right about the presence of Early Man in Arizona during the last Ice Age. The locations where humans originated, however, are still thought to be outside American soil.

15

"To Guide the Ship through the Night"

President of the University of Arizona, 1927–1928

Byron Cummings served as president of the University of Arizona twice: in 1921 and again in 1927 and 1928. Both times he did not seek the presidency but was called upon to use his proven skills as an administrator to fill a temporarily vacant position. The first time was under favorable conditions. Cummings merely assumed some of the president's duties while President Rufus von KleinSmid was traveling abroad. The second time was under extremely difficult circumstances, at a time when the University of Arizona was involved in one of the most challenging crises in its history—a public feud between some of the faculty and the board of regents over university president Cloyd Heck Marvin. Cummings performed admirably on both occasions and was especially skillful in calming the university community after President Marvin was forced to resign in 1927.

Cummings faced many challenges during his term as president, and his capable responses to those challenges are shown in the large body of correspondence generated by Cummings and by individuals who wrote to Cummings, especially Governor George W. P. Hunt, the board of regents, and members of the faculty. This correspondence offers a window into Cummings' renowned administrative skills, his relationship with Governor Hunt and the board of regents, and his philosophy on institutions of higher learning.

The Marvin Presidency

Mary Abbott (1982) has written that Marvin's fifty-two-month tenure at the University of Arizona ended "amidst a turmoil of accusations, hearings, gossip, and politicking." Marvin's term began in September 1922 when he took up the position vacated the year before by Rufus B. von KleinSmid. Marvin had obtained his Ph.D. at Harvard University after studying law at Stanford and was a dean and assistant director at the University of California at Los Angeles. He was selected by the board of regents after a long recruitment with several failed attempts to attract the individuals they wanted. Francis C. Lockwood, dean of the College of Letters, Arts and Sciences, served as acting president during the summer of 1922 until Marvin arrived for the fall semester (Martin 1960).

Within a month of his arrival, President Marvin presented his *Plan of Administration* laying out his vision for the future of the University of Arizona, based on his conception of a modern business approach. That future consisted of a major building program needed by the university, and Marvin used his promotional skills to get a new men's gymnasium constructed and a beautiful new library building built (at a cost of $450,000). The university's water system was finally hooked up to the City of Tucson's water system. In addition, Marvin established the now well-respected College of Law. But he also undertook a number of controversial actions—both to better the university's academic standing and for reasons of "efficiency"—that angered the faculty (Abbott 1982:65). Those actions included the elimination of more than twenty university departments, the reorganization of the Department of Agriculture, the request for the resignation of eleven teachers (including six full professors), and the rescinding of the new faculty constitution approved in 1921. President Marvin believed that he had moved the university twenty years forward, and in 1924 the University of Arizona received national recognition for its academic progress. However, a number of people thought Marvin was harming the morale of the faculty, and they questioned his termination of some of the professors. Marvin responded that he was "cutting dead wood" (Abbott 1982:66).

In the fall of 1923, two of the professors dismissed by Marvin—A. E. Vinson, professor of agricultural chemistry, and de Rosette Thomas, professor of home economics—asked the American Association of University Professors (AAUP) to investigate their terminations from the university. Charles A. Turrell, professor of Spanish, also was part of the original complaint, but he later removed himself during the investigative process. The AAUP issued a balanced report that praised President Marvin for his accomplishments, including a raise in the salary scale, but chastised him for his lack of consideration for some of the older faculty.

Dean Lockwood openly criticized President Marvin and in turn was admonished by the president. Marvin administered the university on his own, without much input from the deans, and many of them were not pleased with his management style. Marvin had even hired teachers without informing the deans of the colleges in which they would teach. However, there was not a consensus of opinion among the deans concerning President Marvin; two influential deans, Gurdon M. Butler of the College of Mines and Engineering and J. J. Thornber of the College of Agriculture, were supporters of Marvin.

Cummings was friends with Dean Butler and Dean Thornber, but he held a different view than they did. In an interview about the controversy, which must have felt like déjà vu because of his similar experience at the University of Utah, Cummings expressed his opinion that Marvin was aggressive and egotistical and that he was "destroying the healthy spirit of the faculty" by "boasting of his accomplishments while ignoring groundwork done in previous years" (Abbott 1982:69). Cummings was also angry at Marvin because the president had backed out on an agreement to purchase several thousand cataloged artifacts from Mexico that Cummings had arranged for the Arizona State Museum when he was excavating at Cuicuilco the year before.

The feud between the president and the faculty created friction in the Tucson community and the rest of the state. The *Arizona Daily Star*, owned by the son of the president of the board of regents (E. E. Ellinwood), supported Marvin, but some prominent citizens wanted Marvin to leave the university. Earnest C. Tuthill, rector of the Grace Episcopal Church in Tucson, appeared before the board of regents in March with a statement of charges against Marvin. Rector Tuthill accused Marvin of "habitual lying" and of damaging the faculty's professional reputations (Abbott 1982:70). Marvin then asked the faculty for a petition of support, but they denied his request.

Hearings were held by the board of regents in mid May for complaints and on June 1 for supporters. During those hearings, Professor G.E.P. Smith and Dean Samuel Fegtly got into a fistfight over Marvin (Windsor 1998:212). Most of the board of regents supported President Marvin, but they also voted to reappoint the six dismissed professors. The *Tucson Daily Independent* opposed the retention of Marvin and published a series of articles that presented the testimonies at the hearings (Martin 1960:148).

Governor Hunt had heard more than he wanted to about President Marvin's continuing problems and, after he was reelected in the fall of 1926, asked Marvin to resign in January 1927. The four members of the board of regents who had supported Marvin—E. E. Ellinwood, John H. Campbell, Cleve W. Van Dyke, and John J. Corrigan—also resigned. Soon thereafter Marvin accepted the presidency at George Washington University, which he ran successfully but with the same aggressive management style for more than thirty years (Windsor 1998). Six years after resigning, Ellinwood would serve again on the Arizona Board of Regents for more than fifteen years (Martin 1960).

A New President

The *Arizona Daily Star* urged the board of regents to appoint Dean Gurdon M. Butler as the new president, but his support of President Marvin eliminated him as a candidate (Windsor 1998:220). In late January 1927, Byron Cummings was appointed acting president by the board of regents. A search committee worked on hiring a new president, and because no suitable candidate was found initially, Cummings was named president in September. A three-person advisory committee was established to assist Cummings: C. T. Vorhies of the Department of Agriculture; E. P. Mathewson of the Department of Mines; and C. Zaner Lesher, registrar. Cummings was in charge of 137 faculty members and around 1,800 students on a seventy-two-acre campus valued at $3 million (Martin 1960). The board of regents gave him a $3,100 raise in his annual salary for his new responsibilities.

Cummings' appointment was met with nearly universal praise, reflecting his popularity and his respect as an administrator. More than forty letters of congratulations arrived from all over the state and the country, written by politicians, educators, businessmen, students, parents of students, and citizens. Governor Hunt (1927a) wrote Cummings on February 1, telling him that the board of regents' action "meets with universal approval." State senator Walter Runke (1927) expressed confidence in Cummings' "splendid ability." Senator W. C. Joyner (1927) informed Cummings that he could think of no one who would be better able "to bring the University back to its former high standards, not only educationally but morally."

Many members of the university faculty also were pleased with Cummings' appointment. Andrew E. Douglass (1927) told Cummings that it was a great relief to learn of his promotion in the Phoenix newspaper. Congratulatory letters came from Dean Lockwood; Dean P. H. Ross, director of the Agricultural Extension Service at the University of Arizona; J. W. Clarson Jr., acting dean of the College of Education; and others.

Rufus B. von KleinSmid (1927), who was then president of the University of Southern California, told Cummings, "I am confident that none other could so quickly and so completely pull the situation together and reset again that pace of progress that we so thoroughly covet for the institution. In scholastic attainment and experience, in vision, in understanding, and in personality, 'thou are the man' for the hour and for the task." T. A. Beal (1927), dean at the University of Utah and a former Latin student of Cummings', noted that he wished Cummings had remained with his institution. E. D. Ryder (1927) of Phoenix informed Cummings that "you may look for my second boy to return soon to finish his course."

Another person to express congratulations was Omar A. Turney, Phoenix archaeologist. Turney (1927) told Cummings that he was very glad to see Cummings appointed as president because "It places the department of Anthropology [Archaeology] in its proper rank due to the splendid museum you have built up."

William V. Whitmore (1927), a medical doctor, wrote an article about Cummings' appointment as president. A former member of the board of regents and chancellor, Dr. Whitmore was eminently qualified to judge Cummings' administrative abilities. He noted that Cummings was a "quiet, most unassuming and courteous gentleman" but was also a person who was willing to make decisions and had the courage of his convictions. Cummings was considered a person with "unquestioned veracity and integrity, tact and sound judgment, broad vision and high ideals." In Whitmore's opinion, Cummings would make a good president because he was thoroughly grounded in the old-fashioned principles of decency, justice, and righteousness.

Cummings went to work on the university's problems immediately, focusing first on faculty and staff morale. He was helped by the positive comments about his character and abilities in an editorial in the February 1 issue of the *Arizona Daily Star* (1927a). Entitled "Get Behind the New President," the editorial said that the appointment of Cummings opened the door for the board of regents to take the university out of politics for the first time in forty years. Under Cummings, it was expected that the "present factionalism, both in Tucson and on the campus, will have a chance to die a natural death." These words are high praise from a newspaper that was opposed to the ouster of President Marvin.

Cummings did not have much time to settle into his new job. On February 2, he assembled the university students and gave them a short speech, which received a standing ovation. He urged the students to seek "beauty, truth, and opportunity" and to seek it quietly and persistently (Cummings 1927a; *Tucson Citizen* 1927a). On February 4, Cummings (1927b) wrote to Governor Hunt stating his primary hopes and concerns for his new job: "We find many things to look after and with our class work this crowds us pretty hard right now, but the spirit on campus seems to be excellent, and we are hoping to be able to guide the ship through the night." The following day, he wrote Robert E. Tally, president of the board of regents, thanking Tally for his suggestions and promising him that Cummings would do everything possible to smooth over the university's difficulties and to get the faculty and staff to cooperate again (Cummings 1927c).

After being on the job only two weeks, Cummings persuaded Senator W. C. Joyner of Pima County to introduce a statewide Antiquities Act in the Arizona Legislature. By the third week of February, Cummings had reviewed the university's previous year's budget and made corrections in President Marvin's annual report. Governor Hunt (1927b) recommended that Cummings attend the legislative meetings on the budget to make sure that "the University gets what is needed." Cummings made the trip to Phoenix as Hunt requested.

In March, Cummings had to deal with the issue of whether or not to fund the new Graduate College recently established by President Marvin. In Cummings' (1927d) opinion, expressed in a letter to Governor Hunt, the money would be better spent for library facilities for graduate students than for paying to administer a Graduate College. Regent Tally (1927b) wrote Cummings and noted that the establishment of the Graduate College by President Marvin had been "hasty and overly progressive" but that it was probably best not to change it at this time. Also in March, Martin Mortenson Jr. (1927) superintendent of Thatcher Public Schools, asked Cummings about the need for entrance requirements to the University of Arizona. Cummings' (1927e) belief that education should build good character is reflected in his reply that "we are merely looking for a good strong intellectual and moral foundation with the inspiration that will give them a big view of life and the service they may render to their fellow men." Acknowledging that "a degree is only a tag," Cummings hoped that those degrees would "stand for equipment and accomplishment."

The month of April was very busy and brought both good and bad news to Cummings. Cummings (1927f) proposed to the board of regents that the university establish its own printing and publishing press because that would increase student involvement in journalism and would be more economical. This proposal was supported by Phi Delta Epsilon, which had undertaken a comprehensive study and found that more than twenty universities had presses and many others wanted them. Furthermore, the University of Utah, where Cummings had formerly taught, had a press that was profitable. However, the estimated $35,000 cost was not well received by the board of regents, and not until much later—in 1969—was Cummings' student Emil Haury able to convince the board of regents to allow the university to have its own press (Thompson 1995:653).

In early April, Governor Hunt (1927c) informed Cummings that the legislature had passed his Arizona Antiquities Act, giving the director of the Arizona State Museum control over all archaeology projects on state land. No sooner had Cummings celebrated this achievement than he had to address the misuse of a controversial entertainment fund by his predecessor. Cummings' (1927g, 1927h) forthright and honest handling of this scandal apparently helped it to fade away quickly without any further harm to the university.

Cummings also responded that month to an inquiry from Edward Ellery (1927a), secretary of Sigma Xi (the Society for the Promotion of Research), about whether or not Sigma Xi should establish a chapter at the University of Arizona. Professor Ellery was concerned about the turmoil left over from Cummings' predecessor but was also interested in the university's new Graduate College. Cummings (1927i) informed Professor Ellery that before the previous summer, graduate work had been done at the university under a committee on graduate studies. Under this system, the university had granted many M.A. degrees and some M.S. degrees but only three Ph.D.'s. President Marvin had established a Graduate College, but he had not gotten approval from the board of regents. In Cummings' opinion, the University of Arizona was not yet well enough equipped to develop a Graduate College and promote upper-level graduate studies. After considering Cummings' comments, Professor Ellery (1927b) decided to defer the installation of Sigma Xi until a new president was appointed "or until the positive effects of the recent rupture in the organization are countered by new forward movements." Cummings (1927j) was disappointed and requested that the university be reconsidered in the future.

In the month of May, Cummings was also forced to address a complaint from Dean Gurdon Butler to the board of regents about the retention of one of Butler's staff, Dr. Davis. Cummings (1927k) became angry that Butler had not brought the complaint to him, and he asked Regent F. J. Crider why Butler "wasn't man enough to come and talk over the thing face to face rather than appealing immediately to the Board of Regents?" Crider (1927a) agreed that Butler should have put his complaint in writing and submitted it to Cummings but recommended that Cummings not undertake any plans that would appear to reduce the organization of any department.

On the first day of June, Cummings gave the university's commencement speech and talked about youth adapting to a changing and progressing world (*Arizona Daily Star* 1927b). Governor Hunt (1927d) then informed Cummings that he had written Glen Frank, president of the University of Wisconsin, and offered Frank the same position at the University of Arizona for a salary of $10,500. Hunt wanted a liberal Progressive (such as Frank) for president and was disappointed not to have heard back yet from Frank. Later that month, Regent Tally (1927c) wrote Cummings and requested that he submit to Tally all the applications for the university president position; Tally assumed that Cummings was not on the search committee because he was a candidate for the position himself. Cummings (1927l) informed Tally that he was not a candidate for the presidency. Sounding like he was on the defensive, Cummings stated that he was "trying to serve the state [as] best we know how, under what all know are trying circumstances." Furthermore, he was "seeking no favors" and had no "personal ambitions."

However, rumors of Cummings' being a candidate for permanent president persisted. In late June, Regent Crider (1927b) wrote Cummings again and stated that "I cannot believe that you are really interested in the job, with your knowledge of the difficulties that would be encountered by any local man." According to Crider, everyone expected that an "outside man" would be best suited for the job, and as long as Cummings was a candidate, "some good men" would be reticent to apply. Cummings was puzzled by Tally's and Crider's letters because he was not a candidate. Cummings (1927m) informed Crider, as he had Tally, that he had no personal ambitions for the presidency.

In early August, one of the candidates for the university president position, Homer Leroy Shantz, visited Arizona and was interviewed by Governor Hunt, Cummings, and others. Crider (1927c) was impressed with Shantz, a professor of botany at the University of Illinois with a Ph.D. from Nebraska, and Crider asked Cummings what he thought. Cummings (1927n) replied that Shantz was "a man of scholarship and excellent personality" and that he seemed to be the best of the men who had applied for the position. Cummings also learned from Governor Hunt that month that the U.S. attorney general had ruled the federal land portion of Cummings' new Arizona Antiquities Act unconstitutional.

Later that month, Cummings took time off from his administrative duties to attend the 1927 Pecos Conference near Santa Fe, New Mexico. He invited several individuals to go along with him and had Emil Haury drive the university car. In addition to Haury and Haury's fiancée, Hulda, Professor Thomas Waterman and student Clara Lee Fraps made the trip (Woodbury 1993). Florence Hawley also had been invited, but her parents refused to let her go without a chaperone. At that conference, the three dozen attendees worked out the famous Pecos classification system for cultures of the American Southwest (Basketmaker I through III and Pueblo I through V).

As the search for a new University of Arizona president intensified in early September, Governor Hunt (1927e) wrote board of regents president Tally and shared his belief that the personality of the person who was selected for president should be carefully considered. Because Cummings was "a lovable character" and was doing a great job, the governor recommended not rushing with a selection and waiting until the end of the year.

At the opening of the fall semester on September 12, Cummings gave a speech to the students (*Tucson Citizen* 1927b). He asked the students to cherish democratic ideals and to realize that their father's reputation or mother's social position would not help them that much. Rather, it was their "own self and what you are able to do that will count most." He also warned them to choose their friends carefully, to try not to be a snob, and to follow a strict schedule and avoid negligence. For Cummings, building a students' character was an essential part of his or her education.

A week later, the *Arizona Daily Star* (Cosulich 1927) interviewed Cummings about his views on education. He pleaded for peace on campus: "Let us give youth something to grow on rather than something to quarrel about." He also argued that an education does not have to involve a conflict between religion and science. This comment may have been in response to an ongoing campaign by the Reverend Richard S. Beal of Tucson to get a state law passed banning the teaching of evolution in Arizona schools. It is interesting to note that Cummings would not allow Arthur I. Brown, a supporter of Reverend Beal, to give a speech concerning their antievolution position on the university campus (Webb 1983b).

The month of September also brought an announcement from the board of regents that they had hired a new president, Homer L. Shantz, but because of previous commitments he would not take office until July 1928 (Martin 1960:150). Cummings was informed that he would be the interim president but could remove the word "acting" from his title. Also that month, Cummings had to address a complaint from Regent Theodora Marsh of Nogales about the university's banking agreements.

In October, Cummings faced two more challenges. One was a complaint by a Hopi delegation that their land was being overrun by cattle and they were not being allowed to perform some of their sacred ceremonies. He also received a request from Governor Hunt that he felt obliged to deny; Hunt (1927f) asked that university employee Albert Roundtree be given a higher salary. Never one to let politics interfere with his sense of justice and fair play, Cummings (1927p) told the governor that Roundtree would not get more money because Roundtree's work had not been very satisfactory and he was unreliable.

Cummings was a fiscal conservative and frugal person and was not readily sympathetic to complaints from university faculty about not having enough money. This was evident when he responded in October to a complaint by Professor James C. Clark of the Electrical Engineering Department. Clark (1927) claimed that because of a lack of money he did not have the equipment he needed. He argued that the lack of financial support for his department would result in "its early stagnation and death." Cummings (1927q) wrote back an uncharacteristically humorous response: "We are sorry to receive your swan song and sincerely hope that this isn't an invitation to any funeral because we haven't funds enough to buy any flowers at this time." On a more serious note, Cummings stated that he thought the department had enough equipment to do excellent teaching and that he was "not trying to kill [the] department or discredit its work." Only three months later, Clark (1928) was happy to report to Cummings that General Electric Company had donated a $412 electrical motor to his department after learning of their need for one.

The end of October was an important occasion for the university because a beautiful new library building was dedicated (Martin 1960:151). Cummings invited former president Rufus B. von KleinSmid and his wife to attend the opening. Von KleinSmid was a guest speaker, and he praised the progress being made at the university and thanked Cummings for his role in that progress (Lutrell 1947).

In early November, Cummings received a letter from W. B. Bizzell (1927), president of the University of Oklahoma in Norman, requesting information about the University of Arizona's policy on forbidding students to drive cars on campus and to date other students. Bizzell's university had banned those activities, and the ban was generating a lot of protests. Cummings (1927r) wrote President Bizzell that the University of Arizona did not restrict the students' use of cars on campus, nor did the university forbid dating among students. According to Cummings, students do not become responsible citizens through attempts "to regulate their lives in petty details." Although Cummings was a strict disciplinarian, he was also a progressive and believed that young people needed to learn to make their own right choices, and thus he was against restricting their freedoms.

In the month of November, Cummings also had to deny another personal request by Governor Hunt (1927g), who asked Cummings if he would allow the daughter of one of Hunt's close friends, T. C. McReynolds, back in school after she had an "indiscretion with a man." Again true to his strong Victorian moral beliefs, Cummings (1927s) told the governor that he could not do so because she had secretly gotten married, had not informed the dean of women as required, and had then withdrawn from the university and lied about the reason for her withdrawal. Cummings argued that "we are here to teach these boys and girls to be frank, straight forward, and honest." Therefore, "any condoning to a disregard for these principles reacts tremendously in breaking down the morale standards of our young people."

Having great respect for Cummings' moral values, Hunt (1927h) wrote back and thanked Cummings for his courteous reply, "which I think covers the situation very well." Hunt noted that he always tried to help his friends but that he did not take offense at Cummings refusal because he had confidence in Cummings' ability and integrity. Furthermore, the governor told Cummings that he appreciated the fact that Cummings was the first university president who had shown Hunt such kindness and courtesy. Hunt had known a few university presidents, having been elected governor of Arizona several times since 1912 (Goff 1973).

In mid December, Governor Hunt (1927i) informed Cummings that because of the governor's concerns about the appearance of undue influence over the university's affairs, he would not be attending the next board of regents meeting as Cummings had requested. Hunt stated that he avoided contacts with the students and faculty, as well as the board of regents, so as to not appear to inject politics into the university's management. The governor also informed Cummings that "there has never been, and probably never will be, a President of the University that I respect more and for whom I have such love and veneration than you." Cummings (1927t) returned the compliment the next day, telling Hunt of Cummings' reciprocal respect and high regards for the governor because Hunt was deeply interested in the best welfare of the university and had "shown a spirit of fairness, justice, and appreciation of what a state university means to the commonwealth."

In January 1928, Homer Shantz visited the University of Arizona and gave a speech in which he praised Cummings' work as president (Martin

1960:151). That month the board of regents began looking at the salary scale of the university to determine whether it should be raised. Cummings was asked his recommendation, and he supported a salary increase. However, Cummings became angry that Professor Charles Pickrell had complained directly to the board of regents about not receiving a salary advance that year, which Cummings felt was totally inappropriate. He wrote to board of regents president Robert Tally and expressed concerns about the manner in which the professor had complained. Cummings (1928d) stated that Pickrell did not get a salary increase that year because his salary was already as high as those in the Agricultural Extension Services. Cummings admonished Pickrell for not discussing the matter with him personally, instead of making indirect complaints to the board of regents.

Cummings also responded that month to an information request from Earl Hudelson (1928), professor of education at the University of Minnesota, about the University of Arizona's policy on class size. Cummings (1928e) reported that the university administration did not like large class sizes but had been forced to expand some classes to thirty-five or even seventy-five students, "beyond what we consider a healthful number." Cummings considered any class over a hundred students a "great mob."

In February, Cummings faced other controversy—a complaint from T. L. Carty, president of the Tucson Typographical Union, that the university was going to use an out-of-state, nonunion publisher to print the university's student body publication, entitled *1928 Desert* (Hunt 1928a, 1928b; Tally 1928a). With Cummings' guidance, the students were able to get an acceptable bid for their publication from a Phoenix printer, and the *1928 Desert* was printed without further controversy. Also that month Cummings (1928f) reported to the governor regarding the pending establishment of the Arizona Pioneers Society headquarters on the campus of the university.

At the end of April, Cummings had to defend himself against accusations from Harvey Zorbaugh (1928), professor at New York University. Professor Zorbaugh was upset with comments Cummings had made about his extension courses at Phoenix Union High School, and he threatened Cummings with an "unpleasant libel suit" for malicious gossip. Cummings (1928h) calmly responded that he was unaware of what Zorbaugh was taking about, except that Cummings had raised the question of why extension courses were being taught in Arizona by a university in New York when the University of Arizona had its own extension course program. Cummings argued that it would be unethical for a University of Arizona staff member to go into the state of New York and organize extension work there. There is no record of Zorbaugh's response in Cummings' archives.

May was the last month of Cummings' correspondence as president, presumably because he then participated in his annual summer field season. Earlier that month, Cummings (1928i) wrote Elsie Lee Turner of the University of California–Berkeley with his opinions about junior colleges. He believed that junior colleges should train students for the semiskilled professions or vocations and teach fundamental courses for freshman and sophomore students who wanted to enter four-year programs. He did not find much value in junior college degrees.

Another educator, David S. Hill (1928), research professor of education at the University of Alabama, asked Cummings about the functions of a university president. The key, in Cummings' (1928j) opinion, was for the president to not only know how to deal with men and women, but also have "endless tact and patience." These are the very same personal qualities that Cummings displayed during his short but important tenure as University of Arizona president.

16

"There Is a Plan and System and Progress in Every Phase"

The Arizona State Museum, 1927–1937

For more than two decades, despite limited funding from the university, Cummings had kept the State Museum open and filled with artifacts from Arizona and around the world. He had a long-term vision for the Arizona State Museum, but it was old-fashioned and focused mostly on increasing the number of items on display and enlarging the museum itself. He paid less attention to key issues of concern today—record keeping, storage conditions, and conservation (Thompson 1995:652). Even his exhibits were like cabinets of curiosity, jammed full of objects having a minimal amount of labeling and explanation. Cummings believed that all objects should be on display, not in storage, so all open spaces were used for display, including tabletops and ceilings. Emil Haury (2004c:133), who began working at the State Museum in 1925, later called this cluttered look "horror vacui." Yet during the difficult times of the 1930s Depression, Cummings was able to achieve one of his long-term goals: the construction of a separate museum building at a prime location on the university campus.

One of Cummings' greatest challenges for the museum had been a lack of adequate staff. According to Haury (2004c), this single factor contributed significantly to Cummings' insufficient attention to museum record keeping and conservation, tasks usually assigned to professional staff at institutions with adequate budgets. Every semester, Cummings would recruit a student volunteer or two to help out in the museum. For more than a decade, Cummings' sister Emma had lived with Byron and Isabelle in Tucson and was his sole paid museum assistant. Raymond Thompson (1995:652) noted that for $50 a month, Emma served as "caretaker, receptionist, duster, docent, guard and tour guide."

The State Museum's budget increased significantly in 1927, when Cummings became president of the university, because the museum's budget was under the direct control of the president (Haury 2004c). Cummings was then able to hire his former graduate student Florence Hawley as catalogue and research assistant. Emma still held her position as assistant, and Haury also continued with his museum duties. With new help, Cummings could expand the museum's hours, and it was open seven days a week, including Sunday afternoons from 2:00 to 4:00 p.m. From then on, Cummings had money to hire his graduate students to work in the State Museum.

The Mission of the State Museum

In mid February of 1929, Cummings published a lengthy article in the *Arizona Daily Star* (1929a) that presented his views on museums and education. To him, the central role of the museum should be to educate students and the public about the prehistoric past in the Southwest, so that their knowledge was not dominated by "superstitions and mystery." The Arizona State Museum collection, which at that time contained around 25,000 catalogued specimens, was to be considered a "laboratory, a demonstration and a show-room in which the facts of the ancient and the modern development of the earth and its inhabitants can be practically presented."

Exhibits of objects, which Cummings called "real things," in his opinion presented the development of humans "in such a clear and forceful manner that the casual visitor, as well as the student, has his knowledge clarified and learns that there is a plan and system and progress in every phase of the universe about him." Furthermore, he noted, archaeological evidence in the Southwest showed that the early Americans overcame many great obstacles and "achieved as great things as early men in other parts of the world." Therefore, Cummings argued, why should Americans not receive credit for their early accomplishments? This was a question other Americans had been asking as well, at a time when there was a concerted search for American origins and values separate from those of Europe (Kammen 1991).

The State Museum displays, in Cummings' opinion, also supplemented and strengthened the work of other University of Arizona departments and enriched the lives of out-of-state visitors. The museum had great potential to educate tourists, many of whom would become citizens of Arizona, he thought, "if they knew her resources more fully." But to accomplish its educational mission, Cummings concluded, the Arizona State Museum needed more room and the means to keep constant the stream of visitors and students that came to see its collections.

Room space at the university was difficult to find, but Cummings worked quickly to take advantage of the construction of the new stadium on the southeastern part of campus. Dedicated in the fall of 1929, the seven-thousand-seat athletic stadium was partly financed by donations raised primarily by E. P. Mathenson (Martin 1960). Cummings donated $250 of his own money. He also made arrangements to move into some of the rooms that would be located in the back of the stadium where it was being closed off for indoor use. He thought the move would expand the museum's collection space.

His enthusiasm for the new museum location was dampened, however, when his beloved wife, Isabelle, passed away the next month. She had been ill for the past year and died at the Mayo Brothers Clinic in Rochester, Minnesota, where she was receiving medical care (*Arizona Daily Star* 1929b; *Tucson Citizen* 1929). Two of Cummings' university colleagues, Andrew E. Douglass and Frank Fowler, served as pallbearers. Members of the P.E.O. and Delphian Society, organizations in which she had been an active participant, attended her memorial. She was buried in the Evergreen Cemetery in Tucson.

Cummings forged on, and in the spring of 1930 the State Museum was moved into its new quarters on the first floor of the west wing of the stadium building. This move did not provide much additional square footage, according to Haury (2004c:141), and the location under the bleachers "was not advantageous to a museum's exhibit needs." Cummings filled the sloping ceiling under the bleachers with dozens of Governor Hunt's donated baskets. Later, a newly acquired mounted buffalo became a favorite of schoolchildren at the museum's new location (Haury 2004c:fig. 4).

Cummings continued to expand the museum's collections during the 1930s, despite the economic depression that strained the university's financial resources. In 1931, he reported that he had arranged, with the assistance of Laura Page of Tucson, a ninety-nine-year loan of a collection of ancient Paleolithic and Neolithic stone implements from the National Museum of St. Germain in France (University of Arizona 1931a:300). Cummings did not record what he exchanged for those artifacts, but an inventory of Southwestern Indian specimens in European museums lists thirty-seven artifacts given in 1931 by the Arizona State Museum to the National Museum of St. Germain (Kaemlein 1967:92–93). Also that year, the Metropolitan Museum of Art in New York agreed to loan the Arizona State Museum a collection of Egyptian artifacts for one year. Furthermore, Harold Gladwin, of the Gila Pueblo Archaeological Foundation, donated to the State Museum artifacts collected from the Little Colorado and Verde rivers in Arizona.

Repeating his frequent refrain about space, Cummings (1931e) wrote E. R. Rieson, dean of the College of Letters, Arts, and Sciences, about the size of laboratory space allotted to the museum in the new stadium building. Cummings argued that his current arrangement would be good for another year or two but would soon be too crowded "to carry on all of the phases of work that our students are able to carry on in their investigations." He requested that a corner of the room in the north end of the stadium be converted from storage to a space where his students could prepare their fossil specimens, in particular the Pleistocene animal skeletons that he and his students had been collecting from locations within the state.

In 1932, Cummings reported that the Arizona State Museum had received from the Southwest Museum in Los Angeles a model of the ancient pueblo that Charles Van Bergen's crew had dug at Casa Grande National Monument and a collection of early red-on-buff pottery recovered from the Grewe site, located near Casa Grande (University of Arizona 1932a:239). In addition, Harold Gladwin donated to the State Museum a collection of pottery from eastern Arizona and a collection of potsherds from other sites, with "full data accompanying them," presumably meaning that their locations were recorded. Finally, the National Museum in Washington (probably meaning Neil Judd) sent the Arizona State Museum a small collection of pottery from Elden Pueblo near Flagstaff. These pots may be some of those recovered in 1926 by Jesse W. Fewkes of the Bureau of American Ethnology in the course of a project that angered Cummings and others and led to establishment of the Arizona Antiquities Act and the founding of the Museum of Northern Arizona.

16.1 Interior of the Arizona State Museum when it was located under the stadium, 1934 (courtesy of Arizona Historical Society/Tucson, #AHS72899)

A photograph of the inside of the Arizona State Museum in 1934, when it was still located at the stadium, shows a room full of glass cases stuffed with artifacts (fig. 16.1). Baskets fill every possible open space on the walls and roof columns. Numerous artifacts are on display, but artifact labels are sparse.

The summer of 1934 was a sad one for Cummings and the museum. On July 7, his sister and faithful museum assistant, Emma, died. She was in her late eighties. For many years Cummings had relied on Emma to keep the museum open during his absence. That year did bring some positive news, however, when Cummings announced that he had obtained a $1,000 grant from the Carnegie Foundation for seven new display cases (University of Arizona 1934a:228).

Finally, a New State Museum

The 1930s were difficult times for many Americans, with more than one-quarter of the nation unemployed. U.S. president Franklin Roosevelt's administration designed a variety of huge federal work programs to put people back to work. Many of these involved large government construction projects. Archaeological excavation and restoration projects on federal land in the Southwest and Southeast were not only eligible, but also desirable because the local communities were expected to benefit economically after the work was done (Fagette 1996).

When the Public Works Administration (PWA) construction program was initiated in the mid 1930s, President Homer Shantz convinced the Arizona Legislature in September 1934 that the board of regents should accept loans and grants from the PWA to construct several new buildings on campus (Collins 1999; Lutrell 1947). These buildings were part of the ten-year building program he had already planned for the university when he first arrived on campus in 1928, but which the Depression had forced him to shelve (Martin 1960). The Arizona Legislature accepted the terms of the PWA financing, which involved an outright gift of 30 percent of construction costs, with the remaining 70 percent paid back as a thirty-year low-interest loan. Altogether, the University of Arizona received $1.02 million from the PWA to implement Shantz's building program.

One of the buildings was a new Arizona State Museum building. Shantz may have included this building—and made it a high priority—as a favor to Cummings since he had performed well as president of the university at a time of great turmoil just before Shantz arrived. As a result, the museum building was one of the first constructed, being completed on December 19, 1935, at a cost of $90,342.57. This attractive, two-story, red brick and sandstone building was designed in an Italian Renaissance style by architect Roy Place and built by J. J. Garfield Building Company.

The new building included rooms for exhibits, classrooms, storerooms, offices, a photographic studio, and a fumigation room. It served not only as the Arizona State Museum, but also as the headquarters for the Department of Archaeology. The building was designed with huge arching windows to provide natural light, but they allowed too much light on the exhibits, and soon some of the windows had to be sealed off. Second-story guardrails in the new museum were used to hang Navajo blankets, and baskets were placed near the ceiling (fig. 16.2).

University funding for the State Museum increased steadily from 1925 to 1930, and then the Depression took its toll (table 16.1). With the exception of 1932, the museum's budget decreased every year from 1930 to

16.2 Interior of the new Arizona State Museum building, 1936 (courtesy of Arizona Historical Society/Tucson, #AHS73191)

1935. Even the increase in 1935 was only to the amount that had been budgeted in 1933. In addition, Cummings and other faculty members took big salary cuts in 1933, averaging about 17 percent (Martin 1960:163). Being a frugal person, Cummings believed that good management meant having money left over in his annual budget. Despite the difficult economic times, he managed to keep the museum open and continued to obtain artifacts for its collection.

In September 1936, Cummings prepared a proposed budget for the next two academic years. Gordon Baldwin was listed as assistant director and part-time cataloger at a salary of $900 annually. For the 1936–1937 budget, Cummings proposed $1,000 for the purchase of the Perry M. Williams collection of Pima and Papago baskets already on loan at the State Museum; $2,400 for new cases; and $1,000 for fieldwork. An authentic Babylonian brick was one of his unusual acquisitions that year (University of Arizona 1937, 1938).

The budget for the 1937–1938 academic year was Cummings' last as di-

TABLE 16.1. Budgets for Arizona State Museum and Department of Archaeology, University of Arizona, 1926–1937

Academic Year, Ending	*Arizona State Museum Budgeted Amount*	*Department of Archaeology Budgeted Amount*
1926	$3,822.11	$5,228.14
1927	$6,223.65	$5,920.18
1928	$6,207.78	$7,427.14
1929	$5,322.78	$7,627.28
1930	$5,247.59	$8,610.65
1931	$6,406.77	$7,392.08
1932	$4,850.24	$9,956.54
1933	$3,788.39	$7,363.68
1934	$4,200.98	$7,646.22
1935	$3,892.73	$8,023.64
1936	$4,373.00	unknown

Sources: University of Arizona 1926b, 1928a, 1929a, 1929c, 1930c, 1931b, 1932b, 1934c, 1935b, 1936b, 1937b.

rector of the Arizona State Museum. In this budget, he requested $2,000 for the Sam E. Day collection of mummies, textiles, and other materials that he had coveted since the early 1920s. He also sought $2,400 for more museum cases and another $1,000 for fieldwork at Kinishba and investigation of caves of the early Archaic period. Furthermore, he proposed raising Baldwin's annual salary to $1,000.

Although Cummings wanted the Arizona State Museum to be "Grand Central Station" for archaeology in Arizona, he had a larger vision than just a single museum in Tucson. He also helped to create museums in several other Arizona communities. These include Fort Lowell historic park in Tucson (1929, dedicated 1963), Tuzigoot Museum near Clarkdale (1934), Smoki Museum in Prescott (1935), and Kinishba Museum (1940) in Whitewater. All but the last museum are still in existence more than a half-century later.

The State Museum, however, remains one of Cummings' greatest legacies. Despite the limitations of his natural history approach, the current reputation of the Arizona State Museum can be partly attributed to his long-term vision and persistent efforts for three decades. He helped make the State Museum one of the most important museums in Arizona and created a foundation that Emil Haury could expand into an internationally known institution. Haury (2004c) continued with Cummings' strong educational mission but also committed the museum to displays that exhibited ideas rather than relics and to the timely publishing of museum research projects.

17

"Shall Arizona Save and Preserve Her Heritage?"

The Arizona Antiquities Act of 1927

Arizona has a large number of ancient ruins scattered across its rugged landscape of mountains, mesas, canyons, and desert valleys. Interest in those ruins has long attracted explorers, commercial pothunters, local amateurs, and professional archaeologists. The 1906 Antiquities Act put the federal government in firm control of archaeology on public land through a permit system for archaeologists. This law allowed the Smithsonian Institution and, ten years later, the National Park Service, to exert a major influence on American archaeology. But enforcement was limited in the Southwest's wide-open spaces, and local citizens were not happy with Washington's control of what they considered their own resources. By the 1910s and later, local archaeology organizations were able to compete for excavation permits with the eastern institutions that had dominated archaeology in the Southwest for decades.

Cummings appears to have wanted to do more than just compete—he wanted to take complete control of Arizona archaeology through a powerful state law. With this law, he would have a legal basis for denying, or approving, archaeology projects in his state. In his view, this law should be applicable both to relic hunters and to prominent eastern-based archaeologists who were excavating in Arizona: Alfred Kidder, Jesse Fewkes, and Earl Morris, for example. Cummings' primary purpose was to ensure that at least a portion of the artifacts retrieved from ancient sites, regardless of who had obtained them, were deposited in the Arizona State Museum. Better there or in another museum within the state, he believed, than in a museum back east. His colleagues at the eastern institutions strongly disagreed with him. They believed that the

Southwest's prehistoric past was not owned by a state but was a national treasure that should be shared with other parts of the country.

Regardless of Cummings' personal motivations, the passage of the 1927 Arizona Antiquities Act was a landmark event for historic preservation in the state. It gave state officials (that is, Cummings) the authority to prevent the illegal removal of artifacts and fossils from state land and to establish professional standards and procedures for archaeologists.

Cummings was not the first to attempt to get an archaeology law in place in Arizona. A group of late-nineteenth-century businessmen in Phoenix became concerned about the destruction of archaeological sites in Arizona through farming and vandalism; in 1895 they founded the Arizona Antiquarian Association in Prescott (Siegel 1975; Wilcox 1988). One of their first projects entailed the stabilization of Montezuma Castle along the Verde River, and the site was declared a national monument in 1906.

In 1897, the Arizona Antiquarian Association unsuccessfully petitioned the Territorial Legislature to pass a law to protect ancient sites in Arizona. When their president, Joshua Miller, died in 1901, the Arizona Antiquarian Association became inactive. In 1926 they were formally disbanded (Wilcox 1987).

A New Archaeology Sheriff in Arizona

The fight for local control of archaeology in Arizona intensified in September 1915 when Byron Cummings moved from Utah to Tucson. Having already been active for a decade in the archaeology of southern Utah and northeastern Arizona, Cummings was well aware of the vandalism of archaeological sites in the Southwest when he arrived at his new job. In a new position of authority, and a nationally known archaeological explorer, he quickly became a spokesperson for the protection of Arizona's prehistoric and historic sites.

It is not clear when Cummings decided that a law protecting Arizona's archaeological resources was needed in Arizona. In early 1916—soon after moving to Arizona—in a letter to supporters of the Arizona Archaeological Society, Cummings expressed his public disapproval of eastern institutions' removal of Arizona's ancient artifacts out-of-state. In this letter, Cummings stated, "Five expeditions from eastern museums are booked for Arizona this summer. Can the state afford to wait any longer without insisting that she keep at least a share of what belongs to her here in her own museum and let her own people have a chance to see and know something of the ancient and modern Indian culture of the region?" (Johnston 1966:43).

The earliest mention in Cummings' archives of his interest in an archaeology law in Arizona appears in 1926. In December of that year he wrote Samuel Day Sr. and apologized for not being able to purchase Day's extensive collection of Basketmaker material that had been offered to President Marvin for $5,000 two years before (Day 1924). A frustrated Cummings (1926f) informed Day that his plans had been "blocked again" and that he would "have to propose a bill to secure the collection." Cummings was given that chance only a few months later, when he was appointed acting president of the University of Arizona. As president, Cummings had contacts with the state legislature, as well as with Governor George Hunt, who was a big supporter of promoting and protecting Arizona's history (Goff 1973).

Several events in 1926 probably contributed to Cummings' seriously contemplating an Arizona Antiquities Act that year. Excavations by Jesse Walter Fewkes at Elden Pueblo that summer infuriated Cummings and the Flagstaff community (Downum 1990). Cummings was already unhappy about excavations in Canyon de Chelly by Earl Morris of the American Museum of Natural History, which had removed a large collection of well-preserved Basketmaker material to New York City (Kidder 1927a). In addition, Morris (1928a) recovered rare artifacts, including cedar bark torches and hafted picks, from a prehistoric salt mine in the Verde Valley in the fall of 1926.

Fewkes (1898) had been excavating sites in Arizona since the 1890s, motivated by the goal of obtaining pottery with designs that could be analyzed to provide support for his tracing of Hopi migration legends. He had worked in the Flagstaff area beginning in April 1900, excavating sites in what is now Wupatki National Monument, and he obtained a large collection of pots from the Black Falls area along the Little Colorado River (Fewkes 1900). After working in various other locations in the Southwest—such as Mesa Verde, Casa Grande, and the Verde Valley—Fewkes decided to return to the Flagstaff region to excavate in Elden Pueblo. As head of the Bureau of American Ethnology (BAE) in Washington, D.C., Fewkes was able to obtain a permit to dig Elden Pueblo because it was located on U.S. Forest Service land.

At the age of seventy-five, Fewkes returned to Flagstaff to dig after receiving some interesting pottery from burials and cremations that had been exposed by a roadcut in Young's Canyon (Downum 1990).[1] These materials were sent to him by J. C. Clarke, custodian at Wupatki National Monument. Clarke's pots were very attractive, "reawakening Fewkes' legendary lust for southwestern pottery specimens" (Downum 1990:357). In Fewkes' (1926a) report on these pots, he chastised the "new archaeologists" for their obsession with stratigraphy and ceramic seriation and supported the validity of his own ideas about Hopi migrations as plotted through pottery designs. His return to Flagstaff was intended to provide further proof of his proposal for a new culture designation for the Flagstaff region, which he called Tokonabi.

Fewkes began his Elden Pueblo excavations in June of 1926, using horses and plows to clear rooms and burial areas of their overburden. Fewkes' talented assistant, BAE ethnologist John P. Harrington, took notes. That summer, Fewkes excavated more than 150 human skeletons and 500 associated pots. He also dug into thirty-four rooms and a rectangular kiva, with the intent that they be reconstructed and that Elden Pueblo become a national monument (Downum 1990; Kelly 1970).

Harold Colton and Byron Cummings were not pleased with Fewkes' work at Elden Pueblo. Disagreements between Colton and Fewkes soon appeared in print. In a report in *Science*, the nation's most prestigious professional journal, Fewkes (1926b) claimed to have discovered Elden Pueblo in May of that year and given the ruin its name. Colton (1927) replied in a February issue of *Science* that he, not Fewkes, had discovered Elden Pueblo, had given it the name Sheep Hill Pueblo, and had published its location in 1918; furthermore, it was Colton who had suggested to Fewkes that he dig Elden Pueblo. Fewkes' (1927a) apology for claiming to have discovered Elden Pueblo was printed in the same issue of *Science*.

When the citizens of Flagstaff realized that Fewkes had shipped all the Elden Pueblo artifacts back to the Smithsonian Institution, they became outraged. J. C. Clarke, Fewkes' guide, told the *Coconino Sun* newspaper in mid August that Fewkes' excavation represented "the latest notable example of hogging of Arizona's archaeological treasures" (Downum

1990:364). Cummings also was quoted in that newspaper article, stating that he had requested that Fewkes leave part of the collection somewhere in Arizona, not necessarily the Arizona State Museum, but Fewkes had refused. Cummings also complained that he was not even allowed the opportunity to examine the pots before they left the state. This incident so offended the local citizens of Flagstaff that they became determined to establish a local museum and research center (Downum 1990). Within a year, the Northern Arizona Society of Science and Art was formed by Harold Colton and Grady Gammage, with Cummings appointed as a member of the board of trustees (Cline 1994). The first exhibits were held in the Flagstaff Women's Club, and Cummings gave the opening lecture on June 2. The current Museum of Northern Arizona buildings were not completed until 1936 (Miller 1991).[2]

Arizona's First Antiquities Act

With the Fewkes incident fresh on his mind, Cummings decided in February 1927, immediately after being appointed acting president of the University of Arizona, that he would pursue passage of an antiquities act in Arizona. He envisioned that this legislation would be written so that the State Museum would have complete control over the excavation of sites within the state as well as the disposition of the artifacts that were retrieved from the sites. Working with Democratic senator William C. Joyner of Pima County, Cummings saw Senate Bill No. 97 introduced into the Eighth Legislature of the State of Arizona on February 16, 1927 (*Journal of the Senate* 1927:297). Although it was a relatively short bill, it had far-reaching implications.

This bill was called "An Act to Prevent Further Despoliation of the Pre-historical Sections of Arizona." It had a preamble that declared,

> WHEREAS for many years the pre-historic ruins of the state have been exploited and ravaged by individuals and scientists alike for commercial purposes, robbing Arizona of its treasure of antiquity, and WHEREAS numerous institutions are being granted permission to excavate the ruins of the state and remove the priceless articles obtained from these ruins to other states and other lands, thus depriving the people of Arizona for all time that which is justly theirs, therefore [Senate Bill No. 97 should be enacted].

The preamble was probably written by Cummings, since it specifically addressed his concern about artifacts going out of state.

As originally drafted, Senate Bill No. 97 required that one-half of all archaeological collections excavated from land in Arizona—whether federal, state, or private land—be deposited in the Arizona State Museum. Violations would be considered a misdemeanor punishable by forfeiture of all materials to the state and a fine not to exceed $500, or imprisonment in the county jail of not more than six months, or both. Cummings' belief that Arizona archaeology should be controlled by the state was supported by Governor George Hunt, a Progressive Democrat who was a strong states' rights advocate and an opponent of federal influence in Arizona.

Senate Bill No. 97 moved through the senate and house surprisingly fast, probably because there were no state appropriations attached to the bill. However, revisions were made to the original bill, much to Cummings' disappointment. On March 2, Republican senator Walter Runke of Coconino County recommended that the bill be modified in two ways. The first was designed to share the state's artifacts with a broader constituency, requiring 50 percent of the collections to go not to the Arizona State Museum but to any public museum in the state of Arizona. The second change, however, solidified Cummings' control of archaeology in the state by requiring that a permit be obtained from the "Archaeological Branch of the University of Arizona and from the Board of Supervisors of the County wherein the same is to be taken." By March 5 the modified bill was passed by the senate unanimously and was then sent to the house.

Although the house approved the bill within a week, Democratic representative Earl C. Slipher of Coconino County recommended two more significant changes (*Journal of the House of Representatives* 1927:508). One was an expansion of the types of ancient sites protected, including fossilized footprints and "hieroglyphics." The other change narrowed the scope of the bill, removing the category of private land from the bill. With these changes, only three representatives, all Democrats, voted against the bill: Nellie T. Bush of Yuma County, Thomas Cowperthwaite of Cochise County, and W. E. Oxsheer of Cochise County.

On March 11, Governor Hunt signed Senate Bill No. 97. The next day the *Arizona Republican* (1927) published a short article on the new law to protect ruins in Arizona. In early April, Hunt (1927a) congratulated

Cummings, requesting that he inform archaeologists of the Southwest Museum in Los Angeles, whom Hunt had learned were planning a dig at Casa Grande National Monument, that they would have to put 50 percent of all the relics they found in the Arizona State Museum. For reasons stated below, Cummings was not able to make this demand of the Southwest Museum project at Casa Grande.

At a Rotary Club talk on July 11 in Tucson, Cummings informed the crowd of the new Arizona law and explained that it had come about because of his disgust that the federal law allowed some of Arizona's choicest collections to be sent east only to be stored in national museums and thereby preventing their study by Arizona students. Cummings mentioned Fewkes' excavations at Elden Pueblo and his out-of-state shipment of five hundred ceramic pots as an example of the problem with the federal law.

Several eastern institutions were soon upset with this new Arizona law, fearing loss of control over their expeditions to Arizona (Wilcox 1988:22). In mid February, only one day after the senate bill was introduced, Alfred Tozzer (1927) of the Peabody Museum at Harvard University wrote Cummings a letter complaining that the law would mean that the Peabody Museum could no longer afford to excavate ruins in Arizona. Clark Wissler (1927) of the American Museum of Natural History believed the law was mostly a bluff but that it "would probably involve us in expense and troublesome litigation if we undertook work at this time." Earl Morris (1927) of the Carnegie Institution stated, "Personally, I am so certain that the law cannot be made to pertain to the lands controlled by the Department of the Interior that I would very much like to go ahead and make a test case of it. However, for diplomatic reasons, I have decided not to do so."

Earl Morris was correct in his assessment of the new Arizona Antiquities Act. In late July, the acting U.S. attorney general, William D. Mitchell (1927), declared the portion of the law that included federal lands to be unconstitutional. This ruling was based on the fact that the State of Arizona had no proprietary or sovereign right to interfere with federal land and the objects obtained from those lands.

Governor Hunt sent Cummings a copy of the attorney general's opinion in early August, and Cummings (1927o) wrote back to the governor thanking him for the copy. Cummings told the governor that he did not agree with the attorney general's ruling and that because private land had been removed from the original senate bill, Cummings would have to work hard to educate private owners about the value of archaeology. He also hoped that the State Museum would be given its fair share of excavation permits and recommended that the state carry out a vigorous campaign of excavation and investigation to "secure our just share of information and material."

Competition for Control of Arizona Archaeology

Dissatisfied that the 1927 Arizona Antiquities Act was applicable only to state land, Cummings was determined to get a more comprehensive act passed. During the next decade he made several attempts to get a new antiquities bill through the Arizona Legislature. However, his attempt to gain control of Arizona archaeology was threatened by a newcomer to Arizona, Odd S. Halseth.

Halseth was a naturalized citizen from Norway and a former student and employee of Edgar L. Hewett (Wilcox 1993). Halseth had been hired in 1927 as director of the newly created Arizona Museum in Phoenix (now called the Phoenix Museum of History). After his resignation the next year, Halseth was hired in 1929 by the City of Phoenix. His new job was to develop the Hohokam ruin called Pueblo Grande into a museum. Halseth was a resourceful and capable administrator, but he had questionable archaeological skills and was a strong-willed, uncompromising person. His contentious nature led to conflicts with other archaeologists, especially those who worked under him at Pueblo Grande, including Julian Hayden, who worked at Pueblo Grande from 1936 to 1940.

Halseth (1929) was appointed chair of the newly formed Southwestern Archaeological Federation (SAF), created to "safeguard archaeology as a science." Composed primarily of archaeologists from institutions in southern California, the seven-member committee of the SAF was ratified by the secretary of the interior, Ray L. Wilbur. The SAF proposed that archaeologists in the Southwest should be certified by a national committee. Cummings was not a member of the SAF, perhaps because he didn't like the idea of a national committee influencing archaeology in his state.

To assist his efforts at developing an archaeology program at Pueblo Grande, Halseth established the Archaeological Commission of the City of Phoenix. Concerned about professionalism in Southwestern archaeology, he wrote Governor John C. Phillips in mid November, explaining the "archaeological situation" in Arizona (Halseth 1929). He complained about pothunting and that artifact collections were leaving the state and recommended that a state archaeological commission be appointed to implement the 1927 Arizona Antiquities Act. Halseth proposed that this commission make a study of archaeological sites in Arizona and be given authority by the Department of the Interior and the secretary of agriculture to inspect applications for excavation on federal land. Governor Phillips obliged Halseth and in January 1930 created the Arizona Archaeological Commission, composed of Halseth, Cummings, and Harold Colton of the fledgling museum in Flagstaff. Halseth was appointed secretary.

Attempts at an Expanded Arizona Antiquities Act

Soon after the creation of the Arizona Archaeological Commission, Cummings began working with Hess F. Seaman, an attorney, to prepare a more comprehensive antiquities act for Arizona. In mid January 1930, Seaman sent Cummings a detailed draft of this proposed bill, which was far broader in scope than the 1927 Arizona Antiquities Act. This proposed bill created a state board of archaeology consisting of three members, one of whom was to be the director of the Arizona State Museum. The board of archaeology would be given the authority to acquire, with the consent of the state board of supervisors, "lands containing valuable prehistoric ruins and artifacts" and to designate the ruins as state archaeological monuments. The board of supervisors in each county would be responsible for excavating, restoring, and maintaining their archaeology monuments, but the board of archaeology would adopt the rules and regulations governing that work. Removal of artifacts from the locations from which they were found, for display or other purposes, also would have to be approved by the board of archaeology. Funding to implement the act was to be obtained from gasoline taxes collected annually by the county but was not to exceed $5,000 for any one monument. This bill failed to pass, probably because of the proposed appropriations.

The Arizona Archaeological Commission triad of Halseth, Cummings, and Colton represented the three most influential local archaeological institutions in Arizona. A fourth was soon to be Harold Gladwin, director of the newly founded Gila Pueblo Archaeological Foundation in Globe. Gladwin was a deep-thinking, iconoclastic financier who adopted Southwestern archaeology in 1924 after making his fortune in the New York stock market (Haury and Reid 1985). Established in the winter of 1927–1928, Gladwin's growing research institution needed pottery for its museum, and he was willing to purchase private collections in addition to obtaining them through surveys and excavations. At a meeting of the Arizona Archaeological Commission, Halseth made accusations about Gladwin's pottery purchases but also about his employment of pothunters to help dig sites and his allowing people to sell artifacts not wanted by the Gila Pueblo Museum (Haury 1988). Halseth felt that these actions encouraged illegal digging on public land, and he called for sanctions. As the commission chair, Cummings was obligated to investigate Halseth's charges; he too was concerned about Gila Pueblo being a private museum and amassing a large artifact collection. Moreover, Gladwin's foundation was California based, with no Arizona members on the board of trustees, a situation that Harold Colton thought caused Cummings to be prejudiced against Gladwin.

Harold Gladwin learned of Halseth's accusations from Colton, who was very impressed with the research efforts of Gladwin's staff, and Gladwin invited Cummings to Gila Pueblo to inspect the facility and listen to Gladwin's side of the story. Cummings visited him in May, under the pretense of examining the pottery collection to determine "the potential value of the Institution in providing material and facilities for study by under-graduates at the University of Arizona" (Haury 1988:27). Present at this meeting, in addition to Cummings and Gladwin, were Mrs. MacCurdy, who was Gladwin's business partner and later became his wife; Roy Kirkpatrick, secretary of the Board of Regents of the University of Arizona; and Charles L. Rawlins, counsel and attorney for Gila Pueblo. Gladwin presented a persuasive defense of his institution, noting that Gila Pueblo was run by a board of trustees that intended for Gila Pueblo to benefit both the people of Arizona and the science of archaeology. Cummings asked Gladwin to put a clause in the Gila Pueblo's trust that would prohibit the future removal of Puebloan collections from Arizona, but Gladwin refused on the grounds that such a clause would be too restrictive. However, Gladwin promised to cooperate fully with any regulations that the commission would make and to continue to obtain permits for all of his excavations in Arizona. Haury (1988:29) later recounted that Cummings was pleased with the results of his investigation and "repeatedly gave assurance of his satisfaction with the manner in which Gila Pueblo was conducting its work." Gladwin made sure that Cummings stayed happy by donating pottery to the State Museum's collections.[3]

That same year, Cummings inspected another archaeological investigation in Arizona by an out-of-state institution—excavations by the Charles Van Bergen–Los Angeles Museum Expedition at Casa Grande National Monument. Julian Hayden, who was working with his father, Irwin, recalled that Cummings was furious when he saw the archaeologists using a horse-drawn plow and fresno scrapers to level trash mounds and that Cummings called Julian a "butcherer" (Hackbarth 2001a:11). Later that day, Irwin Hayden, a 1906 graduate of Harvard, placated Cummings by demonstrating the plow and fresno's effectiveness in removing overburden. Cummings then helped the crew with the excavation of some burials.

The issue of Casa Grande artifacts leaving the state, however, became a heated controversy that eventually caused Governor Hunt to accuse the Los Angeles Museum Expedition of looting Arizona's ruins. In March of 1931, Frank Pinkley, the energetic superintendent of Casa Grande National Monument, objected to Hunt's comments in a letter Pinkley wrote to the editor of the *Coolidge News*. Pinkley (1931) noted that the Los Angeles Museum had spent more than $10,000 on its investigations, which benefited the local community and Casa Grande, and that the display of the artifacts in New York was good publicity for the national monument. However, the Los Angeles Museum did not receive another permit to excavate at Casa Grande after work had been "temporarily" stopped in February of that year (*Coolidge News* 1931), probably due to the influence of Cummings and Halseth (Hackbarth 2001a).

Dueling Antiquities Acts

Apparently unhappy with having Cummings in control of Arizona archaeology, in January 1931 Odd Halseth worked with his Phoenix friends to get his own antiquities bill through the Arizona Legislature. Although he sent copies of his draft bill to Cummings and Colton on January 8, he did not seek their support to ensure passage when he had Representative Gertrude B. Leeper of Maricopa County introduce it on January 19 (*Journal of the House of Representatives* 1931:83). Halseth's House Bill No. 46 proposed the establishment of a system of archaeological permits (with a $100 fee), licenses for all personnel involved in an expedition ($5 each), a statewide archaeological commission to oversee the law, creation of three archaeological districts within the state, and an archaeological inspector with an annual salary of $2,400 to $2,600 plus an expense account.

Cummings realized that Halseth wished to be that archaeological inspector and therefore vigorously opposed the bill, seeing it as a threat to his own attempts to control archaeology in the state. Harold Colton (1931a) told Cummings that Halseth's archaeological district system was not logical and that the archaeological inspector should be one of the commissioners. Colton was also opposed to the fee required for obtaining an archaeological license, calling it an "inexcusable tax on scientific work." Harold Gladwin (1931) was concerned that the archaeological inspector was given too much control.

Less than two weeks after receiving Colton's letter of concern, Cummings sent out his own letters opposing Halseth's bill to his friends in the Arizona house. Representative Rapp wrote back to Cummings that Halseth's bill would be held in committee for further study. Cummings (1931c) also wrote President Homer L. Shantz of the University of Arizona informing him that Governor Hunt, reelected to office again, opposed Halseth's bill because Hunt felt that "the responsibility for the care of the ruins and the keeping track of the work done in the state should devolve, or rest, upon the director of the State Museum, and that all investigations should be tied up as closely as possible with the State University." Furthermore, even if the Arizona State Museum maintained control of archaeology in the state, Cummings did not want to take on the responsibility of having an archaeological inspector "who is desirous of being a little Czar." In Cummings' view, the opportunity for development of the State Museum and the university's Archaeology Department would be "severely curtailed and hampered" if House Bill No. 46 should pass.

On January 30, Democratic representative J. T. Bone of Maricopa County recommended that House Bill No. 46 not be passed. About two weeks later, Democratic representative W. L. Rigney of Maricopa

County, chair of the Committee on Appropriations, recommended a do not pass on House Bill No. 46. It then died in committee.

To counter Halseth's bill, Cummings had his own new antiquities act introduced by Democratic representative D. M. Penny of Pima County in the Tenth Legislature of the State of Arizona in 1931—House Bill No. 137. This bill created an archaeology advisory council, appropriated state money for travel expenses, and allowed the acceptance of federal grant money through the Smithsonian Institution. And, true to Cummings' stubborn nature when he thought he was in the right, it included a section that required 50 percent of all artifacts from federal lands to go to some museum in the state of Arizona.

Harold Colton (1931b) wrote Cummings in February, questioning why federal land was still included in the bill and recommending that the qualifications of the advisory council be specified. Cummings (1931d) wrote back to Colton in March, stating that the issue of federal land permits in Arizona needed the "opinion of some more able court than one Attorney General." However, because the appropriations committee would not approve the proposed expenditure of funds, W. L. Rigney of Maricopa County killed Cummings' Bill No. 137, just as he had killed Halseth's Bill No. 46. No longer president of the University of Arizona, Cummings may not have had the same political power as he did when he was able to get the 1927 state act passed.

Nonetheless, Cummings did not give up on his goal to create a more comprehensive Arizona Antiquities Act. In November 1934, he wrote Senator Paul C. Keefe of Yavapai County about plans for a new archaeology law (Cummings 1934f). This law would cover five main points, including the creation of an archaeology board that could secure and set aside parcels of land with ruins, have the authority to inspect and support all archaeological excavations in the state, and seize and confiscate artifacts in the possession of any dealer or offered for sale in the state. The board of supervisors of each county would maintain the state monuments that were created. Cummings also expressed concern about the federal government, which, in his opinion, "seems very jealous of its authority and control and does not allow any organization to place even a statue or monument of any kind on one of the federal monuments." In December, Cummings (1934i) sent Harold Colton a copy of his five points and urged Colton's support for the passage of a new state archaeology law.

In January 1935, Cummings met with state senator Paul Keefe to prepare another version of the Arizona Antiquities Act. The draft prepared by Keefe proposed the creation of archaeological monuments and that a tenth-of-a-cent gasoline tax be used to fund the implementation of the new law. Cummings (1935k) asked for the addition of language to deal with sellers of artifacts in curio stores and the substitution of the director of the Arizona State Museum for a professor of archaeology as the coordinator of the law, because the former position was "more stable" and is "where it belongs." These are odd comments from the person who held both positions, but it may indicate that Cummings was already thinking about giving up his position as head of the Archaeology Department but staying on as museum director.

Harold Gladwin (1935) requested that Cummings' proposed bill be revised to eliminate the language about the control of buying and selling of artifacts from private land, since that would be declared unconstitutional. Cummings' effort failed again because the tax proposed to fund the new Antiquities Act could not be used for anything but roads.

In 1936 and again in 1937, Cummings was involved in attempts to pass a more comprehensive state archaeology law. Both attempts failed. By that time, however, Cummings was more concerned about the destruction of archaeological sites by pothunters and less with eastern institutions' removal of artifacts out of state. In a November edition of *The Kiva*, Cummings (1936c) asked the rhetorical question, "Shall Arizona Save and Preserve Her Heritage?" In this article, Cummings stated that during the Depression, people had been lenient toward "the destroyers of our ancient history" and that it was time to pass a stronger state law to better protect and preserve Arizona's ruins and historic sites. He requested that readers of *The Kiva* ask their representatives to enact the law he was about to propose in order to "save our rich inheritance . . . from commercial greed and the ignorant seekers for souvenirs and treasure." Furthermore, Cummings argued, the ruins should "be used for the education of the people rather than be despoiled by the selfishness of a few."

To accomplish these goals, Cummings proposed the creation of a commission on state parks and monuments, with members appointed by the governor for six-year terms. Reverting back to his original wishes, Cummings proposed that this commission be given the authority to grant permits to anyone wishing to excavate ruins on state, federal, and private land. His logic was certainly persistent, if fatally flawed.

Emil Haury and the Arizona Antiquities Act

Cummings retired as head of the Department of Archaeology in 1937 and became director emeritus of the Arizona State Museum in 1938. Without his institutional positions of authority, Cummings was no longer a major player in Arizona archaeology and thus was not involved in any further attempts to revise the Arizona Antiquities Act that he had helped pass in 1927. However, taking up Cummings' old torch, the new director of the State Museum, Emil Haury, made a concerted attempt at a new state archaeology law in 1939. Haury's proposal was simple—the creation of an Arizona Commission of Anthropology, appointed by the governor with the advice of the director of the Arizona State Museum. No mention was made of state or private land, and the only appropriations were $300 per year for the travel expenses for each Commissioner and $100 for printing expenses. Haury's bill had the same fate as Cummings' later attempts, and it also failed to pass.

Haury kept pursuing a stronger law, which eventually paid off. In 1950, he negotiated an agreement with the state land commissioner that required archaeologists to get a permit from the Arizona State Museum for work on state land (Thompson 1995:655). A decade later Haury was able to get the Arizona Legislature to pass a comprehensive Arizona Antiquities Act, which serves as the basis for the current state archaeology law (Haury 1960). The 1960 Antiquities Act keeps the Arizona State Museum in control of archaeology on state lands through a system of permits and reporting responsibilities.

18

"A Man of Vision"

Expanding the Archaeology Department

One of the lasting achievements of Byron Cummings in the field of education was his development of the archaeology curriculum at the University of Arizona. After being the sole professor in the Archaeology Department for many years, Cummings' amiable personality and administrative skills won him, in 1927, the appointment of acting president of the university. Using his new status, Cummings increased the budget of the Arizona State Museum and the Archaeology Department and established an archaeology graduate program within the department. His new graduate program required an expanded curriculum, so he added more classes, including a variety of anthropology courses. He and his students also participated in Arizona historical pageants at Casa Grande National Monument in the late 1920s.

Expanding the Archaeology Department

An impressive addition to the Archaeology Department, while Cummings was president, was the hiring of anthropologist Thomas T. Waterman as a visiting professor. Described by Alfred Kroeber (1937) as a brilliant but erratic scholar and a colorful teacher, Waterman received his Ph.D. under Franz Boas at Columbia University. Waterman also attended the 1927 Pecos Conference and is credited by Alfred Kidder with originating the eight-stage Pecos classification system for Southwestern archaeology (Woodbury 1993:92). With the addition of an anthropologist, the department offered courses in linguistics and phonetics. However, after a year of teaching in the Archaeology Department, Waterman accepted a position at the University of Hawaii and then became the territorial historian for Hawaii.

Three of Cummings' best students—Emil Haury, Clara Lee Fraps [Tanner], and Florence Ellis [Hawley]—were accepted into the new graduate program at the University of Arizona. These three individuals went on to have illustrious careers in archaeology, a reflection of the quality of education provided by Cummings. Many of Cummings' other graduate students had successful careers (table 18.1).

At a time when women were not encouraged to seek their own professional careers in America, Cummings was a champion for women's succeeding in archaeology, even though it was a male-dominated discipline. This may have resulted from his Progressive political viewpoint, as well as the fact that women typically outnumbered men in his archaeology classes. Consequently, his admittance of two women into his new graduate program is not surprising.

Clara Lee Fraps was a graduate of Tucson High School and started out as an English major at the University of Arizona, but after attending Cummings' 1923 archaeology class at age eighteen, she decided to change careers (Frontz 1998; Thompson 1998). She attended the first Pecos Conference with Cummings in 1927 as a student, one of the few students invited. After obtaining her master's degree in 1928, she traveled to Europe, at Cummings' suggestion, to visit museums and ancient sites. He then hired her, at $1,500 a year, to teach a variety of classes, including Asian and Egyptian archaeology. Fraps taught twenty-two different classes at the University of Arizona for a total of forty-three years. She also edited *The Kiva* for ten years (Fontana 1985). In January 1936, she married John F. Tanner, and they were lifelong friends with Cummings; she even wrote his obituary (Tanner 1954a, 1954b). Following in Cummings' footsteps, she wrote many newspaper and magazine articles and published twenty articles in *The Kiva*, on Southwestern archaeology and native crafts (Frontz 1998).

Florence Hawley first attended the University of Arizona as an English major at the age of sixteen, and she also became interested in archaeology because of Cummings, receiving her B.A., with distinction, in 1927 (Frisbie 1974, 1991). She made a name for herself early in her career with detailed studies of pottery technology, publishing an important article on pottery pigments in the *American Anthropologist* (Hawley 1929). She

TABLE 18.1. Master's Theses Written under Byron Cummings at the University of Arizona, 1928–1937

Year	Individual	Thesis Title
1928	Clara Lee Fraps	*Archaeological Survey of Arizona*
1928	Emil W. Haury	*The Succession of House Types in the Pueblo Area*
1928	Florence Hawley	*Pottery and Culture Relations in the Middle Gila*
1929	Carl F. Miller	*Prehistoric Irrigation Systems in Arizona*
1930	Luella Haney Russell	*The Primitive Religion of the Southwest*
1930	Charles W. Wisdom	*Elements of the Piman Language*
1931	Norman E. Gabel	*Martinez Hill Ruins*
1931	Frances Gillmor	*The Biography of John and Louisa Wetherill*
1931	John C. McGregor	*Archaeology of the Little Colorado Drainage Area*
1932	Harry T. Getty	*Cultures of the Upper Gila*
1932	William S. Stallings Jr.	*Pueblo Archaeology of the Rio Grande Drainage*
1932	Anna Mae McGrath	*Antiquity of the American Indian*
1933	Henry C. Lockett	*The Prehistoric Hopi*
1933	Hattie G. Lockett	*The Unwritten Literature of the Hopi*
1933	Robert A. Graham	*The Textile Art of the Prehistoric Southwest*
1933	Edward H. Spicer	*The Prescott Black-on-Grey Culture, Its Nature and Relations, as Exemplified in King's Ruin, Arizona*
1933	Louis R. Caywood	*The Archaeology of the Sulphur Springs Valley, Arizona*
1933	Dorothy Frances Gay	*Apache Art*
1933	Eleanor P. Clarke	*Designs on the Prehistoric Pottery of Arizona*
1933	Earl Jackson	*A Survey of the Verde Drainage*
1934	Gordon C. Baldwin	*The Prehistoric Pueblo of Kinishba*
1935	Doris L. Harvey	*The Pottery of the Little Colorado Culture Area*
1935	Helen Forsberg	*A Study of the Skeletal Remains from the Pueblos of Kinishba and Tuzigoot in Arizona*
1935	Martha Jean McWhirt	*Incised Decoration in the Prehistoric Pottery of the Southwest*
1935	Fletcher A. Carr	*The Ancient Pueblo Culture of Northern Mexico*
1936	William A. Duffen	*Development of Human Culture in the San Pedro River Valley*
1936	Esther N. Mahoney	*The Development and Classification of Chihuahua Pottery*
1936	Ruth M. Arntzen	*The Influence of Prehistoric Religious Ceremonies upon the Living Indian Tribes of the Southwest*
1936	Stanley H. Boggs	*A Survey of the Papago People*
1936	Gordon R. Willey	*Methods and Problems in Archaeological Excavation, with Special Reference to the Southwestern United States*
1936	Richard L. Aldrich	*A Survey of Prehistoric Southwestern Architecture*
1937	Linda Y. Guenther	*Gila Polychromes*
1937	Margaret W. Murray	*The Development of the Form and Design in the Pottery of Kinishba*
1937	Alfred Peterson	*Development of Design on the Hohokam Red-on-buff Pottery*
1937	Victor R. Stoner	*The Spanish Missions of the Santa Cruz Valley*

also collected numerous tree-ring specimens from Chaco Canyon in the 1930s, which contributed to the development of the tree-ring dating technique. In 1934, Hawley obtained a Ph.D. from the University of Chicago and accepted a teaching position at the University of New Mexico, where she taught for more than thirty-six years. She taught at least twenty different classes and wrote more than three hundred books, articles, papers, and manuscripts on Southwestern archaeology, anthropology, and history.

Haury was a tall, deliberate, detail-oriented, and somewhat shy person with a good sense of humor (fig. 18.1). As previously stated, he first met Cummings in Kansas in 1925, when the twenty-one-year-old asked Cummings if he could participate in one of Cummings' summer expeditions. After assisting Cummings at Cuicuilco in Mexico, Haury enrolled in the Archaeology Department, earning his B.A. in two years. He later considered it a "lucky break" to have met Cummings and trained under him (Reid 1986). Haury spent several years as Cummings' right-hand man, research assistant, and chauffeur while Cummings was president of the university (Thompson 1995:644). Haury also was given opportunities to work with Andrew Douglass, Cummings' close friend, on tree-ring dating projects. However, as much as Haury admired Cummings as a teacher and humanitarian, he became increasingly uncomfortable with Cummings' "antiquarian approach to archaeological record keeping and inference." Haury had been trained well, for he had learned what his master knew, all the while realizing that as the science of archaeology was rapidly advancing, he could learn even more.

After a short teaching stint with Cummings, Haury decided in 1930 to take the position of assistant director of the Gila Pueblo Archaeological Foundation while also pursuing his Ph.D. at Harvard University (Haury 1988). For his dissertation, he analyzed Frank Hamilton Cushing's field notes and artifacts from the Hohokam village of Los Muertos, southeast of Phoenix. Haury went on to gain national fame for his systematic excavations at Mogollon (Haury 1936a) and Hohokam sites, including returning to Snaketown (Haury 1976), where he had excavated thirty years before (Gladwin et al. 1937). Less than a decade after he graduated from the University of Arizona, Haury returned to replace Cummings as head of the Archaeology Department, immediately changing its name to the Anthropology Department. Haury won many awards in his career. In

18.1 Four of Cummings' archaeology students, 1926 (*left to right*: Florence Hawley, Gladys Phare, Emil Haury, and Clara Lee Fraps) (courtesy of Arizona Historical Society/Tucson, #AHS72899)

1956, he became the first University of Arizona professor to be elected to the National Academy of Sciences (Reid 1986).

Another student of Cummings' in the late 1920s was John C. McGregor, who also had a distinguished career in archaeology, writing a popular textbook on Southwestern archaeology that is now considered a classic (McGregor 1965). McGregor's class notes from a 1928 archaeology class taught by Cummings provide some insight into Cummings' approach to teaching.[1] This class focused on American archaeology but also included discussions on Paleolithic archaeology. According to McGregor's notes, Cummings would pose a question or series of questions to introduce each class. Topics discussed included the development of agriculture, the prehistoric cotton industry, Hopi language, Early Man, relationships between the Southwest and Mexico, prehistory of the Americas, Mayan archaeology, and the extinction of the Neanderthals. McGregor's notes from a 1930 class listed several books on Old World archaeology written by such scholars as Henry Osborn (1918) and Herdman Cleland (1928). In addition, Cummings' outline for his American archaeology class shows that he had a broad anthropological view of human behavior, because his class included discussions on ancient architecture, physical characteristics, subsistence, craft production, social organization, religion, and language.

In 1930, Cummings added a two-semester class in South American tribes. He also helped plan for a spring semester class in tree-ring interpretation, taught by his friend, astronomer Andrew E. Douglass. This class had fifteen people enrolled, many of whom were Cummings' students (Nash 1999). Four of those students—Haury, Hawley, McGregor, and William S. Stallings—contributed to the early development of this important dating method. With Gladwin's support, Haury actively pursued prehistoric wood specimens for dating and soon was credited, along with Lyndon L. Hargrave,[2] another former student of Cummings', for discovering the beam specimen that bridged the gap in Douglass' chronological chart (Haury and Hargrave 1931).

Cummings continued offering his summer field school to both graduate and undergraduate students. His 1930 field school, however, was the last of his famous adventures into the rugged red rock country of northeastern Arizona, before he established a permanent field school at Kinishba Pueblo in east-central Arizona. The 1930 field school was a memorable ten-week trip to the Navajo Mountain region. The students —Maurice and Mayme Burford, Henrietta Cunningham, Marie Gunst, Muriel Hanna, Walter Ormsby, John Hughes, and Ben Shaw—earned eight college credits for a registration fee of $40, in addition to the trip expenses of $150.

These students knew from reading the University of Arizona catalog (1930a) that their work would consist of "excavation, daily discussions, the preparations of maps of the region, charts and plans of the ruins studied and papers on the phases of culture of the people disclosed by the investigations conducted in the region." In addition, students got to meet Harold Colton at the Museum of Northern Arizona, tour Walnut Canyon ruins, inspect Wilson Pueblo with Lyndon Hargrave, attend a Pow-Wow Indian ceremony in Flagstaff, and visit the Hopi mesas before setting up camp at Ben Wetherill's house and excavating in Segazlin Mesa ruins next to Navajo Mountain.

While digging at the Segazlin ruins, one of the students, John Hughes, angered Cummings by refusing to ride a burro to the mesa top and demanding a mule instead. Cummings (1930b) wrote in his journal that he had grown tired of Hughes' negative attitude. The next day Hughes was dismissed from the expedition and was driven back to Flagstaff by Ben Wetherill, where he caught a train back home.

While camped near Segazlin Mesa, the students also got to take a burro ride to the top of Navajo Mountain, observe two Navajo ceremonial dances, explore isolated canyons for ruins with a Navajo guide named Tall Salt, watch a Hopi Snake Dance, visit Rainbow Bridge, and then spend the night sleeping on the rooftops of Betatakin ruins. All in all, it was a trip of a lifetime, as were many of Cummings' summer adventures.

In 1932, John Provinse, a social anthropologist, was hired by Cummings as an assistant professor to teach in the Archaeology Department. Provinse had obtained a law degree from the University of Chicago and was working on his Ph.D. in applied anthropology, which he received in 1934 (Spicer 1966). He married Clara Lee (Fraps) Tanner's sister-in-law, Helen Tanner. In 1936, he taught two classes in primitive society at the University of Arizona. In addition to teaching the ethnology classes, during the summers Provinse assisted Cummings with the excavation of burials in the Prescott region and at Kinishba Pueblo. He then left the University of Arizona to work for the U.S. Soil Conservation Service on the Navajo Reservation.

Continuing to expand his educational program, Cummings added classes on the archaeology of the Mississippi Valley. In 1934, he reported that 275 students were taking classes in the Archaeology Department, with 7 graduate students and 33 undergraduates selecting archaeology as their major subject (Cummings 1934b). Earlier that year, Cummings had been honored by having his portrait painted in oil on canvas by a federal Public Works of Art Project artist, Lucy Drake Marlow (Hall 1974). The next year, 9 students graduated with a B.A. in archaeology, and several students obtained their master's degrees (see table 18.1). At the American Association for the Advancement of Science meeting in Santa Fe, 13 of Cummings' former students honored him with a dinner (*Arizona Daily Star* 1935). Also in 1935, Cummings sponsored an Arizona chapter of the Mu Alpha Nu, an honorary and professional fraternity for anthropologists that organized archaeology and anthropology lectures for the public; most of the charter members were his students.

That same year, Gordon R. Willey received his B.A. from the University of Arizona. Willey had enrolled in the university in the spring of 1931 at the recommendation of his high school history teacher, who admired Cummings. Upon first meeting Cummings, Willey (1988) thought he looked old but soon learned that he was very energetic for a seventy-year-old man, and Willey came to greatly respect him as a teacher and mentor. Willey had wanted to go to the University of Chicago or Harvard University for graduate school but failed to be accepted at either school. Not upset by Willey's attempt to go elsewhere, Cummings was quick to allow Willey to enroll in the master's program at the University of Arizona. Willey (1988:20) especially enjoyed Cummings' seminar on Mexican archaeology and Provinse's courses in physical anthropology and social anthropology, which he saw as a commitment from Cummings to "broaden what had been an archaeology department into an anthropological one." Willey also was pleased that Cummings supported his efforts to write his thesis on methods and problems in archaeological excavations, even though these were not considered to be among Cummings' strengths. Willey felt that, contrary to comments from his critics, Cummings was "a man of vision." In 1939, Willey enrolled in the doctorate program at Columbia University and received his Ph.D. in 1952. He was a professor at Harvard University for thirty-seven years and held the prestigious position of Bowditch Professor of Mexican and Central American Archaeology and Ethnology (Hammond 2003). Perhaps his most well-known publications include a treatise on archaeological method and theory (Willey and Phillips 1958) and a comprehensive history of American archaeology (Willey and Sabloff 1993).

Cummings was considered a tolerant teacher when it came to different ideas. According to Willey (1988:14), he didn't try "to live his students' lives for them; he expected industrious and decent behavior from them, but beyond that their course was their own." However, Willey (1988:12) noted that Cummings "was not fully comfortable with, nor sympathetic to, the push for chronological refinement" that was common during the 1930s. Cummings also was not comfortable with archaeological argument or disputation, although he did discuss, in his classes, differences of opinions with other Southwestern archaeologists. Willey (1988:24) paid Cummings the ultimate compliment for a mentor, stating that Cummings "made you feel that he had confidence in you to do the right thing."

In September 1936, Cummings announced that he was no longer teaching his archaeology of the Southwest class, a course he had taught for twenty-one years. Gordon Baldwin, who had taken the class from Cummings only a few years before, was to teach the class from then on to allow Cummings more time with advanced courses and his duties at the Arizona State Museum (*Arizona Daily Star* 1936). During the 1936–1937 academic year, Cummings' last as a professor, the Archaeology Department offered sixteen different classes in archaeology and anthropology, taught by three professors (Cummings, Provinse, and Fraps) and a newly hired instructor, Harry T. Getty, who had received his master's degree from Cummings in 1932.[3] Classes that year were given in a beautiful new building Cummings had constructed—the Arizona State Museum (table 18.2).

In the last decade of Cummings' teaching career, from 1928 to 1938, more than thirty students received their master's degrees under him. In 1933, Henry Claiborne Lockett and his mother, Hattie, both completed their master's theses on different aspects of Hopi culture. The topics of Cummings' students' theses were very wide ranging and included subjects in archaeology, anthropology, and Southwestern history. Many of the archaeology theses consisted of overviews of the known archaeological sites in a particular region, including the middle Gila River, the Little Colorado River, the Rio Grande, the Prescott area, Sulphur Springs Valley, the Verde River, northern Mexico, the San Pedro River, and the Chihuahuan Desert. Some theses were overviews of particular types of material culture such as house types and other architecture, pottery types, and textiles. Pottery types included Hohokam red-on-buff, Gila polychromes, Chihuahuan pottery, incised pottery, and the pottery of Kinishba Pueblo.

A thesis on analyzing pottery designs was written by Eleanor Clarke, who was killed in a May 1933 accident near Douglas, Arizona.[4] Her thesis was published posthumously as a University of Arizona Social Science Bulletin (Clarke 1935). Other theses under Cummings' supervision dealt with anthropological topics, including religion, art, and language. One thesis was a biography of John and Louisa Wetherill (Gillmor 1931), whom Cummings had befriended early in his career, and another thesis described the Spanish missions of the Santa Cruz Valley (Stoner 1937).

More than three dozen of Cummings' undergraduate and graduate students went on to have highly successful careers in archaeology, anthro-

TABLE 18.2. Professors and Instructors in the Department of Archaeology, 1927–1937

Academic Year	*Professor or Instructor*
1927–1928	Byron Cummings, L.L.D., Sc.D.
	Thomas T. Waterman, Ph.D.
	Emil W. Haury, M.A.
	Clara Lee Fraps, M.A.
1928–1929	Byron Cummings, L.L.D., Sc.D.
	Emil W. Haury, M.A.
	Clara Lee Fraps, M.A.
	Florence Hawley, M.A.
1929–1930	Byron Cummings, L.L.D., Sc.D.
	Emil W. Haury, M.A. (on leave)
	Clara Lee Fraps, M.A.
	Florence Hawley, M.A.
1930–1931	Byron Cummings, L.L.D., Sc.D.
	Clara Lee Fraps, M.A.
	Florence Hawley, M.A.
1931–1932	Byron Cummings, L.L.D., Sc.D.
	Clara Lee Fraps, M.A.
1932–1933	Byron Cummings, L.L.D., Sc.D.
	John H. Provinse, Ph.D. candidate
	Clara Lee Fraps, M.A.
	Florence Hawley, M.A.
1933–1934	Byron Cummings, L.L.D., Sc.D.
	John H. Provinse, Ph.D.
	Clara Lee Fraps, M.A.
1934–1935	Byron Cummings, L.L.D., Sc.D.
	John H. Provinse, Ph.D.
	Clara Lee Fraps, M.A.
1935–1936	Byron Cummings, L.L.D., Sc.D.
	John H. Provinse, Ph.D.
	Clara Lee Fraps, M.A.
1936–1937	Byron Cummings, L.L.D., Sc.D.
	John H. Provinse, Ph.D.
	Clara Lee Fraps, M.A.
	Harry T. Getty, M.A.

Sources: University of Arizona 1927, 1928b, 1929b, 1930b, 1931a, 1932a, 1933, 1934b, 1935a, 1936a, 1937b.

pology, or Southwestern history. A book profiling ten of the most famous archaeologists working in the 1960s featured two of his students: Haury and Willey (Poole and Poole 1968). More than one-third of the master's degrees under Cummings were earned by women. Unlike other prominent male archaeologists in the United States at the time, Cummings promoted female students in their careers (Reyman 1992:74). Several of these women had respected careers in archaeology or anthropology, including Jean McWhirt (Pinkley), Frances Gillmor, and Helen Forsberg (Babcock and Parezo 1988) in addition to Fraps and Hawley. Frances Gillmor received her master's degree in 1931 and published a number of important books and articles on Southwestern anthropology and history. Both Forsberg and McWhirt (Pinkley) obtained their master's degrees from the University of Arizona in 1935. McWhirt worked as an archaeologist at Mesa Verde National Park in Colorado. She married Frank Pinkley's son, Addison, an engineer who was killed during World War II while serving in the U.S. Navy (Schneider-Hector 2003). Pinkley's daughter, Nancy, obtained her B.A. degree in archaeology under Byron Cummings in 1934.[5]

Cummings and the Arizona Pageantry Association

Public events with history components were popular in the early years of Arizona statehood, and historical pageants were common throughout America, serving as celebrations of progress and democracy (Kammen 1991). The American Pageantry Association had been created in 1913, although Santa Fe had held a historical pageant as early as 1911 (Glassberg 1990). In March of 1926, the Arizona Pageantry Association (APA) was established to support plays describing the history of Arizona through fact and legend to promote tourism (Todt 1926). Original members included Governor George Hunt, Arizona historian James H. McClintock, soon-to-be board of regents member Robert E. Tally, President Cloyd H. Marvin of the University of Arizona, and others.[6] McClintock was nominated as president, but the APA secretary, Katherine V. MacRae, was the driving force behind the organization.

The 1926 historical play was held in Compound B of Casa Grande as part of Custodian Frank Pinkley's ongoing efforts to advertise the monument. Governor Hunt opened the November pageant to a huge audience, with 13,000 people attending the three-day event (Clemensen 1992). Garnet Holme of the National Park Service wrote and directed the pageant's four episodes (Russell 1926).

When Cummings assumed President Marvin's duties in 1927, he became involved in the APA. He praised the three-year APA plan by Secretary MacRae, because he believed that historical plays were valuable as a visual education for young people. The 1927 play, directed and partly written by Conrad Seiler, attracted 10,000 visitors to the Casa Grande Ruins for three days in November, but 16,000 people had been expected. In addition, the play was criticized by Pinkley (1927b), who called it a "three-ring circus" that was too long, was disjointed, and had no humor.

In 1928, the APA play was to be at the Grand Canyon, but arrangements fell through. Cummings was nominated as APA president in May of that year and was asked to write the pageant's next play. His biggest concern was artistic and historical accuracy. MacRae, who had fought with the director of the 1926 pageant, resigned that fall in a dispute with Cummings, and Emil Haury was elected APA secretary.

Cummings' pageant was scheduled for March of 1929 at Casa Grande Ruins. His story revolved around the lives of three different prehistoric people: Cave Men, Pithouse Men, and Late Pueblo Men, which included the "peace-loving" people of Casa Grande Ruins (Cummings 1929b, 1929c). Cummings arranged for a group of Navajos and a group of Hopis to perform traditional dances. Athletic contests also were held. Current and recently graduated students were enlisted by Cummings to play characters in his historical play, including Florence Hawley, Clara Lee Fraps, Frances Gillmor, and Henry Lockett. His play was well received, but attendance was only 7,000, less than expected (Clemensen 1992).

Cummings continued as APA president until April 1929. Another contest was held for the next pageant play, with the authors unknown to the four judges, including Frank Pinkley. Thirteen submittals were received, with the winning play having been written by Cummings! His 1930 play involved a Hopi recounting the story of a Hopi princess kidnapped by a Navajo man, and the introduction of gambling by a Navajo, called Clever Hand, to the prehistoric village of Casa Grande. Clever Hand's escapades led to the downfall of the village. There also were Hopi and

Pima dances and athletic contests. Held in March, Cummings' play was well received, and his students were once again involved in a unique outdoor educational experience (Cummings 1930a). However, attendance was lower than previous years—only 5,000 people—and with the Great Depression beginning to impact the state, the Arizona pageant movement was discontinued (Clemensen 1992).

19

"Shortest Possible Statement for a Research Goal"

Excavations in Northern Arizona, 1927–1930

The appointment of Cummings to the presidency of the University of Arizona left him with less time to conduct his archaeological explorations. His plans to dig in the summer of 1927 at Bylas, on the Gila River, and in northern Arizona were canceled at the last minute (Haury 2004b). He was not to be denied his annual summer opportunity to obtain more artifacts for the Arizona State Museum, especially with Earl Morris of the Museum of Natural History having so much success, so he sent out his trusted graduate student Emil Haury. When Cummings finished his time as president the next year, he traveled to northern Arizona to dig a ruin outside Flagstaff, called Turkey Hill Pueblo, returning again the next summer. In 1930, Cummings undertook his last such major expedition into northern Arizona before beginning a long-term summer field school at Kinishba Pueblo in east-central Arizona.

In Search of Basketmaker Caves

Since the mid 1920s, Cummings had been interested in Basketmaker sites present in the Carrizo Mountains, east of the Kayenta region. In 1926, Cummings asked Samuel Day Jr., son of the famous Navajo trader Samuel Day Sr., if he would explore the Carrizo Mountain region for Basketmaker sites for the State Museum. Hinting at his disdain for archaeologists from the East, Cummings (1926f) informed Day that "the state of Arizona ought to have first chance to study that region and save the relics from its ruins." Day agreed with Cummings' request, and for three weeks in April 1927, Day searched out Basketmaker sites and was paid $80 by Cummings for his services.

Only a month after Day's explorations, Alfred Kidder published an article on the various Arizona expeditions of the American Museum of Natural History over the preceding few years. Kidder (1927a) called northeastern Arizona a "happy hunting ground for the archaeologist." He described some of the fabulous material, including well-preserved Basketmaker mummies, which had been found by Earl Morris and Charles Bernheimer in Canyon de Chelly, located a few miles south of the Carrizo Mountains.

Cummings was most likely displeased to know that large quantities of Basketmaker artifacts from Canyon de Chelly were leaving Arizona for New York City. In mid July, he gave Haury $60 and a university vehicle, affectionately called "Old Asthma" by Haury (2004b), and sent his student assistant to a rugged area north of Canyon de Chelly with the command to find some Basketmaker material for the State Museum. Haury (1985:386) thought that Cummings' instructions were "a large order for a novice who had never been there, and the shortest possible statement for a project goal."

One of Haury's first tasks was to visit Cummings' friends in Kayenta, John and Louisa Wetherill, and tour Kiet Siel and Betatakin ruins. With the assistance of a Navajo guide named Paul, Haury then explored the Lukachukai region, north of Canyon de Chelly. Because of Haury's tall stature, he was given the name "Tall Slim Guy" by the Navajos (Elliot 1995:141). Haury was accompanied by Major Lionel F. Brady, curator of geology at the Museum of Northern Arizona, and John Hands and Arthur Hauck, who had already been working in the field for Cummings for several months. Dr. Locke of Illinois and John C. McGregor, another of Cummings' students, joined the group a short while later. McGregor would later become a staff member of the Museum of Northern Arizona and would make a number of contributions to Flagstaff archaeology, including dating the eruption of Sunset Crater to the eleventh century (McGregor 1936).[1]

Haury (2004b) was impressed with the beauty of the Lukachukai Mountains, describing them as great talus slopes topped by vertical cliffs of red sandstones that projected like fingers five hundred feet in height. He decided to excavate a rockshelter named Vandal Cave, so called because it had already been dug into by pothunters. He also spent a day in Painted Cave, sketching the numerous Basketmaker wall paintings, called pictographs (Haury 1945). A talented artist, he made both colored pencil and pastel illustrations of the pictographs.

Ten years later, Haury (1936b) wrote a brief excavation report on Vandal Cave, but considerable information in his field notes was not published in his report. Haury (2004b) noted that despite enduring suffocating dust, blistered hands, and aching muscles, the group met Cummings' expectations for discovering museum-quality items. Early and late Pueblo period structures and at least a dozen burials were excavated. Several mummies from the earlier Basketmaker period were found, as Cummings had hoped. Two of the mummies were wrapped in feather robes and accompanied by multiple baskets and ceramic vessels. In one of the rooms, Haury found a coiled basket painted red and black and in perfect condition. Through the hard work of his talented student, Cummings had been successful, once again, in competing with eastern institutions for Arizona's ancient treasures.

Turkey Hill Pueblo, 1928–1930

In June 1928, Cummings relinquished his duties as president of the University of Arizona and was free to spend the summer as he pleased. He decided to take some students and friends north, out of the heat of Tucson, to excavate a Pueblo site located near Turkey Hill, about nine miles northeast of Flagstaff. This decision may have been influenced by the removal of artifacts from the same area in 1926 by one of Cummings' old adversaries, Jesse Fewkes, director of the Bureau of American Ethnology. Fewkes' excavations at Elden Pueblo were located less than three miles from Turkey Hill Pueblo, and he had uncovered a large collection of painted pots from thirty-four rooms and shipped them all back east, refusing Cummings' plea to leave half of the collection in Arizona (Downum 1990).

Turkey Hill had been recommended to Cummings by Harold Colton of the newly formed Museum of Northern Arizona and was located near Major Brady's camp. Although the site had been badly vandalized by pothunters, Cummings thought the site had potential for containing materials relating to the cultures of the Flagstaff region, which were largely unknown at that time. The village was described as a medium-sized pueblo made of chunks of rock and clay mortar, with plastered room interiors. Some of the rooms were two-story. An outlying group of one-story buildings and the main pueblo surrounded a central plaza. Refuse middens were present northeast and east of the main pueblo.

Cummings' crew included John Hands, Paul and Florence Hawley, the Butler and Crittenden families, John Greene, Bill Perkins, John Wells, and Winslow Walker, who kept a diary of the dig. Excavations were begun on July 3, 1928, in the burial mound to the east of the main structure, where Cummings' crew found thirty-three burials and "secured sufficient pottery and bone and stone implements to give us a fair means of interpreting the cultural development of these people" (Cummings 1929a: 337). Black-on-white and polychrome pottery types at the site indicated extensive trade networks, but most of the pottery was plain red with black interiors.

Burials were found at a depth of 0.5 to 5.5 feet below the surface. Most of the individuals were extended on their side or back, similar to those found at the Elden Pueblo. However, two cremation burials in ceramic jars were found at the edge of the burial area, and Cummings (1929e) wrote in his unpublished report that these were the first Hohokam cremations found that far north. Emil Haury, accompanied by his new wife, Hulda, assisted with the excavation of some of the burials, including the two cremations.

Turquoise earrings and pendants were present in at least nine burials. One of the adult burials had a shell bracelet on its left arm and was accompanied by four ceramic vessels and two dippers, a bone dagger, a painted woven armband and painted baskets with the colors red, green, orange, and blue. Five turquoise ear pendants were lying next to the armband. Another burial, that of an old man, had seven bone daggers laid across his chest, seven arrow points on his left pelvis, three black-on-white bowls on his stomach, a plain jar on his chest, three stone phallic emblems, and two marine shell whistles. Walker (1928) describes a day that started with Cummings irritated with Walker because he was talking too much with Haury "instead of shoveling my head off." Cummings' mood changed for the better later that day, however, when Walker uncovered a burial containing fourteen ceramic vessels.

Only limited excavations were conducted around the pueblo walls that summer, because, according to Walker, they were not allowed to dig the pueblo without a government permit. He wrote in his diary that the crew was forced to quite digging on July 27 because the permit had been delayed in Washington. Walker (1928) stated that it "looks like the dirty work on the part of [Jesse] Nusbaum and [Alfred] Kidder," a comment probably heard from Cummings. These two individuals, alongside whom Cummings had dug at Alkali Ruin in 1908, would continue to be involved in conflicts with Cummings' archaeology activities in the 1930s.

Cummings was a persistent man and was determined to dig again at Turkey Hill Pueblo. In April of 1929, he gave a paper on the results of his excavations at the American Association for the Advancement of Science (AAAS) meeting in Albuquerque. He then returned to Turkey Hill Pueblo, with a permit, in the summer of 1929, intending to do a lot more excavation (Cummings 1929a). Starting in mid June, the digging focused primarily on the pueblo rooms, where Cummings' crew of about ten people continued to uncover burials, this time discovering children interred under the flagstone floors. Field notes record a total of fifty-nine burials combined for 1928–1929.

Excavations of most of the pueblo rooms revealed that many of them had been burned in prehistoric times. Of the thirty-five rooms that were examined, twenty-four were identified as first-story rooms (fig. 19.1). Cummings' photographs indicate that room walls were partially reconstructed for those rooms fully excavated, a common practice for many of his expeditions.

One of the rooms in the main pueblo, number 11, contained an interesting collection of items, including fourteen *Pecten* marine shells, materials for painting, five bone awls, digging tools, two tiny metates, a yucca floor mat, and numerous painted and plain vessels (Cummings 1929e). Room 35 also was of special interest. A little less than 14 feet by 10 feet in overall size, it had the tallest existing wall in the pueblo, 5 feet 9 inches in height. Inside were a clay-lined firepit and numerous ceramic vessels, as well as three bone awls and one bone dagger, four stone axes, twenty-five manos, six stone balls, five rubbing stones, two hammerstones, and chunks of red paint. A happy crew had their picture taken at the site (fig. 19.2).

Obviously pleased with his investigations at Turkey Hill Pueblo, Cummings gave a paper on his 1929 excavations at the April 1930 AAAS meeting in Tucson. In the summer of 1930, Cummings and several students

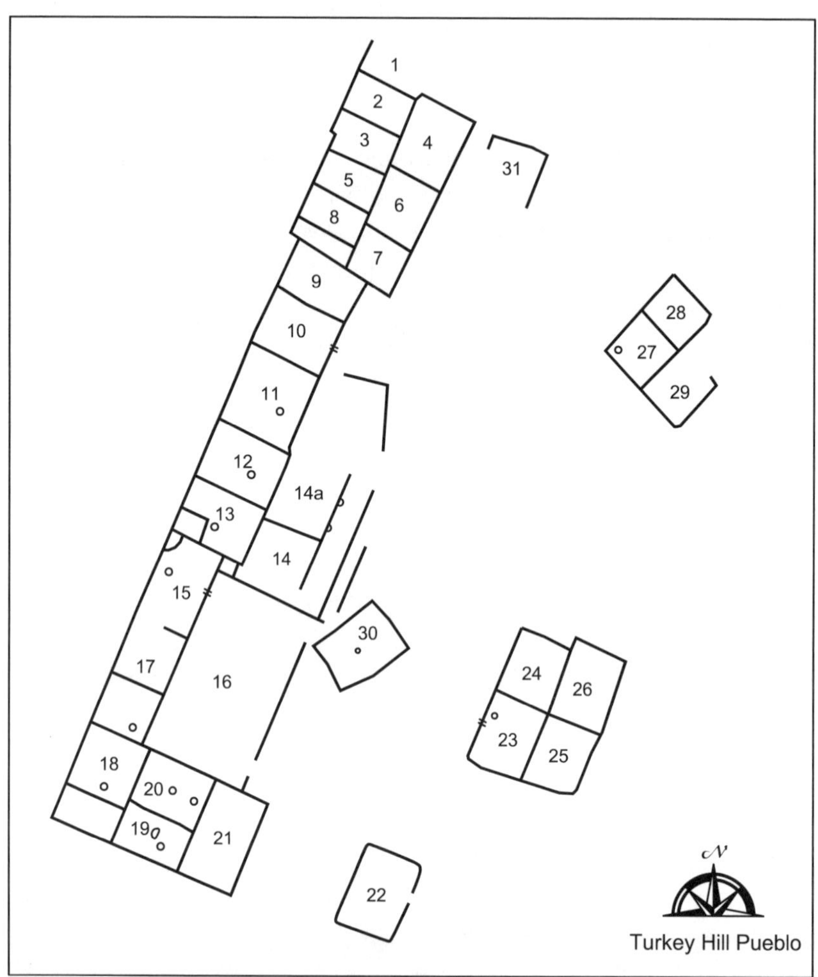

19.1 Cummings' plan map for Turkey Hill Ruin, circa 1929–1930. Room numbers on this map vary from other sketch maps of the site; for example, Room 30 is also listed elsewhere as Room 35.

19.2 Crew photograph for the 1929 Turkey Hill excavations (*bottom row, left to right*: Charles Wisdom, Joseph Hubbard, and Carl Miller; *top, left to right*: Charles McKee, John Hands, Waldo Wedel, and Grenville Goodwin) (courtesy of Arizona Historical Society/Tucson, #AHS73858)

returned to Turkey Hill Pueblo, for a short while, on their way to the Kayenta region. The purpose of this visit was to prepare a map of the site. Cummings (1929e) prepared a brief summary paper of his excavations at Turkey Hill Pueblo, which included detailed information about the burials he exposed, but he never found the time to have his report published.

Another Grand Expedition to Navajo Mountain, 1930

Administrative responsibilities at the University of Arizona kept Cummings from mounting expeditions into the Kayenta area in the late 1920s, and he was not able to return until 1930. He planned another adventurous trip for the summer of that year, spending ten weeks in northeastern Arizona (Cummings 1931a). For three of the ten weeks, he and his assistant Clara Lee Fraps supervised several students, as part of a University of Arizona field school, in the excavation of ruins on top of a mesa on the northeast side of Navajo Mountain. Ruins on top of this oval-shaped mesa, which Cummings called Segazin Mesa (also Segazlin), were already known about, having been partly dug in 1929 by J. Alden Mason.

Cummings' groups used Ben and Myrl Wetherill's new trading post, called Teas-ya-toh ("Water under the Cottonwoods"), as their base camp. It was located only about two miles from the mesa. Charles Van Bergen of the Southwest Museum in Los Angeles and several assistants, including Irwin Hayden and Arthur Woodward, also were investigating the Navajo Mountain region that summer. By mutual agreement, they spent some time excavating alongside Cummings on the mesa top. Another individual in Van Bergen's party, Lionel F. Brady, taught Cummings' students how to use a Brunson compass and an Adelaide and plane table to create an accurate map of the mesa ruins. After a while, the Van Bergen crew left to dig at two cave sites in Desha Canyon (Lindsay et al. 1968).

Cummings (1931h) identified three main groups of ruins on the mesa top: an area of older pithouse rooms, which had plain gray and crude indented pottery; and two other areas of surface pueblos, which had "good" indented coiled, black-on-white, and black-on-red vessels. Cummings' 1930 map of the mesa shows six clusters of ruins (Dean 2002:fig. 6.11). The hundred-foot-high, limestone-capped mesa is steep on all sides and has limited access to its top; consequently, it is a very defendable location. The only unobstructed route to the mesa top is a trail on the talus slope adjacent to the east side of the mesa. A long, linear pueblo was located at the edge of the mesa where the trail joins the mesa top. Cummings' group excavated a kiva and one of the rooms in this cluster of rooms, which was later called the Guardian Pueblo by Glen Canyon Project (GCP) archaeologists, who dug Segazin Mesa ruins in 1960 (Lindsay et al. 1968). Cummings' group also dug another kiva at a pueblo located on the northern part of the mesa, called Tcamahia Pueblo by the GCP. The ruins on this mesa top have been dated to the Tsegi phase, AD 1250–1300, similar to Red House ruin (Dean 2002).

In addition to working at Segazin Mesa, Cummings also spent ten days that summer excavating two small cliff ruins in Long Canyon, a branch of Nitsie Canyon. He found many relics that summer, including well-preserved textiles, twilled yucca baskets and mats, and black-on-white pottery.

Clara Lee Fraps' (1930c) notes from a Cummings lecture that summer indicate how well Cummings understood the importance of looking at stratigraphy within trash deposits at a site: "Look first for refuse heaps, and examine . . . before work in ruin. Debris heaps give good general idea of people who inhabited a village. Wise to trench from margin to center, to undisturbed soil. Old trash heaps should be worked stratigraphically—records for each foot. Also note the manner in which debris have been dumped—stratification." Stratigraphy within a room, however, was given far less emphasis by Cummings.

Fraps (1930a, 1930b) wrote a series of lively articles on their 1930 trip for the *Arizona Daily Star*, keeping Tucson citizens up-to-date on the Archaeology Department's latest adventures. Cummings (1930b) kept a detailed journal of their journey but, as with so many of his other expeditions, never wrote a report on their excavations. However, in October of that year, Cummings, Fraps, and three students (Marie Gunst, Muriel Hanna, and Walter Ormsby) gave illustrated presentations on their trip at the fall meeting of the Arizona Archaeological and Historical Society in Tucson.

20

"Weird, Thrilling, Spectacular"

Archaeology and Tourism in the Prescott and Verde River Regions, 1931–1934

The 1930s Depression strained the local economies of many towns in Arizona, and some aggressively pursued increased tourism through promotion of their natural and historical resources. One of those communities was Prescott, which at the time billed itself as "The Friendly Town." Cummings' personal involvement in the development of an archaeology museum in Prescott, called the Smoki Museum, is directly related to this push for tourist attractions, but it also involved competition over control of central Arizona archaeology. This competition led to conflicts between local and out-of-state institutions and between professional and amateur archaeologists. The increased archaeological attention, sponsored by both Arizona citizens and the federal government, resulted in a much better understanding of the prehistoric cultures of the Prescott and Verde Valley regions. Cummings' students played a major role in this advance of knowledge through their excavations of several important sites, providing data later used by Harold Colton to define the Prescott Culture in central and western Arizona (Colton 1939) and the Southern Sinagua Culture of the Verde Valley (Colton 1946).

Early Archaeology of the Prescott and Verde Regions

Except for the early investigations of Cosmos Mindeleff and Jesse W. Fewkes, the archaeology of the Prescott and Verde River region had been largely ignored by professional archaeologists working in Arizona until the early 1930s. Mindeleff (1896), who worked for the Bureau of American Ethnology in Washington, D.C., recorded more than fifty sites along the 150-mile-long Verde River, which begins northeast of Prescott and flows southward into the Salt River east of Phoenix. In addition to farmland along the river, this environmentally diverse region contained other valuable resources such as red argillite for carved stone jewelry and salt deposits that were widely traded. The talented Mindeleff identified village ruins on the valley bottom and in elevated defensive positions, cliff ruins, boulder-lined sites, towers, irrigation ditches and reservoirs, and numerous "cavate" lodges carved out of limestone cliffs.

Jesse W. Fewkes (1912b) of the Smithsonian Institution followed with a brief survey of the upper Verde region in 1905 and 1906. He noted that almost every high hill adjacent to the tributaries of the Verde River was crowned with a ruin, some of which appeared to be fortified. Fewkes (1912b:187) did not believe that the upper Verde region had once been occupied by descendants of the Pueblo Indians but instead argued that the local inhabitants had been a "mixed blood" related to the Yavapai, Walapai (Hualapai), and Havasupai Indians who lived in west-central Arizona in historic times.

Harold Gladwin, in search of the northern and western boundaries of the Red-on-Buff Culture (Hohokam) of the Sonoran Desert, directed two pottery inventories of 185 sites in the Prescott and Verde region from 1927 to 1930 (Gladwin and Gladwin 1930a, 1930b). He believed that red-on-buff pottery had been made by a culture different from the prehistoric people of central Arizona, who had made a black-on-gray decorated pottery, and that the Verde River marked the western frontier of the Pueblo Culture (Gladwin and Gladwin 1930a).

James W. Simmons and the Black-on-Gray Culture

The excavations of a gray-haired but energetic and feisty Prescott citizen, James W. Simmons, brought renewed interest to the region after Gladwin's surveys. Simmons had little formal training in archaeology but read everything he could get his hands on, and he understood the importance of careful excavation and record keeping after helping John Harrington take notes and photographs during Fewkes' excavations at Elden Pueblo in 1926 (Kelly 1970). Simmons also wrote letters to several Southwestern archaeologists, including Alfred Kidder and Earl Morris, seeking their advice. In February of 1931, Alfred Kidder (1931b) wrote Simmons to inquire about his interesting clay figurine collection from the Groom Creek area, southeast of Prescott. Simmons invited Kidder to visit the Prescott area.

Kidder was still very interested in Arizona archaeology, having completed his famous excavations at Pecos Pueblo in New Mexico, and he accepted Simmons' invitation. In late July of that year, Kidder and his wife, Madeleine, spent two days examining several sites in the Prescott area with Simmons. Kidder promised Simmons that he would consider organizing an expedition to the region in the near future, if Cummings and Harold Colton of the Museum of Northern Arizona did not object. After Kidder spoke with Cummings at the Pecos Conference that summer, Cummings visited Simmons and told Simmons that he objected to Kidder's working the Prescott region because there were other archaeologists just as good as Kidder and that Kidder's gang wanted to "hog it all" (Simmons 1933b).

Cummings then met with the Yavapai County Chamber of Commerce and solicited the assistance of several prominent Prescott citizens, helping them form the Yavapai Archaeological Committee. Charles Elrod, of the Rio Grande Oil Company and head of a civic group called the Smoki, was selected to chair the committee. Other members of this committee were historian Sharlot Hall, artist Kate T. Cory, A. H. Favour, Lester Ruffner, and Grace Sparkes.[1] When the committee complained that the State Museum had done little to promote the archaeology of the Prescott region, Cummings offered to put up $300 to pay for excavations in the region if the committee would match it; with that money Cummings would hire Simmons to dig for six months at $100 a month (Simmons 1933b). The committee also planned to build a local museum to hold the materials that Simmons recovered, showcasing the local prehistoric cultures and creating a tourist attraction.

That fall, Cummings wrote Simmons and told him that it was okay if he worked with Kidder and the Carnegie Institution as long as they got started right away and "do not sap the legitimate resources of Arizona for the benefit of outside intruders" (Simmons 1933b). Kidder, however, decided not to compete with Cummings for the Prescott region, because, in Simmons' (1933b) words, Kidder "thought it best to let the little runt have his own way." Soon thereafter, money was available to hire Simmons at $100 a month for six months, expenses included, as Cummings had promised.

King's Ruin

In November, Simmons began conducting excavations on behalf of the Yavapai Archaeological Committee to obtain archaeological specimens representative of the prehistoric people who made black-on-gray pottery. He chose to dig at a small pueblo ruin on the King Brothers Ranch in Chino Valley, about thirty-five miles northwest of Prescott. This site was located on a prominent rise overlooking Chino Creek, a tributary of the Verde River. The site had a noticeable mound, but Simmons focused instead on a burial area to the northeast, where he knew he would find the best-preserved artifacts. He used a pick and shovel, a trowel, and a screen. By mid December, he was digging through eighteen inches of snow covering the ground, which forced him to quit for the winter.

Cummings traveled to Prescott in January of 1932 to give one of his famous lantern-slide lectures. He informed the group that later in the year he would be sending up a number of his students to conduct excavations at King's Ruin. Cummings offered to have Simmons come down to Tucson during the winter and dig with Cummings' students in milder weather, but Simmons did not have enough money to support himself there.

Simmons resumed digging in May 1933. He was allowed to continue excavating burials when Cummings and more than a dozen students showed up in June to dig the pueblo. The students focused on cleaning out the rooms of this small pueblo, which was ninety feet in length and forty-three feet in width. Altogether, Simmons (1936) recovered fifty-seven human burials and one cremation at King's Ruin, although Edward Spicer (1936b) listed fifty-five in his report. Many of these burials had log coverings, and some graves contained two or three individuals. Eight of the burials contained individuals with the lower parts of their faces painted green. One individual was buried with a mosaic frog pendant on his or her chest. Another burial yielded a skeleton with 410 turquoise beads in three strands on the right wrist. Some of the burials had fibrous pillows emplaced under the heads of the deceased. These materials were later deposited by Simmons in the Smoki Museum.

Twenty-six-year-old Edward ("Ned") H. Spicer was put in charge of the University of Arizona dig at King's Ruin.[2] Cummings donated money for expenses, as did the Arizona Archaeological and Historical Society (Cummings 1933c). Newly hired Assistant Professor John Provinse of the University of Arizona and student Gordon C. Baldwin participated in the excavations. These investigations revealed a transitional pithouse occupation (Cummings 1953:22) and a later surface pueblo of twelve rooms, probably two stories in height. Tree-ring dates reported by Baldwin (1939a) dated the site to the mid 1000s, although it was later dated more accurately to AD 1204 (Bannister et al. 1966).

The King Brothers Ranch excavations were among the first systematic investigations of the Prescott Black-on-Grey Culture, and the project stands as a pioneering work in the Prescott region. Edward H. Spicer (1933) wrote his thesis on the excavations, and he and Louis R. Caywood (1936) published a combined report on King's Ruin and Fitzmaurice Ruin in a University of Arizona Social Science Bulletin. Acknowledging that the Verde Valley and adjoining areas were "still question marks in the archaeological notebook," Spicer's (1936b:7) report put the Prescott Culture on the Southwestern archaeology map. However, Spicer was not overly impressed with the Prescott Culture's artistic abilities, especially compared to the artisans of the San Juan River region of northeastern Arizona, stating that the Prescott black-on-gray pottery "stands almost alone for its determined ugliness" (Spicer 1936b:6). Illustrations of several pots in his report show a whimsical nature to the painted designs that give them a certain country charm (fig. 20.1).

Simmons' important role in the development of the Prescott Culture has not been fully recognized. Indeed, Simmons (1933b) was not pleased with the university's work at King's Ruin, later commenting that the students received little supervision from Cummings, because he either was away on political trips or was busy with cooking and cleaning, and they "went through the site like the German army thru Belgium." Simmons gathered several bags of broken pottery at the site after Cummings left and sent them to State Museum, which probably did not humor Cummings, who was generally interested only in whole or partial pots.

20.1 Example of ceramic design on pottery from King's Ruin (redrawn from Spicer 1936:fig. 7)

In August, Simmons was asked by Chairman Elrod if he would put his extensive collection of artifacts into the excavated rooms of King's Ruin to serve as a museum, but Simmons refused on the grounds that the artifacts would not be adequately cared for there. He was then told that he would no longer conduct excavations on behalf of the Yavapai Archaeological Committee, even though there was one month left on his contract. Simmons, however, continued to dig on his own at King's Ruin after Cummings' students left at the end of summer.

Cummings' and Simmons' relationship soured even further that fall when Cummings visited Simmons in December, offering Simmons $1 for letting Spicer analyze the ceramics in his collection. When Cummings failed to acknowledge Simmons' excavations in newspaper articles about Prescott archaeology, Simmons (1933a) told Harold Gladwin that Cummings "seems to be devoid of common ordinary ethics." Simmons later moved south to the Salt River valley and Hohokam archaeology, digging the La Ciudad platform mound for the Heard family (Wilcox 1987) and the Pueblo Grande platform mound for Odd Halseth (Downum 1993).

Mercer Ruin

Cummings also expanded his activities in 1932 to the east, into the Verde River region, with the assistance of Clarence R. King. After a reconnaissance in the spring, Cummings organized a summer exploration of the Verde River by Earl Jackson and several other graduate students, the results of which were reported in Jackson's (1933) master's thesis. More than thirty sites were recorded, many of which Mindeleff had previously visited, including a very large ruin above Lime Creek that was later called Mercer Ruin. Jackson also excavated two pithouses at Calkins Ranch along the lower Verde River (*Arizona Daily Star* 1933). Jackson (1933: 100) disagreed with Winifred and Harold Gladwin (1930a) that the Verde was the western frontier of the Pueblo Culture and argued instead that the material culture of the region exhibited more influence by the Hohokam to the south.

Concerned about increased pothunting activity in the Verde region, Cummings (1932c) hired Thomas L. Mercer, for $50 a month, to serve as a caretaker for sites on the Verde River. Cummings used $500 donated by Harold Colton the year before. Mercer (1932) reported to Cummings that he had chased off pothunters and that Odd Halseth had brought a group to tour Verde ruins for two weeks but that they had done no excavating. Limited excavations were subsequently undertaken by Cummings and his students at Mercer Ruin, named by Earl Jackson after its caretaker. This multistory structure contained more than two hundred rooms and had well-built walls made of dressed tabular masonry chinked with smaller stones.[3] It also had an unusual four-foot-thick, isolated wall that was more than 160 feet long, located at the southeast end of the ruin.

Stephanie Whittlesey (1997) has provided an interesting account of a controversy involving Cummings and Mercer Ruin. Cummings and a large group of students visited Mercer Ruin in early April. In his typical exuberance after inspecting ruins, Cummings boasted to the *Arizona Republic* (1932) that Mercer Ruin was an "Archaeological Prize." This comment generated a negative response from Charles M. Morgan (1932) in the April 8 issue of the *Jumping Cactus*, a weekly Phoenix newspaper. Morgan chastised Cummings for spending taxpayers' money and using twenty-seven students to "discover" a ruin that had been long ago mapped by Mindeleff (1896:plate XII) and commonly known to the local ranchers and prospectors for years. Morgan accused Cummings either of faking the discovery or of being ignorant of his own business, both of which were inexcusable for the head of the Archaeology Department at the University of Arizona. Morgan (1932) also attacked Cummings' integrity: "We heartily condemn the practice of giving false or misleading publicity to facts already established and unhesitatingly condemn those who think only of strutting themselves before the public yet give no thought to protecting our prehistoric ruins from vandalism, scientific or otherwise." To counter this attack, Cummings wrote a series of letters to Maricopa County, the Arizona State Highway Department, the U.S. Forest Service, and Governor Hunt, in which he expressed his concerns about the vandalism that could result from publicity about Mercer Ruin. Cummings (1932b) also informed Mrs. Emery Oldaker, of the Arizona Museum in Phoenix, that he suspected that Odd Halseth was behind the negative *Jumping Cactus* article. Cummings had hoped to partner with the Arizona Museum and obtain federal New Deal money to excavate Mercer Ruin but was unsuccessful in that effort.

Fitzmaurice Ruin

During the summer of 1933, Cummings also coordinated excavations of Fitzmaurice Ruin, seven miles northeast of Prescott, by graduate student Louis R. Caywood. Fitzmaurice Ruin was located on a ridge overlooking Lynx Creek, a tributary of the Agua Fria River, which flows south into the Salt River. Fitzmaurice Ruin contained more than fifty rooms constructed of local granite blocks and had already been partly excavated by James Simmons, who had dug forty-three burials at the site in 1930. Cummings wished to work out further details of the Black-on-Gray Culture, so he decided to follow up on the King's Ruin excavation with another site in the Prescott region. He chose Fitzmaurice Ruin because of its proximity to Prescott, its large size, and its location on the periphery of the Black-on-Gray Culture. Work began in early June.

After outlining the general plan of excavation, Cummings returned to Tucson and "left the details to be worked out" by Caywood and Spicer, and by Frank Keller Jr., a student engineer (Spicer and Caywood 1936: 87). Some of the costs of the dig were financed by the Delphian Society and by local patrons. Excavations revealed three types of room construction, with the earliest being a pithouse similar to the ones found at King's Ruin. Decorated pottery types were mostly Prescott black-on-gray and black-on-brown bowls and ollas, but a variety of imported ceramics also were present, including polychromes from Tusayan and white-on-red vessels from the upper Verde region. In addition, many shell artifacts (in particular, beads and carved pendants) were recovered from the site.

Tuzigoot

One of the most important investigations ever undertaken in the Verde region began in the fall of 1933, when an extensive excavation was undertaken by Cummings and the federal government at a large pueblo called Tuzigoot ("Crooked Lake" in Apache, for nearby Pecks Lake). This large ruin was located on the top of a narrow ridge about one hundred feet above the Verde River floodplain, near the modern town of Clarkdale in central Arizona. Earl Jackson (1934) had recommended the site for excavation because no sites in the Verde Valley had yet been systematically excavated. At Cummings' request, money from the federal Civil Works Administration (CWA) was obtained by Grace Sparkes, secretary of the Yavapai Chamber of Commerce and the work relief representative for Yavapai County. The site was owned by the United Verde Copper Company, which supported the investigation and later allowed the site to be made into a national monument.

The purpose of Cummings' excavations at Tuzigoot was to completely dig the main ruin, conduct partial reconstruction of some rooms, and display the excavated artifacts at the site. To accomplish the latter goal, a small building, called an "annex," was built next to the main ruin. This excavation and museum plan was similar to the one Cummings was undertaking at the same time at Kinishba Pueblo in eastern Arizona.

Because of their previous experience at King's Ruin and Fitzmaurice Ruin, Caywood and Spicer were put in charge of the excavations at Tuzigoot, under Cummings' oversight but largely in his absence. The work took place from October 31, 1933, to June 1, 1934 (Caywood and Spicer 1935; Spicer and Caywood 1935). Harry T. Getty and Gordon C. Baldwin, Cummings' assistants in the Arizona State Museum, also supervised the CWA laborers. Initially, money from the federal Emergency Relief Administration (ERA) was used to hire a crew of eight men. On November 24, CWA (Project No. P-10) money was available to hire forty-eight workmen for excavation and restoration and several women for cleaning artifacts and reconstructing pottery. An old distilled water store in Clarkdale served as both laboratory and classroom,[4] with Caywood in charge of this facility (Smith 1983). More than 150 pots from the Tuzigoot site were reconstructed in this building (fig. 20.2). When the CWA program was eliminated by Congress the next year, Sparkes was able to get money

20.2 Inside Tuzigoot ceramic laboratory, circa 1934 (courtesy of Arizona State University, Hayden Library Arizona Collection, #HD 3890.A7 09X V.1 Ariz.)

from the Emergency Relief Administration to finish the work (Project No. 12-F2-14). Combined CWA and ERA money spent on Tuzigoot totaled $27,575.00. Most of this was spent on labor, with an impressive 34,065 total man-hours used (Warner 1935:50).

Altogether, 86 of the 110 rooms at Tuzigoot were excavated by the CWA (Caywood and Spicer 1935). Some of the excavation techniques are unclear, and there are no notes for sixteen of the rooms (Hartman 1976). Except for a few earlier rooms built with river cobbles, room walls were constructed with irregular chunks of local limestone and sandstone. About fifteen rooms were identified as two stories in height. Most of the rooms were bigger, at least 18 feet by 12 feet, than those of other ruins in the region. Except for a few storage rooms, the vast majority of the rooms were living rooms that would have been entered from an opening in their roof. Three periods of construction were defined at Tuzigoot, and these are still valid today. Tree-ring specimens dated the pueblo from AD 1137 to 1386, but an earlier occupation is evident as well. Thus, the site was in use for about three centuries.

A plaza or courtyard was present in the northern part of the main group of rooms at Tuzigoot (fig. 20.3). No kivas were found, which is typical for the region (Mindeleff 1896:257). However, one rectangular room in the center of the pueblo on top of the ridge had a raised bench against one wall and floor partitions that suggested it may have been a ceremonial room. The burials of seven children were found beneath the floor of this room, and three other burials were present under the southeast corner of the raised platform.

The excavation and restoration of Tuzigoot involved the moving of 5,000 cubic yards of earth and the reconstruction of 20,000 cubic yards of masonry (Hartman 1976). Caywood and Spicer (1935) believed that Tuzigoot had not been built according to a preconceived plan, but had grown through time and that approximately 450 people had lived there in the 1200s.

The refuse heaps on the west and east slopes of the main ruin were trenched to locate burials. Three stratigraphic blocks also were dug into this refuse. Altogether, 411 burials were found at Tuzigoot, some containing more than one person, for a total of 429 individuals. About one-third of the burials were below the floors of the rooms, including more than 160 children and infants. One room contained 14 children and 1 adult. Similar to what was found at King's Ruin, the faces of some of the deceased had been painted green. Well-crafted jewelry adorned some individuals, including several mosaics made with worked pieces of turquoise and red shell. Shell jewelry was very common, with fourteen different species of shell represented.

One individual, who appeared to be a priest, was wrapped in a fine matting and was accompanied by several ceramic vessels. He was wearing outstanding jewelry, including thirteen carved shell bracelets on his left arm; a string of tiny shell and stone beads, more than twelve feet in length, and three frog mosaic pendants around his neck; another five-foot-long string of 2,542 red and black beads around his left wrist; a string of black beads alternating with turquoise pendants on his right wrist; and a twenty-four-foot-long string of beads, which had probably been sewn into his clothing, around his knees.

Another person had two turquoise earrings and an armband made of wood with turquoise mosaics. One of the child burials contained a small wooden bow, two feet in length, and part of an arrow. More than a dozen Jeddito yellowware vessels, made at ancestral Hopi villages to the north-

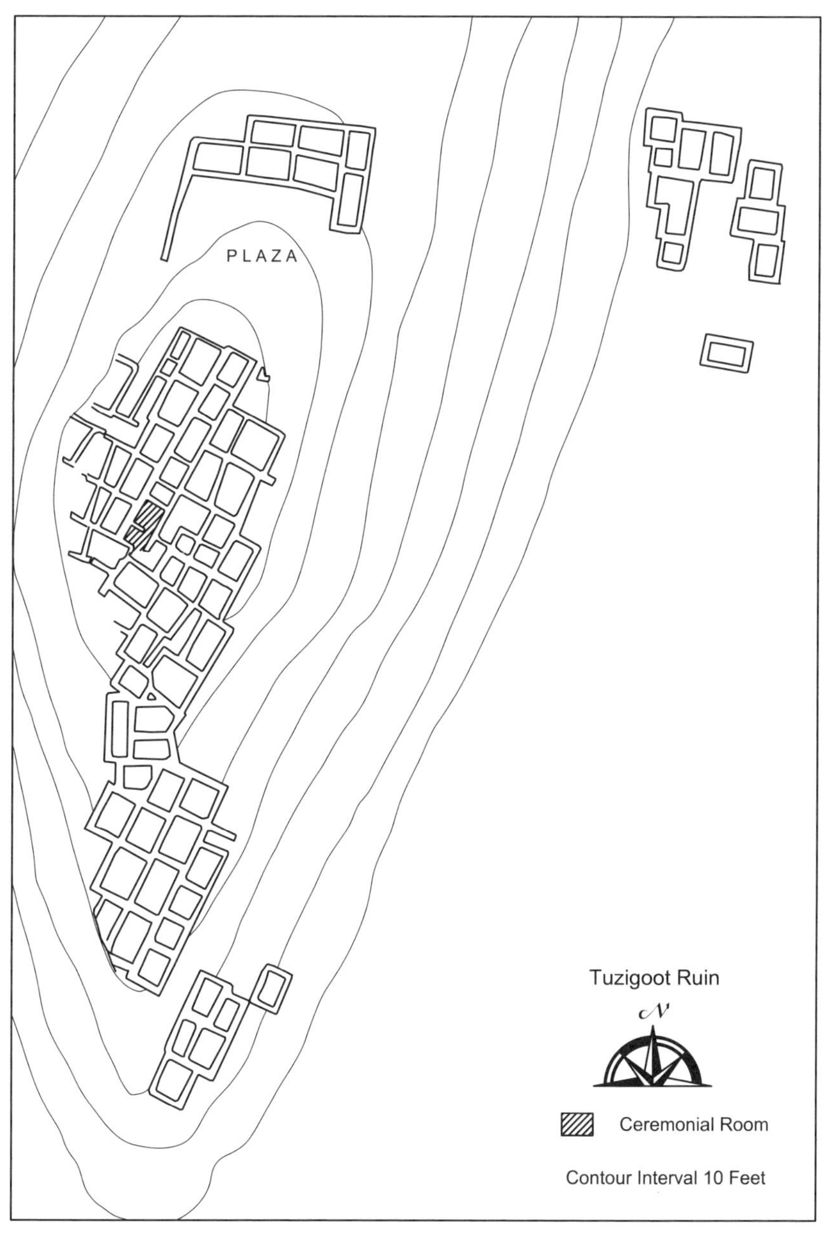

20.3 Tuzigoot Ruin plan view (redrawn from Caywood and Spicer 1935:fig. 3)

east, had been placed with the Tuzigoot burials, including the priest mentioned above (Anderson 1992). According to Caywood and Spicer, the abundance of exquisite jewelry indicated that the inhabitants had been a prosperous and industrious people, among whom leisure, wealth, trade, and esthetic taste had been well developed.

Five new types of decorated pottery were identified at Tuzigoot, reflecting multiple cultural influences. These included black-on-gray, white-on-red, red-on-buff, and black-on-white types, but most of the pots were a plain redware (Tuzigoot red) and a coarse brownware (Verde brown). Many of the black-on-white vessels at Tuzigoot were imported from the Flagstaff region. Curiously, Prescott black-on-gray represented only 11 percent of the decorated pottery at Tuzigoot. This mixture of different cultural styles prevented the excavators from declaring that the archaeology of the Verde region represented an independent culture.

Cummings made several unsuccessful attempts in the mid 1930s to make Tuzigoot a state monument. His efforts to preserve the site finally paid off when Tuzigoot was declared a national monument on July 25, 1939. However, the pueblo's reconstructed roofs were badly damaged during the winter of 1939–1940, and the wall reconstruction done by the CWA was deemed substandard. Consequently, many of the walls were reconstructed by the National Park Service in 1940–1941 and in 1953. Additional acreage was added to the monument in 1966 (Hartman 1976).

Montezuma Castle

In addition to Tuzigoot, Cummings also was able to get CWA money for the excavation and restoration of the famous five-story cliff dwelling at Montezuma Castle National Monument, twenty miles to the southeast. This picturesque ruin contains more than forty-five rooms, with some of the rooms dug into the limestone cliff. Its multistory square rooms contain only a few windows and doors, giving it the appearance of a medieval castle.

Beginning the week before Christmas of 1933, Earl Jackson supervised five to ten CWA laborers in restoring walls in Montezuma Castle and excavating burials at the base of the cliff. They worked until mid April of the next year. Sallie Pierce assisted with laboratory analysis. More than twenty pottery types representing thirteen ceramic wares were identified, providing evidence of widespread trade. Jackson and Pierce wrote a report in 1934, but it was not published for twenty years. In that report, Earl Jackson and Sallie Pierce Van Valkenburgh (1954:vi) thanked Cummings for his advice on field techniques. Jackson and Pierce (Van Valkenburgh/Brewer/Harris) went on to have long careers with the National Park Service.

The Smoki Museum

Today the Smoki Museum is a proud local institution in Prescott. Its origin came about during the Great Depression, which severely hurt the central Arizona mining and ranching economy and stimulated the Yavapai Chamber of Commerce to promote the scenic and historic qualities of Prescott for tourism dollars (Maxwell 1982). The secretary of the Yavapai Chamber of Commerce, who also served as the county's immigration commissioner, Grace M. Sparkes, was instrumental in these efforts. She had worked for the Yavapai Chamber of Commerce since 1910 and was also in charge of Prescott Pioneer Days and the Northern Arizona State Fair.

One of the popular cultural attractions in Prescott was a group of Anglo businessmen, called the Smoki People, who dressed up like Hopi Indians and performed dances, including the Hopi Snake Dance. The Smoki began in 1921 as a component of the Prescott Pioneer Days celebration. Their history was colorfully described in a sixteen-page pamphlet written by Sharlot Hall (1922), well-known author and curator of the original Governor's Mansion in Prescott. The Smoki became such an attraction that in 1926 they performed in Philadelphia. Prescott Chamber of Commerce promotional fliers (in the Grace Sparkes Papers at Arizona State University) described the Smoki dance as "weird, thrilling, spectacular." The success of the Smoki encouraged them to construct a stone building for their headquarters at the Prescott City Park, where the city council gave them a parcel of land next to a historic cemetery. Construction of this stone building, designed to store the Smoki's paraphernalia and serve as a museum, was financed through local donations that had been collected for the past two years. Construction began in January 1931, and stone quarried from the nearby Granite and Pine Dells area was used for construction material (Maxwell 1982).

A wing of the Smoki building served as a local museum. However, some citizens complained about the use of the name "Smoki" for the museum, because not everyone was enamored with the Smoki Lodge, so the Smoki dedicated a parcel of land next to their building for a separate museum.

In March 1933, the Arizona Legislature passed the State Welfare Act, which created a State Board of Public Relief, qualifying the state for federal New Deal money. With the capable assistance of Grace Sparkes, Civil Works Administration (CWA) funds were obtained from the federal government to construct a "Smoki building annex" beginning in the fall of 1933. CWA Project No. P-44, one of nine awarded to Yavapai County, provided $15,132.65 in labor and $13,523.53 in materials for the new museum. Construction consumed 24,368 person-hours before the CWA was phased out by Congress in March 1937. To complete the museum, Sparkes was able to get an additional $2,107.88 in material costs, paid with funds from the Emergency Relief Administration (Project No. 13-B2-31).

Pleased with the progress of the new Prescott museum and the local citizens' cooperation with the State Museum, Cummings (1934c) wrote a letter to University of Arizona president Shantz and recommended that the "Prescott Museum" be made a branch of the State Museum. Cummings informed President Shantz that the chamber of commerce and the Smoki People thought that the institution would have "greater prestige with the people of Prescott and be assured of greater permanency" if it were a branch of the Arizona State Museum and connected with the University of Arizona. Furthermore, they felt that "its work could thus be kept up to a higher standard, be made a real educational influence in the community, and thus bring the University and the people of Prescott and Yavapai County in closer sympathy and cooperation." Cummings supported their efforts because he believed that the two museums could be very helpful to each other.

Cummings recognized that to maintain the Prescott museum as a branch of the State Museum, a consistent source of funding would be required. He estimated that the Prescott museum could be run with about $2,000 a year, and the people in Prescott claimed they could raise most of this amount. In case they were not able to do so, Cummings suggested that the state subsidize the Prescott organization to the amount of $500 to $1,000 annually. This money would be well spent, Cummings argued, in promoting the best welfare of the state. He further stated that at a time when the state's mining and cattle industries were hurting, "various communities in the state must capitalize on their greatest resources—the climate and the educational advantages the state affords the growing youths and the weak adults under the most healthy surroundings." Those educational advantages, in Cummings' view, included the opportunities for learning about past human life in a museum.

Cummings proposed that the people of Prescott donate the grounds and museum to the University of Arizona in exchange for being granted State Museum branch status. This museum was to be governed by a five-member board of control, of which one member would be the director of the State Museum and the other members appointed by the chamber of commerce and the Yavapai Archaeological Society. In addition, the people of Prescott would be required to meet at least one-half of the expense of its annual maintenance. In addition to the board of control, the university's board of regents was to be assigned the responsibility of seeing that the work of the museum would be conducted in accord with the "best standards," that the collections would be properly preserved, and that investigations would be carried forward as time and money became available.

The University of Arizona's budget during the mid 1930s was very tight, and the proposal to fund a museum off campus was not favorably received. The chamber of commerce and the Smoki Committee, however, continued on with the completion of their new museum. The Smoki Lodge decided to call the new building the Smoki Public Museum.

The formal opening of the Smoki Museum was held on May 29, 1935. Cummings delivered one of the opening speeches, along with Homer R. Wood, chairman of the Yavapai County Welfare Board; Floyd Williams, president of the Yavapai County Chamber of Commerce; Roy Young, chief of the Smoki People; and Russell E. Insley, president of the Yavapai Archaeological Society. Louis Caywood, Tuzigoot park ranger, gave a lecture on archaeology. The opening program included a statement on the importance of archaeology and museums. It declared that a museum can become a clearinghouse of information and "an establishment of definite value as well as a place of interest to the curious." It closed by inviting people to become associated with the museum and to help make it a landmark for Prescott and the state of Arizona.

Malcolm Cummings served as director of the Smoki Museum for a short while in 1935 before it closed for the winter. In the summer of that year, Malcolm excavated a prehistoric masonry compound at the Prescott fairgrounds. He also unearthed two large mountain sheep heads carved from sandstone (M. Cummings 1936).

The Smoki Museum is still open to the public more than seventy years after it was built and is now a Prescott and Arizona landmark. It has never been affiliated with the Arizona State Museum. The Smoki Museum and Tuzigoot National Monument, which has more than 100,000 visitors annually, continue to be important tourist attractions for Yavapai County.

21

"A Profitable Chapter in the Life History of Man"

Cummings' Vision of an Outdoor Museum at Kinishba, 1931–1937

Four miles southwest of Fort Apache in eastern Arizona exists an imposing set of stone ruins that are situated among juniper trees on both sides of a deep ravine. The Apache call this ancient pueblo Kinishba, meaning "Brown House," a name derived from the color of the rocks used to build the pueblo. The broad valley in which Kinishba is located is bounded by high plateaus and mesas and drained by the White River, which runs from east to west and eventually joins the Salt River. This beautiful green-and-brown setting was once home to an industrious farming community that participated in an extensive trade network, connecting with other prehistoric cultures to the east, south, and north.

Adolph Bandelier (1892), the intrepid explorer of the Southwest, was the first Anglo to record Kinishba Pueblo, which he did during a visit in April 1883. He described a village settlement organized into two main groups, with scattered smaller buildings. Walter Hough (1903) observed that no professional excavations had taken place before then and that most previous digging probably had been done by soldiers stationed at the nearby Fort Apache in the 1870s. Nor would any organized excavation happen at Kinishba until Byron Cummings took an interest in the site half a century later.

In the summer of 1930, while on an expedition to northern Arizona with his annual summer field school, Cummings was told about Kinishba by a teacher at the Fort Apache Indian school. Cummings' summer and fall were already planned, so it wasn't until the spring of 1931 that he, along with several students, conducted a preliminary survey of Kinishba. Impressed with the number and size of ruined buildings in eight separate groups at the site, four on each side of a deeply incised wash, Cummings decided to excavate Kinishba with a few students and friends (fig. 21.1). Cummings then dedicated himself to Kinishba for fifteen years, excavating and restoring portions of three of the ruin groups, as well as building a small museum next to the restored Group I ruins on the east side of the wash. His plan was to create an outdoor and indoor museum with restored pueblo rooms, unrestored but excavated rooms, and museum display cases full of artifacts. Kinishba would become an educational experience for visitors, where they would learn about a "profitable chapter in the life history of man" (Cummings 1940a:117). Cummings' work at Kinishba is now legendary, but unfortunately, his restoration work and the museum building deteriorated over time, and now portions of the restored Kinishba are back in ruins.

What motivated Cummings to establish a permanent camp for an annual return to the same site, after years of exploring the red rock country of the Navajo Nation? Jeff Reid and Stephanie Whittlesey (1989:8) have suggested that Cummings was lonely and depressed from the loss of his beloved wife, Isabelle, in November of 1929 and was looking for an excavation project to keep him occupied. This may be true, but Cummings was by then in his seventies, and he simply may have decided to settle down a little. In 1928 and 1929 he had excavated Turkey Hill Pueblo near Flagstaff, and the idea of spending his summers in pine-tree country while digging into an important prehistoric pueblo was obviously appealing. In the preface to Cummings' (1940a:vii) book on the pueblo, the Hohokam Museums Association expressed hope that the story of Kinishba would "provide a source of understanding for the great pre-history of the Southwest and lend permanence to the story of a scientific triumph." With his Kinishba excavations and restorations, Cummings may have wished to accomplish something that would stamp his legacy on the Southwest, similar to what Alfred Kidder (1931a, 1932, 1936a) had done so spectacularly at Pecos Pueblo in New Mexico and Earl Morris (1928b) had done at Aztec Ruins in Colorado, or what his nephew, Neil Judd (1954c, 1964), had accomplished at Pueblo Bonito in Chaco Canyon.

The site's having received little scientific attention made Kinishba attractive to Cummings (1940a:xi), but he noted that it also "seemed the most promising for investigation because it represented the period of

21.1 Cummings at Kinishba, late 1930s (courtesy of Arizona Historical Society/Tucson, #PC29F.2A)

the highest development of prehistoric Pueblo Culture, was situated near the highway [State Route 73] and easily accessible and its location on the reservation would insure its protection." These are good reasons, since Cummings planned on developing the ruin into a national monument.

1931 Field Season

Early in the summer of 1931, Cummings applied to the secretary of the interior for a permit to excavate Kinishba, suggesting that his decision to dig there that summer had been made hastily. He received his permit on July 15; one of the conditions of the permit was that the artifacts, conveniently for Cummings, were to be stored at the Arizona State Museum (Dixon 1931).

Less than a week later, Cummings and a handful of students were digging into Kinishba. They continued until September 8 (Cummings 1931b). One of those students was Gordon C. Baldwin, who would later write his master's thesis on Kinishba and become assistant director of the Kinishba project and also the Arizona State Museum.[1] Five or six other students worked with Cummings that summer, including Florence Hawley, who had been one of his first master's students to graduate, in 1928. Hawley collected 286 wood specimens to be used for tree-ring dating (Nash 1999:213). The dig was not a university field school, so the students earned no credit that summer.

One of the first things Cummings did was a surface survey of the site to obtain a collection of the broken pottery. He also dug three long trenches into the south slope of Ruin Group II, finding several burials. Nine rooms in Group II and three rooms in Group I were excavated (Cummings 1940a:xi). The results of the excavations were valuable enough to convince him that he had chosen the right site.

1932 Field Season

From July 12 to the first week of September in 1932, as many as seventeen people worked with Cummings, including newly hired University of Arizona assistant professor John H. Provinse, who was assigned the title of assistant director (Cummings 1932a). More than a dozen students worked that summer at Kinishba, including graduate students from

Yale University, the University of Illinois, and the University of South Dakota (*Arizona Daily Star* 1932a). Several of the University of Arizona students went on to get their master's degrees under Cummings, including Louis Caywood, William Duffen, Earl Jackson, and Edward Spicer. Ben Wetherill, who by that time had considerable experience in Southwestern archaeology, also participated.

That summer the crew dug thirty-five to forty rooms at Kinishba (fig. 21.2). Several were two-story, as indicated by examination of the stratified fill of a room that revealed a firepit high above the lower floor. In some instances these second floors were still intact, containing not only firepits but also an associated floor artifact assemblage. Cummings also trenched into the refuse mounds for burials, which were excavated under the supervision of Provinse. Tree-ring samples collected by Hawley the year before had been analyzed and revealed occupation dates of 1260 to 1316, firmly establishing Kinishba as part of the Late Pueblo period (Baldwin 1938a:20). Toward the end of summer, a test pit was sunk at the northwest corner of Group II, revealing the remains of a pithouse that predated the pueblo.

In October, the Arizona Archaeological and Historical Society held its fall meeting at the Player's Theatre in the University Stadium. Cummings and Provinse wowed the audience with a program on their excavations at Kinishba and sites excavated by Cummings' students during that same summer at King's Ruin in Big Chino Valley, near Prescott (*Arizona Daily Star* 1932b). Artifacts and skeletons from Kinishba were shown to the audience.

1933 Field Season

With the Depression beginning to severely impact the University of Arizona's budget, in 1933 Cummings had to cut back on his Kinishba operations. Nonetheless, twenty-one rooms and part of a large patio or courtyard were excavated by more than a dozen students and volunteers (Cummings 1933e, 1939d). Two Apache Indians also assisted with the excavations. One of the rooms was subterranean and rectangular and had a small antechamber. This room seemed to be ceremonial, although it did not have the characteristics of a formal kiva. Cummings also reconstructed a room in the southwest corner of Ruin Group I. That summer

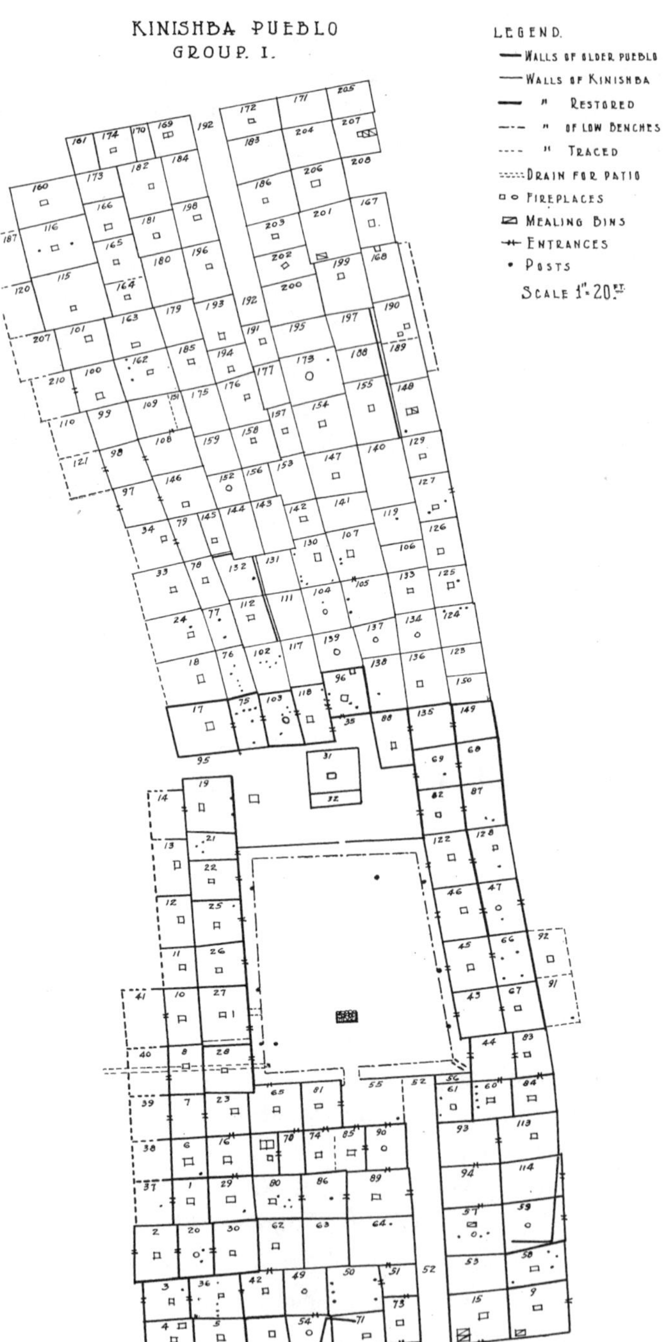

21.2 Plan map for Kinishba Group I ruins (Cummings 1940a)

Cummings (1940a:xiii) allowed women to camp at the site, with the tents of men and women set up in separate areas of the property. Before then, the women had commuted daily from Fort Apache.

1934 Field Season

By the next spring, Gordon Baldwin (1934) had completed his master's thesis on Kinishba. Cummings then submitted that thesis with his request for another permit to dig. Cummings had big plans for the summer of 1934 at Kinishba, since the university had agreed to give credits for participation in the dig, helping to finance the operations and thereby relieving the impact on the State Museum's budget. Twenty students and volunteers participated, each paying $5 per week for board (Cummings 1939d). Some of the crew members were individuals who stopped by for a few weeks at a time, including Cummings' son, Malcolm. Two of the students—Victor Stoner and Fletcher Carr—later received their master's degrees under Cummings. Because the crew was so large, Cummings hired a cook. Cummings (1934j) had unsuccessfully requested that Civilian Conservation Corps (CCC) laborers be assigned to work at Kinishba. He was able to hire two Apache laborers again.

Altogether, sixteen rooms and two patios were excavated that summer (Cummings 1934a; Jones 1935). In addition, five rooms were partially or completely reconstructed. Cummings (1934k) had asked for the loan of a truck from Superintendent William Donner of the Indian Service, but none was available. Fortunately, some of Cummings' friends in Miami, Arizona, provided him with an old truck—said to be worth $50—that was used to haul dirt away from excavated rooms (Jones 1935).

Cummings' recording techniques were generally systematic, with individual rooms assigned numbers and serving as the basic provenience location. Excavation within a room was done in arbitrary levels, typically six inches in thickness, with most rooms containing between five and seven levels. Plan maps were made of each level, and artifacts were recorded according to their location within that level. A master catalog for artifacts was kept, beginning with number 1, and each artifact was assigned a number within the catalog. Unfortunately, the catalog contains only a description of the artifact and not its specific provenience information within the room in which it was found.

That summer Cummings submitted his plans to construct a museum building and custodian quarters next to the ruins. In August, Cummings was taken to the hospital in Phoenix with a sciatic problem, forcing him to use a walking cane. He recovered, and the following November, thinking even more about his future, he informed Superintendent Donner of his plans to develop Kinishba as a future national monument (Cummings 1934k).

1935 Field Season

By the mid 1930s, archaeologists had learned to take advantage of the funding opportunities provided by President Roosevelt's New Deal work programs (Fagette 1996). Early in 1935, Cummings (1935) asked Superintendent William Donner for $6,000 from the commissioner of Indian affairs to hire twenty Apache laborers for six months and to improve the primitive well at Kinishba. Jesse Nusbaum, consulting archaeologist for the National Park Service, approved the twenty Apache laborers and issued a permit. The Department of the Interior also loaned Cummings a truck, and the U.S. Forest Service provided small timbers from forest thinning projects to be used for roof reconstruction at Kinishba.

Up to twenty-seven Apache workers, each paid $1.50 per day, and around two dozen students and volunteers excavated and reconstructed rooms that summer (Cummings 1935g, 1935j). It was a diverse crew, coming from as far away as California, Iowa, Missouri, Nebraska, New Mexico, New York, Rhode Island, Texas, Utah, and Washington, D.C. (Cummings 1939d). Two of the notable students included Richard Aldrich and Jean McWhirt. The Reverend Victor Stoner participated for a second season. In addition, a geology field school was established at Kinishba that year, headed by Professor R. J. Leonard.

Cummings (n.d.b) explained his reasons for hiring so many Apache laborers: "Both the Indians and white men need a practical and definite demonstration of the life of these ancient people to remove the mass of superstition and romance that has grown up around these ruins of the early population of Arizona and their relationships to the living tribes that still occupy more than one-third the area of this state." Working at Kinishba, Cummings believed, would teach the Apache to have more pride and greater faith in themselves.

With dozens of Apache and Anglos working together, more than twenty rooms were restored, and around twenty rooms and a patio were excavated. One of the unusual finds, from Room 76, was a copper bell from Mexico. In Room 64, twelve burials, mostly infants, were found under the floor.

Helen Forsberg (1935) wrote her master's thesis that year on the burials at Kinishba, and Gordon Baldwin (1935a:30) published new tree-ring dates from wood specimens that he had collected over the last two years. These dates were obtained from Group I and ranged from AD 1238 to 1306, similar to Hawley's tree-ring dates. David Jones (1935), another student of Cummings', wrote a summary article on Kinishba for *The Kiva* that fall.

One of Cummings' more famous students, Gordon Willey, later wrote about his experience at Kinishba in 1935. Willey (1988) remembers that Cummings had built a cook shack and another building that was used as a dining and lecture hall, which also served as headquarters for the site. Cummings kept his personal office and sleeping quarters in two restored rooms at the southern end of the pueblo. Willey remembered that Cummings had a sense of humor. Soon after Willey arrived, Cummings asked him if he "was ready to do some excavating." Willey (1988:16–17) recalled this momentous occasion:

> I responded with an eager affirmative, inwardly enjoying the surprise that I had been the one to be singled out to begin the real archaeological work while my companions continued with the tents or enlarged the cook house. Could my pith helmet, which I still wore, I thought, with some panache, have at last worked its magic and given me a sudden status. But no, given my shovel, I was dispatched some distance up the ravine to dig a new latrine for the women's camp.

Willey was later assigned to work with David Jones, excavating a room with a pick and shovel. They removed four or five feet of room fill in a little over a week until they discovered the floor.

Willey remembered that Cummings was an excellent raconteur during the evening lectures, telling captivating stories about his many adventures. On the Fourth of July, the entire group attended a fair in Whitewater. Cummings won the senior hundred-yard dash, and Willey won the junior hundred-yard dash. There were also trips to watch Apache dances, held at night and often lasting from sundown to sunrise. In mid August, Cummings took the group on a tour to visit several major ruins in northeastern Arizona and northwestern New Mexico.

After completing the 1935 field season at Kinishba, Cummings (1935m) wrote Superintendent Donner with his ambitious proposal to construct a nine-room masonry building to house a museum, a laboratory, a storeroom, and custodian's quarters. Sketch plans were included and a budget estimate of $10,032 prepared. A supporter and friend of Cummings, Superintendent Donner (1935) quickly approved his plans.

1936 Field Season

For the 1936 field season, Cummings received approval to use $2,500 of Superintendent Donner's Emergency Conservation Work (ECW) money for Apache laborers. That summer, about two dozen students and a similar number of Apache laborers excavated thirty rooms and restored forty rooms, two of them two-story (Mott 1936). The students included Stanley Boggs and Paul Gebhard, who would later attend Harvard University for their Ph.D.'s, and other well-known students such as Paul Ezell, Thomas Hale, Dorothy Mott, Frederick Scantling, and Albert Schroeder. Margaret Murray and James Schaeffer also worked that summer and later became the National Park Service's custodians at the site when Cummings left in the mid 1940s.

Three interesting individuals who dug at Kinishba in 1936 were Don Worcester and his mother and sister from Tempe. Worcester (1990) later remembered having befriended one of the Apache workers, David Kane, who always had an extra horse for him to ride. When not excavating, Worcester would ride all over the Apache reservation, checking on Kane's cattle and horses and visiting his friends. Kane tried to give one of his black stallions to Worcester as a gift, but it was too wild and they could not corral it to take it back to Tempe.

Worcester spent much of his time at Kinishba working on restoring rooms. He shared a tent with Paul Gebhard for a while, and then they moved into one of the reconstructed rooms in the pueblo. An Apache warned them that there were "Chindees" (ghosts) in the room because a burial had been found under the floor. Worcester had learned that children at Kinishba were buried under room floors, apparently to be near their mother. Perhaps it was a coincidence, but Gebhard became ill and had to return home. Worcester was fine, but he always remembered hearing snakes chase mice around the rafters of the reconstructed room!

Cattle roamed the site that summer, causing some damage, so Cummings (1936e) asked Superintendent Donner if Donner could assist with funding for a fence around the site. Approximately four miles of fence and a gate were needed to enclose the forty acres that included the eight ruin groups. In the fall, Jesse Nusbaum visited Kinishba to inspect the site because he was concerned that Cummings had submitted very brief reports, only one to two pages in length, on his annual work. Apparently satisfied with what he saw, Nusbaum later approved another season of work by Cummings. It may have helped that one of Cummings' students, Dorothy C. Mott (1936), published a four-page summary article on Kinishba in the November issue of *The Kiva*. In addition, Gordon Willey (1936) provided a detailed plan map of the work done at Kinishba in his master's thesis that year.

1937 Field Season

A turning point in the history of Cummings' Kinishba project occurred in 1937. Because he was forced to retire as head of the Archaeology Department that year, it was the last summer that he could use Kinishba as a University of Arizona field school. Realizing that he would need new supporters for his work, in April he invited three members of the newly formed Hohokam Museums Association to visit him at Kinishba. That organization would provide critical financial support for his work there for the next few years.

Cummings also sought help from the National Park Service. On April 10, he wrote two letters to Harold Ickes, secretary of the Department of the Interior. One letter expressed the need for a museum and custodian building at the site and requested that Kinishba be declared a national monument (Cummings 1937a). The other letter requested his summer excavation permit and $2,835 for ECW laborers and $120 for 120 sacks of cement (Cummings 1937b). These requests were passed on to Jesse Nusbaum, who recommended that the excavation permit be issued and money for the Apache laborers be allotted, but Nusbaum did not approve the construction of the museum building. Nusbaum did not want the National Park Service to build a museum that then had no commitment for future funding for its operations. He had experienced the difficulties of operating a museum without dedicated annual appropriations when he was the director of the Laboratory of Anthropology in Santa Fe in the early 1930s (Stocking 1982).

From mid June to mid August, several of Cummings' students and friends excavated and restored portions of Kinishba. Cummings charged students $6 per week that summer to pay for food expenses. In addition, approximately twenty-five Apache workmen were financed, at $1 each per day, by CCC funds through the Indian Service. Gordon Baldwin was appointed assistant director. Field notes identify at least nine different people who excavated nine rooms. Several others worked on restorations, and a detailed topographic map of the site was prepared by Walter Atwell. By the end of the summer, a total of fifty-nine rooms had been restored, and another twenty-six were ready for roofs. In addition, Margaret Murray (1937) completed her master's thesis on Kinishba pottery. Disappointingly, in mid September, Oscar L. Chapman (1937), assistant secretary of the Department of the Interior, deferred for two years Cummings' request for national monument status for Kinishba.

Kinishba was the first permanently based archaeological field school in Arizona (Gifford and Morris 1985). Between 1934 and 1937, Cummings trained at least seventy students in archaeological excavation techniques at Kinishba. Many of those students went on to have successful careers in archaeology or anthropology. Cummings' successor, Emil Haury, moved the university's field school to Forestdale in 1939 and a few years later to Point of Pines. The reign of Kinishba as an Arizona student-learning center was over with the retirement of Cummings as a university professor. But Cummings was not yet finished with Kinishba.

22

"A Very Unpopular Move"

Cummings' Involuntary Retirement and the Hohokam Museums Association

As the Depression dragged on during the late 1930s, the Arizona Legislature was forced to keep cutting the University of Arizona's budget. One means by which to save money was to replace older professors who had been at the university for some time with younger professors, who were paid lower salaries. Professor Byron Cummings, young in spirit but more than seventy-five years of age, was caught in this administrative move. The resulting changes in Cummings' academic responsibilities gave him more time to write, and he subsequently published three books based on his archaeological and anthropological experiences. To assist his tireless efforts to promote archaeology to the public, he and a friend, Mrs. Anna Child Bird, organized a new support group called the Hohokam Museums Association, which lasted from 1937 to 1946. At a time when Cummings no longer had institutional support, this organization arranged important social functions for him and his supporters and assisted with funding his excavations and publications.

Cummings' Involuntary Retirement

In late March 1937, President Paul S. Burgess of the University of Arizona announced that the board of regents had recommended that several professors over seventy years of age should be retired. Cummings was one of those professors, and he was not happy when he learned that he would lose both of his jobs: as head of the Archaeology Department and as director of the State Museum. As the paper had done throughout his career when he had something to tell the public, the *Arizona Daily*

Star (1937) soon printed a story quoting Cummings about his displeasure with the university. The headline of this story said it all: "Dean Protests 'U' Retirement." In this article, Cummings stated that he was willing to give up his position as head of the Department of Archaeology to Emil Haury but wished to retain his position as director of the State Museum because "certain plans I have made for it can be carried out and accomplished better by me than others." Clearly unhappy to lose his museum position, he proclaimed, "If there are any complaints about the quality of my work, I think I should be given a chance to be heard before the Board of Regents takes action." Cummings let his supporters and detractors know that "there are times when one has to stand up for his rights and I feel I have a right to the museum, and to more courteous treatment than I have received in the last few days."

Cummings was angered by the manner in which he had learned of his impending retirement. In his statement, he said that he had been informed by Dean Emil R. Riesen of the College of Liberal Arts, that University of Arizona president Paul S. Burgess had asked Haury to take over for Cummings at both his university positions. Cummings claimed that he had not been told by President Burgess or by the board of regents of this change in his academic status. He acknowledged that he had recommended Haury to follow him as department head but had made it clear to Haury that Cummings wanted to stay on at the State Museum.

It is interesting to note that 1937 was also the last year of the seven-year work agreement Emil Haury had made with Harold Gladwin of Gila Pueblo in exchange for support of his doctorate from Harvard University (Haury 1988). In other words, Haury was free to pursue a different direction in his career. Another interesting twist is that Dean Riesen was Haury's brother-in-law (Thompson 1995:649).

Because of his unhappiness at losing both of his university positions, Cummings informed the *Daily Star* (1937) that a number of university alumni and students had started a movement to protest Cummings' involuntary retirement from the museum. The *Daily Star* also interviewed President Burgess about Cummings' statements, and the president simply stated that it was "obviously a matter of policy." He noted that since 1934 the board of regents had been considering retiring faculty over seventy years in age (at part-time pay) and hiring younger professors at smaller salaries but that because of a lack of money no action had been taken.

The *Tucson Citizen* (1937) also wrote a story strongly supporting Cummings, stating that "ripe knowledge is the fruit of ripe years." The *Citizen* criticized the university for the way in which they handled Cummings' retirement, quoting Shakespeare's King Lear: "How sharper than a serpent's tooth to have a thankless child." The *Citizen* hoped that the university administration "will exert itself only to honor and gratify the distinguished, still vigorous savant, rather than humiliate him."

The announcement of Cummings' forced retirement brought a storm of protests from his friends and admirers. A family friend and supporter of Cummings, Mrs. Anna Child Bird, helped orchestrate letters of protest to the board of regents, to the governor, and to the university. Another friend, Bessie B. Loveless (1937), told Cummings that she had talked with many people in the state and found that his removal from the State Museum was "a very unpopular move." Sounding assured that something could be done on Cummings' behalf, Mrs. Loveless told him that there were "a lot of people with you" and that he should "stand pat."

Upon hearing of Cummings' retirement, in early April Senator Carl Hayden sent a four-page letter to E. E. Ellinwood, president of the board of regents. The contents of this letter suggest that Cummings had spoken to Hayden about his desire to remain as the director of the State Museum. Senator Hayden (1937) informed Regent Ellinwood, as "one old friend to another," that he was "strongly of the opinion that the Nation, and Arizona in particular, will be the loser if Professor Cummings is permitted at this time to retire from the directorship of the museum." Hayden (1937) provided these insightful words about Cummings' future:

> There comes a time when most of us wish to lay aside the tools of our active years in order to put the finishing touches on our life's work. Professor Cummings apparently has reached this period in his long and useful career and doubtless is impatient to leave the classroom in younger hands while he, himself, devotes all his energy to completing the museum and to preparation of his scientific reports. I sincerely trust that the Board of Regents may find it possible to provide all necessary aid in order that his investigations may reach their logical conclusion.

Hayden urged that Cummings should now spend his time preparing publications on his years of excavations "under the seal of the University in order that Arizona may rest firmly on the pedestal to which Professor

Cummings has raised it among institutions engaged in archaeological investigation." In Hayden's view, Cummings should be permitted to do his writing where the collections would be readily accessible. Obviously that meant he should be retained at the State Museum.

Grace M. Sparkes (1937), secretary of the Yavapai Chamber of Commerce and a member of the Yavapai Archaeological Committee, wrote to Governor R. C. Stanford in early April, lodging her protest against Cummings' retirement. She stated that the news had been received "with a shock by those who know of his many years of untiring, unselfish effort and work to develop archaeology to where it now stands in Arizona." Furthermore, she warned that Cummings' forced retirement would have a deleterious impact, for it would take years "for Arizona to live down the stigma which will be placed upon it." She pleaded with the governor that Cummings not be "discarded simply because he has reached a certain age," because, in her opinion, he "is too valuable and useful man for such treatment."

That same day in April, Mrs. Eva M. Scales of Atzcapotzalco, Mexico, wrote E. E. Ellinwood to express her regret and protest. Mrs. Scales (1937) noted that the excavations he had directed at the pyramid of Cuicuilco had been "one of the most valuable contributions made to Mexican archaeology." She urged that for the University of Arizona's own sake, it needed to see "that Dr. Cummings stays on the job!"

Thomas Hale (1937), a student at the University of Arizona and former president of the Arizona Archaeological and Historical Society, also wrote to Ellinwood (with a copy to the governor) about his admiration for Cummings. Hale had known Cummings for eight years and had observed "his great capacity for the work in which he is engaged, as a painstaking educator, as Director of the Museum, and as a kindly and lovable man." In Hale's opinion, Cummings was capable of carrying on his work "with the energy and mental activity of a man half his age."

Sharlot M. Hall (1937), Prescott author and historian, wrote Cummings a letter from Phoenix to express her sympathy for his predicament. Hall had known Cummings for a long time, and she let him know how she felt about the situation: "I am thinking of those rough red hills of the north where you were working when I said that you were needed at the University of Arizona. You came—and did a glorious work—but I am ashamed of the payment you are getting now. It is a strange world we live in—where a fine experience and learning are measured by year—when all the world's best work, has been done by mature minds—minds now scoffed at." Hall was clearly upset at the way Cummings' retirement had been handled.

W. B. Taylor (1937) of Harwichport, Massachusetts, and formerly of Salt Lake City, Utah, wrote Cummings on June 29 to tell him that Taylor had information about Cummings' retirement that might be of interest to him. Taylor was retired and an amateur archaeologist who hung around Harvard University because of his interest in anthropology. He stated that in the spring of 1936 he had heard gossip from one of the anthropology students at Harvard that Emil Haury was "trying to oust you and get your job." When Taylor read about Cummings' involuntary retirement, he wrote Governor Stanford a letter about the gossip he had heard at Harvard. The governor's response, if any, is unknown.

Cummings' retirement was a difficult issue for the University of Arizona, but some individuals in the university's administration believed that it was time for younger leadership. There also were increasing complaints that Cummings had not written up reports on many of his expeditions. A letter from James W. Simmons (1933b) to Harold Gladwin four years earlier provides some insight into this issue. One of Governor George Hunt's aides, Lynn Lockhart, had informed Simmons that the governor had become concerned about the lack of reports from Cummings and had suggested that he be retired on reduced pay with a secretary so he could write up his long-awaited reports. No action was taken at that time, but the issue appears to have been under discussion in some political circles for a while.

Realizing that they had a problem on their hands, the university administration talked to Cummings about his desire to remain as director of the State Museum. Determined to have the Harvard-trained Haury run the State Museum, Alfred Atkinson, the new president of the University of Arizona, offered Cummings a deal whereby he could stay at the State Museum as director emeritus at one-half salary, but Haury would administer the museum's operations. In late January, President Atkinson (1938a) wrote a letter to Cummings, offering this new arrangement—subject to the approval of the board of regents—which would take effect July 1 of that year. President Atkinson commented, "I know you will be pleased to be relieved of the details of administration, and the appointment of director emeritus will give you continuing recognition of the large service which you have rendered to the upbuilding of archaeology at the University of Arizona and in the country generally."

President Atkinson told Cummings that he could finish his work at Kinishba Pueblo for the next two years as he requested. In addition, Atkinson hoped that Cummings would complete the reports on his many explorations, which Cummings had been unable "to put in shape because of the heavy demands on your time throughout the past years." The publication of these reports, Atkinson argued, "will round out your record of attainment in a way that will be permanent and will be an inspiration to the archaeologists throughout the decades and centuries ahead." This formal approach to Cummings' writing responsibilities during his half-time employment in his position as director emeritus suggests that Haury had had a hand in the president's statements.

Cummings accepted the offer, which paid him a half-time annual salary of $2,100 ($27,300 in 2003 dollars). He also was allowed access to the State Museum collections. In mid February, President Atkinson (1938b) wrote a letter to Cummings informing him that the board of regents had approved of his appointment as director emeritus. Atkinson wished Cummings "many years of sound health, so that you may continue to work with your present vigor and effectiveness."

Hohokam Museums Association

Although Cummings had created the Arizona Archaeological and Historical Society (AAHS) as a support group, in 1937 he sought another way to gain additional help for his research and writing expenses, perhaps because the AAHS was too closely tied to the Department of Archaeology. This opportunity came about when he befriended a remarkable woman in her early eighties, Mrs. Anna Child Bird. Bird resided in Massachusetts but visited Tucson on a regular basis because of her love of the Southwest and its native peoples. In addition, her daughter, Edith, lived in Tucson and was married to Robert P. Bass, former governor of New Hampshire from 1911 to 1913. Mrs. Bird was married to Charles Sumner Bird and was well connected socially, having been the first women member of the National Republican Committee in the 1920s.

Bird became a big supporter of Cummings' archaeological research and was the "founder and moving spirit" of a new support group called the Hohokam Museums Association. This group was dedicated to the encouragement of archaeological work in Arizona in general and of Cummings' work in particular, but it was especially interested in sharing Cummings' archaeology with the public. Publications, of course, were one way to do that.

The idea for a Hohokam Museums Association (HMA) was discussed in March 1937, the same month Cummings learned of his retirement.[1] On April 4, 1937, the HMA adopted its constitution and by-laws with the motto "Truth Leads Men." Cummings was elected president; Hubert H. d'Autremont, treasurer; and Anna McGrath, a former student of Cummings', secretary. In addition, an executive committee and advisory council were established. A professional-looking pamphlet (published with the date 1938–1939) stated the purpose of the HMA: "To promote public interest in the museums of the State of Arizona, to enlarge their collections, to augment and improve existing facilities for display purposes within them, and to endeavor to make of the museum a factor of continually increasing importance in the cultural life of each community." This mission statement seems tailored to Cummings' needs at the State Museum, and he may have assisted in its composition. The pamphlet listed membership costs from $1 for regular membership to $100 for life membership. Cummings contributed $50 as a patron member. Potential members were encouraged to join, with an invitation that stated, "You are cordially invited to add your influence and co-operation to this great cause."

Altogether, 406 members of the HMA are known (Wilcox 2001). Members resided in fifteen different states other than Arizona, including states in the Midwest and East. Occupations included lawyers, artists, bankers, newspaper editors, hospital staff, businessmen, insurance workers, law enforcement officers, University of Arizona faculty, and others. Interestingly, no out-of-state professional archaeologists were identified, although there were several students and instructors in the Department of Archaeology at the University of Arizona.

Several prominent faculty and administrators of the University of Arizona were members of the HMA, including President Atkinson. In addition, Everett E. Ellinwood, president of the board of regents, and his wife were members. President Atkinson was popular with members of the HMA, perhaps because he brokered the deal with Cummings for his position of director emeritus, and the group honored Atkinson with a reception and dinner on February 16, 1938. More than three hundred people attended.

In late 1937, the Bird family was sympathetic to Cummings' fragile state of mind and invited him to accompany them to the Bective House near Navan, Ireland, and to make a journey to ancient Tara. Atkinson, also concerned about Cummings, encouraged him to take leave and go on the trip. In October, Cummings finally traveled to one of the countries he had always wanted to visit. After his Ireland experience, Cummings took advantage of being overseas and continued on to Italy, Syria, and another place he had always wanted to explore—Egypt (Cummings and Cummings n.d.:197).

In Cairo, he spent three days in November visiting museums and two days examining pyramids. While there, he rode a camel, climbed to the top of the Great Pyramid of Cheops, and crawled through the galleries of the King's Chamber. To add even more excitement to his experience, he met with the famous Egyptologist George A. Reisner and his wife, who were working at the pyramids. Professor Reisner had trained Alfred Kidder in field methods at Harvard University nearly thirty years before. Cummings was very impressed with their work but noticed that the professor was losing his sight. The Temple of Luxor and the tombs in the Valley of the Kings were also on Cummings' Egyptian itinerary. From Alexandria, he sailed to New York, arriving back in the United States the second week of December. This exciting trip may have helped sooth the resentment he felt toward the university concerning his position at the State Museum.

The HMA raised interest and money for their coffers through a series of exciting public lectures and social dances. Cummings contributed an illustrated lecture every year. After 1938, programs also included amateur motion pictures on a variety of topics. For example, Cummings showed a movie of his Ireland trip.

In 1938, Cummings was still in control of Kinishba, and he planned his future around the Brown House. The HMA provided some critical funding for his work at Kinishba in the late 1930s and early 1940s, and he invited them for an annual weekend powwow at Kinishba to repay them, a 420-mile round trip from Tucson. Apache dances, as well as the singing of "The Star Spangled Banner," were typically part of the program at these Kinishba powwows.

23

"There Is Much Work Yet to Be Done"

Final Years at Kinishba, 1938–1947

Cummings' retirement from the Archaeology Department in 1937 and from the State Museum the next year freed him from his typical heavy load of teaching and administrative responsibilities. His director emeritus status gave him time to complete his Kinishba excavations and restorations and to build the museum that he had long envisioned for the site. He also had time to write up a report on his work at Kinishba. For the next eight years, he lived in a reconstructed room in Ruin Group I, trying to fulfill his goals for Kinishba.

1938 Field Season

In 1938, Cummings worked at Kinishba for nine straight months, from mid April to mid December. Field notebooks indicate that more than two dozen volunteers and Apache laborers excavated more than forty rooms that year (Cummings 1938a, 1938c). In addition, twenty or more rooms were reconstructed, including a three-story room. Student John D. Fletcher drove the old Ford truck, and his salary and insurance was paid by the Hohokam Museums Association (HMA). One of the Apache workers, Turner Thompson, became Cummings' close friend. Although deaf, Thompson was one of Cummings' most dependable and cooperative workers for two seasons (Cummings 1952).

Work was begun in earnest that year on the museum building, with the concrete foundation poured, the water and sewer trench dug, and the cesspool built by mid December. Gordon Baldwin published two articles on Kinishba that year: a summary of his master's thesis in *American An-*

tiquity (1938a) and an article in *Southwestern Lore* (1938c) on unusual pottery at the site. Cummings (1938a) wrote a short article on Kinishba for a fall issue of *The Kiva*.

1939 Field Season

In 1939, tensions began to develop between Cummings and Emil Haury, partly because Haury began reorganizing the Arizona State Museum and making requests of Cummings about undocumented objects in the museum. Haury also asked for the return of the State Museum's camping equipment from Kinishba so he could use it for his field school in Forestdale that summer. Cummings (1939e) sent some equipment back but kept a few of the tents and the kitchen utensils, and he suggested that Haury purchase new equipment with the State Museum budget.

In mid May, Haury wrote Cummings a letter requesting that Cummings prepare a report on his work at Kinishba to be included in the university president's annual report. In that letter, Haury (1939) asked Cummings to provide information on "complete financial assistance both direct and indirect," including money from the HMA. Cummings (1939f) became indignant about Haury's request, writing him immediately to inform him that Kinishba was not a university or State Museum project and had not really been one for several years. Other than his own half-salary, paid by the university, Cummings argued that the "State Museum has put nothing into the project since we began giving summer courses and the government furnished Apache laborers." In the firmest language he could muster, Cummings told Haury, "Don't try to control everything in the state just yet." Upon receipt, Haury forwarded the letter to President Atkinson. Sensing Cummings' unhappiness with the university, Atkinson (1939) told Haury to forget the Kinishba report.

More determined than ever to complete his work at Kinishba, Cummings steadily continued his excavations and restorations. In 1939, about twenty rooms were dug. By the end of that season, a total of ninety-two ground-floor rooms and forty-eight second-story rooms had been restored. Cummings was paid a salary from the Civilian Conservation Corps (CCC) for supervising Apache laborers who worked on restoration. The HMA provided a Ford truck and again paid the salary for a driver. Much to Cummings' delight, that year the museum building and custo-

23.1 Excavated but unrestored portion of Kinishba, with museum in background (courtesy of Arizona Historical Society/Tucson, #PC29F.3A)

dian's quarters were completed with financial assistance from the Indian Service (fig. 23.1).

Unfortunately, CCC support for Apache laborers at Kinishba was terminated at the end of September. The HMA solicited more money from the federal government for Cummings' restorations, but John Collier (1939), commissioner of Indian Affairs, responded that no additional money was available and reminded Mrs. Bird that the government had already spent $20,000 on Kinishba restorations.

Perhaps to repair Cummings' and Haury's deteriorating relationship, in December 1939, Emil Haury was elected to the advisory council of the HMA. In addition, a Miss Page requested that Cummings' photograph be taken by Esther Henderson and placed in the State Museum. That year Gordon Baldwin (1939a) published another article on Kinishba in *American Antiquity*; the article annoyed Cummings because he had been working on his Kinishba book at the time and felt that Baldwin had undermined the book's importance. Baldwin (1939b) wrote a letter of apology

23.2 Kinishba reconstructed, looking north (courtesy of Arizona Historical Society/Tucson, #PC29F.3B)

to Cummings, explaining that he was merely following up on his 1938 *American Antiquity* article.

1940 Field Season

The year 1940 was a turning point in Cummings' work at Kinishba. He had excavated into this prehistoric pueblo for nine years and had accumulated a huge amount of information and artifacts from the site. He learned in January that he would no longer receive his annual salary of $1,680 from the CCC or the use of Apache labor because the federal work program had been shut down by Congress (Maulding 1940). Without Apache laborers or students from the University of Arizona, Cummings decided not to undertake any excavations that year; rather, he focused on developing the museum grounds and exhibits and finishing his book on Kinishba (fig. 23.2). That summer, Cummings (1940d) was among five hundred Native Americans who witnessed an Apache lightning ceremony near a house that had been struck by lightning. In October, Cummings (1940b) requested from Haury a loan of specific Kinishba artifacts stored at the State Museum. Haury (1940) obliged, offering a loan of seventeen ceramic vessels, several pieces of shell and turquoise jewelry, and 350 gypsum pendants for the Kinishba museum.

Cummings' Kinishba Book

Under pressure to write a comprehensive report on his excavations, Cummings put his energy that year into completing his long-awaited book on Kinishba. As the book was going through production, he was forced to address the question of who would get credit for publication. The University of Arizona administration felt that the university should be credited, but Cummings was still resentful toward the university because of the way his retirement had been handled three years before. In late August, this disagreement reached a crescendo when President Atkinson (1940a) requested that Cummings allow the University of Arizona Publications Committee to review the book before it was published. Cummings (1940c) resented the implication and informed President Atkinson that the HMA had provided most of the funding for its publication and therefore should get publication credit. Reminded that as director emeritus, he was still a university employee, Cummings offered a compromise in which both the HMA and the University of Arizona were to be credited on the title page. In late September, his book was approved by the publications committee (Atkinson 1940b).

Although Cummings (1940b) believed that there was "much left to be done at Kinishba if all of the problems arising are to be settled," he was ready to reveal his story of the pueblo. In mid December, his book was published with the title *Kinishba: A Prehistoric Pueblo of the Great Pueblo Period*. It was a hardcover book, 128 pages in length, and sold for $3.50. The book had a detailed map of the main ruin and 119 illustrations, including more than 90 black-and-white photographs and 35 beautiful color plates prepared by Henry Lockett, Courtney R. Jones, and Donald Sayner.[1]

Cummings took a generalist approach when writing his Kinishba book, aiming more toward a broad public audience than toward his professional colleagues. The book is not a detailed account of every room and burial, nor is it a systematic examination of the artifacts recovered from the site. Rather, Cummings provided a concise summary that includes a short history of the project and the highlights of his findings. In his description of the architecture, he noted that earlier rooms were made with an ashlar design, mostly from sandstone but also including some blocks of lava and limestone. Later walls were constructed with chinking stones used to fill in gaps, similar to classic Chacoan architecture in New Mexico. Juniper and pine trees were used for roof supports and crossbeams.

Group I, where Cummings did the most excavating, was described as having 210 rooms, two inner courts (patios), and three entrances. But Cummings selected only a few of the more than 220 rooms that were excavated at the site as examples for illustration and discussion. Among these are Room 6, which contained twenty-one stone balls, and Room 16, which had a set of mealing bins. Room 27 contained an altar stone and other objects, such as twenty-six deer pelvic bones, that indicated it might have been a ceremonial chamber. Room 30 had an impressive number (1,141) of gypsum pendants made from local materials. Room 168 had six children buried under its floor, and Room 198 contained a painted stone tablet altar. Unfortunately, we are told little or nothing about the many other rooms at the site.

Only general information was presented about Kinishba burials. Altogether, most of the burials in the Group I ruins were those of children, who were often wrapped in cotton blankets and rolled into a rush mat or had a mat laid over them. Some graves had a "roof" of poles and bark covered with earth. Many of the skeletons showed evidence of dental cavities and ulcerations of the jaw, and others were arthritic. Some of the burials had crania shapes, indicating that the back of the individual's head had been intentionally flattened at a young age. Three cremations were found, suggesting some influence from the Hohokam in southern Arizona.

Artifact descriptions focused on the more interesting items. These include beautiful painted pots, shell and stone jewelry, stone animal effigies (deer, bear, and birds), and numerous pieces of ground and powdered minerals used for paint. Cummings also gave totals for some artifact types: 270 stone axes, 625 bone awls and 50 bone daggers (see Olsen 1980), 2 copper bells, and 2 stone lip plugs. But rather than presenting a

23.3 Cummings' (1940a:78) sketch of a Roosevelt style black-on-white jar from Kinishba

full description of the artifacts, such as Kidder (1931a, 1932, 1936a) had done for his Pecos Pueblo excavations, Cummings chose to write some colorful, romantic text about the wonderful craft items that the people of Kinishba had created. He argued that Kinishba pottery displays "evidence of individual freedom and taste [so] that one feels sure these artists were not held down by a multitude of conventionalities. Their styles were chaste and harmonious, their designs balanced and symmetrical. There are not clashing of loud colors. Contrast is employed, but the lines so arranged to give an effect of light and shade and which brings out the details of each design clearly" (Cummings 1940a:92). But we can only accept Cummings' word and look at the sample of vessels illustrated (fig. 23.3), because he provided little actual data about individual pots and their proveniences through which to evaluate or better understand his conclusions.

According to Cummings, people from three different time periods had lived at Kinishba—a conclusion based on architectural characteristics. The earliest people were represented by pithouses, scattered in three different locations. Under the current pueblo was evidence of an earlier pueblo that postdated the pithouse people. The last configuration of Kinishba had been built during the Great Pueblo period, a time when the pueblo had served as a central station in an extensive trade network that included the Anasazi, Mogollon, Hohokam, and others. Cummings believed that the drying up of the local water source, not warfare, had caused the abandonment of the Kinishba pueblo in the late fourteenth century.

In his conclusions, Cummings expressed his vision for Kinishba. He hoped that the ruin and museum would make the prehistoric people come alive to the visitor and would become a clearinghouse of ideas and information profitable to both Apaches and Anglos (Cummings 1940a: 117).

Family, friends, and students of Cummings' who had worked at the site were thrilled that he had finally published the results of years of excavations at Kinishba. The HMA played an important role in helping finance the $4,417.37 in publishing costs for the book, contributing $1,755 of the association's money. Mrs. Bird donated $600. Cummings wrote a personal check for $53.66 to cover the shortage between receipts and disbursements.

To Cummings' supporters, the book was a triumphant achievement. But not everyone was thrilled with his book. Especially critical were archaeologists working on the Mogollon culture, who eagerly sought data on Kinishba because it was considered a Mogollon site. Paul S. Martin of the Field Museum in Chicago had responded favorably to Haury's (1936a) pioneering publication on the Mogollon only a few years earlier. But in a 1941 issue of the *American Anthropologist*, Martin wrote a very negative review of Cummings' book. Martin was clearly disappointed that Cummings had not attempted to understand the role of Kinishba within the context of Mogollon regional and chronological developments.

Some of Martin's (1941a:654) comments were damning statements about Cummings' approach to archaeology, such as that "there were regrettable features about his report, the most important of which are the lack of insight into what archaeology stands for and a lack of synthesis and theoretical approach." Martin (1941a:655) stated that Cummings' book gave the impression that "specimens are collected as one might collect postage stamps." He complained that Cummings did not cite other authorities whose work was relevant and that his classification system (Archaic, Pithouse, and Great Pueblo) was inadequate. Martin was critical of the lack of provenience information and the lack of specific details about architecture and artifacts, stating that meager data did not justify the specialist's long wait. He also stated that the careless method of presentation would not attract the layman.

Martin was right on the first account but wrong on the second. Laymen did enjoy Cummings' book, as indicated by the positive letters Cummings received from many friends and former students. For example, an old colleague, Edgar Hewett (1941), sent Cummings a letter in May that stated, "how greatly I appreciate this piece of work." But most professional archaeologists have generally ignored the book because of its lack of details, especially spatial information.

Cummings was furious with Martin's review. So were some of Cummings' supporters. John McGregor, a former graduate student of Cummings' and a staff member of the Museum of Northern Arizona, wrote Cummings in late October to offer sympathy. McGregor (1941) wanted to convey his "disgust" at the manner in which Martin had reviewed Cummings' book, calling it "the most biased and unfair report I have ever read in such a paper." He recommended that Cummings just ignore it. But Cummings would not do so.

On November 17, Cummings wrote two letters from Fort Apache. A typed letter went to Paul (Ralph) Linton, editor of the *American Anthropologist*, and a handwritten letter went to Paul Martin. Cummings (1941b) told Dr. Linton that "the spirit manifest in his [Martin's] so-called review has no place in the columns of the *American Anthropologist*." Martin's review, in Cummings' opinion, was "petty, sneering, and misrepresents the facts."

Cummings (1941c) used even stronger language in his letter to Paul Martin, beginning it with "Heil the Great Paul Martin!" He then commented, "How charming it will be from now on that all other archaeologists can just sit back and wait for Paul Martin to do their thinking and interpreting for them!" Accusing Martin of being "Hitlerian" in his approach, Cummings asked if Martin's judgment of others was anything but "accept my ideas and standards or off goes your head!" Cummings then responded to his own rhetorical question:

> No, Mr. Martin, neither science nor men are produced by petty, carping criticism or slurs and innuendoes. American archaeology needs no self-imposed censor or dictator. We are fighting for freedom of speech and the

> right to work out our own salvation on the same plane with others in peaceful and harmonious development. You have a right to your opinions and their expression, but you have no human right in that expression to vent your personal animosity and seek to destroy the reputation and nullify the efforts of any other human being.

Cummings closed his letter by inviting Martin to visit Kinishba to see how mistaken Martin was in his judgment of the work done there.

Ralph Linton (1941) wrote Cummings back in late November, acknowledging that Martin's review was "unduly severe" but that Linton had followed the *American Anthropologist*'s policy of publishing reviews as they were received. Paul Martin (1941b) also wrote Cummings back in December, stating that he regretted "very much that you took my review of your book in a personal way." He assured Cummings, "What I had to say reflected in no way upon your personal character." It may not have, but it certainly reflected upon Cummings' professional reputation, and for that he was in some ways devastated.

Martin's negative review only added to Cummings' sense of betrayal by his profession. Earlier that year, Superintendent Donner (1941a) had asked J. W. Jamison, state administrator for the Works Progress Administration (WPA), if there was a possibility that the WPA could hire Cummings and two or three Apache laborers to fix damage to the roofs that had been caused by a very wet winter the year before. Jamison (1941) denied Donner's request on the pretext that the project was too small to be cost-effective and too isolated to be properly administered.

Donner also wrote Senator Hayden asking whether the senator could find a government position for Cummings. Donner (1941b) acknowledged that Cummings was in his eighties but asserted that he acted much younger. He noted that Cummings "still feels his retirement very keenly which seems to be the principal reason for his wanting to stay away from Tucson." He also requested that Kinishba be turned into a national monument so that Cummings' "interest and time in this project would not have been in vain." Senator Hayden (1941) made an effort to find something for Cummings, but there were few government archaeology jobs available, and his age precluded him from other government positions.

The Kinishba Museum in the 1940s

On April 26, 1941, the Kinishba Museum was officially dedicated. A visitor log was started that was kept for ten years. In its first year, 716 people visited the museum—coming from more than three dozen states—but attendance slowed considerably during the war. In September, Senator Ernest McFarland (1941) wrote a letter to John Collier requesting that Kinishba be declared a national monument. The request was denied because of the excuse that Kinishba would be better cared for by the Indian Service (Zimmerman 1941). To make matters even worse, heavy rains damaged the new museum's roof that winter, and Cummings had to replace it with a new roof.

A year later, Cummings (1942a) prepared a five-year budget for the years 1943 to 1948. It was an ambitious budget, designed to address the remaining museum development that Cummings envisioned for the site. He wanted to rebuild roofs on restored rooms ($2,500) and paint them reddish brown ($500); repair portions of the nonrestored rooms in the Group I ruins ($1,000); buy primitive furniture for the restored rooms ($500); build a road from Highway 73 ($500); build a porch in front of the museum ($500); purchase display cases ($2,000); construct a telephone system ($400); build a lighting system ($500); buy a hot water tank ($100); and purchase an estimated $2,500 in general materials for five years. In addition, $2,700 was earmarked for an Indian assistant for five years with an annual salary of $540. The $15,400 cost for Cummings' five-year program, however, was not well received by the Indian Service during wartime, and Cummings was left with little financial support for Kinishba. He again wrote Harold Ickes of the Department of the Interior asking for national monument status for Kinishba but was again turned down (Cummings 1942b).

At the March 1943 meeting of the HMA, Cummings reported on the need for a front porch and sign for the Kinishba Museum. He also recommended reconstructing some guest rooms in the ruin and renting them for revenue. The executive committee also expressed sympathy concerning the unfortunate death of Mrs. Bird in Massachusetts in the fall of 1942. Cummings (1943) wrote to Mrs. Bird's daughter, Edith, and told her that her mother's "activity and resourcefulness were an inspiration to all." Without Mrs. Bird's energy and drive, and given the full retirement of Cummings from the State Museum soon thereafter, the HMA slowly died.

Because Cummings' five-year budget had been rejected in 1942, Superintendent Donner (1944) requested that Cummings prepare a budget for the year 1945. Cummings (1944b) proposed a total of $1,265 to be spent on repairing the roofs of nine rooms and the employment of two or three people. One (presumably Cummings) was to be a caretaker for the period from September 1944 to June 1945 at $50 a month, and the other or others would lend assistance during the summer. In late August, Cummings (1944c) told Superintendent Donner that he had to repair many of the reconstructed roofs because the materials he had used—a commercial mixture of emulsified asphalt and soil recommended by Standard Oil officials—did not hold up to the winter and summer rains as he had been led to believe. Cummings' notes are very sketchy concerning his reconstruction activities, but he apparently replaced the defective roof coverings with cement, which turned out to be just as ineffective.

To complement the back porch he had built onto the museum two years before, Cummings finished his construction of a front porch. He also completed his excavations of Ruin Group IV and partially rebuilt four more rooms. In October, Cummings (1944a) was happy to report in an issue of *Museologists* that he was still "going strong" on his eighty-third birthday and was greatly encouraged because the Indian Service had included Kinishba Ruins and the museum in its annual budget. He expressed hope that the Indian Service and the public would come to appreciate Kinishba as a valuable asset. In November, he was saddened to hear of the death of his long-time friend, John Wetherill.

Although Cummings began to have trouble with his eyesight, he refused to give up on his deep-seated vision for an outdoor and indoor museum at Kinishba. He continued working at the site when the weather permitted, spending winters with Malcolm in southern California. Joyce and Joseph Muench published two articles on Cummings and Kinishba in *Natural History* (1946a) and the *Arizona Highways* magazine (1946b). Cummings told the authors about his sparse lifestyle—he had no electricity, no phone, no refrigeration, and no batteries for his radio. His life had changed drastically from twenty years earlier, when he and Isabelle had lived luxuriously in the University of Arizona's president's house and he had been chauffeured around by Emil Haury in the university's Lincoln Towncar.

Also in 1946, the Indian Service hired James B. Shaeffer and his wife, Margaret Murray Shaeffer, as custodians for Kinishba. Cummings lived in one of the reconstructed rooms. Such hard accommodations for a man in his eighties proved to be too much, and after a visit in 1947, Cummings left Kinishba disillusioned and depressed.

What to Do with Kinishba?

The National Park Service finally fulfilled Cummings' wish to give formal protection to Kinishba by declaring the site eligible for national historic landmark status in 1964. Cummings' former student, Albert H. Schroeder, had filled out the nomination form on October 1, 1962.[2] In February 1965, Kinishba was declared a national historic landmark. This designation, however, did not help Kinishba's rapid decline, because little money was spent on the landmark and it continued to deteriorate over time.

Byron Cummings spent fifteen years of his life working at Kinishba (fig. 23.4). His work represented an opportunity for him to leave a personal legacy of his tireless dedication to Southwestern archaeology and to provide an outdoor educational experience for students, Anglo visitors, and Apaches who lived in the area. He faced many difficult challenges during the Depression of the 1930s but managed to scrape together enough money from the University of Arizona, the Indian Service, government work relief programs, students, and friends to fund his annual excavations and reconstructions.

Cummings tried to bring the people of Kinishba alive through the reconstruction of its architecture and the display of interesting materials in the museum he built next to the ruin. Experiencing this reconstructed great pueblo could take the visitor back in time: "One can let his imagination have full play and conjure back the scenes of that great court long ago. He can vision its work and its gossip, its wails of sorrow and its shouts of laughter, its dances and its processions, and listen for the echo of its chants and prayers as they weirdly ascended to heaven" (Cummings 1940a:117). Unfortunately, Kinishba today does not conjure up those visions. Rather, as Jeff Reid and Stephanie M. Whittlesey (1989:8) have

23.4 Reg Mannings' *Arizona Republic* cartoon of Cummings at Kinishba

commented, "It is profoundly sad that Cummings' vision for Kinishba—a monument to Native Americans of the past, present, and future—has evaporated in the stark light of another day." But there is hope for resurrection, however, because the Fort Apache Historic Preservation Office has been stabilizing Kinishba, and the National Park Service is giving it some attention as well. Kinishba's potential may not yet have been fully realized.[3] Perhaps Cummings' vision for Kinishba has not completely evaporated.

24

"Something Besides a Few Scraps of Paper That May Blow Away"

Cummings the Writer and His Twilight Years

When one examines regional and material culture summaries on Southwestern archaeology published in the early twentieth century, Byron Cummings' name is usually absent, because he wrote few technical papers or comprehensive site reports—the types of written material that become part of the overall body of cited archaeological literature. Cummings wrote many articles, as well as a few books, but almost all were tailored toward a public or student audience. He gathered an abundance of archaeological data, more than many other archaeologists of greater fame, but analyzed little of it in detail; and he frequently did not write adequate reports, if any at all, on his excavations. Cummings was not alone in his failure to write up the results of his excavations, but he stands out because he excavated so many sites and excavated at a time when those sites were still in pristine condition. Thus, Cummings epitomizes the nineteenth-century Victorian archaeologist who was driven to obtain relics to fill museum cases but placed far less emphasis on addressing research questions that could be examined through analysis of the collected material.

Cummings the Writer

Cummings authored more than forty articles, pamphlets, and books from 1910 to 1953 (see Hill 1950). He also wrote a number of unpublished manuscripts that are now in his archives at the Arizona Historical Society Library in Tucson. Most of the published articles are short, descriptive summaries that are very readable but contain limited archaeological data and provenience information. Many of these articles, however, are full of colorful prose that provides insight into Cummings' thought processes.

Cummings' first two professional publications were written in 1910: a forty-five-page report on archaeology of the San Juan area in the *Bulletin of the University of Utah* (Cummings 1910a) and a ten-page article on natural bridges in Utah in the *National Geographic Magazine* (Cummings 1910b). During the next ten years, when he was leading annual expeditions to retrieve thousands of artifacts from dozens of undisturbed sites in northeastern Arizona, Cummings published only three short articles and wrote no detailed site reports. One article was on prehistoric kivas of the San Juan drainage in the *American Anthropologist* (Cummings 1915a), another was a pamphlet on prehistoric textile fabrics of the Southwest (Cummings 1915b), and the third was a general article on the national monuments of Arizona in *Art and Archaeology* (Cummings 1920).

By the early 1920s, Cummings had developed a reputation for not writing up his excavations. Alfred Kidder ([1924]1962:219n.42), in his now classic book on Southwestern archaeology, commented that the "publication of [Cummings'] notes will throw much light on many now obscure problems." Cummings then excavated the Cuicuilco Pyramid in Mexico in the mid 1920s; that work remains one of his best-reported investigations (Cummings 1923a, 1923b, 1933b). Still, those publications do not constitute a comprehensive report.

Southwestern archaeologists began urging Cummings to report on his many excavations. John Hands—who had assisted Cummings with excavations at Cuicuilco, the Silverbell Road site, and at Turkey Hill—complained to the *Tucson Citizen* (1931) about Cummings' lack of reports. Cummings' reply in the same article summed up his view of the matter: "he was a teacher and not an author." This is a telling comment because it acknowledges that Cummings did not consider himself a social scientist. To other archaeologists, it was not a satisfactory answer.

In the mid 1930s, Lyndon Hargrave, assistant director of the Museum of Northern Arizona and a former student of Cummings', asked for a summary of the excavations Cummings had conducted in northeastern Arizona. Hargrave (1935:14) summarized Cummings' three-page response in a survey report of that region and commented that it was unfortunate that "many things have prevented the publication of . . . [Cummings'] findings."

When the University of Arizona offered Cummings a half-salary position as director emeritus of the State Museum, this offer was specifically contingent on his writing archaeology reports on his many excavations. Old friends also put pressure on him to write. Senator Elbert D. Thomas (1939) of Utah, a former student of Cummings', wrote him a charming letter pleading with him to publish:

> I got a pain in the leg the other day and it made me realize that Tomie '06 is no longer a sprightly youth. The best teacher he ever had, Dean Cummings, cannot be listed among the babes of the woods. Now what I am thinking about is this. You have tucked away in that remarkable, rather positive head of yours, a lot of information about certain things that no one else has or will have. Writing may have been invented to fool those who could not write but civilization has found other uses for it. . . . My point is simply this, get that information of yours down on something besides a few scraps of paper that may blow away. Put it in a book.

With the added encouragement of people like Senator Thomas, Cummings became motivated, and he set about the task of writing.

The first major writing project he decided to tackle was a book on Kinishba, and he began working earnestly on that project while continuing to excavate and stabilize the site. Cummings (1938a) first wrote a four-page summary of Kinishba for *The Kiva*. The following year, three articles were published: two on an Apache girls' puberty ceremony he had observed (Cummings 1939a, 1939b), and a reminiscence of his early experiences in northeastern Arizona with Edgar Hewett (Cummings 1939c).

The publishing of Cummings' (1940a) book on Kinishba soon produced acrimony between him and a critical reviewer, Paul Martin. According to John McGregor (1987), Cummings was deeply hurt by Martin's review, and it temporarily discouraged him from further writing. Nonetheless, Cummings reported on the Segazlin Mesa ruins that year in a four-page article in *The Kiva* (Cummings 1941a) and wrote a review of George C. Vaillant's *Aztecs of Mexico* (Cummings 1941b). Four years later, after the war, Cummings (1945) described some unusual prehistoric kivas near Navajo Mountain in a seven-page article in *The Kiva*. The two *Kiva* articles reported data collected by Cummings many years earlier during his field expeditions.

Upon retiring from his responsibilities at Kinishba in 1947, Cummings felt abandoned by two institutions he had once respected: the University of Arizona and the National Park Service. Undoubtedly his feeling of loneliness was exacerbated by the fact that his mentor and colleague, Edgar Hewett, had died the year before. To get away from the Tucson crowd, Cummings decided to live on a forty-acre ranch near Hayden that he and a family friend, Mrs. Mertice Knox, had purchased in 1936. This property, called the Orr Ranch, contained a large ruin, which had prompted him to buy the place. His intentions were to live in a small house on the property and, as a memorial to his sister Emma, to excavate the ruin "where work would be undisturbed and my control unquestioned" (Cummings and Cummings n.d.:209). Unfortunately for Cummings, when he arrived at the ranch he found the house to be in terrible shape and beyond his ability to repair. Feeling defeated in his ambitions, he later wrote that "facing an impossible situation, all contact with former associates and the work of a lifetime slipping away, I awoke to the fact that struggling to bring back a way of life that for me had gone was a hopeless task" (Cummings and Cummings n.d.:210).

Erma Judd, a niece who lived in Tucson, picked him up at the ranch and drove him to her home. On the way, Cummings came up with another plan. "Still in the race," he later wrote, "I must look ahead, not over my shoulder, in order to create a new life" (Cummings and Cummings n.d.:210). That new life began with Cummings asking Ann Chatham, recently retired from the Indian school at Fort Apache, to marry him (fig. 24.1). She accepted, and on October 17, 1947, the two were married at the Trinity Presbyterian Church in Tucson. They got along very well together, even though she was fifty-five years old and a Democrat from Georgia and he was eighty-seven years old and a Republican from New York.

Cummings and his new wife made plans to build their own home at 220 Stefan Road in Halcyon Acres, east of Tucson.[1] Byron, Ann, and two Apache friends designed and built most of the house, with Ann laying the foundation stone in November. They moved into the house on January 25, 1948. Friends soon found their way to the house to visit regularly.

In 1949, Byron and Ann traveled to Salt Lake City and the University of Utah, where he received a rousing welcome from the football team. They also took a trip to New Brunswick, New Jersey, in June and met

24.1 Ann Chatham and Byron Cummings, circa 1940s (courtesy of Arizona Historical Society/Tucson, #PC29F.21B)

with six classmates on the sixtieth anniversary of Cummings' graduation from Rutgers College. Ernest Cummings, a nephew from Syracuse, New York, showed up at the reunion with a plan to drive the three of them on a tour through New Jersey and New York. They also traveled to Silver Springs, Maryland, to visit with Byron's nephew Neil Judd, recently retired from his position at the Smithsonian Institution in Washington, D.C. Judd arranged for yet more get-togethers, this time with Cummings and former University of Utah students living in Washington, D.C., and for a luncheon at the famous Cosmos Club with National Park Service and Indian Service officials. On the way back to Arizona, Cummings and his wife drove through the South, visiting the area in Georgia where Ann used to teach.

After arriving back in Tucson, Cummings spent his time planting and tending a garden. On September 19, 1950, a reception was held at his home for his birthday. More than two hundred former students and friends attended, and hundreds of letters and telegrams came from all over the country, expressing their best wishes. One of those letters was from the president of the United States, Dwight Eisenhower. In honor of Cummings' lifetime achievements, an edited volume was compiled in his name, with twenty-one articles written by former students. It was called *For the Dean: Essays in Anthropology in Honor of Byron Cummings on His Eighty-Ninth Birthday, September 20, 1950* (Hohokam Museums Association and Southwest Monuments Association, 1950).

With Ann's strong encouragement and loving assistance, Byron Cummings set about writing his books. In December 1952, Arizona Silhouettes published more than two thousand copies of a short book, called *Indians I Have Known*, about several of Cummings' Native American friends. This fifty-six-page book sold for $2.50 for a clothbound edition and $1.50 for the paperback. The book profiled more than a dozen Navajo, "Pahute," Ute, and Apache Indians: Hoskinini Begay, Huddlechusley (Huddlechessy), Sam Chief, Navajo Tom, Navajo Bill, Hosteen (Hostein) Jones, Glad Hand, Sitsosie (possibly Sie Soci), Noscha Begay (Nasja Begay), Johnny Benow, Turner Thompson, Nathan Antonio, and Chief Baha Alchesay.

Cummings Publication Council

In 1953, Cummings finally published his book on Southwestern archaeology, entitled *First Inhabitants of Arizona and the Southwest: An Authoritative Study of the Lives, Customs, Arts, and Crafts of Pre-historic Dwellers in the Great Southwest.* Ann was of considerable help in the production of this book because Cummings' eyesight had been giving him serious problems, and he dedicated the book to her. Otis Chidester also assisted with the book's production. The book was financed by the Cummings Publication Council, a group set up in March 1952 to help fund his writing projects through donations and the money remaining from the dissolved Hohokam Museums Association. The council's officers were Dale King, chairman and executive secretary of the Southwest Monuments Association; Otis Chidester, vice-chairman, of Tucson High School; Mrs. Herbert D'Autremont, treasurer, from Tucson; Clara Lee Tanner, secretary, Department of Anthropology at the University of Arizona; Ann Cummings, custodian of manuscripts, from Tucson; Mitzi Zipf, publicity chairman, from Mesa; and Dan McGrew, publisher, from Phoenix. A solicitation for funds by the council included the following statement: "Help us let Byron Cummings talk to you through the printed page and remind you of the many times you enjoyed his discussions in the class room and in the halls of the University."[2]

Materials in Cummings' archives at the Arizona Historical Society indicate that he had written most of this book by the early 1940s but had been unable to find a publisher willing to print it with all the black-and-white and color photographs that he wanted in the book. The University of Arizona turned down his publishing proposal in 1943. Cummings, however, was not to be denied his book, especially after all the criticism he had faced over not writing about his excavations. That he was able to publish it privately, albeit ten years later, is a testament to his persistence and his many friends and admirers.

First Inhabitants of Arizona and the Southwest is 251 pages in length and profusely illustrated with more than 250 black-and-white photographs (many of them Cummings' original field photographs), 29 color plates of exemplary artifacts, nearly a dozen pen-and-ink drawings, several tables, and a few maps (Cummings 1953). The book was priced at $6. McGrew Printery of Phoenix, which had submitted the lowest bid—around $6,200 for two thousand copies—was responsible for printing the book.

Cummings' 1953 book is organized into five chapters: Introduction; Homes, Agriculture, and Mining; Manufactures; Religion; and Conclusion. Cummings (1953:vii) states in the preface that the purpose of the book was "to bring before young students and the public an outline of the life and attainments of the people who occupied the great Southwest before the coming of the Spanish into this region." Always the educator, he stated that his book was for students and the public, not for other archaeologists. Therefore, the book was written in a general and nontechnical style that made it highly readable but limited its use for comparative purposes. Too many of the details desired by archaeologists, Cummings (1953:vii) argued, obscured "the great object of all education, which is the presentation of truth clearly and forcefully." Cummings knew who his audience would be but failed to recognize that many archaeologists were hoping to see a book that provided details concerning the results of decades of excavations that Cummings had undertaken but never wrote up.

In Cummings' mind, Southwestern archaeologists were obsessed with differences in prehistoric cultures and paid too little attention to their similarities. Thus, his book was written as a very general treatment of more than two millennia of prehistory, with a focus on the general evolution of the house form in the Southwest from cave to pithouse to pueblo. An admirer of Lewis Morgan's (1881) comparative study of houses, Cummings (1953:ix) believed that the home was the "foundation and source of all those influences that have led to progress and greater human happiness." This significance of the home in the past was consistent with Cummings' own sense of Victorian morality and its importance on home life. His domestic focus was part of the American public's image of Pueblo life at that time, an image that emphasized Puebloan peoples' communal labor, social harmony, and artistic or spiritual qualities (Hinsley 1996:198).

Although Cummings (1953) acknowledges the four main prehistoric cultures of the Southwest (Hohokam, Anasazi, Mogollon, and Patayan) in his preface, nowhere within the book are archaeological materials organized according to one of those culture areas. Rather, he treats the Southwest as a monolithic culture, undergoing the same changes that brought about progress for all people in all places. This general approach made the book frustrating for archaeologists who wished to know about the material culture excavated by Cummings in a particular location.

The only locational, or provenience, information in Cummings' book is the occasional mention of the canyon or site in which objects were found. His overly generalized method of data presentation is not conducive to intrasite analysis, such as plotting the distribution patterns of specific artifacts or architectural features. Thus, it is difficult to use Cummings' data for reconstructing human behavior within a site or a specific area. The book is a beautiful and well-illustrated overview for beginning students and the public but is of limited use for professional archaeologists. Cummings' book was considered a magnificent achievement by his supporters but was a major disappointment to his archaeological critics.

Byron Cummings' long and happy life came to an end on the afternoon of May 21, 1954. Governor Howard Pyle (1954) sent Ann a telegram expressing his condolences: "Arizona is so much poorer today for the loss of a great man. No one can ever measure Dean Cummings' personal contribution to the University, or to our knowledge and understanding of our own state. With you I mourn a fine mind and a gentle soul. We can only be grateful that we had him with us so long and so usefully." Byron Cummings was cremated and buried at the Evergreen Cemetery in Tucson, alongside his first wife, Isabelle.[3] The Southwest had truly lost a great man.

The Cummings Publication Council continued with their publishing plans after Cummings' death. One of the projects they considered was Cummings' autobiography, which he had worked on but not completed. Examination of this manuscript, called *Trodden Trails* by Cummings (1958), revealed that it needed considerable editing and was incomplete for the latter years, especially for the period 1915 to 1945. Ann Cummings and Mitzi Zipf agreed to coordinate the completion of the autobiography by soliciting information from former students, but the effort required was too much for them; Jeane and Malcolm Cummings eventually completed the task. Their version, which remains unpublished, was originally called *The Dean of Kinishba*, but the title was changed to *Natani Yazzi: The Little Captain* (n.d.). The manuscript contains useful information about Cummings' personal life, especially his early years before he moved west, but provides only brief sketches of his archaeological expeditions and professional activities.

In 1957, the Cummings Publication Council decided to reprint Cummings' earlier publications on his explorations of natural bridges in Utah and Arizona. On the fiftieth anniversary of the discovery of the Rainbow Bridge, the council (1959) published three thousand copies of Bulletin No. 1, a compilation of short articles written by Cummings and others. These include "The Discovery of Rainbow Bridge" (by Neil Judd); "Statement of Stuart M. Young"; "Recollections of Malcolm Cummings"; "Notes on Discovery of Betatakin" (by John Wetherill); a reprint of a chapter out of *Indians I Have Known* (Cummings 1952); and reprints of two articles by Cummings (1910a, 1910b) on natural bridges in Utah. The cost of this forty-six-page booklet was $1. The council also reprinted Cummings' (1933b) report on his Cuicuilco excavations as Bulletin No. 2, which could also be purchased for $1.

Soon after Cummings' death, colleagues and friends memorialized him by writing about his many accomplishments. They were obligated, however, to address his lack of site reports. Walter A. Kerr, professor emeritus at the University of Utah and a former Latin student of Cummings', wrote a tribute to Cummings one year after his death. Professor Kerr (1955:149) noted that "many have wondered why Dean Cummings . . . did not write more of the scientific facts of these early expeditions." Cummings' response when asked that question by Kerr was, "I am anxious to get as much for our museum as I can before the large eastern schools fill their museums with our material. Writing can be done later. I say let's get what we can before it is too late." And he did get what he could, recovering thousands of artifacts from Arizona sites that have limited provenience information and, therefore, have limited scientific value.

Neil Judd, Cummings' nephew and his former Latin student, was a great admirer of Cummings. But he too was disappointed with Cummings' lack of reports: "It is an incalculable loss to Southwestern archaeology that much of his field work remains unrecorded as to details. Cummings never found the necessary leisure for writing. Teaching and administrative responsibilities crowded every daylight hour and diverse other obligations constantly intervened" (Judd 1954b:155). Judd also commented that a fire in Cummings' garage in 1949 had destroyed some of his notes and his library. Even without this fire, it is doubtful that Cummings would have been able, nor would he have desired, to write several detailed site reports so late in his life.

Archaeologists and Site Reports

Between 1938 and 1953, Cummings wrote several articles and three books but no site reports, unless one considers the 1940 Kinishba book a site report. Site reports are very demanding and are best written when the data are fresh in one's mind. To expect Cummings to write up his whole life in the twilight years of his late seventies and eighties was unrealistic and unfair, even for his seemingly unlimited energy.

Cummings' difficulties in writing reports were not unique to him in

American archaeology. Alfred Kidder (1932), although a prolific writer, wrote about the problems in reporting archaeological excavations. In the introduction to his famous report on the artifacts of Pecos Ruin in New Mexico, Kidder noted archaeologists' tendency to overemphasize artifacts and the effect of this focus on their ability to adequately report their findings. His comments were applicable to many archaeologists at the time but could have been meant for Cummings:

> Being human, he enjoys as much as anyone else the thrill of discovery; he naturally likes to work where exciting finds reward his efforts. His museum wants specimens, digging, particularly rich sites, is fun; study of collections is laborious, writing is downright hard work. And not seldom, he takes the easiest way and becomes a treasure seeker. He collects and collects, and promises himself that some day he will write. But his writing is usually postponed and, as writing requires thinking, that troublesome process is also generally put off (Kidder in Woodbury 1973:133).

When writing about Cummings' accomplishments, Jeff Reid and Stephanie Whittlesey (1989:14) have stated that "compared to academic administrators, his record is substantial; compared to Professor Emeriti, his record is phenomenal." Unfortunately, they noted, "It is an established lament of Southwestern archaeology that Cummings committed little of [his] early explorations to print." But let us not forget his outstanding contributions in the education of students and the public on the values of archaeology, his passage of the first Arizona Antiquities Act, his establishment of an archaeology graduate program, his building of the Arizona State Museum facility, and his many administrative accomplishments.

Epilogue

How does one evaluate a person's life, his accomplishments and failures? Cummings believed strongly that there was a great plan in the universe and that people either advance the plan or retard it. Education was the key to enlightenment, he felt, and he dedicated his life to the education of men and women, helping them to advance their parts in the great plan. As a scientist, Cummings might be said to have failed to advance the development of Southwestern prehistory as much as he could have because he wrote so few archaeology reports. His lack of reports is unquestionably a blemish on his scientific record. Nonetheless, most of his artifacts are cataloged at the State Museum, and much information remains to be gleaned from his field notes and photographs.

Reflecting on his own career, Emil Haury (1985) recognized Cummings and Edgar Hewett as true pioneers in Southwestern archaeology but noted that they excavated sites primarily to retrieve specimens for their own western museums before the objects ended up in eastern museums. In contrast, Haury and his colleagues excavated sites to address research problems through analysis of data collected during their excavations and from careful descriptions of the artifacts. Haury acknowledged that detailed site reports did not appear in the Southwest until the 1930s, toward the end of Cummings' long career.

Curtis Hinsley (1981:190) has argued that American archaeology developed during the Age of Science and Industry, when society bestowed hero status on explorers. Cummings enjoyed his status as a famous explorer, but he always remained a humble hero. A truly kind and caring man, Cummings clearly is a shining example of a person advancing the various communities in which he worked and lived. With his classroom instruction, his frequent lectures, and his constant stream of newspaper articles, he helped to create a sense of wonder and beauty for natural history and a feeling of respect for Native Americans. His love of the Southwest was passed on to others through his training, mentoring, and being a friend to hundreds of students and members of the public. He enthusiastically promoted the emotional, spiritual, and mythological qualities of the southwestern landscape and fought hard for the preservation of its native traditions and ancient ruins.

Cummings' former student and close friend Clara Lee Tanner (1954a: 19) praised him for his sterling character: "A man can be measured but partially in his scientific attainments, in the positions he holds in life, in the words he speaks or writes on paper; his greater worth lies in his relation to his fellow men and women with whom he came in contact. He gave freely of inspiration, of knowledge, he gave willingly and without reservation. Personal gain was of no concern to him, for whatever he had that another might profit through sharing that should be and was shared." Andrew Douglass (1950:7), another lifelong friend, stated that Cummings' genuine concern for his students had a strong influence on them, conveying "those intangible forces of right and wrong that ordinary teaching does not necessarily give to the student." Neil Judd (1950:27) recalled how Cummings strived to awaken in his students "increasing respect for honest effort and clean living."

Perhaps Cummings' own words best express his philosophy on correct living:

> We may catch the shafts of light that here and there penetrate our ignorance, thus learning to smooth the threads and weave in our part of the design in harmony with the rest; or in our self-assurance, we may rend the threads and leave a place frayed and broken for some more skillful and wiser spirit to restore. The task is ours. Shall we play our part skillfully and sincerely, or shall we fritter away the time allotted in contention and waste?[1]

True to his beliefs, Cummings wove in his part of the design skillfully and sincerely.

Notes

CHAPTER 1. *"One of the Leading Figures in Southwestern Archaeology"*

1. Cummings was on the boards of the Arizona State School for the Deaf and Blind, the Museum of Northern Arizona, the School of American Archaeology and the Laboratory of Anthropology in Santa Fe, the Chamber of Commerce of Tucson, and the Young Mens Christian Association. He also was active in the American Association for Engineers; Salt Lake City Board of Education; International Society of Archaeologists; Southwest Division of the American Association for the Advancement of Science (serving as president in the mid 1920s); American Anthropological Association; American Association of Museums; Institute of Social Science; Utah Academy of Sciences; American Indian Defense Association; Indian Arts and Crafts Committee; University Club, Rotary Club; and the Phi Beta Kappa, Phi Kappa Phi, Sigma Xi, and Delta Upsilon social fraternities.

2. The definition of tourism varies, but it generally means the activity of someone who travels to and stays for a while outside his or her usual environment, either for leisure or for business (Wrobel and Long 2001). Thus, tourists bring outside money into a community, providing additional revenues for local businesses and taxes for local governments.

3. Christy Turner (1962), Andrew Christenson (1987b), Laurie Webster (1991), and David Wilcox (2002) have compiled partial lists of sites investigated by Byron Cummings, but no comprehensive list for his entire career yet exists, and the accuracy of such a list would be constrained by the incomplete nature of his field notes. According to Christenson (1987b), Cummings excavated ninety-six sites in the Kayenta region alone.

4. This paper was written for the Arizona Writers Project as part of the Works Progress Administration (WPA); a copy is on file at the Arizona State Library Ar-

chives and Public Records in Phoenix (Records Group 91, box 5). Cummings' paper was not included in the final Arizona State Guide (Works Progress Administration 1940).

CHAPTER 2. *"If We Live, at All, Let Us Be Alive"*

1. U.S. census records for 1850.

2. The exact date of Byron Cummings' birth is a subject of debate—he used both 1860 and 1861. Both dates appear in his obituaries and other records, including published biographies. In a 1923 questionnaire from his alma mater, Rutgers University (College), Cummings stated that his birthday was September 20, 1861. However, the National Archives and Records Administration contains Civil War pension records filed by his mother stating that his date of birth was September 22, 1860. Affidavits by close relatives of the family, dating 1866, also swear that he was born on that date. Neil Judd (1954), Cummings' nephew and longtime colleague, claimed that Cummings was born in 1860 (but on September 20). In addition, the U.S. census record for July 1870 states that "Brion" Cummings, son of Moses and Roxana Cummings, was nine years of age at that time, and thus he would have been born in 1860.

3. Cummings' class notes are on file at the Arizona Historical Society in Tucson (MS 200).

CHAPTER 3. *"The Climate Is Delightful, the Scenery Unsurpassed"*

1. The address of Cummings' house in Salt Lake City was 936 East Eleventh South Street.

2. The University of Chicago's graduate program was started in 1892 (Ryan 1939:114). Cummings may have been attracted to its School of Greek Language and Literature and its School of Latin Language and Literature.

CHAPTER 4. *"Archaeology of Our Own Region"*

1. See, for example, Arizona Biography (1930).

2. The spelling of this individual's name is different in each of the accounts of the expedition, with variants including Nashja-Begay (Judd 1927), Nasja-begay (M. Cummings 1940), and Noscha-Begay (Cummings 1952). Zane Grey (1972) wrote about his 1913 adventures with Nasja Bega.

3. The University of Utah has more than 2,100 cataloged artifacts collected by Cummings.

CHAPTER 9. *"The Organizing and Building Up of Our University Museum"*

1. The Territorial Museum was originally sponsored by Gila County representative George W. P. Hunt (who later served several terms as governor), and his bill was passed on April 7, 1893 (Wilder 1942:26). Territorial governor N. O. Murphy recommended that the museum should be part of the University of Arizona, established in 1885, and governed by the board of regents.

2. Cummings had tried to hire Emma in early 1915 to assist him with his small museum at the University of Utah, but he was told by the secretary of the board of regents there that because of a university nepotism rule, he could not do so.

3. E. John Hands and his brother, Frank, homesteaded a ranch in Pinery Canyon in southeastern Arizona and staked several mining claims, one of which they sold to John O. Fife of Chicago in 1915 for $120,000 (Hayes 1999).

CHAPTER 11. *"A Mexican Pompeii"*

1. Cummings' correspondence indicates that he conducted excavations in 1922 at San Cristobal de la Llave in Vera Cruz. ASM (A-18, 00121).

2. Byron and Isabelle visited the famous ruin of Mitla, near Oaxaca, when they were in Mexico. He wrote a fanciful novel, called *Bolzan: Priest of Mitla*, which was never published. Malcolm drew illustrations for this novel.

3. Edward H. Spicer (1936) analyzed some of the Cuicuilco skeletal material and wrote a paper summarizing the results.

CHAPTER 12. *"A Good Detective Story"*

1. Bent's log recorded the names of three Mexican laborers who did much of the digging and thus were the first to discover some of the artifacts: Antonio Carella, Richard Balancuela, and L. Albuquez.

2. Curiously, Douglass' role in the Silverbell lead artifact controversy is not mentioned in his biography (Webb 1983a). His archives in the Special Collections at the University of Arizona, however, contain a wealth of information about his involvement in this bizarre story.

3. The newspapers reported that the offer was for $15,000, but in a letter written by President Shantz in 1930, he states that it was $16,000.

CHAPTER 13. *"Life to Them Had Ceased to Be a Struggle for Existence"*

1. During that time period, Cummings and his students also examined sites along the San Pedro River that he thought might have been visited by Father Eusebio Francisco Kino during his travels in the early eighteenth century.

CHAPTER 14. *"Why Shouldn't Man Have Been Created on American Soil?"*

1. This skeleton was originally identified as a mammoth, which at the time were called *American incognitum* because so little was known about them and their environment. Paul Semonin (2000) has argued that during the eighteenth century, the mammoth/mastodon was thought of as an American monster that proved that the natural history of the American continent was not inferior to Europe's. Mastodons (*Mammut americanum*) and mammoths (*Mammuthus columbi*) are different species, but both are distantly related to modern-day elephants, and both lived during the Ice Age in North America. The mastodon was slightly smaller and sometimes had two pairs of tusks.

2. Other fossil remains recovered from the Double Adobe site later by archaeologists from Gila Pueblo Archaeological Foundation and the Arizona State Museum include ancient horse, camel, and dire wolf (Waters 1998:125).

CHAPTER 17. *"Shall Arizona Save and Preserve Her Heritage?"*

1. Jesse Walter Fewkes died in poor health in 1930, only three years after his Elden Pueblo excavations.

2. Harold Colton put up a sign at the Museum of Northern Arizona that said, "This museum exhibits ideas not things" (Miller 1991:37). This sign may have been, in part, a reaction to Cummings' object-oriented approach.

3. Harold Gladwin was awarded an honorary Doctor of Letters by the University of Arizona in 1951, one year after he dissolved the Gila Pueblo Archaeological Foundation and donated its collections to the university. Between 1928 and 1950, Gladwin's team published thirty-nine reports, called "The Medallion Papers" (Haury and Reid 1985).

CHAPTER 18. *"A Man of Vision"*

1. Cummings' class notes are located at the Arizona Historical Society in Tucson (MS 200).

2. Lyndon L. Hargrave was a hydrographer for the Roosevelt Dam in Arizona who became an archaeologist at the urging of Byron Cummings. He was hired as curator of archaeology at the Museum of Northern Arizona and initiated the first archaeology classes at the Arizona State Teachers College in Flagstaff (now Northern Arizona University). He became an expert on bird bones in archaeological sites and published one of the first systematic descriptions of pottery types in Arizona in 1932 (Taylor and Euler 1980).

3. Harry T. Getty was a quiet and modest person hired by Cummings first as a

museum assistant and then as an instructor in the Archaeology Department. He continued to work at the university after Cummings retired and was employed there for a total of thirty-eight years (Thompson 1996). He wrote his dissertation on an anthropological study of a Mexican American community in Tucson for a Ph.D. under Robert Redfield, in 1950, at the University of Chicago. He also conducted research on the San Carlos Apache cattle industry and worked on Fiji and in Slovenia.

4. Eleanor Parker Clarke's death occurred from a fractured skull when the rear tire blew out on the car that Anna Mae McGrath was driving, causing the vehicle to roll over (*Arizona Daily Star* 1933b). Clarke was one of four students and a professor in the car on their way back to Tucson from the American Association for the Advancement of Science conference in Las Cruces, New Mexico. Professor John Provinse and Earl Jackson also received broken bones, but they recovered. Louis Caywood and McGrath were not seriously hurt.

5. Some of the other individuals not mentioned in the text who studied under Cummings and went on to have successful careers in archaeology or anthropology include George Cattanach, E. T. Hall Jr., Roy Lassiter, Maud Makemson, William Smith, Carr Tuthill, and Irene Vickrey.

6. The Arizona Pageantry Association's meeting minutes and correspondence are located in the archives of the Arizona State Museum (A-247 to A-249).

CHAPTER 19. *"Shortest Possible Statement for a Research Goal"*

1. John C. McGregor's interest in archaeology began when he ducked into the State Museum as a new freshman on campus to avoid being hazed because he sported a new mustache that was reserved for seniors (McGregor 2003). Cummings talked with him and suggested that he take archaeology classes, which he did. He received his master's degree under Cummings and after undertaking pioneering work on the Cohonina Culture of the Flagstaff region while at the Museum of Northern Arizona, he had a distinguished career as an anthropology professor at the University of Illinois.

CHAPTER 20. *"Weird, Thrilling, Spectacular"*

1. Grace M. Sparkes Papers, Arizona Historical Foundation, Tempe (MSS 12, box 10).

2. Edward H. Spicer received a Ph.D. in social anthropology from the University of Chicago in 1939 after studying the Yaqui Indians in southern Arizona. He taught at the University of Arizona from 1939 to 1940 and from 1946 to 1978. His 1962 book, *Cycles of Conquest*, is in its eleventh printing.

3. Joseph Crary (1991) has argued that Mercer Ruin is a platform mound, but Stephanie Whittlesey (1997) disagrees with this hypothesis.

4. In January 1934, Yavapai Indians became upset when a local citizen placed a prehistoric skeleton on display in the store window. The Yavapai claimed that it was one of their former chiefs. Cummings had the skeleton taken off display in exchange for keeping the bones and the associated grave goods for study.

CHAPTER 21. *"A Profitable Chapter in the Life History of Man"*

1. Gordon C. Baldwin later earned his Ph.D. from the University of Southern California, worked for the National Park Service, and authored more than sixty-five articles and books, including several western novels.

CHAPTER 22. *"A Very Unpopular Move"*

1. In some versions of this group's title, "Museum" was singular. The Hohokam Museums Association meeting minutes are present in the Cummings Papers, Arizona Historical Society (MS 200, box 10).

CHAPTER 23. *"There Is Much Work Yet to Be Done"*

1. Donald Sayner was interviewed by the author in 2002, and he had many fond memories of his experience at Kinishba with Cummings.

2. Albert Schroeder began his distinguished archaeology career when he attended a lecture by Cummings in New York in the mid 1930s and Cummings invited Schroeder to enroll in the Archaeology Department in Tucson. Schroeder's (1940) master's thesis, completed under Emil Haury, was on a 1938–1940 Works Progress Administration archaeology project administered by Odd Halseth, city archaeologist at Pueblo Grande Museum in Phoenix. Schroeder supervised the excavation of dozens of Hohokam trash mounds in the Salt River Valley, with each mound systematically trenched and their ceramics analyzed.

3. Reid and Whittlesey (1997:272) have suggested that Kinishba could be one of the camps of the Coronado Expedition of 1540 called Chichilticale, or Red House, where a vanguard army of about seventy-five horsemen, twenty-five foot-soldiers, several native allies, and a small herd of cattle rested for two days on their way to Cíbola (a Zuni village). If this is true, then Kinishba has additional significance.

CHAPTER 24. *"Something Besides a Few Scraps of Paper That May Blow Away"*

1. Cummings had previously lived at 1444 East Third Street, at 615 East Second Street, and at Fremont and Sixth Street in Tucson.

2. Cummings Publication Council meeting minutes are on file at the Arizona Historical Society (MS 200, box 10, f. 118).

3. Cummings' second wife, Ann, also is buried in the same plot as Byron; they share a common headstone. Their grave plot is located midway into section 14 B, north of the Evergreen Cemetery maintenance shop. Ann passed away on March 13, 1963, at age seventy. In 1947, she received the Department of Interior's Meritorious Service Award for her twenty-two years of teaching in the Indian Service.

EPILOGUE

1. Unpublished note in Cummings Papers, Arizona Historical Society (MS 200).

References

ARCHIVES

ACMNM	Angélico Chavéz Library, Museum of New Mexico (includes Edgar Hewett Papers, AC 105)
AF	Amerind Foundation
AHS	Arizona Historical Society, Tucson (includes Byron Cummings Papers, MS 200; and Thomas Bent Papers, MS 1122)
AIA	Archaeological Institute of America
ASLAPR	Arizona State Library, Archives, and Public Records
ASM	Arizona State Museum
FANHL	Fort Apache National Historic Landmark
LOA	Laboratory of Anthropology, School of American Research
MNA	Museum of Northern Arizona
NAUSC	Northern Arizona University Special Collections
PGM	Pueblo Grande Museum
RUA	Rutgers University Archives
SM	Smoki Museum
UASC	University of Arizona Libraries Special Collections

REFERENCE MATERIALS

Abbott, C. C. "Paleolithic Man in North America." *Science* 20 (1892): 70–71.

Abbott, Mary Huntington. "The Marvin Affair." *Journal of Arizona History* 23, no. 2 (1982): 59–80.

Adams, Richard E. W. *Prehistoric Mesoamerica*, rev. ed. Norman: University of Oklahoma Press, 1991.

Aldrich, Richard L. *A Survey of Prehistoric Southwestern Architecture*. Unpublished master's thesis, Department of Archaeology, University of Arizona, 1936.

Ambler, J. Richard, Alexander J. Lindsay Jr., and Mary Anne Stein. *Survey and Excavations on Cummings Mesa, Arizona and Utah, 1960–1961*. Museum of Northern Arizona Bulletin no. 39, Glen Canyon Series no. 5. Flagstaff, 1964.

Anderson, Keith M. "Excavations at Betatakin and Keet Seel." *Kiva* 37 (1971): 1–79.

———. *Tuzigoot Burials*. National Park Service Publications in Anthropology 60. Tucson: Western Archeological and Conservation Center, 1992.

Arizona Biography. *History of Arizona Biographical*, vol. 4, pp. 14–15. Phoenix: Record Publishing, 1930.

Arizona Board of Public Welfare. *Outstanding Projects—Work Division. Emergency Relief Administration of Arizona, 1935*, 2 vols. Arizona Historical Foundation.

Arizona Daily Star. "Tablets Found Here Bear Inscription of '800 A.D.'," September 21, 1924.

———. "Pyramid Found on 'Hunch' of Dean Cummings," October 3, 1925a.

———. "Two Tucsonans Given Honors by Scientists," October 23, 1925b.

———. "Log of Excavations Kept by Discoverers of Relics," December 13, 1925c.

———. "Tucson Artifacts Bear Out Mormon Traditions Except Dates, Says Elder," December 16, 1925d.

———. "Tucson's Crossword Puzzle," December 21, 1925e.

———. "Cummings Firmer than Ever in Belief Tucson Artifacts Are Genuine," January 19, 1926a.

———. "Bearded White Man of Toltecs May Be Israel III of Artifact Fame," February 17, 1926b.

———. "Artifact Find Loses Support of University," February 18, 1926c.

———. "Three Latin Text Books Contain All Phrases on Artifacts, Says Fowler," March 7, 1926d.

———. "Cave Folks Ancestors of Pueblo Instead of Victims, Cummings Finds," September 30, 1926e.

———. "Get Behind the New President," February 1, 1927a.

———. "Trust in Youth," June 1, 1927b.

———. "Leaden Spear-Shaft Found in Location of Famed Artifacts," February 17, 1928.

———. "Museum Work and Education," February 17, 1929a.

———. "Mrs. Byron Cummings Dies; Funeral to Be Held Friday," November 13, 1929b.

———. "Full Text of Dr. Cummings' Report on Alleged Artifacts," January 21, 1930.

———. "Work on Pueblo Ruins to Go On," May 27, 1932a.
———. "Picture of Prehistoric Life Painted by Geologists Here," October 18, 1932b.
———. "Girl Student of U Critically Injured in Douglas Accident," May 5, 1933.
———. "Cummings Will Lead Expedition," April 12, 1934a.
———. "Bonita Canyon Caves Explored," April 25, 1934b.
———. "Dr. Cummings Discovers Old Burial in Cave at Safford," November 13, 1934c.
———. "Former Students Honor Teacher," May 10, 1935.
———. "Cummings Quits Course He Taught for 21 Years," September 30, 1936.
———. "Dean Protests 'U' Retirement," March 27, 1937.
Arizona Gazette. December 28, 1928.
Arizona Republic. "Huge Pueblo Is Uncovered," March 7, 1932.
———. "Dr. Cummings to Visit Ruins," April 25, 1934a.
———. "Archaeological Find Is Made near Safford," November 12, 1934b.
Arizona Republican. "The Leaden Artifacts," February 19, 1926.
———. "Governor Signs Bill to Protect Ruins," March 12, 1927.
Arizona Wildcat. "Dean Cummings Is Spending Winter in Mexican Work," November 26, 1924.
Arntzen, Ruth M. *The Influence of Prehistoric Religious Ceremonies upon the Living Indian Tribes of the Southwest*. Unpublished master's thesis, Department of Archaeology, University of Arizona, 1936.
Atkinson, Alfred. Letter to Byron Cummings, July 20, 1937, AHS.
———. Letter to Byron Cummings, January 24, 1938a, AHS (MS 200, box 1, f. 9).
———. Letter to Byron Cummings, February 15, 1938b, AHS (MS 200).
———. Memorandum to Emil W. Haury, May 25, 1939, ASM (A-468, 00097).
———. Letter to Byron Cummings, August 20 and 26, 1940a, AHS (MS 200, box 1, f. 11).
———. Letter to Byron Cummings, September 20, 1940b, AHS (MS 200, box 1, f. 11).
———. Letter to Byron Cummings, July 5, 1944, AHS (MS 200).
Babcock, Barbara A., and Nancy J. Parezo. *Daughters of the Desert: Women Anthropologists and the Native American Southwest, 1880–1980*. Albuquerque: University of New Mexico Press, 1988.
Bacon, George A. Letter of recommendation for Byron Cummings, July 6, 1891, AHS (MS 200, box 1, f. 1).
Baldwin, Gordon C. *The Prehistoric Pueblo of Kinishba*. Unpublished master's thesis, Department of Archaeology, University of Arizona, 1934.
———. "Dates from Kinishba Pueblo." *Tree-Ring Bulletin* 1, no. 4 (1935a): 30.

———. "Our Heritage from the Desert." *Arizona Alumnus*, December 15, (1935b): 2–3.
———. "The Pottery of Kinishba." *Kiva* 3, no. 1 (1937): 1–4.
———. "Excavations at Kinishba Pueblo, Arizona." *American Antiquity* 4 (1938a): 11–21.
———. "Proclamation," 1938b, AHS (MS 200).
———. "A New Pottery Type from Eastern Arizona." *Southwestern Lore* 4, no. 2 (1938c): 21–26.
———. "The Material Culture of Kinishba." *American Antiquity* 4 (1939a): 314–327.
———. Letter to Byron Cummings, June 6, 1939b, AHS (MS 200).
Ball, Phyllis. *A Photographic History of the University of Arizona 1885–1985*. Tucson: privately printed, 1986.
Bandelier, Adolph F. "Reports by A. F. Bandelier on His Investigations in New Mexico during the Years 1883–84." In *Fifth Annual Report of the Archaeological Institute of America*, pp. 55–98. Cambridge, MA: J. Wilson and Son, 1884.
———. *Final Report on Investigations among the Indians of the Southwestern United States, Carried on Mainly in the Years from 1880 to 1885*, part 2. Papers of the Archaeological Institute of America. Cambridge, MA: Peabody Museum of American Archaeology and Ethnology, Harvard University, 1892.
Bannister, Bryan, Elizabeth A. M. Gell, and John W. Hannah. *Tree Ring Dates from Arizona* NQ*: Verde-Showlow-St. Johns Area*. Tucson: Laboratory of Tree Ring Research, 1966.
Beal, T. A. Letter to Byron Cummings, April 8, 1927, UASC (AZ 420).
Beals, R. L., George W. Brainerd, and William Smith. *Archaeological Studies in Northeast Arizona: A Report on the Archaeological Work of the Rainbow Bridge-Monument Valley Expedition*. Berkeley: University of California Press, 1945.
Beauregard, Donald. *Deseret Evening News*, July 24, 1909.
Bender, Harold H. Letter to Byron Cummings, February 3, 1927, ASM (A-0697).
Benson News. "Evidence of Ancient Man in Sulphur Springs Valley Is Uncovered by U.A. Professor," November 6, 1926.
Bent, Thomas W. Letter to editor, *Arizona Daily Star*, March 4, 1926.
———. Letter to Byron Cummings, February 23, 1929, ASM (A-192, 00048).
———. Letter to Byron Cummings, January 22, 1930, ASM (A-192, 00054).
———. *The Tucson Artifacts*, 1964, unpublished manuscript, AHS (MS 1122).
Bernheimer, Charles. "Encircling Navajo Mountain with a Pack Train." *National Geographic Magazine* 43 (February 1923): 197–224.
———. *Rainbow Bridge: Circling Navajo Mountain and Explorations in the 'Badland' of Southern Utah and Northern Arizona*. Garden City, NY: Doubleday, Page, 1924.

Bizzell, W. B. Letter to Byron Cummings, November 2, 1927, UASC (AZ 420).
Blackburn, Fred M., and Ray A. Williamson. *Cowboys and Cave Dwellers: Basketmaker Archaeology in Utah's Grand Gulch*. Santa Fe, NM: School of American Research, 1997.
Bloom, Lansing B. "Meeting of the Southwestern Division, A.A.A.S., Phoenix, Feb. 15–18." *El Palacio* 29, no. 6 (1926): 123–126.
Boas, Franz. "International School of American Archaeology in the Valley of Mexico." *American Anthropologist* 14 (1912): 192–194.
Boggs, Stanley H. *A Survey of the Papago People*. Unpublished master's thesis, Department of Archaeology, University of Arizona, 1936.
Boyden, Eddie. "Mysterious People Lived 10,000 Years Ago in Mexico." *San Francisco Chronicle*, March 6, 1923.
Brace, Martha A. "On the Road and in the Field in 1919: The University of Arizona Summer Archaeological Field Season." *Kiva* 51, no. 3 (1986): 189–200.
Broda, Johanna. "The Sacred Landscape of the Aztec Calendar Festivals: Myth, Nature, and Society." In *To Change Place: Aztec Ceremonial Landscapes*, ed. David Carrasco, pp. 74–120. Niwot: University Press of Colorado, 1991.
Brown, Herbert H. "A Pima-Maricopa Cemetery." *American Anthropologist* 8 (1906): 688–690.
Burg, David F. *Chicago's White City of 1893*. Lexington: University Press of Kentucky, 1976.
Canon-Tapia, E., G. P. L. Walker, and E. Herrero Bervera. "Magnetic Fabric and Flow Direction in Baslatic Pahoehoe Lava of Xitle Volcano, Mexico." *Journal of Volcanology and Geothermal Research* 65 (1995): 249–263.
Carr, Fletcher A. *The Ancient Pueblo Culture of Northern Mexico*. Unpublished master's thesis, Department of Archaeology, University of Arizona, 1935.
Caywood, Louis R. *The Archaeology of the Sulphur Spring Valley, Arizona*. Unpublished master's thesis, Department of Archaeology, University of Arizona, 1933.
———, and Edward H. Spicer. *Tuzigoot: The Excavation and Repair of a Ruin on the Verde River near Clarkdale, Arizona*. Berkeley, CA: National Park Service, Field Division of Education, 1935.
Chamberlin, Ralph V. *The University of Utah: A History of Its First Hundred Years, 1850–1950*. Salt Lake City: University of Utah Press, 1960.
Chapman, Oscar C. Letter to Byron Cummings, December 12, 1934, ASM (A-204, 0013).
———. Letter to Byron Cummings, September 17, 1937, AHS (MS 200, box 1, f. 8).
Chavenet, Beatrice. *Hewett and Friends: A Biography of Santa Fe's Vibrant Era*. Santa Fe: Museum of New Mexico Press, 1983.

Christenson, Andrew L. "The Last of the Great Expeditions: The Rainbow Bridge/Monument Valley Expedition, 1933–1938." *Plateau* 58, no. 4 (1987a): 1–32.

———. *Archaeological Exploration and Research in the Kayenta Anasazi Region: A Synoptic History*. Black Mesa Archaeological Project. Carbondale: Southern Illinois University Press, 1987b.

———. *Annotated Bibliography of Tsegi Canyon, Navajo Nation, Arizona: Natural History, Archaeology, Ethnology with Notes on Art and Literature*. Prescott: privately printed, 2002.

Clark, James C. Letter to Byron Cummings, October 3, 1927, UASC (AZ 420).

———. Letter to Byron Cummings, January 17, 1928, UASC (AZ 420).

Clarke, Eleanor P. *Designs on the Prehistoric Pottery of Arizona*. Bulletin 5, no. 4. Social Science Bulletin 9. Tucson: University of Arizona, 1935.

Cleland, Herdman F. *Our Prehistoric Ancestors*. New York: Coward-McCann, 1928.

Clemensen, A. Berle. *Casa Grande Ruins National Monument, Arizona: A Centennial History of the First Prehistoric Reserve, 1892–1922*. Denver: National Park Service, 1992.

Cline, Platt. *Mountain Town: Flagstaff's First Century*. Flagstaff, AZ: Northland Publishing, 1994.

Collier, John. Letter to Mrs. Charles [Anna Child] Bird, October 24, 1939, AHS (MS 200, box 10).

Collins, William S. *The New Deal in Arizona*. Phoenix: Arizona State Parks, 1999.

Colton, Harold S. "Some Notes on Elden Pueblo." *Science* 65 (1927): 141–142.

———. Letter to Byron Cummings, January 12, 1931a, ASM (A-678).

———. Letter to Byron Cummings, February 20, 1931b, ASM (A-678).

———. Letter to Byron Cummings, January 8, 1935, ASM (A-204, 0014).

———. *Prehistoric Culture Units and Their Relationships in Northern Arizona*. Museum of Northern Arizona Bulletin 17. Flagstaff, 1939.

———. *The Sinagua: A Summary of the Archaeology of the Region of Flagstaff, Arizona*. Museum of Northern Arizona Bulletin 22. Flagstaff, 1946.

———. "Reminiscences in Southwest Archaeology: IV." *Kiva* 26 (1961): 1–7.

Comfort, Mary A. *Rainbow to Yesterday: The John and Louisa Wetherill Story*. New York: Vantage Press, 1980.

Conn, Steven. *Museums and American Intellectual Life, 1876–1926*. Chicago: University of Chicago Press, 1998.

Cook, E. H. Letter of reference for Byron Cummings, 1891, AHS (MS 200, box 1, f. 1).

Cook, Harold J. "Definite Evidence of Human Artifacts in the Pleistocene." *Science* 62 (1925): 459–460.

———. "The Antiquity of Man in America." *Scientific American* 137 (November 1926): 334–336.

Coolidge News. "San Carlos Will Be Under Water in Three Months, Dr. Cummings Hastens Excavations of Ruins near Town," January 12, 1929.

———. "Van Bergen Men at Ruins Discontinue Work Temporarily," February 19, 1931.

Cordova, Carlos F. de A., Ana Lillian Martin del Pozzo, and Javier Lopez Camacho. "Paleolandforms and Volcanic Impact on the Environment of Prehistoric Cuicuilco, Southern Mexico City." *Journal of Archaeological Science* 21 (1994): 585–596.

Cosulich, Gilbert. "Roman Relics Found Here Baffle Science," *Arizona Daily Star*, December 13, 1925a.

———. "If Cummings Says They're Genuine, They Are, Declare Tucsonans," *Arizona Daily Star*, December 23, 1925b.

———. "President of University Finds Hard Work Answer to Living for 66 Years," *Arizona Daily Star*, September 20, 1927.

Covey, Cyclone. *A Roman Jewish Colony in America from the Time of Charlemagne through Alfred the Great*. New York: Vantage Press, 1975.

Crary, Joseph S. *An Archaeological Survey of the Lower Verde Area: A Preliminary Report*. Paper presented at the 64th Annual Pecos Conference, Nuevo Casas Grandes, Chihuahua, Mexico, 1991.

Crider, F. J. Letter to Byron Cummings, May 28, 1927a, UASC (AZ 420).

———. Letter to Byron Cummings, June 29, 1927b, UASC (AZ 420).

———. Letter to Byron Cummings, August 5, 1927c, UASC (AZ 420).

Cummings, Byron. Letter to Isabelle McClaury, June 9, 1895, NAUSC (MS 219).

———. Letter to Edgar Hewett, July 7, 1906a, ACNMN (AC 105).

———. Letter to Thomas D. Seymour, July 20, 1906b, AIA.

———. Letter to Edgar Hewett, March 14, 1907a, ACNMN (AC 105).

———. Letter to Edgar Hewett, September 17, 1907b, ACNMN (AC 105).

———. Letter to Edgar Hewett, September 14, 1908a, ACNMN (AC 105).

———. Letter to Edgar Hewett, November 9, 1908b, ACNMN (AC 105).

———. Letter to Edgar Hewett, January 11, 1909a, ACNMN (AC 105).

———. Letter to Edgar Hewett, March 6, 1909b, ACNMN (AC 105).

———. Letter to Edgar Hewett, June 28, 1909c, ACNMN (AC 105).

———. Letter to Edgar Hewett, October 22, 1909d, ACNMN (AC 105).

———. Letter to Edgar Hewett, December 27, 1909e, ACNMN (AC 105).

———. Field notes, 1909f, ASM (A-0198).

———. "The Ancient Inhabitants of the San Juan Valley." *Bulletin of the University of Utah* 3, no. 3, part 2 (1910a): 1–45.

———. "The Great Natural Bridges of Utah." *National Geographic Magazine* 21, no. 2 (1910b): 157–167.
———. Letter to Edgar Hewett, January 25, 1910c, ACNMN (AC 105).
———. Letter to Edgar Hewett, April 14, 1910d, ACNMN (AC 105).
———. Letter to Edgar Hewett, June 27, 1910e, ACMNM (AC 105).
———. Letter to Edgar Hewett, August 3, 1910f, ACMNM (AC 105).
———. Letter to Edgar Hewett, December 14, 1910g, ACMNM (AC 105).
———. Letter to Edgar Hewett, September 3, 1911, ACNMN (AC 105).
———. Field notes, 1914, ASM (A-198).
———. "Kivas of the San Juan Drainage." *American Anthropologist* 17, no. 2 (1915a): 172–282.
———. "Textile Fabrics of the Cliff Dwellers." Paper presented at the National Association of Cotton Manufacturers 98th meeting, Boston, April 29, 1915b.
———. Letter to President Joseph Kingsbury, March 6, 1915c, AHS (MS 200, box 1, f. 3).
———. Expense Account for 1915 Summer Field Season, 1915d, ASM (A-468, 00051).
———. Expense Account for 1916 Summer Field Season, ASM (A-468, 00052).
———. Expense Account for 1917 Summer Field Season, ASM (A-468, 00053).
———. "The National Monuments of Arizona." *Art and Archaeology* 10, nos. 1–2 (1920): 27–36.
———. "A Mexican Pompeii." *Literary Digest*, August 26, 1922a.
———. Field notes for Cuicuilco, 1922b, ASM (A-0199).
———. "Cuicuilco, the Oldest Temple Discovered in North America." *Art and Archaeology* 16, nos. 1–2 (1923a): 51–58.
———. "Ruins of Cuicuilco May Revolutionize Our History of Ancient America." *National Geographic Magazine* 44, no. 2 (1923b): 202–220.
———. "Arizona State Museum Forms Basis for Preserving Early Cultures." *Arizona Alumnus* 1, no. 3 (1924a): 3–4, 11.
———. *State Museum, University of Arizona, Report for the Year of 1923–1924*, 1924b, ASM.
———. Letter to Gilbert Grosvenor, November 1, 1924c, ASM (A-199).
———. Field notes for Cuicuilco, 1924–1925, ASM (A-199).
———. Final report to the National Geographic Society, 1925a, ASM (A-199).
———. "Ancient Canals of Casa Grande." *Progressive Arizona* 3, no. 5, (1926a): 9–10, 43.
———. "Cuicuilco and the Archaic Culture of Mexico." *Scientific Monthly* 23 (1926b): 289–304.
———. "Problems of a Scientific Investigator." *Science* 63 (1926c): 321–324.

———. "White Man's Discovery of the Rainbow Bridge." *Progressive Arizona and the Great Southwest* 3, no. 1 (1926d): 23–24.
———. Letter to Gilbert Grosvenor, April 17, 1926e, ASM (A-0003).
———. Letter to Sam Day, December 3, 1926f, NAUSC (MS 89).
———. "Greetings." *Arizona Alumnus* 4, no. 3 (1927a): 3.
———. Letter to Governor George Hunt, February 4, 1927b, UASC (AZ 420).
———. Letter to board of regents president Robert E. Tally, February 5, 1927c, UASC (AZ 420).
———. Letter to Governor George Hunt, March 1, 1927d, UASC (AZ 420).
———. Letter to Martin Mortenson Jr., April 16, 1927e, UASC (AZ 420).
———. Letter to the board of regents, April 2, 1927f, UASC (AZ 420, box 5, f. 23).
———. Letter to Governor George Hunt, April 11, 1927g, UASC (AZ 420).
———. Letter to Governor George Hunt, April 16, 1927h, UASC (AZ 420).
———. Letter to Edward Ellery, April 11, 1927i, UASC (AZ 420).
———. Letter to Edward Ellery, May 24, 1927j, UASC (AZ 420).
———. Letter to Regent F. J. Crider, May 24, 1927k, UASC (AZ 420).
———. Letter to Regent Robert Tally, June 25, 1927, UASC (AZ 420).
———. Letter to Regent F. J. Crider, July 12, 1927m, UASC (AZ 420).
———. Letter to Regent F. J. Crider, August 10, 1927n, UASC (AZ 420).
———. Letter to Governor George Hunt, August 16, 1927o, UASC (AZ 420).
———. Letter to Governor George Hunt, October 26, 1927p, UASC (AZ 420).
———. Letter to James C. Clark, October 26, 1927q, UASC (AZ 420).
———. Letter to W. B. Bizzell, November 25, 1927r, UASC (AZ 420).
———. Letter to Governor George Hunt, November 10, 1927s, UASC (AZ 420).
———. Letter to Governor George Hunt, December 11, 1927t, UASC (AZ 420).
———. "The Casa Grande Pageant Will Be Held in March." *Progressive Arizona and the Great Southwest* 7, no. 4 (1928a): 16.
———. "Cochise of Yesterday." *Arizona Old and New* 1, no. 4 (1928b): 9–10, 25–28.
———. "Archaeological Fieldwork in North America during 1927." *American Anthropologist* 30, no. 3 (1928c): 503.
———. Letter to Regent Robert Tally, January 25, 1928d, UASC (AZ 420).
———. Letter to Earl Hudelson, January 26, 1928e, UASC (AZ 420).
———. Letter to Governor George Hunt, February 18, 1928f, UASC (AZ 420).
———. Letter to Robert E. Tally, March 12, 1928g, UASC (AZ 420).
———. Letter to Harvey Zorbaugh, April 30, 1928h, UASC (AZ 420).
———. Letter to Elsie Lee Turner, May 1, 1928i, UASC (AZ 420).
———. Letter to David S. Hill, May 19, 1928j, UASC (AZ 420).
———. "Archaeological Fieldwork in North America during 1928." *American Anthropologist* 31, no. 2 (1929a): 337.

———. "The Arizona Pageant of 1929." *Progressive Arizona and the Great Southwest* 8, no. 2 (1929b): 24–25.
———. "Life of the Casa Grande Indians as Told in Pageantry." *Progressive Arizona and the Great Southwest* 8, no. 3 (1929c): 15–16.
———. Gila Bank Ruins, field notes, 1929d, AHS.
———. *Turkey Hill Ruin*, unpublished report, 1929e, AHS (MS 200, box 3).
———. Letter to C. L. Walker, February 2, 1929f, ASM (A-248).
———. Letter to Thomas Bent, February 25, 1929g, Thomas Bent Papers, ASM (A-192, 00053).
———. "An Outline of the Casa Grande Ruins Pageant." *Progressive Arizona and the Great Southwest* 10, no. 3 (1930a): 16–17, 27.
———. *Expedition* (journal), 1930b, AHS (MS 200, box 4, f. 42).
———. 1930c, AHS (MS 200, box 5, f. 63).
———. "Archaeological Fieldwork in North America during 1930." *American Anthropologist* 33, no. 3 (1931a): 462–463.
———. *Kinishba Ruin near Fort Apache, Arizona: A Preliminary Report on the First Season's Work, July 20–Sept. 1*, 1931b, ASM (A-143).
———. Letter to President Homer L. Shantz, January 24, 1931c, ASM (A-678).
———. Letter to Harold Colton, March 27, 1931d, ASM (A-678).
———. Letter to Dean E. R. Rieson, June 3, 1931e, ASM (A-0468, 00151).
———. Letter to Secretary of the Interior Ray L. Wilber, June 17, 1931f, FANHL.
———. Letter to James W. Simmons, October 29, 1931g, ASM (A-50).
———. Segazlin field notes, 1931h, ASM (AA-10).
———. *Kinishba—The Brown House: Report on the Progress*, 1932a, ASM (A-143).
———. Letter to Mrs. Emery E. Oldaker, May 7, 1932b, ASM.
———. Letter to Harold Colton, May 29, 1932c, MNA (MS 207-1-68).
———. "Pithouses at Hohokam Park near Tucson." *Pan-American Geologist* 9, no. 4 (1933a).
———. *Cuicuilco and the Archaic Culture of Mexico*. University of Arizona Bulletin 9, no. 8, Social Science Bulletin 4. Tucson, 1933b.
———. "Archaeological Fieldwork in North America during 1932." *American Anthropologist* 35, no. 3 (1933c): 486.
———. *Antiquity of Man in the Americas*, 1933d, unpublished manuscript, Tucson.
———. *Kinishba*, 1933e, unpublished manuscript, AHS (MS 200).
———. Letter to Harold Ickes, July 5, 1933f, FANHL.
———. Letter to Jesse Nusbaum, July 7, 1933g, ASM.
———. Letter to Jesse Nusbaum, July 8, 1933h, AHS (MS 200, box 1, f. 7).
———. "Hohokams Described by Cummings," *Tucson Magazine*, June 14, 1933i.

———. *Report: Kinishba Ruin near Fort Apache, Arizona, Season of 1934*, 1934a, ASM (A-413).
———. Letter to Earl S. Miers, January 9, 1934b, RUA.
———. Letter to President Homer Shantz, February 1, 1934c, ASM (A-0165).
———. Letter to President Homer Shantz, April 18, 1934d, ASM (A-0165).
———. Letter to Glen McEuen, November 3, 1934e, ASM (A-204, 0004).
———. Letter to Senator Paul C. Keefe, November 20, 1934f, ASM (A-678).
———. Letter to M. P. McEuen, November 21, 1934g, ASM (A-204, 0010).
———. Letter to Harvey L. Mott, November 21, 1934h, ASM (A-204, 0011).
———. Letter to Harold Colton, December 4, 1934i, ASM (A-678).
———. Letter to Henry A. Wallace, June 21, 1934j, FANHL.
———. Letter to Superintendent William Donner, November 11, 1934k, FANHL.
———. "Archaeological Field Work in North America during 1934: Arizona." *American Antiquity* 1, no. 1 (1935a): 50.
———. "Arizona Advances." *Museologist* 2 (1935b): 7.
———. "The Archaeology of the Southwest." *Kiva* 1, no. 1 (1935c): 1–2.
———. "Primitive Man in America." *Kiva* 1, no. 1 (1935d): 2–3.
———. "Old Fort Lowell Park." *Kiva* 1, no. 1 (1935e): 4.
———. "Primitive Pottery of the Southwest." *Kiva* 1, no. 2 (1935f): 1–8.
———. "Progress of the Excavation at Kinishba." *Kiva* 1, no. 3 (1935g): 1–4.
———. "Pleistocene Man in America." *Pan-American Geologist* 64, no. 2 (1935h): 155–156.
———. *Martinez Hill Ruins*, unpublished report, 1935i, AHS (MS 200).
———. *Report: Kinishba Ruins near Fort Apache, Arizona, October 19, 1935*, 1935j, ASM (A-143, 00113).
———. Letter to R. C. Kunzell, January 26, 1935k, ASM (A-678).
———. Letter to Superintendent William Donner, February 17, 1935l, FANHL.
———. Letter to Superintendent William Donner, October 11, 1935m, FANHL.
———. Letter to Harold Ickes, October 16, 1935n, ASM (A-204, 0018).
———. "The Bride of the Sun." *Kiva* 1, no. 5 (1936a): 1–4.
———. "Navajo Sand Paintings." *Kiva* 1, no. 7 (1936b): 1–2.
———. "Shall Arizona Save and Preserve Her Heritage?" *Kiva* 2, no. 2 (1936c): 5–8.
———. "The Archaeology of Arizona." Arizona Writers Project, Works Progress Administration, 1936d, manuscript, ASLAPR (Records Group 91, box 5, film file 51.27.2).
———. Letter to William Donner, September 15, 1936e, FANHL.
———. Letter to Harold Ickes, April 10, 1937a, FANHL.
———. Letter to Harold Ickes, April 10, 1937b, FANHL.

———. "Kinishba Pueblo: The Brown House." *Kiva* 4, no. 1 (1938a): 1–4.
———. "Kivas of the San Juan Drainage." *Kiva* 3, nos. 7–8 (1938b): 25–30.
———. Kinishba, field notes, 1938c, AHS (MS 200, box 5, f. 50).
———. "Apache Puberty Ceremony for Girls." *Kiva* 5, no. 1 (1939a): 1–4.
———. "An Apache Girl Comes of Age." *Indians at Work* 7 (1939b): 37–39.
———. "Early Days in Utah." In *So Live the Works of Men, 70th Anniversary Volume Honoring Edgar Lee Hewett*, ed. Donald D. Brand and Fred E. Harvey, pp. 117–120. Albuquerque: University of New Mexico Press, 1939c.
———. *The Record of Kinishba*, 1939d, unpublished manuscript, AHS (MS 200).
———. Letter to Emil W. Haury, February 25, 1939e, ASM (A-468, 00091).
———. Letter to Emil W. Haury, May 20, 1939f, ASM (A-468, 00098 and 00099).
———. *Kinishba: A Prehistoric Pueblo of The Great Pueblo Period*. Phoenix: Republic and Gazette Printery, 1940a.
———. Letter to Emil W. Haury, October 3, 1940b, ASM (A-468).
———. Letter to Alfred Atkinson, August 21, 1940c, AHS (MS 200, box 1, f. 11).
———. *The Lightning Ceremony of the Apache Indians*, 1940d, unpublished manuscript, AHS (MS 200, box 5).
———. "Segazlin Mesa Ruins." *Kiva* 7, no. 1 (1941a): 1–4.
———. Letter to Paul [Ralph] Linton, November 17, 1941b, AHS (MS 200, box 1, f. 12).
———. Letter to Paul S. Martin, November 17, 1941c, AHS (MS 200, box 1, f. 12).
———. Letter to Mrs. McGrath, September 22, 1942a, AHS (MS 200, box 10, f. 114).
———. Letter to Harold Ickes, 1942b, FANHL.
———. Letter to Mrs. Robert P. Bass, March 21, 1943, AHS (MS 200).
———. *Museologists*, October 1944a, AHS (MS 200).
———. Letter to William Donner, August 1944b, FANHL.
———. Proposed budget for Kinishba, 1944–1945, 1944c, FANHL.
———. "Some Unusual Kivas near Navajo Mountain." *Kiva* 10, no. 4 (1945): 30–35.
———. *Indians I Have Known*. Tucson: Arizona Silhouettes, 1952.
———. *First Inhabitants of Arizona and the Southwest*. Tucson: Cummings Publication Committee, 1953.
———. *Trodden Trails*, 1958, manuscript, Cummings Publication Council, AHS.
———. *Nomenclature in Southwestern Archaeology*, n.d.a, manuscript, AHS (MS 200, box 6, f. 70).
———. *Restoration of Kinishba and the Apache Laborers*, n.d.b, manuscript, AHS (MS 200, box 6, f. 72).
———. Gila Bank Ruin, field notes, n.d.c, AHS (MS 200).

Cummings, Byron, and Lousia Wade Wetherill. "A Navajo Folk Tale of Pueblo Bonito." *Art and Archaeology* 14, no. 3 (1922): 132–136.

Cummings, Emma. "Sand Pictures in the Arizona State Museum at Tucson." *Kiva* 1, no. 7 (1936): 2–4.

Cummings, Jeane, and Malcolm B. Cummings. *Natani Yazzi: Little Captain*, n.d., manuscript on file, AHS (MS 200).

Cummings, Malcolm. "Mountain Sheep Effigies." *American Antiquity* 2 (1936): 130–132.

———. "I Finished Last in the Race to Rainbow Bridge." *Desert Magazine* (May 1940).

Cummings Publication Council. *The Discovery of Rainbow Bridge, the Natural Bridges of Utah, and the Discovery of Betatakin: Commemorating the 50th Anniversary of Its Discovery, August 14, 1909*. Cummings Publication Council Bulletin 1. Tucson, 1959.

Cushing, Frank Hamilton. "Preliminary Notes on the Origin, Working Hypothesis, and Primary Researches of the Hemenway Southwestern Archaeological Expedition." In *Congres International des Americanistes, Compte-Rendu de Septieme Session, Berlin, 1888*, pp. 151–194. Berlin: W. H. Kühl, 1890.

Dalton, O. E. Letter to A. E. Douglass, December 19, 1924, UASC (AZ 72, box 147).

Damon, Paul E., and Austin Long. "Arizona Radiocarbon Dates." *Radiocarbon* 4 (1962): 246–247.

Darwin, Charles. *On the Origin of Species, Or The Preservation of Favoured Races in the Struggle for Life*. London: J. Murray, 1859.

Day, Samuel, Sr. Letter to Cloyd Marvin, March 24, 1924, NAUSC (MS 89).

Dean, Jeffrey S. *Chronological Analysis of Tsegi Phase Sites in Northeastern Arizona*. Papers of the Laboratory of Tree-Ring Research 3. Tucson: University of Arizona, 1969.

———. "Late Pueblo II–Pueblo III in Kayenta Branch Prehistory." In *Prehistoric Culture Change on the Colorado Plateau: Ten Thousand Years on Black Mesa*, ed. Shirley Powell and Francis E. Smiley, pp. 121–158. Tucson: University of Arizona Press, 2002.

Deseret Evening News. "University Archaeology Expedition Made Important Discoveries," September 13, 1913.

Deseret News (Salt Lake City). September 2, 1909.

Dick, Herbert W., and Albert H. Schroeder. "Lyndon Hargrave: A Brief Biography." In *Collected Papers in Honor of Lyndon Lane Hargrave*, pp. 1–8. Papers of the Archaeological Society of New Mexico no. 1. Santa Fe, 1968.

Dixon, Joseph M. Letter to Byron Cummings, July 15, 1931, FANHL.

Donner, William. Letter to Byron Cummings, October 18, 1935, FANHL.

———. Letter to John Collier, August 4, 1936a, FANHL.

———. Letter to Byron Cummings, December 3, 1936b, FANHL.

———. Letter to J. W. Jamison, March 22, 1941a, FANHL.

———. Letter to Senator Carl Hayden, November 17, 1941b, AHS (MS 200, box 1, f. 12).

———. Letter to Byron Cummings, 1944, FANHL.

Douglas Daily Dispatch. "Cummings Thinks Man Lived nearby 40,000 Years Ago," October 30, 1926a.

———. "Cummings Has New Proof of Ancient Man," October 31, 1926b.

Douglass, Andrew E. "Dating our Prehistoric Ruins: How Growth Rings in Timbers Aid in Establishing the Relative Ages of the Ruined Pueblos of the Southwest." *Natural History* 21, no. 2 (1921): 27–30.

———. Letter to British Museum, November 5, 1924, UASC (A-272, box 147).

———. "Lead Alloy Spear Exhumed Wednesday, March 4, 1925, at a Point on the Silverbell Road, Nine Miles from the Observatory," 1925a, UASC (A-272, box 147).

———. Letter to Byron Cummings, March 14, 1925b, UASC (A-272, box 147).

———. Letter to Byron Cummings, February 1, 1927, AHS (MS 200, box 1, f. 5).

———. "The Secret of the Southwest Solved by Talkative Tree Rings." *National Geographic Magazine* 56, no. 6 (1929): 736–770.

———. "Our Friend, Byron Cummings." In *For the Dean: Essays in Anthropology in Honor of Byron Cummings on His Eighty-ninth Birthday, September 20, 1950*. Tucson: Hohokam Museums Association, and Santa Fe: Southwestern Monuments Association, 1950.

Douglass, William B. Letter to Walter Hough, August 4, 1909a, NAUSC.

———. Letter to Walter Hough, November 24, 1909b, NAUSC.

———. "The Discovery of Rainbow Natural Bridge." *Our Public Lands* 5 (1955): 8–9, 14–15.

Downum, Christian E. "From Myths to Methods: Intellectual Transitions in Flagstaff Archaeology, 1883–1930." In *Perspectives on Southwestern Prehistory*, ed. Paul E. Minnis and Charles E. Redman, pp. 351–366. Boulder, CO: Westview Press, 1990.

———. "Relief Archaeology." In *Archaeology of the Pueblo Grande Platform Mound and Its Surrounding Features*, vol. 1: *Introduction to the Archival Project and History of Archaeological Research*, ed. Christian E. Downum and Todd W. Bostwick, pp. 137–192. Pueblo Grande Museum Anthropological Papers no. 1. Phoenix, 1993.

Duffen, William Neil, II. *Development of Human Culture in the San Pedro River Valley*. Unpublished master's thesis, Department of Archaeology, University of Arizona, 1936.

Eighth Arizona Legislature. *Bill Number 97: Arizona State Antiquities Act*, March 11, 1927, ASM (A-678).

Elder, Clayburn C. Letter, June 24, 1957, AHS (MS 200, box 9, f. 97).

Ellery, Edward. Letter to Byron Cummings, April 4, 1927a, UASC (AZ 420).

———. Letter to Byron Cummings, May 11, 1927b, UASC (AZ 420).

Elliot, Melinda. *Great Excavations: Tales of Early Southwestern Archaeology*. Santa Fe: School of American Research Press, 1995.

Evans, Susan Toby, and David L. Webster, eds. *Archaeology of Ancient Mexico and Central America: An Encyclopedia*. New York: Garland Publishing, 2001.

Excelsior, "Un Describrimiento de Gran Merito Arqueológico," July 22, 1922, ASM (A-697).

Fagan, Brian M. *The Great Journey: The Peopling of Ancient America*. London: Thames and Hudson, 1987.

Fagette, Paul. *Digging for Dollars: American Archaeology and the New Deal*. Albuquerque: University of New Mexico Press, 1996.

Fagin, Nancy L. "Closed Collections and Open Appeals: The Two Anthropology Exhibits at the Chicago World's Columbian Exposition of 1893." *Curator* 27, no. 4 (1984): 249–264.

Federal Civil Works Administration. *Interesting Programs in Arizona*, 1934, ASLAPR.

Federal Writers Project. [1940]. *Arizona: A State Guide*. Revised by Joseph Miller. New York: Hastings House, 1966.

Ferg, Alan, and William D. Peachy. "An Atlatl from the Sierra Pinacate." *Kiva* 64 (1998): 175–200.

Fewkes, Jesse Walter. "A Report on the Present Condition of a Ruin in Arizona Called Casa Grande." *Journal of American Ethnology and Archaeology* 2 (1892): 176–193.

———. *Archaeological Expedition to Arizona in 1895*. Bureau of American Ethnology Seventeenth Annual Report, Part 2, pp. 519–742. Washington, DC, 1898.

———. "Pueblo Ruins near Flagstaff, Arizona: A Preliminary Notice." *American Anthropologist* 2 (1900): 422–450.

———. "Excavations in Casa Grande, Arizona, in 1906–1907." *Smithsonian Miscellaneous Collections* 50 (1907): 289–329.

———. "Prehistoric Ruins of the Gila Valley." *Smithsonian Miscellaneous Collections* 52, no. 5 (1909): 1–15.

———. *Preliminary Report on a Visit to the Navajo National Monument*. Bureau of American Ethnology Bulletin 50. Washington, DC, 1911.

———. "Casa Grande, Arizona." In *Twenty-eighth Annual Report of the Bureau of American Ethnology*, pp. 25–179. Washington, DC, 1912a.

———. "Antiquities of the Upper Verde River and Walnut Creek Valleys, Arizona." In *Twenty-eighth Annual Report of the Bureau of American Ethnology, 1906–1907*, pp. 180–220. Washington, DC, 1912b.

———. "An Archaeological Collection from Young's Canyon, near Flagstaff, Arizona." *Smithsonian Miscellaneous Collections* 77, no. 10 (1926a): 403–436.

———. "Elden Pueblo." *Progressive Arizona* 3, no. 6 (1926b): 13–14, 30.

———. "Elden Pueblo." *Science* 64 (1926c): 508.

———. "The Elden Pueblo." *Science* 65 (1927a): 209.

———. "Explorations and Field Work of the Smithsonian Institution in 1926: Archaeological Fieldwork in Arizona." *Smithsonian Miscellaneous Collections* 78, no. 7 (1927b): 207–232.

Fletcher, Alice. Letter to Byron Cummings, April 11, 1908, ACMNM (AC 105).

Fogelson, Raymond D. "The Red Man in the White City." In *Columbian Consequences*, vol. 3: *The Spanish Borderlands in Pan-American Perspective*, ed. David H. Thomas, pp. 73–90. Washington, DC: Smithsonian Institution, 1991.

Fontana, Bernard L. "*The Kiva*: A Half Century of Southwestern Anthropology." *Kiva* 50, no. 4 (1985): 175–182.

Forsberg, Helen. *A Study of the Skeletal Remains from the Pueblos of Kinishba and Tuzigoot in Arizona*. Unpublished master's thesis, Department of Archaeology, University of Arizona, 1935.

Fowler, Don D. "Models of Southwestern Prehistory, 1840–1914." In *Rediscovering Our Past: Essays on the History of American Archaeology*, ed. Jonathan E. Reyman, pp. 15–34. Avebury, UK: Aldershot, 1992.

———. "Harvard vs. Hewett: The Contest for Control of Southwestern Archaeology, 1904–1930." In *Assembling the Past: Studies in the Professionalization of Archaeology*, ed. Alice B. Kehoe and Mary Beth Emmerichs, pp. 165–211. Albuquerque: University of New Mexico Press, 1999.

———. *A Laboratory for Anthropology: Science and Romanticism in the American Southwest, 1846–1930*. Albuquerque: University of New Mexico Press, 2000.

———, and John F. Matley. "The Palmer Collection from Southwestern Utah, 1875." In *Miscellaneous Paper 20, Anthropological Papers* 99, pp. 17–42. Salt Lake City: University of Utah Press, 1978.

Fraps [Tanner], Clara Lee. *Archaeological Survey of Arizona*. Unpublished master's thesis, Department of Archaeology, University of Arizona, 1928.

———. "University Party Inspects Ruins in Northern Arizona," *Arizona Daily Star*, July 7, 1930a.

———. "Cummings Leads Expedition to Other Ruins of Arizona," *Arizona Daily Star*, August 31, 1930b.

———. Field notes for Archaeology 310, 1930c, AHS (MS 200, box 4, f. 42).

———. "Tanque Verde Ruins." *Kiva* 1, no. 4 (1935): 1–4.

Frisbie, Theodore R. "A Biography of Florence Hawley Ellis." In *Collected Papers in Honor of Florence Hawley Ellis*, ed. Theodore R. Frisbie, pp. 1–11. Papers of the Archaeological Society of New Mexico 2. Santa Fe, 1974.

———. "Florence Hawley Ellis, 1906–1991." *Kiva* 57, no. 1 (1991): 93–97.

Frontz, Kim. "An Annotated Bibliography of the Writings of Clara Lee Tanner." *Kiva* 64, no. 1 (1998): 61–87.

Gabel, Norman. *Martinez Hill Ruins*. Unpublished master's thesis, Department of Archaeology, University of Arizona, 1931.

Gamio, Manuel. "Arqueologia de Atzcapotzalco, D.F. Mexico." In *Eighteenth International Congress of Americanists, Proceedings*, pp. 180–187. 1913.

———. "Las Excavations del Pedregal de San Angel y la Cultura Arcaica del Valle de Mexico." *American Anthropologist* 22 (1920): 127–143.

———. "The Sequence of Cultures in Mexico." *American Anthropologist* 26 (1924): 307–322.

Gay, Dorothy Frances. *Apache Art*. Unpublished master's thesis, Department of Archaeology, University of Arizona, 1933.

Getty, Harry T. *Cultures of the Upper Gila*. Unpublished master's thesis, Department of Archaeology, University of Arizona, 1932.

Gifford, Carol A., and Elizabeth A. Morris. "Digging for Credit: Early Archaeological Field Schools in the American Southwest." *American Antiquity* 50 (1985): 395–411.

Gillmor, Frances. *The Biography of John and Lousia Wetherill*. Unpublished master's thesis, Department of Archaeology, University of Arizona, 1931.

———, and Louisa Wade Wetherill. *Traders to the Navajos: The Story of the Wetherills of Kayenta*. Boston: Houghton, Mifflin, 1934. Reprinted, Albuquerque: University of New Mexico Press, 1953.

Gladwin, Harold S. "Excavations at Casa Grande, Arizona, February 12–May 1, 1927." *Southwest Museum Papers* 2 (1928): 7–30.

———. Letter to Byron Cummings, January 24, 1931, ASM (A-678).

———. Letter to Senator Paul Keefe, February 5, 1935, ASM (A-678).

———, Emil W. Haury, E. B. Sayles, and Nora Gladwin. *Excavations at Snaketown: Material Culture*. Medallion Papers 25. Globe, AZ: Gila Pueblo Archaeological Foundation, 1937.

Gladwin, Winifred, and Harold S. Gladwin. *The Red on Buff Culture of the Gila Basin*. Medallion Papers 3. Globe, AZ: Gila Pueblo Archaeological Foundation, 1929.

———, and ———. *The Western Range of the Red-on-buff Culture*. Medallion Papers 5. Globe, AZ: Gila Pueblo Archaeological Foundation, 1930a.

———, and ———. *An Archaeological Survey of the Verde Valley*. Medallion Papers 6. Globe, AZ: Gila Pueblo Archaeological Foundation, 1930b.

Glassberg, David. *American Historical Pageantry: The Uses of Traditon in the*

Early Twentieth Century. Chapel Hill: University of North Carolina Press, 1990.

Goff, John S. *George P. Hunt and His Arizona*. Pasadena, CA: Socio Technical Publications, 1973.

Gonzalez, Silvia, Alenjandro Pastrana, Claus Siebe, and Geoff Duller. "Timing of the Prehistoric Eruption of Xitle Volcano and the Abandonment of Cuicuilco Pyramid, Southern Basin of Mexico." In *The Archaeology of Geological Catastrophes*, ed. W. J. McGuire, D. R. Griffiths, P. L. Hancock, and I. S. Stewart, pp. 205–224. Geological Society Special Publication no. 171. London, 2000.

Gould, Lewis L., ed. *The Progressive Era*. Syracuse, NY: Syracuse University Press, 1974.

Graham, Robert. *The Textile Art of the Prehistoric Southwest*. Unpublished master's thesis, Department of Archaeology, University of Arizona, 1933.

Grand Valley Times (Moab). "The Explorers," June 21, 1907.

———. September 2, 1909a.

———. "Jealousy Besets Gov't Official," October 1, 1909b.

Gregory, Herbert E. *Geology of the Navajo Country: A Reconnaissance of parts of Arizona, New Mexico, and Utah*. United States Geological Survey Professional Paper 93. Washington, DC, 1917.

Grey, Zane. *Riders of the Purple Sage*. New York: Harper and Brothers, 1912.

———. *The Rainbow Trail*. New York: Harper and Brothers, 1915.

———. "Nonnezshe, the Rainbow Bridge." In *Rainbow Trails: Early-Day Adventures in Rainbow Bridge Country*, compiled by James E. Babbitt, pp. 26–36. Page, AZ: Glen Canyon Natural History Association, 1990.

Grosvenor, Gilbert. Letter to Byron Cummings, January 12, 1925, ASM (A-199).

Guenther, Linda Young. *Gila Polychromes*. Unpublished master's thesis, Department of Archaeology, University of Arizona, 1937.

Guernsey, Samuel J. *Explorations in Northeastern Arizona*. Papers of the Peabody Museum of American Archaeology and Ethnology 12, no. 1. Cambridge, MA: Harvard University, 1931.

———, and Alfred V. Kidder. *Basket Maker Caves of Northeastern Arizona, Report on the Explorations, 1916, 1917*. Papers of the Peabody Museum of American Archaeology and Ethnology 8, no. 2. Cambridge, MA: Harvard University, 1921.

Gulick, Luther H. *The Efficient Life*. New York: Doubleday, Page, 1913.

Guthe, Carl E. "Reflections on the Founding of the Society for American Archaeology." *American Antiquity* 32 (1967): 433–440.

Hackbarth, Mark R. "Archival Studies." In *The Grewe Archaeological Research Project*, vol. 3: *Synthesis*, ed. Douglas B. Craig, pp. 1–34. Tempe: Northland Research, 2001a.

———. "Appendix A: Grewe Site Annotated Bibliography." In *The Grewe Archaeological Research Project*, vol. 3: *Synthesis*, ed. Douglas B. Craig, pp. 149–189. Tempe: Northland Research, 2001b.

———. "Newspaper Accounts." In *The Grewe Archaeological Research Project*, vol. 3: *Synthesis*, ed. Douglas B. Craig, pp. 200–208. Tempe: Northland Research, 2001c.

Hale, Thomas. Letter to Regent E. E. Ellinwood, April 4, 1937, AHS (MS 200, box 1, f. 8).

Haley, Bruce. *The Healthy Body and Victorian Culture*. Cambridge, MA: Harvard University Press, 1978.

Hall, Daniel A. *Federal Patronage of Art in Arizona from 1933-1943*. Unpublished master's thesis, Arizona State University, 1974.

Hall, Sharlot. *The Story of the Smoki People*. Prescott, AZ: Prescott Courier, 1922.

———. Letter to Byron Cummings, 1937, AHS (MS 200, box 1, f. 8).

Hallman, Peter R. "When Byron Cummings Discovered Arizona's 'Ice Age.'" *Kiva* 65 (1999): 125–142.

Halseth, Odd. Letter to Governor John C. Phillips, November 15, 1929, PGM.

Hammond, Norman. "Obituary: Gordon Randolph Willey, 1913-2002." *Antiquity* 22 (2003): 431–433.

Hargrave, Lyndon L. *Report on Archaeological Reconnaissance in the Rainbow Plateau Area of Northern Arizona and Southern Utah: Based upon the Fieldwork of the Rainbow Bridge-Monument Valley Expedition of 1933*. Berkeley: University of California Press, 1935.

Harris, Charles H., III, and Louis R. Sadler. *The Archaeologist Was a Spy: Sylvanus G. Morley and the Office of Naval Intelligence*. Albuquerque: University of New Mexico Press, 2003.

Hartman, Dana. *Tuzigoot: An Archaeological Overview*. Research Paper 4, Archaeological Report 4. Flagstaff: Museum of Northern Arizona, 1976.

Hartmann, Gayle H., and Sharon F. Urban. "The Arizona Archaeological and Historical Society: Its First Seventy-Five Years." *Kiva* 56, no. 4 (1991): 329–357.

Harvey, Doris L. *The Pottery of the Little Colorado Culture Area*. Unpublished master's thesis, Department of Archaeology, University of Arizona, 1935.

Hassell, Hank. *Rainbow Bridge: The Illustrated History*. Logan: Utah State University Press, 1999.

Haury, Emil W. *The Succession of House Types in the Pueblo Area*. Unpublished master's thesis, Department of Archaeology, University of Arizona, 1928.

———. *Gila Pueblo Conference Summary*, 1931, ASM (A-0091, 00003).

———. *The Canyon Creek Ruin and the Cliff Dwellings of the Sierra Ancha*.

Medallion Papers 14. Globe, AZ: Gila Pueblo Archaeological Foundation, 1934.

———. *The Mogollon Culture of Southwestern New Mexico*. Medallion Papers 20. Globe, AZ: Gila Pueblo Archaeological Foundation, 1936a.

———. "Vandal Cave." *Kiva* 1, no. 6 (1936b): 1–4.

———. "Ball Courts." In *Excavations at Snaketown: Material Culture*, by Harold S. Gladwin, Emil W. Haury, E. B. Sayles, and Nora Gladwin, pp. 36–49. Medallion Papers 25. Globe, AZ: Gila Pueblo Archaeological Foundation, 1937.

———. Letter to Byron Cummings, May 15, 1939, ASM (A-468, 00096).

———. Letter to William Donner, October 22, 1940, FANHL.

———. *Painted Cave, Northeastern Arizona*. Amerind Foundation 3. Dragoon, AZ, 1945a.

———. *The Excavations of Los Muertos and Neighboring Ruins in the Salt River Valley, Southern Arizona*. Papers of the Peabody Museum of American Archaeology and Ethnology 24, no. 1. Cambridge, MA: Harvard University, 1945b.

———. "The Naco Mammoth." *Kiva* 18, nos. 3 and 4 (1952): 1–20.

———. "The Lehner Mammoth Site." *Kiva* 21, nos. 3 and 4 (1956): 23–24.

———. "The Arizona Antiquities Act of 1960." *Kiva* 26, no. 1 (1960): 19–24.

———. "Cuicuilco in Retrospect." *Kiva* 41, no. 2 (1975): 195–200.

———. *The Hohokam, Desert Farmers and Craftsmen: Excavations at Snaketown*. Tucson: University of Arizona Press, 1976.

———. "Concluding Remarks." In *The Cochise Cultural Sequence in Southeastern Arizona*, ed. E. B. Sayles, pp. 158–166. Anthropological Papers of the University of Arizona no. 42. Tucson, 1983.

———. "Reflections: Fifty Years of Southwestern Archaeology." *American Antiquity* 50, no. 2 (1985): 383–394.

———. "Gila Pueblo Archaeological Foundation." *Kiva* 54, no. 1 (1988): 1–77.

———. "Cuicuilco Diary: June 11–September 12, 1925." *Journal of the Southwest* 45, no. 1 (2004a): 55–91. Emil Walter Haury Centennial, ed. Loren Haury.

———. "Diary of the U of A Archaeological Expedition: July 13–August 26, 1927." *Journal of the Southwest* 45, no. 1 (2004b): 95–112. Emil Walter Haury Centennial, ed. Loren Haury.

———. "Reflections on the Arizona State Museum: 1925 and Ensuing Years." *Journal of the Southwest* 45, no. 1 (2004c): 129–164. Emil Walter Haury Centennial, ed. Loren Haury.

———, Ernst Antevs, and John F. Lance. "Artifacts with Mammoth Remains, Naco, Arizona." *American Antiquity* 19, no. 1 (1953): 1–24.

———, and Lyndon L. Hargrave. "Recently Dated Ruins in Arizona." *Smithsonian Miscellaneous Collections* 82, no. 11 (1931): 4–120.

———, and J. Jefferson Reid. "Harold Sterling Gladwin 1883–1983." *Kiva* 50, no. 4 (1985): 271–283.
———, E. B. Sayles, and William W. Wasley. "The Lehner Mammoth Site, Southeastern Arizona." *American Antiquity* 25 (1959): 2–30.
Hawley [Ellis], Florence M. *Pottery and Culture Relations in the Middle Gila*. Unpublished master's thesis, Department of Archaeology, University of Arizona, 1928.
———. "Prehistoric Pottery Pigments in the Southwest." *American Anthropologist* 31, no. 4 (1929): 731–754.
———. *The Significance of the Dated Prehistory of Chetro Ketl, Chaco Canyon, New Mexico*. Monograph Series 1, no. 1. Albuquerque: University of New Mexico, 1934.
———. *Field Manual of Southwestern Pottery Types*. Bulletin 291, Anthropological Series 1. Albuquerque: University of New Mexico, 1936.
Hayden, Carl. Letter to Regent E. E. Ellinwood, April 2, 1937, AHS (MS 200, box 1, f. 8).
———. Letter to William Donner, May 17, 1941, FANHL.
Hayden, Julian D. *Excavations, 1940, at University Indian Ruin, Tucson, Arizona*. Technical Series 5. Tucson: Southwestern Parks and Monuments Association, 1957.
Hayes, Alden C. *A Portal to Paradise: 11,537 Years, More or Less, on the Northeast Slope of the Chiricahua Mountains*. Tucson: University of Arizona Press, 1999.
Hazard, R. B. Letter to Byron Cummings, August 23, 1935, FANHL.
Heiser, Robert F., and Jerry Bennyhoff. "Archaeological Investigations of Cuicuilco, Valley of Mexico, 1956." *Science* 127 (1958): 161–180.
———, and ———. "Archaeological Investigations at Cuicuilco, Mexico, 1957." In *National Geographic Society Research Reports 1955-1960, Projects*, pp. 93–104. Washington, DC, 1972.
Hewett, Edgar L. "Report of the Director." *American Journal of Archaeology* 11 (1907a): 51–60.
———. Letter to Byron Cummings, April 24, 1907b, ACNMN (AC 105).
———. Letter to Byron Cummings, December 3, 1907c, ACNMN (AC 105).
———. *Progress Report for the First Half of 1908 to the Committee on American Archaeology*. Santa Fe, NM: School of American Research, 1908.
———. *Report of the Director of American Archaeology*. Santa Fe, NM: School of American Research, 1909a.
———. Letter to Byron Cummings, January 8, 1909b, ACNMN (AC 105).
———. Letter to Byron Cummings, summer 1909c, ACNMN (AC 105).
———. *The School of American Archaeology*. Bulletin 2. Santa Fe: Archaeological Institute of America, 1910a.

———. Letter to F. W. Holmes, July 9, 1910b, AIA.
———. *The School of American Archaeology*. Bulletin 3. Santa Fe: Archaeological Institute of America, 1911a.
———. Letter to Byron Cummings, January 6, 1911b, ACNMN (A 105).
———. *The School of American Archaeology*. Bulletin 4. Santa Fe, NM: Archaeological Institute of America, 1912.
———. "Report of the Director, 1912." *Old Santa Fe: A Magazine of History, Archaeology, Genealogy, and Biography* 1, no. 1 (1913): 118–128. Santa Fe, NM: Old Santa Fe Press.
———. Letter to Byron Cummings, October 21, 1916, ACNMN (A 105).
———. *Ancient Life in the American Southwest, with an Introduction on the General History of the American Race*. New York: Bobbs-Merrill, 1930.
———. Letter to Byron Cummings, May 5, 1941, AHS (MS 200, box 1, f. 12).
Hill, David S. Letter to Byron Cummings, May 5, 1928, UASC (AZ 420).
Hill, Gertrude. "Annotated Bibliography of Papers by Byron Cummings." In *For the Dean: Essays in Anthropology in Honor of Byron Cummings on his Eighty-ninth Birthday, September 20, 1950*, pp. 5–9. Tucson: Hohokam Museums Association, and Santa Fe: Southwestern Monuments Association, 1950.
Hinsley, Curtis M., Jr. *The Smithsonian Institution and the Development of American Anthropology, 1846–1910*. Washington, DC: Smithsonian Institution Press, 1981.
———. "Ethnographic Charisma and Scientific Routine: Cushing and Fewkes in the American Southwest, 1879–1893." In *Observers Observed: Essays on Ethnographic Fieldwork*, ed. George W. Stocking Jr., pp. 53–69. History of Anthropology 1. Madison: University of Wisconsin Press, 1983.
———. "Edgar Lee Hewett and the School of American Research in Santa Fe, 1906–1912." In *American Archaeology Past and Future: A Celebration of the Society for American Archaeology, 1935–1985*, ed. David Meltzer, Don D. Fowler, and J. A. Sabloff, pp. 217–233. Washington, DC: Smithsonian Institution, 1986.
———. "The Promise of the Southwest: A Humanized Landscape." In *The Southwest in the American Imagination: The Writings of Sylvester Baxter, 1881–1889*, ed. Curtis M. Hinsley and David R. Wilcox, pp. 181–233. Tucson: University of Arizona Press, 1996.
Hinton, Ralph J. *The Handbook of Arizona: Its Resources, History, Towns, Mines, Ruins and Scenery*. San Francisco: Payot Upham, 1878.
Hodge, Frederick W. "Prehistoric Irrigation in Arizona." *American Anthropologist* 6 (1893): 323–330.
Hofstadler, Richard. *The Age of Reform: From Bryan to F.D.R.* New York: Random House, 1955.

Hohokam Museums Association, 1938–1939, pamphlet, AHS (MS 200, box 10, f. 110).
Hohokam Museums Association and Southwestern Monuments Association. *For the Dean: Essays in Anthropology in Honor of Byron Cummings on his Eighty-ninth Birthday, September 20, 1950*. Tucson: Hohokam Museums Association, and Santa Fe: Southwestern Monuments Association, 1950.
Hollinger, David A. "Inquiry and Uplift: Late Nineteenth Century American Academics and the Moral Efficacy of Scientific Practice." In *The Authority of Experts: Studies in History and Theory*, ed. Thomas L. Haskell, pp. 142–156. Bloomington: Indiana University Press, 1984.
Holmes, William H. "Modern Quarry Refuse and the Paleolithic Theory." *Science* 20 (1892): 295–297.
———. "On the Antiquity of Man in America." *Science* 47 (1918): 561–562.
———. "The Antiquity Phantom in American Archaeology." *Science* 62 (1925): 256–258.
———. "Jesse Walter Fewkes." *American Anthropologist* 33 (1931): 92–97.
Hough, Walter. "Archaeological Field Work in Northeastern Arizona: The Museum Gates Expedition of 1901." In *Report of the United States National Museum for 1901*, pp. 279–358. Washington, DC: Government Printing Office, 1903.
Hrdlička, Aleš. *Skeletal Remains Suggesting or Attributed to Early Man in North America*. Bureau of American Ethnology Bulletin 33. Washington, DC: Smithsonian Institution, 1907.
———. "Recent Discoveries Attributed to Early Man in America." Bureau of American Ethnology Bulletin 66. Washington, DC: Smithsonian Institution, 1918.
Huckell, Bruce B., Lisa W. Huckell, and Steven Shackley. "McEuen Cave." *Archaeology Southwest* 13, no. 1 (1999): 12.
Hudelson, Earl. Letter to Byron Cummings, ca. January 1928, UASC (AZ 420).
Hunt, George. Letter to Byron Cummings, February 1, 1927a, UASC (AZ 420).
———. Letter to Byron Cummings, February 24, 1927b, UASC (AZ 420).
———. Letter to Byron Cummings, April 8, 1927c, UASC (AZ 420).
———. Letter to Byron Cummings, June 3, 1927d, UASC (AZ 420).
———. Letter to Regent Robert Tally, September 9, 1927e, UASC (AZ 420).
———. Letter to Byron Cummings, October 13, 1927f, UASC (AZ 420).
———. Letter to Byron Cummings, November 9, 1927g, UASC (AZ 420).
———. Letter to Byron Cummings, November 17, 1927h, UASC (AZ 420).
———. Letter to Byron Cummings, December 10, 1927i, UASC (AZ 420).
———. Letter to Byron Cummings, February 8, 1928a, UASC (AZ 420).
———. Letter to Byron Cummings, February 23, 1928b, UASC (AZ 420).

Huntington, Archer M. Letter to A. E. Douglass, October 18, 1924, UASC (AZ 72, box 147).
Huntington, Ellsworth. "The Fluctuating Climate of North America, Part I: The Ruins of the Hohokam." *Geographical Journal* 40, no. 3 (1912): 264–280.
Jackson, Earl. *A Survey of the Verde Drainage*. Unpublished master's thesis, Department of Archaeology, University of Arizona, 1933.
———, and Sallie Pierce Van Valkenburgh. *Montezuma Castle Archaeology*. Southwest Monuments Archaeology Technical Series 3, no. 1. Tucson, 1954.
Jacobs, Mike. "The St. Mary's Hospital Site." *Kiva* 45, nos. 1–2 (1979): 119–130.
Jamison, J. W. Letter to William Donner, 1941, FANHL.
Janetski, Joel C. "150 Years of Utah Archaeology." *Utah Historical Quarterly* 65, no. 2 (1997): 100–133.
Jeppson, Joseph H. *The Secularization of the University of Utah to 1920*. Unpublished Ph.D. dissertation, Department of Education, University of California, Berkeley, 1973.
Jett, Stephen. "The Great 'Race' to 'Discover' Rainbow Natural Bridge in 1909." *Kiva* 58, no. 1 (1992): 3–66.
Johnston, Bernice. "Fifty Years of the Arizona Archaeological and Historical Society." *Kiva* 32: 2 (1966): 41–56.
Jones, David. "Progress of the Excavations at Kinishba." *Kiva* 1, no. 1 (1935): 1–4.
Jones, Howard M. Letter to Byron Cummings, June 5, 1944, AHS (MS 200, box 1, f. 14).
Journal of the House of Representatives. Phoenix: Eighth Arizona Legislature, 1927.
Journal of the House of Representatives. Phoenix: Tenth Arizona Legislature, 1931.
Journal of the Senate. Phoenix: Eighth Arizona Legislature, 1927.
Joyner, W. C. Letter to Byron Cummings, February 3, 1927, AHS.
Judd, Neil M. Letter to Edgar Hewett, September 12, 1910a, ACNMN (AC 105).
———. Letter to Edgar L. Hewett, December 18, 1910b, ACMNM (AC 105).
———. *Archaeological Observations North of the Rio Colorado*. Bureau of American Ethnology Bulletin 82. Washington, DC: Smithsonian Institution, 1926.
———. "The Discovery of Rainbow Bridge." *National Parks Bulletin* 9, no. 4 (1927): 7–16.
———. *The Excavation and Repair of Betatakin*. U.S. National Museum, Publication 2828. Washington, DC: Smithsonian Institution, 1931.
———. "Pioneering in Southwestern Archaeology." In *For the Dean: Essays in Anthropology in Honor of Byron Cummings on His Eighty-ninth Birthday, September 20, 1950*. Tucson: Hohokam Museums Association, and Santa Fe: Southwestern Monuments Association, 1950.

———. "Introduction." In *Indians I Have Known*, by Byron Cummings, p. xi. Tucson: Arizona Silhouettes, 1952.
———. "Byron Cummings, 1860–1954." *American Anthropologist* 56 (1954a): 871–872.
———. "Byron Cummings, 1860–1954." *American Antiquity* 20 (1954b): 154–157.
———. *The Material Culture of Pueblo Bonito*. Smithsonian Miscellaneous Collections 124 (1954c).
———. "Reminiscences in Southwestern Archaeology." *Kiva* 26 (1960): 1–6.
———. *The Architecture of Pueblo Bonito*. Smithsonian Miscellaneous Collections 147, no. 1 (1964).
———. *Men Met along the Trail: Adventures in Archaeology*. Norman: University of Oklahoma Press, 1968.
Kaemlein, Wilma R. *An Inventory of Southwestern American Indian Specimens in European Museums*. Tucson: Arizona State Museum, University of Arizona, 1967.
Kammen, Michael. *Mystic Chords of Memory: The Transformation of Tradition in American Culture*. New York: Alfred A. Knopf, 1991.
Kankainen, Kathy, ed. *Treading in the Past: Sandals of the Anasazi*. Salt Lake City: Utah Museum of Natural History and the University of Utah Press, 1995.
Keefe, Paul. Letter to C. R. Kuzell, March 25, 1935, ASM (A-678).
Kelly, Dorothea S. *McEuen Cave Report*. Manuscript sent to Harold Gladwin, Gila Pueblo Archaeological Foundation, 1937.
Kelly, Isabel T. *The Hodges Ruin: A Hohokam Community in the Tucson Basin*. Anthropological Papers of the University of Arizona no. 30. Gayle H. Hartman, ed. Tucson: University of Arizona Press, 1978.
Kelly, Roger E. "Elden Pueblo: An Archaeological Account." *Plateau* 42 (1970): 79–91.
[Kelly, William H.] "University Ruin." *Kiva* 1, no. 8 (1935): 1–4.
Kennedy, David M. "Overview: The Progressive Era." *Historian* 37 (1975): 53–468.
Kerr, Walter A. "Byron Cummings, Classic Scholar and Father of University Athletics." *Utah Historical Quarterly* 23 (1955): 145–160.
Kidder, Alfred Vincent. "Explorations in Southwestern Utah in 1908. *American Journal of Archaeology* 14 (1910): 337–359.
———. *An Introduction to the Study of Southwestern Archaeology, with a Preliminary Account of the Excavations at Pecos*. Papers of the Southwestern Expedition no. 1. Cambridge, MA: Yale University Press, 1962. Reprint of the original 1924 version with an introduction by Irving Rouse.

———. "The Museum's Expedition to Canon de Chelly and Canon del Muerto, Arizona." *Natural History* 27 (1927a): 202–209.

———. *The Pottery of Pecos*, vol. 1. Papers of the Southwestern Expedition, Phillips Academy. New Haven, CT: Yale University Press, 1931a.

———. Letter to James W. Simmons, February 23, 1931b, ASM (A-49).

———. *The Artifacts of Pecos*. Papers of the Southwestern Expedition no. 6. New Haven, CT: Publications for Phillips Academy by Yale University Press, 1932.

———. *The Pottery of Pecos*, vol. 2. Papers of the Southwestern Expedition, Phillips Academy. New Haven, CT: Yale University Press, 1936a.

———. "Speculations on New World Prehistory." In *Essays in Anthropology: In Honor of Alfred Louis Kroeber*, ed. Robert H. Lowie, pp. 143–151. Berkeley: University of California Press, 1936b.

———. "Sylvanus Grisworld Morley, 1883–1948." In *Morleyana*, ed. A. J. O. Anderson. Santa Fe, NM: School of American Research, 1950.

———, and Samuel J. Guernsey. *Archaeological Explorations in Northeastern Arizona*. Bureau of American Ethnology Bulletin 65. Washington, DC: Smithsonian Institution, 1919.

Kraeling, Emil G. H. Letter to Byron Cummings, October 20, 1925, ASM (A-192, 00002).

Kroeber, Alfred L. *Native Culture of the Southwest*. University of California Publications in American Archaeology and Ethnology 23, no. 9. Berkeley, 1928.

———. "Thomas Talbot Waterman." *American Anthropologist* 39, no. 3 (1937): 527–529.

Lambert, Marjorie F. "Karl Ruppert, 1895–1960." *American Antiquity* 27 (1961): 101–103.

Lange, Charles H., and Carroll L. Riley. *Bandelier: The Life and Adventures of Adolf Bandelier, American Archaeologist and Scientist*. Salt Lake City: University of Utah Press, 1996.

Lee, Ronald. "An Old and Reliable Authority: An Act for the Preservation of American Antiquities," Raymond H. Thompson, ed. *Journal of the Southwest* 42, no. 2 (2000).

Levine, Mary Ann. "Creating Their Own Niches: Career Styles among Women in Americanist Archaeology between the Wars." In *Women in Archaeology*, ed. Cheryl Claasen, pp. 9–39. Philadelphia: University of Pennsylvania Press, 1994.

Lindsay, Alexander J., Jr., J. Richard Ambler, Mary Anne Stein, and Philip M. Hobler. *Survey and Excavations North and East of Navajo Mountain, Utah, 1959–1962*, Bulletin no. 45, Glen Canyon Series no. 8. Flagstaff: Museum of Northern Arizona, 1968.

Linford, Laurence D. *Navajo Places: History, Legend, Landscape.* Salt Lake City: University of Utah Press, 2000.

Linton, Ralph. Letter to Byron Cummings, November 28, 1941, AHS (MS 200, box 1, f. 12).

Lister, Robert H., and Florence C. Lister. *Earl Morris and Southwestern Archaeology.* Albuquerque: University of New Mexico Press, 1968.

Lockett, Hattie Green. *The Unwritten Literature of the Hopi.* Social Science Bulletin 4, no. 4. Tucson: University of Arizona, 1933.

Lockett, Henry Claiborne. *The Prehistoric Hopi.* Unpublished master's thesis, Department of Archaeology, University of Arizona, 1933.

Lockwood, Francis C. Letter to Byron Cummings, March 27, 1927.

Lopez-Camacho, J. "Estratigrafia de la Piramide de Cuicuilco en Retrospectiva." *Cuicuilco* 27 (1991): 35–46.

Los Angeles Times. "Prehistoric Ruins May Tell Facts of Ancient American Civilization," May 6, 1923.

———. "Arizona Dean to Get Rutgers Degree," June 7, 1924.

Loveless, Bessie B. Letter to Byron Cummings, March 31, 1937, AHS (MS 200, box 1, f. 8).

Lovering, T. S. Notarized statement, 1925, AHS (MS 1122).

Lummis, Charles F. *Sixth Annual Report.* Fifth Bulletin, Southwest Society of the Archaeological Institute of America. Boston, 1910.

Lutrell, Estelle. *History of the University of Arizona, 1885-1926, Supplementary Data, 1926-1947,* 1947, UASC.

Maguire, Don. "Report of the Department of Ethnology, Utah World's Fair Commission." In *Utah at the World's Columbian Exposition.* Salt Lake City: Press of the Salt Lake Lithographing Co., 1894.

Mahoney, Esther N. *The Development and Classification of Chihuahua Pottery.* Unpublished master's thesis, Department of Archaeology, University of Arizona, 1936.

Mahoney, Ralph. "Old Roman Relics? Scientists Still Are Puzzled by Archaeological Discovery of 1924." *Arizona Days and Ways Magazine,* January 8 (1956).

Martin, Douglas. *The Lamp in the Desert: The Story of the University of Arizona.* Tucson: University of Arizona Press, 1960.

Martin, Paul S. "Review of Kinishba: A Prehistoric Pueblo of the Great Pueblo Period, by Byron Cummings." *American Anthropologist* 43 (1941a): 653–654.

———. Letter to Byron Cummings, December 1, 1941b, AHS (MS 200, box 1, f. 12).

Martin del Pozzo, A. L., C. Cordova, and J. Lopez. "Volcanic Impact on the

Southern Basin of Mexico during the Holocene." *Quaternary Research* 43/44 (1997): 181–190.

Martinez Hill Ruins, 1935, unpublished report, AHS (MS 200, box 5, f. 45).

Maulding, J. Atwood. Letter to Byron Cummings, January 3, 1940, AHS (MS 200, box 11).

Maxwell, Margaret F. "The Depression in Yavapai County." *Journal of Arizona History* 23 (1982): 209–228.

May, Dean L. *Utah: A People's History*. Salt Lake City: University of Utah Press, 1987.

May, Stephen J. *Zane Grey: Romancing the West*. Athens: Ohio University Press, 1997.

McEuen, Glen. Letter to Byron Cummings, October 26, 1934, ASM (A-204, 0002).

McEuen, M. P. Letter to Byron Cummings, November 18, 1934, ASM (A-204, 0008).

McFarland, Ernest. Letter to John Collier, November 4, 1941, FANHL.

McGrath, Anna Mae. *Antiquity of the American Indian*. Unpublished master's thesis, Department of Archaeology, University of Arizona, 1932.

McGregor, John C. *Archaeology of the Little Colorado Drainage Area*. Unpublished master's thesis, Department of Archaeology, University of Arizona, 1931.

———. "Dating the Eruption of Sunset Crater, Arizona." *American Antiquity* 2 (1936): 15–26.

———. Letter to Byron Cummings, October 22, 1941, AHS (MS 200, box 1, f. 12).

———. *Southwestern Archaeology*. 2nd ed. Urbana: University of Illinois Press, 1965.

———. *Archaeological Reminiscences*, 1987, manuscript on file at Department of Anthropology, Northern Arizona University.

———. Letter to Todd Bostwick, March 25, 2003, PGM.

McWhirt, Jean. *Incised Decoration in the Prehistoric Pottery of the Southwest*. Unpublished master's thesis, Department of Archaeology, University of Arizona, 1935.

Meltzer, David J. "On 'Paradigms' and 'Paradigm Bias' in Controversies over Human Antiquity in America." In *The First Americans: Search and Research*, ed. Tom D. Dillehay and David J. Meltzer, pp. 13–49. Boca Raton, FL: CRC Press, 1991.

Mercer, Thomas L. Letter to Byron Cummings, July 27, 1932, AHS (MS 200).

Merriman, George B. Letter of recommendation for Byron Cummings, professor of math and astronomy, Rutgers College, New Brunswick, N.J., April 18, 1891, AHS (MS 200, box 1, f. 1).

Miller, Carl F. *Prehistoric Irrigation Systems in Arizona.* Unpublished master's thesis, Department of Archaeology, University of Arizona, 1929.

Miller, Jimmy H. *The Life of Harold Sellers Colton: A Philadelphia Brahmin in Flagstaff.* Tsaile, AZ: Navajo Community College, 1991.

Miller, William C. "1661 Chas Arnod or 1861 Anno D? at Inscription House Ruin." *Plateau* 40, no. 4 (1968): 143–147.

Mindeleff, Cosmos. "Aboriginal Remains in the Verde Valley, Arizona." *Bureau of American Ethnology Thirteenth Annual Report*, pp. 176–261. Washington, DC, 1896.

Mitchell, William D. Letter to Secretary of the Interior, July 30, 1927, ASM (A-678).

Montezuma Journal (Cortez). September 2, 1909.

Montgomery, Henry. "Prehistoric Man in Utah." *Archaeologist* 2, no. 8 (1894).

Moore, James R. *The Post Darwinian Controversies: A Case Study of the Protestant Struggle to Come to Terms with Darwin in Great Britain and America, 1870–1900.* Cambridge, UK: Cambridge University Press, 1979.

Moreno, Teresa K. "Accelerator Mass Spectometry Dates from McEuen Cave." *Kiva* 65, no. 4 (2000): 343–360.

Morgan, Charles M. "Dean Simply Fluts when Arizona Republication Shrieks about New Find of Old, Old Ruin," *Jumping Cactus*, April 8, 1932.

Morgan, Lewis Henry. *Ancient Society, or Researches in the Lines of Human Progress from Savagery through Barbarism to Civilization.* New York: Henry Bolt, 1877.

———. *Houses and House Life of the American Aborigines.* Contributions to North American Ethnology 4. Washington, DC: Government Printing Office, 1881.

Morris, Earl H. Letter to Clark Wissler, July 26, 1927, Correspondence Files, Department of Anthropology, American Museum of Natural History.

———. *An Aboriginal Salt Mine at Camp Verde, Arizona.* Anthropological Papers of the American Museum of Natural History 30. New York, 1928a.

———. *Excavations in the Aztec Ruin.* Anthropological Papers of the Museum of Natural History 26. New York, 1928b.

Mortenson, Martin, Jr. Letter to Byron Cummings, March 21, 1927, UASC (AZ 420).

Mott, Dorothy C. "Progress of the Excavation at Kinishba." *Kiva* 2, no. 1 (1936): 1–4.

———. "Kinishba, Prehistoric Pueblo of the Great Pueblo Period." *Kiva* 6 (1940): 1–4.

Mott, Harvey L. "14,000,000 Yesterdays in Arizona," *Arizona Republic*, July 4, 11, 18, and 25, 1937.

Muench, Joyce, and Joseph Muench. "Kinishba: The Brown House of Long Ago." *Natural History* 55, no. 3 (1946a): 114–119.

———, and ———. "The Dean of the Southwest." *Arizona Highways* 22, no. 4 (1946b): 28–31.

Muller, Florencia. *La Cerámica de Cuicuilco B: Un Rescate Arqueológico*. Mexico City: Instituto Nacional de Antropologia e Historia, 1990.

Murray, Margaret W. *The Development of the Form and Design in the Pottery of Kinishba*. Unpublished master's thesis, Department of Archaeology, University of Arizona, 1937.

Nash, Stephen Edward. *Time, Trees, and Prehistory: Tree-Ring Dating and the Development of North American Archaeology 1914–1950*. Salt Lake City: University of Utah Press, 1999.

———, ed. *It's About Time: A History of Archaeological Dating in America*. Salt Lake City: University of Utah Press, 2000.

New York Herald. "Fossil Bone of Elephant Found in Arizona Mine," June 27, 1926.

New York Times. "15 Professors Out of Utah University," March 20, 1915.

———. "Puzzling Relics Dug Up in Arizona Stir Scientists," December 13, 1925a.

———. "Arizona University Will Study 'Relics,'" December 14, 1925b.

———. "Asserts 'A.D.' Shows 'Relics' Are Frauds," December 15, 1925c.

———. "Bogus Relics of the Past Tempt Collectors," December 20, 1925d.

Nichols, Deborah L. "Basketmaker III: Early Ceramic-Period Villages in the Kayenta Region." In *Prehistoric Culture Change on the Colorado Plateau: Ten Thousand Years on Black Mesa*, ed. Shirley Powell and Francis E. Smiley, pp. 66–76. Tucson: University of Arizona Press, 2002.

Ninth Arizona Legislature. *Senate Bill Number 100*, 1929, ASM (MU IA: Legislative History).

Nusbaum, Rosemary, ed. *Tierra Dulce: Reminiscences from the Jesse Nusbaum Papers*. Santa Fe: Sunstone Press, 1980.

Olsen, Sandra L. "Bone Artifacts from Kinishba Ruin: Their Manufacture and Use." *Kiva* 46, nos. 1–2 (1980): 39–67.

O'Neill, William L., ed. *The Progressive Years: America Comes of Age*. New York: Dodd, Mead, 1975.

Opening of the Smoki Museum, brochure, May 19, 1935, SM.

Osborn, Henry Fairfield. *Men of the Old Stone Age, Their Environment, Life, and Art*. 3rd ed. New York: C. Scribner, 1918.

Patrick, H. R. *The Ancient Canal Systems and Pueblos of the Salt River Valley, Arizona*. Phoenix Free Museum Bulletin 1. 1903.

Pepper, Choral. "Terra Calalus, U.S.A. (775–900 A.D.)." *Desert Magazine* (December 1980): 21–24.

Perez-Camp, M., A. Pastrana, and H. Gomez-Rueda. *Projecto Arquelogico Cuicuilco: Archivo del Conejo de Arqueologia.* Mexico City: Instituto Nacional de Antropologia e Historia, 1995.

Peterson, Alfred. *Development of Design on the Hohokam Red-on-buff Pottery.* Unpublished master's thesis, Department of Archaeology, University of Arizona, 1937.

Pinkley, Edna T. *Casa Grande: The Greatest Valley Pueblo of Arizona.* Tucson: Arizona Historical Society, 1926.

Pinkley, Frank. "The Southwestern Monuments." In *Annual Report of the Director of the National Park Service for 1924* (1925): 148–150.

———. Letter to Stephen Mather, April 19, 1927a, ASM (MS15).

———. Letter to Mrs. MacRae, November 11, 1927b, ASM (A-248).

———. Letter to Katherine MacRae, November 29, 1927c, ASM (A-248).

Poole, Lynn, and Gary Poole. *Men Who Dig Up History.* New York: Dodd, Mead, 1968.

Price, Ira M. Letter to Byron Cummings, November 5, 1925, ASM (A192, 00014).

Prudden, T. Mitchell. "The Prehistoric Ruins of the San Juan Watershed of Utah, Arizona, Colorado, and New Mexico." *American Anthropologist* 5 (1903): 224–288.

Pyle, Howard. Telegram to Ann Cummings, May 1954, AHS (MS 200).

Reid, J. Jefferson. "Emil Walter Haury: The Archaeologist as Humanist and Scientist." In *Emil W. Haury's Prehistory of the American Southwest*, ed. J. Jefferson Reid and David E. Doyel, pp. 3–17. Tucson: University of Arizona Press, 1986.

———, and Stephanie M. Whittlesey. *Byron Cummings' Architectural Reconstruction of Kinishba: An Archival Analysis.* Whitewater, AZ: Fort Apache National Monument, 1989.

———. *The Archaeology of Ancient Arizona.* Tucson: University of Arizona Press, 1997.

Reyman, Jonathon E. "Women in American Archaeology: Some Historical Notes and Comments." In *Rediscovering Our Past: Essays on the History of American Archaeology*, ed. Jonathon E. Reyman, pp. 69–80. Avebury, UK: Aldershot, 1992.

Roosevelt, Theodore. "Across the Navajo Desert." *The Outlook* 105 (1913): 309–317. Reprinted in *Rainbow Trails: Early-Day Adventures in Rainbow Bridge Country*, compiled by James E. Babbitt, pp. 37–52. Page, AZ: Glen Canyon Natural History Association, 1990.

Rothman, Hal. *Preserving Different Pasts: The American National Monuments.* Urbana: University of Illinois Press, 1989.

———. *Navajo National Monument: A Place and Its People, An Administrative*

History. Southwest Cultural Resources Center Professional Papers no. 40. Santa Fe, 1991.

———. "Ruins, Reputations, and Regulation: Byron Cummings, William B. Douglass, John Wetherhill, and the Summer of 1909." *Journal of the Southwest* 35 (1993): 318–340.

Rubens, Violet. 1919, unpublished field school paper, AHS (MS 200).

Runke, Walter. Letter to Byron Cummings, January 31, 1927, AHS (MS 200, box 1, f. 5).

Ruppert, Karl. *The Caracol at Chitzen Itza, Yucatan, Mexico*. Carnegie Institution of Washington Publication 454. Washington, DC, 1935.

———, J. Eric S. Thompson, and Tatiana Proskouriakoff. *Chichen Itza, Architectural Notes and Plans*. Washington, DC: Carnegie Institution of Washington, 1952.

———, ———, and ———. *Bonampak, Chiapas, Mexico*. Carnegie Institution of Washington Publication 602. Washington, DC, 1955.

Russell, Frank. "The Pima Indians." In *Twenty-sixth Annual Report of the Bureau of American Ethnology, 1904–1905*, pp. 3–389. Washington, DC: Government Printing Office, 1908. Reprint, Tucson: University of Arizona Press, 1980.

———. "The Pageant Beautiful at Casa Grande." *Progressive Arizona* 3, no. 4 (1926): 17, 44.

Russell, Luella Haney. *The Primitive Religion of the Southwest*. Unpublished master's thesis, Department of Archaeology, University of Arizona, 1930.

Ryan, W. Carson. *Studies in Early Graduate Education: The Johns Hopkins University, Clark University, the University of Chicago*. Bulletin no. 30. New York: Carnegie Foundation for the Advancement of Teaching, 1939.

Ryder, E. D. Letter to Byron Cummings, February 9, 1927, AHS (MS 200, box 1, f. 5).

Salt Lake Tribune. "Archaeological Expedition Suffers Greatly on the Desert, Thrilling Tale Told of Trip across Monument Valley," September 5, 1915.

Sanders, W. T., J. R. Parsons, and R. S. Stanley. *The Basin of Mexico: Ecological Processes in the Evolution of A Civilization*. New York: Academic Press, 1979.

Sarle, C. J. Letter to Thomas Bent, February 20, 1929, AHS (MS 1122).

Sayles, Edward B., and Ernst Antevs. *The Cochise Culture*. Medallion Papers 29. Globe, AZ: Gila Pueblo Archaeological Foundation, 1941.

———, with Joan A. Henley. *Fantasies of Gold: Legends of Treasures and How They Grew*. Tucson: University of Arizona Press, 1968.

Scales, Eva M. Letter to Regent E. E. Ellinwood, April 3, 1937, AHS (MS 200, box 1, f. 8).

Schavelzon, Daniel. *La Piramide de Cuicuilco: Album Fotographico*. Mexico City: Fondo de Cultura Economica, 1983.

Schneider-Hector, Dietmar. *Sundipped Memories of Frank Pinkley: A "Man on the Lone Post" at Casa Grande Ruins National Monument, Arizona*. Hillsboro, NM: Percha Creek Press, 2003.

Schroeder, Albert H. *A Stratigraphic Survey of Pre-Spanish Trash Mounds in the Salt River Valley, Arizona*. Unpublished master's thesis, Department of Anthropology, University of Arizona, 1940.

Science News Bulletin 70. "Uncovers Mexican Pompeii; Extends History Centuries," August 5, 1922.

Scott, Douglas D. "Pioneering Archaeology in Southwestern Colorado: The Kidder and Morley Years." In *Why Museums Collect: Papers in Honor of Joe Ben Wheat*, ed. Meliha S. Duran and David T. Kirkpatrick, pp. 203–211. Papers of the Archaeological Society of New Mexico no. 19. Santa Fe, 1993.

Seattle Times. "University News," March 1, 1923.

Semonin, Paul. *American Monster: How the Nation's First Prehistoric Creature Became a Symbol of National Identity*. New York: New York University Press, 2000.

Siegel, David N. "Legislation for the Protection and Preservation of Archaeological Remains in Arizona." *Kiva* 40 (1975): 315–326.

Simmons, James W. Letter to Harold Gladwin, November 10, 1932, ASM (A-20).

———. Letter to Harold Gladwin, January 7, 1933a, ASM (A-20, 0028).

———. Letter to Harold Gladwin, February 21, 1933b, ASM (A-20, 0032-54).

———. *The King Pueblo*. Arizona Writers Project, Works Progress Administration, 1936, ASLAPR (Records Group 91, box 5, film file 51.27.2).

Smith, Elmer R. "Utah Anthropology, an Outline of Its History." *Southwestern Lore* 16, no. 2 (1950): 22–23.

Smith, Watson. "The Archaeological Legacy of Edward H. Spicer." *Kiva* 49, nos. 1–2 (1983): 75–79.

Smoot, Reed. Letter to Byron Cummings, July 2, 1910, ACMNM (AC 105).

Snead, James E. *Ruins and Rivals: The Making of Southwest Archaeology*. Tucson: University of Arizona Press, 2001.

Sonnichsen, C. L. *Tucson: The Life and Times of an American City*. Norman: University of Oklahoma Press, 1982.

Sparkes, Grace M. Letter to Governor R. C. Stanford, April 3, 1937, AHS (MS 200, box 1, f. 8).

Spicer, Edward H. *The Prescott Black-on-Grey Culture, Its Nature and Relations, as Exemplified in King's Ruin, Arizona*. Unpublished master's thesis, Department of Archaeology, University of Arizona, 1933.

———. "Archaic Skeletal Material from Cuicuilco, Valley of Mexico," 1936a, unpublished manuscript, ASM, Spicer Collection (A-87).

———. *Two Pueblo Ruins in West Central Arizona*. University of Arizona Bulletin no. 7, Social Science Bulletin no. 10. Tucson: University of Arizona, 1936b.

———. *Cycles of Conquest: The Impact of Spain, Mexico, and the United States on the Indians of the Southwest, 1533–1960*. Tucson: University of Arizona Press, 1962.

———. John H. Provinse, 1887–1965. *American Anthropologist* 68, no. 4 (1966): 990–994.

———, and Louis Caywood. *Tuzigot Ruins Near Clarkdale, Arizona*. Prescott: Yavapai County Chamber of Commerce, 1935.

Springer, Frank. "The Field Session of the School of American Archaeology." *Science* 23, no. 827 (1910): 622–624.

Spry, William. Letter to Byron Cummings, February 2, 1910, AHS (MS 200, box 1, f. 2).

Stallings, William S., Jr. *Pueblo Archaeology of the Rio Grande Drainage*. Unpublished master's thesis, Department of Archaeology, University of Arizona, 1932.

———. "Southwest Dated Ruins: I." *Tree-Ring Bulletin* 4, no. 2 (1937).

Stocking, George W., Jr. "The Santa Fe Style in American Archaeology: Regional Interest, Academic Initiative and Philanthropic Policy in the First Two Decades of the Laboratory of Anthropology." *Journal of the History of Behavioral Sciences* 18 (1982): 3–19.

Stoner, Reverend Victor R. *The Spanish Missions of the Santa Cruz Valley*. Unpublished master's thesis, Department of Archaeology, University of Arizona, 1937.

Tally, Robert. Letter to Byron Cummings, March 2, 1927a, UASC (AZ 420, box 5, f. 19).

———. Letter to Byron Cummings, March 5, 1927b, UASC (AZ 420).

———. Letter to Byron Cummings, June 22, 1927c, UASC (AZ 420).

———. Letter to Byron Cummings, February 1, 1928a, UASC (AZ 420).

———. Letter to Byron Cummings, February 15, 1928b, UASC (AZ 420).

———. Letter to Byron Cummings, March 1928c, UASC (AZ 420).

Talmadge, James E. "Salt Lake City: The Desert That Has Blossomed as the Rose." In *Historic Towns of the Western United States*, ed. Lyman P. Powell, pp. 479–508. New York: Knickerbocker Press, 1901.

Tanner [Fraps], Clara Lee. "Tanque Verde Ruins." *Kiva* 1 (1935): 1–4.

———. "Blackstone Ruin." *Kiva* 2, no. 3 (1936): 9–12.

———. "Byron Cummings, 1860–1954." *Kiva* 20, no. 1 (1954a): 1–21.

———. "A Dedication to the Memory of Byron Cummings, 1861–1954." *Arizona and the West* 20, no. 4 (1954b): 303–306.

———. *Prehistoric Southwestern Craft Arts*. Tucson: University of Arizona Press, 1976.

Taylor, Walter W., and Robert C. Euler. "Lyndon Lane Hargrave, 1896–1978." *American Antiquity* 45, no. 3 (1980): 477–482.

Taylor, W. B. Letter to Byron Cummings, June 29, 1937, AHS (MS 200, box 1, f. 8).

Thomas, Elbert D. Letter to Byron Cummings, September 9, 1939, AHS (MS 200, box 1, f. 10).

Thompson, Raymond H. "Emil W. Haury and the Definition of the Southwestern Archaeology." *American Antiquity* 60, no. 4 (1995): 640–660.

———. "Harry Thomas Getty." *Anthropology Newsletter* 37, no. 1 (1996): 47.

———. "Obituary: Clara Lee Tanner, 1905–1997." *Kiva* 64, no. 1 (1998): 53–60.

———. "Edgar Lee Hewett and the Political Process." *Journal of the Southwest* 42 (2000): 273–381.

Todt, William C., Jr. "The Arizona Pageant." *Progressive Arizona* 3 (1926): 7–8.

Tombstone Epitaph. "San Pedro Goes on Rampage," September 30, 1926a.

———. "Fossilized Bones of Pre-historic Animal Are Found," October 24, 1926b.

———. "Evidence of Ancient Man in Sulphur Springs Valley Is Uncovered by U.A. Professor," November 4, 1926c.

Tozzer, Alfred. Letter to Byron Cummings, February 17, 1917 [1927], ASM (A-678).

Tucson Citizen. "Arizona Archaeologist to Continue Excavation Work at Old Pyramid in Mexico," September 1, 1922.

———. "The Oldest Temple in North America," January 13, 1924.

———. "Inscribed Plate Found near City May Unfold Story of an Early Race Here, Belief Now," February 1, 1925a.

———. "Aborigine Pit House over 1000 Yrs. Old Is Located near Tucson," November 17, 1925b.

———. "Dean Scoffs at Idea of Putting Museum with Livestock Exhibits," November 22, 1925c.

———. "Leaden Relics Genuine, States U. of A. Archaeologist, Who Replies to Doubting Thomases," December 14, 1925d.

———. "Relics Are to Be Given to U., Bent Declares," December 16, 1925e.

———. "Collegian May Have 'Planted' Leaden Relics, Belief of Some," January 14, 1926a.

———. "Odohui, Mexican Sculptor, Made Leaden Figures, Recalls Ruiz, Friend of Lime Kiln Family," January 17, 1926b.

———. "Scientist Had Returned from Eastern Visit," January 18, 1926c.

———. "Home of Odohui now Fixed at Lime Kiln by Pioneer Rancher," January 20, 1926d.

———. "Artifacts 'Puerile' Toys, Ransome Avers; Caliche Was Dumped," February 1926e.

———. "Plan of Phoenix to Build Rival Museum Scorned by Cummings," April 18, 1926f.

———. "Dean Cummings Returns from Summer's Trip," September 13, 1926g.

———. "Adobe Wall Built by Pueblo People Located by Students," October 5, 1926h.

———. "Lusty Rah Is Given Him, Presented by Students' Chief," February 2, 1927a.

———. "Acting President Cummings Welcomes Students, not as Visitors, but as Picked Men," September 12, 1927b.

———. "Excavations Will Start Feby. 6th," February 4, 1928.

———. "Mrs. Byron Cummings Laid to Rest with Hundreds Paying Tribute to Her Life of Splendid Service," November 15, 1929.

———. "Pioneer Arrives, Blood in Eye," December 28, 1931.

———. "Cummings to Go on Field Trip," November 18, 1935.

Turner, Christy G., II. *A Summary of the Archaeological Explorations of Dr. Byron Cummings in the Anasazi Culture Area*. Flagstaff: Museum of Northern Arizona Technical Series 5, 1962.

Turney, Omar A. "When the Salt River Valley Was Watered by a Great Prehistoric System of Canals," *Arizona Republican*, November 29, 1922.

———. *The Land of the Stone Hoe*. Phoenix: Arizona Republican, 1924.

———. Letter to Byron Cummings, September 29, 1925, ASM (A-193).

———. Letter to Byron Cummings, February 7, 1927, AHS (MS 200).

———. "Antiquity of Man in America." *Arizona Old and New* 1, no. 3 (1928): 7–8, 29–31.

———. "Prehistoric Irrigation." *Arizona Historical Review* 2, nos. 1–4 (1929): 1–163.

Universal, El. "Un Sensational Describimiento de Arqueologia," July 10, 1922, ASM (A-697).

University of Arizona. "Twenty-Fourth Annual Catalogue 1914–1915, Announcements for 1915–1916," *University of Arizona Record* 8, no. 1 (1915).

———. "Twenty-Fifth Annual Catalogue 1915–1916, Announcements for 1916–1917." *University of Arizona Record* 9, no. 4 (1916).

———. "Twenty-Sixth Annual Catalogue 1916–1917, Announcements for 1917–1918." *University of Arizona Record* 10, no. 4 (1917).

———. "Twenty-Seventh Annual Catalogue 1917–1918, Announcements for 1918–1919." *University of Arizona Record* 11, no. 4 (1918).

———. "Twenty-Eighth Annual Catalogue 1918–1919, Announcements for 1919–1920." *University of Arizona Record* 12, no. 2 (1919).

———. "Twenty-Ninth Annual Catalogue 1919–1920, Announcements for 1920–1921." *University of Arizona Record* 13, no. 1 (1920a).

———. "Annual Report of the Board of Regents of the University of Arizona for the Fiscal Year Ending June 30, 1920, Part II, Financial Statement." *University of Arizona Record* 14, no. 3 (1920b).

———. "Thirtieth Annual Catalogue 1920–1921, Announcements for 1921–1922." *University of Arizona Record* 14, no. 4 (1921a).

———. "Summer School in Spanish and Mexican Archaeology." *University of Arizona Record* 14, no. 5 (1921b).

———. "Thirty-First Annual Catalogue 1921–1922, Announcements for 1922–1923." *University of Arizona Record* 15, no. 4 (1922a).

———. "Announcement for the Academic Year 1922–1923." *University of Arizona Record* 16, no. 1 (1922b).

———. "Announcement for the Academic Year 1923–1924, Record of University Activities for the Academic Year, 1922–1923." *University of Arizona Record* 16, no. 3 (1923).

———. "Announcement for the Academic Year 1924–1925, Record of University Activities for the Academic Year, 1923–1924." *University of Arizona Record* 17, no. 2 (1924a).

———. "Annual Report of the Board of Regents of the University of Arizona for the Fiscal Year Ended June 30, 1924." *University of Arizona Record* 17, no. 4 (1924b).

———. "Announcement for the Academic Year 1925–1926, Record of University Activities for the Academic Year, 1924–1925." *University of Arizona Record* 18, no. 2 (1925).

———. "Announcement for the Academic Year 1926–1927, Record of University Activities for the Academic Year, 1925–1926." *University of Arizona Record* 19, no. 2 (1926a).

———. "Annual Report of the Board of Regents of the University of Arizona for the Fiscal Year Ended June 30, 1926." *University of Arizona Record* 19, no. 4 (1926b).

———. "Announcement for the Academic Year 1927–1928, Record of University Activities for the Academic Year, 1926–1927." *University of Arizona Record* 20, no. 2 (1927).

———. Annual Report of the Board of Regents of the University of Arizona for the Fiscal Year Ended Jun 30, 1927." *University of Arizona Record* 20, no. 4 (1928a).

———. "Announcement for the Academic Year 1928–1929, Record of University Activities for the Academic Year, 1926–1927, Register of Students, 1927–1928." *University of Arizona Record* 21 no. 2 (1928b).

———. "Annual Report of the Board of Regents of the University of Arizona for the Fiscal Year Ended June 30, 1928." *University of Arizona Record* 21, no. 4 (1929a).
———. "Announcement for the Academic Year 1929–1930, Record of University Activities for the Academic Year 1927–1928, Register of Students, 1928–1929." *University of Arizona Record* 22, no. 2 (1929b).
———. "Annual Report of the Board of Regents of the University of Arizona for the Fiscal Year Ended June 30, 1929." *University of Arizona Record* 22, no. 4 (1929c).
———. "Announcement for the Summer Session 1930." University of Arizona Record 23, no. 1 (1930a).
———. "Announcement for the Academic Year 1930–1931, Record of University Activities for the Academic Year 1928–1929, Register of Students, 1929–1930." *University of Arizona Record* 23, no. 2 (1930b).
———. "Annual Report of the Board of Regents of the University of Arizona for the Fiscal Year Ended June 30, 1930." *University of Arizona Record* 23, no. 4 (1930c).
———. "Announcement for the Academic Year 1931–1932, Record of University Activities for the Academic Year 1929–1930, Register of Students, 1930–1931." *University of Arizona Record* 24, no. 2 (1931a).
———. "Annual Report of the Board of Regents of the University of Arizona for the Fiscal Year Ended June 30, 1931." *University of Arizona Record* 24, no. 4 (1931b).
———. "Announcement for the Academic Year 1932–1933, Record of University Activities for the Academic Year 1930–1931, Register of Students, 1931–1932." *University of Arizona Record* 25, no. 2 (1932a).
———. "Annual Report of the Board of Regents of the University of Arizona for the Fiscal Year Ended June 30, 1932." *University of Arizona Record* 25, no. 4 (1932b).
———. "Announcement for the Academic Year 1933–1934, Record of University Activities for the Academic Year 1931–1932." *University of Arizona Record* 26, no. 3 (1933).
———. "Announcement for Summer Session 1934." *University of Arizona Record* 27, no. 2 (1934a).
———. "Announcement for the Academic Year 1934–1935, Record of University Activities for the Academic Year 1932–1933." *University of Arizona Record* 27, no. 3 (1934b).
———. "Annual Report of the Board of Regents of the University of Arizona for the Fiscal Year Ended June 30, 1934." *University of Arizona Record* 27, no. 5 (1934c).

———. "Announcement for the Academic Year 1935–1936, Record of University Activities for the Academic Year 1933–1934." *University of Arizona Record* 28, no. 3 (1935a).
———. "Annual Report of the Board of Regents of the University of Arizona for the Fiscal Year Ended June 30, 1935." *University of Arizona Record* 28, no. 5 (1935b).
———. "Announcement for the Academic Year 1936–1937, Record of University Activities for the Academic Year 1934–1935." *University of Arizona Record* 29, no. 3 (1936a).
———. "Annual Report of the Board of Regents of the University of Arizona for the Fiscal Year Ended June 30, 1936." *University of Arizona Record* 29, no. 5 (1936b).
———. "Announcement for the Academic Year 1937–1938, Record of University Activities for the Academic Year 1935–1936." *University of Arizona Record* 30, no. 3 (1937).
———. "Annual Report of the Board of Regents of the University of Arizona for the Fiscal Year Ending June 30, 1938." *University of Arizona Record* 31, no. 5 (1938).
Utah Chronicle. March 30, 1915.
Veysey, Laurence R. *The Emergence of the American University*. Chicago: University of Chicago Press, 1965.
von KleinSmid, Rufus B. Letter to Byron Cummings, June 22, 1915, AHS (MS 200, box 1, f. 3).
———. Letter to Byron Cummings, February 21, 1927, AHS (MS 200, box 1, f. 5).
Walker, Franklin D. *Archaeology Report*, September 23, 1919, unpublished manuscript, AHS (MS 200).
Walker, Winslow. *Diary*, 1923, ASM (87-5).
———. *Diary*, 1928, ASM (87-5).
Walla Walla Bulletin. "Remnants of Old Civilization Shown to Archaeologists," February 27, 1923.
Ward, Albert E. "Inscription House: Two Research Reports." *Museum of Northern Arizona, Technical Series* 16 (1975): 1–17.
Warner, Florence M. *Outstanding Projects—Work Division: Emergency Relief Administration in Arizona 1935*. Phoenix: Arizona Board of Public Welfare, 1935.
Waterman, Thomas T. "Culture Horizons in the Southwest." *American Anthropologist* 31, no. 3 (1929): 367–400.
Waters, Michael R. *The Geoarchaeology of Whitewater Draw, Arizona*. Anthropological Papers of the University of Arizona. Tucson: University of Arizona Press, 1986.

———. "The Sulphur Springs Stage of the Cochise Culture and Its Place in Southwest Prehistory." *Kiva* 64, no. 2 (1998): 115–135.

Wauchope, Robert. "Alfred Vincent Kidder, 1885–1963." *American Antiquity* 31, no. 2 (1965): 149–171.

Weadock, J. F. "Dean Cummings Tells of 10,000 Year Old Temple in Old Mexico," September 13, 1925.

Weaver, Muriel Porter. *The Aztec, Maya, and Their Predecessors: Archaeology of Mesoamerica.* 3rd ed. New York: Academic Press, 1993.

Webb, George E. *Tree Rings and Telescopes: The Scientific Career of A. E. Douglass.* Tucson: University of Arizona Press, 1983a.

———. "Tucson's Evolution Debate, 1924–1927." *Journal of Arizona History* 24 (1983b): 1–12.

———. *Science in the American Southwest: A Topical History.* Tucson: University of Arizona Press, 2002.

Webster, Laurie. *Accession Notes, Cummings Field Seasons, 1915–1930*, 1991, ASM.

Wedel, Waldo R. "Obituary: Neil Merton Judd, 1887–1976." *American Antiquity* 43, no. 3 (1978): 399–402.

Wetherill, John. Letter to Byron Cummings, November 6, 1910, ACMNM (AC 105).

———. "Notes on Discovery of Betatakin." *Plateau* 27, no. 4 (1955): 23.

Whitmore, Opal LeBaron. Letter to Byron Cummings, November 16, 1938, AHS (MS 200).

Whitmore, William V. "Our New President," 1927, AHS (MS 200, box 9).

Whittlesey, Stephanie M. "An Overview of Research History and Archaeology of Central Arizona." In *Vanishing River: Landscape and Lives of the Lower Verde Valley*, ed. Stephanie M. Whittlesey, Richard Ciolek-Torrello, and Jeffrey H. Altschul, pp. 59–141. Tucson: SRI Press, 1997.

Whorton, James C. *Crusaders for Fitness: The History of American Health Reformers.* Princeton: Princeton University Press, 1982.

Wilcox, David R. *Frank Midvale's Investigation of the Site of La Ciudad.* Arizona State University Anthropological Field Studies no. 19. Tempe, 1987.

———. "The Changing Context of Support for Archaeology and the Work of Erich F. Schmidt." In *Erich F. Schmidt's Investigations of Salado Sites in Central Arizona: The Mrs. W. B. Thompson Archaeological Expedition of the American Museum of Natural History*, ed. John W. Hohmann and Linda B. Kelley, pp. 11–27. Museum of Northern Arizona Bulletin 56. Flagstaff, 1988.

———. "Pueblo Grande as Phoenix: Odd Halseth's Vision of a City Museum." In *Archaeology of the Pueblo Grande Platform Mound and Its Surrounding Features*, vol. 1: *Introduction to the Archival Project and History of Archaeologi-*

cal Research, ed. Christian E. Downum and Todd W. Bostwick, pp. 97–137. Pueblo Grande Museum Anthropological Papers no. 1. Phoenix, 1993.

———. *Data Tables on Members of the Hohokam Museum Association, Tucson, 1937–1946*. Flagstaff: Museum of Northern Arizona, 2001.

———. "Creating a Firm Foundation: The Early Years of the Arizona State Museum." Paper presented at the American Anthropological Association, Washington, DC, 2002.

———, and Charles Sternberg. *Hohokam Ballcourts and Their Interpretation*. Arizona State Museum Archaeological Series no. 160. Tucson: University of Arizona, 1983.

Wilder, Carleton S. "The Arizona State Museum History." *Kiva* 7 (1942): 26–31.

Willey, Gordon R. *Methods and Problems in Archaeological Excavation, with Special Reference to the Southwestern United States*. Unpublished master's thesis, Department of Archaeology, University of Arizona, 1936.

———. *Portraits in American Archaeology: Remembrances of Some Distinguished Americanists*. Albuquerque: University of New Mexico Press, 1988.

———, and Philip Phillips. *Method and Theory in American Archaeology*. Chicago: University of Chicago Press, 1958.

———, and Jeremy A. Sabloff. *A History of American Archaeology*. 3rd ed. New York: W. H. Freeman, 1993.

Williams, Stephen. *Fantastic Archaeology: The Wild Side of North American Prehistory*. Philadelphia: University of Pennsylvania Press, 1991.

Wilson, Harold G. "Junior Odohui Was Eccentric, Fimbres Avers," *Tucson Citizen*, February 16, 1926.

Windsor, David L. "The Marvin Affair—A Bizarre University of Arizona Presidency." *Smoke Signals* 70 (1998): 209–224.

Wisdom, Charles W. *Elements of the Piman Language*. Unpublished master's thesis, Department of Archaeology, University of Arizona, 1930.

Wissler, Clark. Letter, June 14, 1927, p. 23 in David R. Wilcox, "The Changing Context of Support for Archaeology and the Work of Erich F. Schmidt." In *Erich F. Schmidt's Investigations of Salado Sites in Central Arizona: The Mrs. W. B. Thompson Archaeological Expedition of the American Museum of Natural History*, ed. John W. Hohmann and Linda B. Kelley, pp. 11–27. Museum of Northern Arizona Bulletin 56. Flagstaff, 1988.

Woodbury, Richard B. *Alfred V. Kidder*. New York: Columbia University Press, 1973.

———. *Sixty Years of Southwestern Archaeology: A History of the Pecos Conference*. Albuquerque: University of New Mexico Press, 1993.

Woodward, Arthur. *The Grewe Site, Gila Valley, Arizona*. Los Angeles Museum of History, Science and Art, Occasional Papers 1. 1931.

Worcester, Don. *A Visit from Father and Other Tales of the Mojave*. College Station: Texas A and M University Press, 1990.
Work Projects Administration. *Arizona: A State Guide*. Flagstaff: Arizona State Teachers College, 1940.
Wright, George F. *Man and the Glacial Period*. New York: Appleton, 1892.
———. *Origin and Antiquity of Man*. Oberlin, OH: Bibliotheca Sacra, 1912.
Wrobel, David M., and Patrick T. Long, eds. *Seeing and Being Seen: Tourism and the American West*. Lawrence: University Press of Kansas, 2001.
Zahniser, Jack L. "Late Prehistoric Villages Southeast of Tucson, Arizona, and the Archaeology of the Tanque Verde Phase." *Kiva* 31, no. 3 (1966): 103–204.
Zimmerman, William, Jr. Letter to Senator Ernest McFarland, November 14, 1941, FANHL.
Zorbaugh, Harvey. Letter to Byron Cummings, April 1928, UASC (AZ 420).

Index

About the Author

Todd Bostwick has been conducting archaeological research in the Southwest for more than twenty-five years. He has a master's degree in anthropology and a Ph.D. in history from Arizona State University (ASU). Bostwick has been the Phoenix city archaeologist for fifteen years, with his office located at the Pueblo Grande Museum National Historic Landmark. He also is a faculty associate in the History Department at ASU. He has authored various articles and books on Southwestern archaeology and history, including *Landscape of the Spirits: Hohokam Rock Art at South Mountain Park* (2002), published by the University of Arizona Press.